ARIS & PHILLIPS CLASS

GREEK ORATORS I

Antiphon & Lysias

translated with commentary and notes by

M. J. Edwards and S. Usher

Aris & Phillips is an imprint of
Oxbow Books, Park End Place, Oxford OX1 1HN

ISBN 0-85668-247-0

First published 1985, corrected edition 1987,
reprinted 1993, 2005

A CIP record for this book is available from the British Library.

Printed and bound by Antony Rowe Ltd, Eastbourne

CONTENTS

PREFACE

This contribution to the expanding series of Aris & Phillips Classical Texts follows the general lines of earlier volumes. The Antiphontean part of the book is the work of Michael Edwards, while Stephen Usher wrote the Lysianic part and the General Introduction. We wish to thank the proprietors of Teubner Verlag, Stuttgart and of the Clarendon Press, Oxford for permission to use their texts of Antiphon and Lysias (respectively) as the bases for ours. Thanks are also due to Professor Douglas MacDowell, from whose published work and private discussion and correspondence we have benefited greatly; and to Professor Malcolm Willcock, whose idea this volume was.

ABBREVIATIONS

(1) Ancient Authors

Aes.	Aeschines
Aeschyl.	Aeschylus
Ammian.Marc.	Ammianus Marcellinus
And.	Andocides
Ant.	Antiphon
Ar.	Aristophanes
Arist.	Aristotle
Apollod.	Apollodorus
Callim.	Callimachus
Cic.	Cicero
Democr.	Democritus
Dem.	Demosthenes
Dinarch.	Dinarchus
Diod.	Diodorus Siculus
Diog.Laert.	Diogenes Laertius
D.H.	Dionysius of Halicarnassus
Epicharm.	Epicharmus
Eupol.	Eupolis
Eur.	Euripides
Gorg.	Gorgias
Hermog.	Hermogenes
Hdt.	Herodotus
Hes.	Hesiod
Hesych.	Hesychius
Hippoc.	Hippocrates
Hom.	Homer
Hor.	Horace
Is.	Isaeus
Isoc.	Isocrates
Lyc.	Lycurgus
Lys.	Lysias
Pi.	Pindar
Pl.	Plato
Plut.	Plutarch
Quint.	Quintilian
Sext.Emp.	Sextus Empiricus
Soph.	Sophocles
Steph.Byz.	Stephanus Byzantinus
Theog.	Theognis
Theophrast.	Theophrastus
Thuc.	Thucydides
Xen.	Xenophon

(2) Periodicals

AJP	American Journal of Philology
ASNP	Annali della Scuola Normale Superiore di Pisa
CB	Classical Bulletin
CP	Classical Philology
CQ	Classical Quarterly
GRBS	Greek, Roman and Byzantine Studies
REG	Revue des Études Grecques
Rh.Mus.	Rheinisches Museum für Philologie
TAPA	Transactions and Proceedings of the American Philological Association

For other abbreviations see Bibliography

GENERAL INTRODUCTION

ORATORY BEFORE RHETORIC

The reader of Homer soon becomes aware of the importance of the spoken word in his story. Many of his heroes are accomplished orators, who earn as much respect for their eloquence as for their martial prowess; and their speeches often mark turning-points in the action. Observing the brilliance of Nestor, Odysseus and Agamemnon and its effect upon their audiences, later critics of systematic rhetoric disparaged the pioneering pretensions of its exponents by claiming that its techniques had been evolved and refined in that distant heroic age, so that the best speakers in the *Iliad* and *Odyssey* exhibited, in pristine form, all of the finest qualities of persuasive oratory.[1] There is even evidence for instruction[2] and competition[3] in eloquence in Homeric society. But it must be doubted whether, among semi-literate people, teaching could have included material which required close study, or indeed extended beyond general precepts of the simplest kind. Homeric oratory appears as spontaneous utterance, without regular plan and showing only such intellectual subtlety as the speaker might have been expected to deploy on the spur of the moment.[4] The presence of formulae and stock topics in it suggests that these may have formed part of the teaching material: perhaps orators, like poets, learned their craft with the aid of formulae.[5] However this may be, the speeches themselves are less notable for their rational and dialectical content than for their appeal to the emotions, particularly those of anger and fear. This should cause no surprise, since as autocratic leaders Odysseus and Agamemnon were not mentally conditioned to use reasoned argument when their primary purpose was simply to make their decisions known to their subjects and call upon them to carry them out. Their oratory was not so much deliberative as nortatory. But the existence of some kind of forensic oratory is attested in the description of a scene depicting a trial for homicide on the Shield of Achilles.[6] In this, after the contending parties have stated their points of view, each member of a panel of elders delivers his judgment of the case, and the one whose judgment seems the best is awarded two talents of gold. The scene raises many interesting questions about the administration of justice in early Greek society, but the question which concerns the present discussion is that of whether the elders who spoke had received any training in oratory and/or law, or whether (as seems more likely) wisdom born of experience was all that they needed in order to arrive at judgments which could satisfy their younger fellow-citizens.

5

A search for vestiges of formal rhetoric in **Hesiod** is even less rewarding, in spite of the tone and general purpose of his didactic poetry. His description of oratory as a gift of the Muses (*Theogony* 80-93) which enables kings to control their people contains a suggestion of divinely-inspired, effortless fluency rather than training. In the *Works and Days* the nearest approach to an oratorical manner is found in the passages addressed directly to his brother Perses (213ff,286ff), but even here the tone is hortatory, very much in the direct style of the Homeric speeches.

Later literature provides two trial scenes. The first, the *Hymn to Hermes*, belongs perhaps to the sixth century, and describes a dispute between Apollo and Hermes in which the latter employs argument from probability and is also accused of bribing a witness. But the speeches show no clear partition. The second is the trial scene in Aeschylus *Eumenides*, which is late enough to have come under the influence of early rhetorical teaching, and does not therefore properly belong to a survey of oratory before that teaching became available.

RHETORIC IN THE FIFTH CENTURY

It was not until political conditions were favourable that rhetoric flourished at all levels of society. Neither monarchy nor oligarchy afforded these conditions. It was only when all citizens enjoyed sovereign power to decide on political and judicial issues that the art of persuasion was called upon to marshal all its resources. Leaders in a democracy were, by definition, obliged to persuade the people to adopt their policies. In Athens, democracy entered the most positive phase of its development early in the fifth century, at the time of the Persian Wars (491-479 B.C.) During this time some crucial decisions were made by the Popular Assembly, and the man who guided them in these decisions was Themistocles. He persuaded the Athenians to enlarge their fleet before Xerxes' great invasion,[7] and so prepared them for the naval victory at Salamis. It is of interest to learn from biographical sources that Themistocles' powers of mass persuasion were not acquired without instruction. He is said to have received this from an otherwise unknown teacher named Mnesiphilus, who is described as a student of *sophia* (wisdom applied to practical matters).[8] In the accounts of Herodotus and Plutarch he appears as Themistocles' mentor in all aspects of his political career, which must have included what he said as well as what he did.[9] Plutarch also describes Mnesiphilus as a forerunner of the sophists,[10] who differed from him only in their greater professionalism and more formalised teaching, which undoubtedly included the techniques of public speaking. Finally, in his speech to the wavering Greeks on the eve of Salamis, Themistocles is reported by Herodotus to have contrasted the better with the worse in man's nature, and urged the Greeks to choose the better.[11] Unless Herodotus is guilty of literary anachronism, this speech is an early example of the antithetical style which dominated Athenian oratory for many years.

Progress towards more general availability of instruction in public speaking depended upon the publication of rhetorical handbooks. Ancient authorities are unanimous in tracing the first of these to Sicily.[12] There is no good reason to reject this tradition, but it needs qualification. Corax and Tisias were respectively master and pupil, but since they are usually mentioned together as the first writers of rhetorical handbooks, it is impossible to distinguish their individual contributions. However, the fact that Corax came into prominence at the time of the expulsion of the tyrants from Sicily (c.467 B.C.) is probably significant. Having previously acted in some sort of advisory capacity to the tyrants Hieron and Gelon, he was well placed to enter the political arena as a deliberative speaker on their departure.[13] Recognising the characteristics of a popular audience, he devised a form of oratory which exploited these characteristics. He saw that a large assembly must be initially settled down and made receptive, then presented with factual and argumentative material, and finally be given a summary and an emotionally charged ending in order to carry its judgment in the direction desired by the speaker.[14] This is clearly the first proposition of the tripartite division of a speech on which subsequent subdivisions were based. Corax was also interested in various forms of argument, and may have done pioneering work in the use of argument from probability.[15] But from this point onwards it becomes increasingly difficult to distinguish his contribution from that of Tisias. Evidence that Corax actually wrote anything on rhetoric is extremely tenuous, and perhaps it is this difference that separates the two. Just as no written teaching can safely be ascribed to Corax, so no separate and original theory can safely be ascribed to Tisias. His contribution probably lay in committing Corax's teaching, together with the fruits of their joint experience and thinking, to publishable form.[16] It may have been his elaboration of earlier work that produced the fourfold division (prooemium, narrative, proof, epilogue) of the classical Attic speech,[17] and he may have begun a classification of topics.[18] It was in his hands also that probability (*eikos*) argument assumed greater sophistication and was adapted for wider use. This broadening and elaboration of earlier teaching established Tisias as the main forerunner, according to the biographical tradition, of the first generation of Attic orators.

POLITICAL AND FORENSIC ORATORY

It must be emphasised that, throughout its early development, any distinction between political and forensic (or judicial) oratory is artificial. Not only did political subject-matter figure prominently in speeches delivered in the courts, but also the commonplace topics, types of argument and methods of arousing emotion were the same. This is not surprising, since the Popular Assembly (*Ecclesia*) and the Popular Courts (*Dikasteria*) comprised the same citizens, often in the same numbers. The differences arose later through the circumstances of their development, and perhaps even more through the obsession of theorists with classification.[19] In the fifth century interest centres chiefly upon political oratory and the rise of the *rhetor*, or political speaker, which was one of the most important products of the emergent Athenian democracy.[20] Although a degree of self-assurance might be expected of a man who embarked on a career in public life, it was a new and unfamiliar environment for many *parvenu* politicians. Such men found assistance from the teaching of the sophists, whose claims to be able to impart skill in a wide range of subjects included politics: indeed, it was upon their ability to train politicians that they laid the greatest store.[21] The teaching methods of the sophists probably varied according to the ability and experience of their pupils and to the fees which individuals could afford to pay. The standard method involved the use of set rhetorical discourses, which the pupil learned by heart.[22] These discourses used mythical or imaginary subjects to illustrate topics and types of argument which could be applied to similar situations in real life.[23] Sophists also illustrated rhetorical techniques through their own lectures,[24] incorporating passages which aimed at the same effects as a live oration.[25] Finally, they held discussions on a philosophical level with their more intelligent pupils and with other sophists on political, legal and ethical subjects of perennial interest.[26] Of the sophists who contributed to the development of rhetoric in the fifth century, Protagoras of Abdera was the first. He taught his pupils how to argue for and against the same case,[27] at length and in brief;[28] and he treated topics of general application, or *communes loci*.[29] More interestingly, he was concerned with grammar and the correct use of words,[30] a study shared by Prodicus of Ceos,[31] who also studied emotional appeal.[32] Thrasymachus of Calchedon developed this study, and made prose a more potent medium for arousing emotion by stylistic means, including the use of rhythm.[33] Finally, Gorgias of Leontini realised, beyond the bounds of refinement, the powers of the word in a style which incorporated balanced clauses, assonance and poetic vocabulary to such excess that he found few imitators, though the principles which he applied were influential, especially upon the style of Isocrates.[34]

Taught by these sophists and their various methods, aspirants to political fame faced a further challenge when they mounted the rostrum. Their audience expected them to speak without a text. Part of the magnetism of the most popular speakers came from their apparent spontaneity of thought, emotion and utterance.[35] But their oral masterpieces survived only in the memory of their audiences, for very few were published, and those mostly under unusual circumstances.[36] Nevertheless, the best of these oratorical virtuosi certainly influenced the style of deliberative oratory. For example, Pericles developed a penchant for striking imagery - Aegina was "the stye in the eye of the Piraeus"[37] ; with the death of the young men of Athens in a battle "the spring had gone out of the year"[38]; and the Boeotians, riven by civil war, were "like holm-oaks that are beaten down by knocking against one another".[39] That this kind of imagery became a feature of the style of the greatest Greek orator, Demosthenes,[40] can have been no accident, since he regarded Pericles as his guiding model,[41] and by following his example acknowledged that the political orator owed his audience the obligation of expressing himself memorably, since they looked to him for edification as well as advice. Moreover, his success in promoting his policies depended on their recollection of his main arguments, and there could be no better way of assisting this recollection than by highlighting them with images of the kind illustrated above. Again, a speaker who wished to appear spontaneous could have only limited recourse to the handbooks of rhetoric, and when he found it necessary to develop arguments on the standard deliberative themes of justice, expediency, possibility and opportunity, he must impress his own personal stamp upon them. Hence the art of political oratory was peculiarly difficult to learn,[42] and Isocrates was only being honest and realistic when he said that he could teach it only to pupils with special gifts.[43]

The conditions faced by the litigant in the law-courts were somewhat different and less demanding. Although the law required him to present his case in person, the availability of professional speechwriters alleviated his ordeal, if he could afford their services. Next, although it was probably normal for the litigant to memorise the speech,[44] it is unlikely that inability to do so could cause him to lose his case.[45] On the other hand, the speechwriter was judged by the same professional standards as the political orator. Although lawsuits tended to involve many recurrent situations which afforded him more opportunities than his political counterparts to utilise the common topics provided by the handbooks, his skills were fully extended, especially in the more difficult cases, in evaluating the relative importance of factors which might vary considerably from one case to another - the seriousness of the charge, the state of the law in regard to it, the extent of popular prejudice against his client or his alleged crime, and the political climate at the time of the trial. These factors also decided the relative lengths of prooemium, narrative, proof and epilogue. Having met these technical requirements, the speechwriter faced judgment on a higher aesthetic plane. There was a discerning reading public for forensic, as for ceremonial (epideictic) oratory, and there can be little doubt that perceived literary merit as much as success in the courtroom secured the survival of the speeches of Antiphon and Lysias. These speeches owed less to the handbooks, and to the mechanical application of their rules and commonplaces, than those of the many hack speechwriters whose work was lost and forgotten soon after it was written. But their literary distinction was of a peculiar kind, at least as conceived by critics. In the fourth century Alcidamas, while arguing in his pamphlet *Against the Sophists* for the superiority of impromptu over written oratory, said that the most effective forensic speeches are those which imitate the style of extemporising speakers.[46] Isocrates, who opposed Alcidamas' main thesis and classed forensic oratory, on the basis of current practice, as "written" composition, nevertheless describes its recommended style as "that which gives the impression of having been spoken in a simple manner and without embellishment",[47] and does not disagree with this view. The idea of art concealing art which this suggests, and which the critic Dionysius of Halicarnassus later echoes in his *Essay on Lysias* (8), appears to be a point in which Isocrates and Alcidamas are in substantial agreement in regard to forensic oratory. In view of their disagreement on almost all other matters, it is reasonable to believe that the appearance of artless simplicity was a characteristic which those who read forensic speeches generally looked for in the early fourth century, satisfying as it did both the literary reader and the potential client. There was no conflict between the two. The latter wanted a speech which he could deliver naturally, without speaking out of character but at the same time narrating the facts and presenting the arguments convincingly, and arousing the emotions of the jury in his favour. In the eyes of the former, a speech which met these criteria seemed to deserve no less praise than a fine poem or a piece of display oratory.[48]

This view of the nature of Attic Oratory expressed or implied by contemporaries provides a point of reference from which to approach the orations themselves. They are the published texts of speeches, most of which were made in actual trials. The speechwriter had the opportunity of hearing the evidence and some of the main arguments of his opponents on as many as three occasions before the trial.[49] He also had time after the trial for reflection and some revision. But such revision was probably superficial and did not include any substantial alteration in the presentation of material,[50] except possibly by way of abbreviation in some instances.[51] In his preparation of the final version of the speech for publication the speechwriter was subject to a tension between the need to set his own authentic stamp upon it (both in order to confound imitators and to establish his own credit), and the need to demonstrate his adaptability to different types of case and client. It is this mixture of common authorial features and individual treatment that informs the best Attic speeches. As to their arrangement and construction, the modern reader's main interest is in the speechwriter's application of the received rules of division, the amount of space he devotes to commonplaces, digressions, personal attacks on opponents and emotional appeal, and how the proportion of all these factors corresponds with the needs of the case. Our judgment is to some extent hampered by the fact that, in all but a few instances, we do not have the speeches delivered by the opposition, and in most cases we do not know the outcome. But these are minor misfortunes compared with the opportunity the speeches give us to enjoy the only Greek literature which serves both artistic and practical purposes in equal measure, and which affords a fresh and vital medium for the study of Greek history, law, society and morals.

NOTES TO GENERAL INTRODUCTION

1. Philodemus *Rhetorica* Fr.21 (Vol.2, 111 Sudhaus) appears to be the earliest clear reference to this controversy. See also Quint.10.1.46. Critics liked to trace the characteristics of the Three Styles back to Homeric speakers (Quint.12.10.64). Other refs.: Sopatros *in Hermog.* W V 6,3; Plut. *De Vita et Poesi Homeri* 92ff.; Radermacher, *AS*, 9-10; G. Kennedy, 'The Ancient Dispute over Rhetoric in Homer', *AJP* 78 (1957) 23-35.
2. Hom. *Il.*9.442-3.
3. Hom. *Il.* 15.284; Quint.2.17.8.
4. For discussions of the characteristics of Homeric oratory, see Kennedy, *APG*, 35-39; F. Solmsen, 'The Gift of Speech in Homer and Hesiod', *TAPA* 85 (1954) 1-15; M. Delaunois, *Le plan rhétorique dans l'éloquence grecque d'Homère à Démosthène* (Brussels, 1959) 7-16.
5. So Kennedy, *APG*, 36. But the presence of formulae in the speeches may be merely an extension of the poet's technique.
6. Hom. *Il.* 18.497-508. For a recent discussion, see MacDowell, *LCA*, 18-21, and his n.11 for bibliography.
7. Hdt. 7.144; Plut. *Them.* 4.1.
8. Plut. *Them.* 2.4.
9. Hdt. 8.57-8. R.J. Lenardon, *The Saga of Themistocles* (London, 1978) 22-23, regards Mnesiphilus as an important formative influence on Themistocles' political career.
10. *loc.cit.* (n.8).
11. 8.83.
12. Plato *Phaedr.* 267a, 273 a-d; Arist. *Soph.El.* 33(183b 29); Cic. *Inv.* 2.2.6-7, *Brutus* 12.46; Quint.3.1.8; Sopatros *in Hermog.* W V 6, 14. For other ancient refs. see Radermacher, *AS*, 11-27; and for a modern review of the evidence, G. Kennedy, 'The Earliest Rhetorical Handbooks', *AJP* 80(1959) 169-178.
13. Troilus in *Proleg. Syll.* 52. The whole tradition is carefully examined by S. Wilcox, 'Corax and the Prolegomena', *AJP* 64 (1943) 1-23, and he concludes that the historian Timaeus was the source of the tradition which gave primacy to deliberative oratory.
14. Anonym. in *Proleg. Syll.* 24.
15. Arist.*Rhet.*2.24.11; D.A.G. Hinks, 'Tisias, Corax and the Invention of Rhetoric', *CQ* 34 (1940) 63.
16. So Radermacher, *AS*,31, following Susemihl.
17. Though the evidence is confused, the four *partes orationis* (on which see Hinks, *op.cit.*(n.15) 66-69) are more likely to be the work of Tisias than anyone else, reflecting his interest in forensic rather than deliberative oratory. See Kennedy, *op.cit.*(n.12) 177-178.
18. See Süss 2ff.

19. Aristotle distinguished three kinds of oratory: deliberative, forensic and epideictic (*Rhet*.1.3). But before him this division is never clearly defined. It does not appear in Plato *Phaedrus*, and Isocrates, while expressing disdain for 'speeches made about private cases' (4 *Paneg*.11), does not indicate whether he considers his own discourses to be 'deliberative' or 'epideictic', and of course avoids referring to the speeches which he himself composed for the lawcourts. After a very thorough examination of the evidence, S.Wilcox concluded that instruction in the fifth century included both deliberative and forensic oratory ('The Scope of Early Rhetorical Instruction', *HSCP* 53(1942) 121-155). This seems to confirm the uncertainty of the distinction.
20. See W. Pilz, *Der Rhetor im attischen Staat* (Weida,1934).
21. Plato *Meno* 71e, 91a-b. G.B. Kerferd, *The Sophistic Movement* (Cambridge, 1981) 17ff.
22. Arist. *Soph.El.* 183b 36.
23. Surviving examples include Gorgias *Helen* (which may be humorous in intent) and *Palamedes* (which has a more practical forensic tone); Antisthenes *Ajax* and *Odysseus*; and Isocrates *Helen* and *Busiris*.
24. They liked to give their public appearances the trappings of a dramatic performance. See Kerferd, *op.cit*.(n.21) 28-9.
25. Arist.*Rhet*.3.14.9.
26. Kerferd, *op.cit*. (n.21) 30.
27. Seneca *Epist*.88.43; Steph.Byz. s.v. *Abdera*.
28. Plato *Protag*.334e.
29. Cic.*Brutus* 12.46; Quint.3.1.12.
30. Plato *Phaedr*.267c, *Crat*.391b; Arist.*Rhet*.3.5.5; Suidas s.v. *Protagoras*; Quint.3.4.9; Diog.Laert.9.52.
31. Plato *Euthyd*.277e, *Protag*.337a-c.
32. Arist.*Top*. 112b 21; Quint.3.1.12.
33. Arist.*Rhet*.3.1.7;3.8.4; Cic.*Orat*.52.175. There is also a tradition which credits Thrasymachus with fundamental influence in the development of prose style generally. See D.H. *Isaeus* 3,20; G.M.A. Grube, 'Thrasymachus, Theophrastus and Dionysius of Halicarnassus', *AJP* 73 (1952) 251-267 attacks this tradition. For a discussion of the problems, see H. Gotoff, 'Thrasymachus of Calchedon and Ciceronian Style', *CP* 75 (1980) 297-301.
34. See Radermacher, *AS*, 42-66; and for further bibliography MacDowell, *Gorgias: Encomium of Helen* (Bristol,1982) 7-8.
35. On the effectiveness of extempore speaking see Alcidamas, *De Sophistis*, esp.9-10. H.J. Milne, *Alcidamas and his Relation to Contemporary Sophistic* (Diss.Bryn Mawr, 1924) argues that this pamphlet is earlier than Plato *Phaedrus* and Isoc. *Ag.Soph*. On the importance of extempore speaking for political oratory, see Hudson-Williams 68-73.

36. See Plato *Phaedr*. 257d. The earliest extant deliberative speech may be Andocides, *On the Peace with Sparta*. It was probably composed when he was in exile. See Kennedy, *APG*, 204.
37. Arist.*Rhet*. 3.10.7.
38. *id*. 1.7.34; 3.10.7.
39. *id*. 3.4.3.
40. See G. Ronnet, *Étude sur le Style de Démosthène dans les Discours Politiques* (Paris, 1951).
41. Hermog. *Id*.2.9 (Sp.2.392).
42. Aristotle argues (*Rhet*.3.17) that political oratory is more difficult than forensic oratory because its subject-matter concerns the future, not the past.
43. 13 *Ag.Soph*.10, 14-15; 14 *Antid*.189,191.
44. Ar.*Knights*, 347-350.
45. See Usher (1976) 36-37.
46. 13.
47. *Panath*. 1-2.
48. Isocrates' frequent disparagement of forensic oratory is due to its popularity among readers who would, in his opinion, be more edified by studying discourse of the kind he wrote (4 *Paneg*.11;88; 15 *Panath*.271).
49. (1) When the case was submitted to an arbitrator (*diaitētēs*).
    (2) At the preliminary hearing (*anakrisis*).
    (3) On the entry of a special plea (*paragraphē*) by the defendant. See Harrison, *LA* 2,64-66, 94-104, 105-131.
50. Lavency, *ALJA*, 190.
51. Many speeches are shorter than the time that would have been allotted to them in the actual trial. See Lavency, *ALJA*, 191.

Select Bibliography

1. *Oratory and Rhetoric*
   F. Blass, *Die attische Beredsamkeit* (Leipzig, 1887-98,repr. 1962)
   (= Blass,*AB*).
   I. Bruns, *Das literarische Porträt der Griechen* (Berlin,1896).
   D.L. Clark, *Rhetoric in Graeco-Roman Education* (New York,1957).
   J.F. Dobson, *The Greek Orators* (London,1919).
   H. Gomperz, *Sophistik und Rhetorik* (Leipzig,1912).
   P. Hamberger, *Die rednerische Disposition in der alten* Τέχνη
   'Ρητορικἠ (Paderborn,1914).
   H.L. Hudson-Williams, 'Political Speeches in Athens', *CQ* N.S.1
   (1951) 68-73.
   R.C. Jebb, *The Attic Orators from Antiphon to Isaeus* (London, 1893
   repr.1962) (= Jebb, *AO*).
   G. Kennedy, *The Art of Persuasion in Greece* (Princeton,1963) (=
   Kennedy,*APG*).
   H. Kroll, *Rhetorik*, in Pauly *RE* Suppl.7 (1940).
   M. Lavency, *Aspects de la logographie judiciaire attique* (Louvain,
   1964)(= Lavency,*ALJA*).
   J. Martin, *Antike Rhetorik: Technik und Methode* (Munich,1974).
   O. Navarre, *Essai sur la rhétorique grecque avant Aristote* (Paris,
   1900).
   W. Pilz, *Der Rhetor im attischen Staat* (Weida,1934).
   L. Radermacher, *Artium Scriptores* (Vienna,1951) (= Radermacher,
   AS).
   R. Volkmann, *Die Rhetorik der Griechen und Römer* (Leipzig,1885).
   W. Wyse, *The Speeches of Isaeus* (Cambridge,1904).

2. *Antiphon and Lysias*
   U. Albini, 'Antifonte logografo', *Maia* 10(1958) 38-65.
   U. Albini, 'Rassegna di studi Lisiani', *Atene e Roma* 14-16 (1954)
   56-67.
   U. Albini, 'Lisia narratore', *Maia* 5 (1952) 182-190.
   U. Albini, 'L'orazione lisiana per l'invalido', *Rh.Mus.*95 (1952) 328-338.
   J.J. Bateman, 'Lysias and the Law', *TAPA* 89 (1958) 276-285.
   J.J. Bateman, 'Some Aspects of Lysias' Argumentation', *Phoenix* 16
   (1962) 157-177.
   F. Berbig, *Über das Genus Dicendi Tenue des Redners Lysias* (Küstrin,
   1871).
   P.S. Breuning, 'On the Date of Antiphon's Fifth Oration', *CQ* 31 (1937)
   67-70.
   O. Büchler, *Die Unterscheidung der redenden Personen bei Lysias*
   (Heidelberg, 1936).
   C. Cucuel, *Essai sur la langue et le style de l'orateur Antiphon* (Paris,
   1886).

14

W.L. Devries, *Ethopoiia, A Rhetorical Study of the Types of Character in the Orations of Lysias* (Baltimore, 1892).
A. Dihle, *Studien zur griechischen Biographie* (Göttingen,1956).
A.P. Dorjahn, 'Anticipation of Arguments in Athenian Courts', *TAPA* 66 (1935) 274-295.
A.P. Dorjahn & W.D. Fairchild, 'Antiphon and Improvisation', *CB* 50 (1973) 29-31.
K.J. Dover, 'The Chronology of Antiphon's Speeches', *CQ* 44 (1950) 44-60 (= Dover, *CAS*).
K.J. Dover, *Lysias and the Corpus Lysiacum* (Berkeley,1968) (= Dover, *LCL*).
B. Due, *Antiphon, A Study in Argumentation* (Copenhagen,1980).
H. Erbse, 'Antiphons Rede über die Ermordung des Herodes', *Rh.Mus.* 120 (1977) 209-227.
H. Erbse, 'Lysias-Interpretationen', (*Festschrift Ernst Kapp* (Hamburg, 1958)).
F. Ferckel, *Lysias und Athen* (Würzburg,1937).
D. Ferrante, *Antifonte, Peri tou Hērōidou phonou* (Naples,1972).
C.W. Francken, *Commentationes Lysiacae* (Utrecht,1865).
V. Fumarola, 'Il problema storico, civile e litterario di Lisia', *Atene e Roma* 10 (1965) 49-65.
P. Grau, *Prooemiengestaltung bei Lysias* (Diss.Erlangen,1971).
D.H. Holmes, *Index Lysiacus* (Bonn,1895).
D.G. Lateiner, *Lysias and Athenian Politics* (Diss.Stanford,1971).
T.C. Loening, 'The Autobiographical Speeches of Lysias and the Biographical Tradition', *Hermes* 109 (1981) 280-294.
W. Motschmann, *Die Charaktere bei Lysias* (Munich,1905).
F.A. Müller, *De Elocutione Lysiae* (Diss.Halle,1887).
A.C. Palau, 'Ipotesi per un "giallo" antico', *Helikon* 17 (1977) 193-209.
F. Scheidweiler, 'Antiphons Rede über den Mord an Herodes', *Rh.Mus.* 109(1966) 319-338.
U. Schindel, 'Untersuchungen zur Biographie des Redners Lysias', *Rh.Mus.* 110(1967) 32-52.
U. Schindel, 'Der Mordfall Herodes', *Nachr.der Akad.der Wiss. in Göttingen* 8 (1979) 1-41.
K. Schön, *Die Scheinargumente bei Lysias* (Paderborn,1918).
F. Solmsen, *Antiphonstudien* (Berlin,1931).
S. Usher, 'Individual Characterisation in Lysias', *Eranos* 63 (1965) 99-119.
S. Usher, 'Lysias and his Clients', *GRBS* 17 (1976) 31-40.
S. Usher, 'A Statistical Study of Authorship in the Corpus Lysiacum', *Computers and the Humanities* 16 (1982) 85-105 (with D.Najock).
F.L.van Cleef, *Index Antiphonteus* (Cornell,1895).
W. Voegelin, *Die Diabole bei Lysias* (Basel,1943).

3. *Language and Style*
   P. Chantraine, *La stylistique grecque* (Paris,1951).
   J.D. Denniston, *Greek Prose Style* (Oxford,1952).

J.D. Denniston, *The Greek Particles* (Oxford,1954).

K.J. Dover, *Greek Word Order* (Cambridge,1960).

H. Frisk, *Studien zur griechischen Wortstellung* (Göteborg,1933).

W.W. Goodwin, *Syntax of the Moods and Tenses of the Greek Verb* (repr.London,1966) (= *GMT*).

W.W. Goodwin, *A Greek Grammar* (repr.London,1976).

R. Kühner & B. Gerth, *Ausführliche Grammatik der griechischen Sprache* (Hannover,1955).

E. Norden, *Die antike Kunstprosa* (Leipzig,1898).

E. Schwyzer & A. Delbrunner, *Griechische Grammatik* (Munich, 1939-1953).

4. *History, Law and Society*

A. Böckh, *Die Staatshaushaltung der Athener* (Berlin,1886).

R.J. Bonner, *Evidence in Athenian Courts* (Chicago,1905).

R.J. Bonner, *Lawyers and Litigants in Ancient Athens* (New York, 1969) (=Bonner, *LL*).

R.J. Bonner & G. Smith, *The Administration of Justice from Homer to Aristotle* (repr.New York,1968) (= Bonner & Smith, *AJHA*).

E.W. Bushala, 'Torture of Non-Citizens in Homicide Investigations', *GRBS* 9 (1968) 61-68.

S. Cataldi, 'La restituzione della terra ai Mitilenensi e le rinnovate *xumbolai* tra Atene e Mitilene', *ASNP* 6(1976) 15-33.

P. Cloché, *La Restauration démocratique à Athènes en 403 av.J.C.* (Paris,1915) (= Cloché,*RDA*).

J.K. Davies, *Athenian Propertied Families 600-300B.C.* (Oxford, 1971) (= Davies,*APF*).

G.E.M. De Ste Croix, 'Notes on Jurisdiction in the Athenian Empire', *CQ* N.S.11 (1961) 94-112, 268-280.

A.P. Dorjahn, *Political Forgiveness in Old Athens* (Evanston,1946).

K.J. Dover, *Greek Popular Morality* (Oxford,1974) (= Dover,*GPM*).

M. Gagarin, 'The Prosecution of Homicide in Athens', *GRBS* 20 (1979) 301-323.

M. Gagarin, *Drakon and Early Athenian Homicide Law* (Yale,1981).

P. Gauthier, 'Les *XENOI* dans les textes athéniens de la seconde moitié du Ve siècle av. J.-C.', *REG* 84 (1971) 43-79.

P. Gauthier, *Symbola* (Nancy,1972).

G.Glotz, *La solidarité de la famille dans le droit criminel en Grèce* (Paris,1904).

A.W. Gomme, A. Andrewes & K.J. Dover, *A Historical Commentary on Thucydides*, 5 vols. (Oxford,1945-81) (= Gomme,*HCT*).

M.H. Hansen, *Eisangelia* (Odense,1975).

M.H. Hansen, *Apagoge, Endeixis and Ephegesis against Kakourgoi, Atimoi and Pheugontes* (Odense,1976) (= Hansen, *AEE*).

M.H. Hansen, 'The Prosecution of Homicide in Athens: A Reply', *GRBS* 22 (1981) 11-30.

A.R.W. Harrison, *The Law of Athens*, 2 vols. (Oxford 1968,1971) (= Harrison, *LA*).

C.Hignett, *A History of the Athenian Constitution to the End of the Fifth Century B.C.* (Oxford, 1952) (= Hignett, *HAC*).

W.K. Lacey, *The Family in Classical Greece* (London,1968) (= Lacey, *FCG*).

F. Lämmli, *Das attische Prozessverfahren in seiner Wirkung auf die Gerichtsrede* (Paderborn,1938).

J.W. Lipsius, *Das attische Recht und Rechtsverfahren mit Benutzung des attischen Prozesses*, 4 vols. (Leipzig, 1905-1915) (= Lipsius, *AR*).

J.O. Lofberg, *Sycophancy in Athens* (Chicago,1917).

D.M. MacDowell, *Andocides: On the Mysteries* (Oxford,1962).

D.M. MacDowell, *Athenian Homicide Law* (Manchester,1963). (= MacDowell, *AHL*).

D.M. MacDowell, *The Law in Classical Athens* (London,1978) (= MacDowell, *LCA*).

R. Meiggs, *The Athenian Empire* (Oxford,1972).

B.D. Merritt, 'Athenian Covenant with Mytilene', *AJP* 75 (1954) 359-368.

G.R. Morrow, 'The Murder of Slaves in Attic Law', *CP* 32 (1937) 210-227.

U.E. Paoli, 'Il reato di adulterio in diritto attico', *Studia et Documenta Historiae et Iuris* 16 (1950) 123-182.

P.J. Rhodes, *The Athenian Boule* (Oxford,1972) (= Rhodes, *AB*).

P.J. Rhodes, *A Commentary on the Aristotelian Athenaion Politeia* (Oxford,1981) (= Rhodes, *CAAP*).

G. Smith, 'Dicasts in the Ephetic Courts', *CP* 19 (1924) 353-358.

W. Süss, *Ethos* (Leipzig,1910).

G. Thür, *Beweisführung vor den Schwurgerichtshöfen Athens (Die Proklesis zur Basanos)* (Vienna,1977).

G.E. Underhill, *A Commentary on the Hellenica of Xenophon* (Oxford,1900).

U.von Wilamowitz-Moellendorff, *Aristoteles und Athen* (Berlin, 1893).

The Text (Antiphon)

The text of Antiphon is derived from two manuscripts only, which are independent and of equal authority: A, the Crippsianus (Brit. Mus. Burneianus 95) of the thirteenth century, and N, the somewhat younger Oxoniensis (Bodl. Misc. 208). It has long been agreed that the other surviving MSS. are all dependent on A. N was revised by its copyist (N. corr.1) and at least one corrector (N corr.2; these alterations were mere conjectures); while A was also corrected by its copyist (A corr.1) and by a second hand as far as 84 (A corr.2, in a different colour ink; the source of these corrections is completely uncertain).

The works most commonly referred to in the *apparatus criticus*, after the earliest editions of Aldus (1513, the *editio princeps*) and Stephanus (1575), are:

J.G. Baiter and H. Sauppe, *Oratores attici* (Zürich, 1839).
I. Bekker, *Oratores attici*, vol.1 (Oxford, 1822).
F. Blass, *Antiphontis orationes et fragmenta* (Leipzig, 1881).
P.P. Dobree, *Adversaria ad Antiphontem* (Berlin, 1875).
C. Fuhr, *Animadversiones in oratores atticos* (Bonn, 1877); 'Excurse zu den attischen Rednern', *Rh. Mus*. 33 (1878) 565-599.
L. Gernet, *Antiphon, Discours* (Paris, 1923).
G.A. Hirschig, 'Selectae emendationes et observationes in Antiphonte', *Philologus* 9 (1854) 728-739.
R.C. Jebb, *Selections from the Attic Orators* (London, 1888).
V. Jernstedt, *Antiphontis orationes* (Petersburg, 1880).
E. Mätzner, *Antiphontis orationes XV* (Berlin, 1838).
F. Pahle, *Antiphontis orationes critica ratione* (Jever, 1874).
J.J. Reiske, *Oratorum graecorum vol. VII* (Leipzig, 1773).
H. Sauppe, *Quaestiones Antiphonteae* (Göttingen, 1861).
T. Thalheim, *Antiphontis orationes et fragmenta* (Leipzig, 1914).

Further on the text, and with a fuller bibliography, see Thalheim.

The Text (Lysias)

The text of Lysias in this edition is based on that of Hude (Oxford, 1912), but a number of changes necessitated by later work has been made.

The parent manuscript is Palatinus Heidelbergensis 88 (12th Century) (X). It contains corrections (X^C), some in the hand of the original scribe ($X^C(1)$); other corrections by a later hand (X^r), and alternative readings (X^S). Marcianus 422 (15th Century) (H) is derived from the same archetype, but contains only Sp. 1 from the Lysianic Corpus. This manuscript was preferred to X by H. Schenkl (*Wiener Studien* 3 (1881) 81-5), but he was not followed by Hude. Of the remaining manuscripts, all derived from X or H, the most important is Laurentianus 57 (15th Century)(C), which Bekker used as the chief manuscript for his edition (Oxford, 1822; Berlin, 1823). Others used by Hude include Vaticanus Palatinus 117 (15th Century) (P), and to a lesser extent Vaticanus 66 (15th Century)(M), Vaticanus 1366 (15th Century) (N) and Urbinas 117 (15th Century) (O). As in the text of Antiphon, the Leiden *editio princeps* of Aldus Manutius (1513) and the edition of Stephanus (1575), supply some important readings, perhaps from lost manuscripts.

In the *apparatus* of both texts, absence of a source reference signifies a reading of the principal manuscripts.

The following works are referred to in the *apparatus criticus*:

A. Auger, *Lysiae Opera Omnia* (1783).
J. Bake, *Scholica Hypomnemata* Vol.II,III (*Mnem.7.8*).
T. Bergk, 'Epistola ad Schillerum in Schilleri Andocide', *Philologus* 14 (1859).
F. Blass, Notes in *Rhein.Mus.* 21 (1866) and Bursian's *Jahresbericht* 1,2,9,21,30 (1873-1883).
C.G. Cobet, *Oratio de Arte Interpretandi* (Leiden, 1847).
A. Contius, (Antoine Leconte, 1517-86), *Emendationes*.
A. Coraes, *Mnem.*2,3,9 (1853-70).
A. Emperius, *Observationes Brunsvigae* (1833); *Adversaria in Opusculis* p.313.
C. Francken, *Commentationes Lysiacae* (1865).
J. Franz, *Diss. de Locis Quibusdam Lysiacis* (Munich, 1830).
F.V. Fritzsche, *Emendationum Lys.*p.1 (Rostock, 1867);*Adversariorum* p.x (Rostock, 1873).
H. Frohberger, *Philol.* 15,19,29; *Phil. Ang.*II ff.
G. Gebauer, *De Praeteritionis Formis apud Oratores Atticos* (Leipzig, 1874); *De Hypotacticis et Paratacticis Argumenti ex Contrario Formis apud Oratores Atticos* (Zwicau, 1877).
H.G. Hamaker, *Quaestiones Nonnullis Lys.Orat.* (Leiden, 1843).

L.F. Herbst, *Suppl.Jahr.Kl.Phil.* 1857.
F.C. Hertlein, *Konjecturen zu Griech.Prosaikern.* Prog.Wertheim 1862.
H.van Herwerden, *Analecta Critica ad Lysiam.* Traiect.ad Rhen. 1868.
R.B. Hirschig, *Miscellanea Philologica et Paedagogica,* Fasc.1 (Amsterdam, 1850); *Mnem.*25.
J. Markland, *Lusiou ta perigenomena...accedunt J.Mark...conjecturae* (1739).
P.J. Maussac, *Harpocrationis Dictionarium in Decem Rhetores* (1614).
P.R. Müller, *De Emendandis Aliquot Locis Lysiae.* Prog.Rossleb. 1858; *Beitrage zur Kritik des Lysias.* Prog.Merseburg 1862,1866,1873.
G.G. Pluygers, 'Ad Lysiae Orationes', *Mnem.*11.
J.O. Sluiter, *Emendationum Lys.Fascic.Prog.*(Neostrelitz, 1852).
J. Taylor, *Lusiou ta perigenomena....interpretatione....donavit J. Taylor* (1739).
A. Weidner, *Jahrb.f.Phil.*87.
A. Westermann, *Commentationes in Script. Graec.* 4-6 (Leipzig, (1853-6); *Quaestionum Lysiacarum* 1-3 (Leipzig, 1859-65).

Editions:

Stephanus (1575) (Marginalia by Brulart de Sillery (1756)); Bekker (1822-3); Dobson (1828); Foertsch (1829); Franz (1831); Baiter-Sauppe (Zürich, 1839, hence 'Turicenses'); Scheibe (2nd.ed. 1852); Westermann (1854); Cobet (1863); Thalheim (1901); Gernet-Bizos (1924-26); Lamb (1930).
Select Orations: Bremer (1845); Rauchenstein-Fuhr (1848-99); Herwerden (1863); Frohberger-Gebauer-Thalheim (1866-95); Shuckburgh (1882); Weidner (1888); Morgan (1895); Jebb (1899); Adams (1905).

Antiphon

Most of the details of Antiphon's life before his emergence among the leaders of the oligarchic revolution in 411 are obscure. Our main sources are Thucydides 8.68 and the *Life* of Antiphon wrongly ascribed to Plutarch, from which our other authorities (the anonymous *genos Antiphōntos* found in the MSS.; Philostratus, *Lives* 1.15; Photius, cod.259) seem to derive and whose author in turn drew on Caecilius of Caleacte, the originator of the canon of ten Attic orators. Unfortunately, the later sources confuse the orator with at least two different Antiphons, the one executed by the Thirty (Xen. *Hell.* 2.3.40) and the tragedian put to death by the tyrant Dionysius (Arist. *Rhet.* 2.6.27), and so when [Plutarch] mentions an Antiphon conversing with Socrates (cf. Xen. *Mem.* 1.6) doubts arise as to whether this 'sophist' Antiphon was the same person as the orator. Further on this old chestnut see J.S. Morrison, 'Antiphon', *Proc. Cam. Phil. Soc.* 187 (1961) 49–58; H.C. Avery, 'One Antiphon or two?', *Hermes* 110 (1982) 145–158 (who argue against the view adopted by most scholars that we should distinguish the two, as did Didymus, ap. Hermog. *peri id.* 2.385-6 Walz).

Antiphon was born in the deme of Rhamnus in c.480. [Plutarch]'s statement that his father Sophilus was a sophist seems untenable, since Sophilus would have been an old man before the sophistic movement became prominent at Athens (and a confusion of Sophilus/sophist could easily have arisen). Antiphon's grandfather was a partisan of the Peisistratids (cf. Ant. frg.1 Thalheim) and his family background would have been influential in forming Antiphon's own oligarchic tendencies. But while Antiphon favoured the old-style government his thoughts were also shaped by the new culture of Athens, and even if we reject the equation of orator and sophist the influence on Antiphon of the Sicilian rhetoric can clearly be seen in two ways. Firstly in the field of theory, where Antiphon is credited with writing a three-volumed rhetorical handbook (*technē*; cf. frgg. 71-76 Th; its authenticity was denied by Pollux 6.143, = frg. 74) and a collection of proems and epilogues (see the proem, heading n.). More doubtful is the tradition that he opened a school in Athens (cf. Plato, *Menex.* 236a; Avery, *art. cit.*, 156, with n.39) and was Thucydides' teacher (perhaps an inference from Thucydides' praise of the orator in 8.68). Secondly in the practical application of the new rhetoric, Antiphon was generally regarded as the first *logographos*, or writer of speeches for money (as [Plut.] 832c; Ammian. Marc. 30.4.5; Quint. 3.1.11; on his accompanying reputation for avarice see Avery, *art. cit.*, 152-153). The need for such speechwriters arose as a direct result of the subtle argumentation and polished style that the

Sicilians taught, and there was none better at the time than Antiphon.

But a consequence of Antiphon's ability was that he gained a reputation for cleverness (*deinotēs*), which made him suspect to the people and prevented him from enjoying a successful political career. His sharp intellect, which supposedly earned him the nickname 'Nestor' ([Plut.] 832e), is shown by the *Tetralogies*, in which both sides of a case are argued (always assuming these are authentic works of Antiphon; see recently on this much disputed question Avery, *art. cit.*, 155-156, who favours Antiphon's authorship). Antiphon therefore sought to gain influence by his speechwriting and put his skills to practical use in the cause of Athens' oppressed allies. This is indicated both in the *Herodes* speech (composed for a Mytilenean) and in the fragments (as the speeches for the Lindians and Samothracians on the matter of their tribute, frgg.25-33, 49-56 Th). Antiphon may well have been acting here as a member of one of the oligarchic clubs (*hetaireiai*) which were working behind the scenes against the democracy (cf. Ar. *Wasps* 1269-70, 1301-02; Avery, *art. cit.*, n.34; additionally, Antiphon attacks the corruption of democratic officials in speech 6, perhaps written for an oligarchic sympathiser, and he reviles Alcibiades in a polemical pamphlet, frg. 66, = Plut. *Alcib.* 3); and he probably played a crucial role in bringing these clubs together in 411. But Antiphon's triumph was short-lived, as the new Council of 400 divided into two factions, the extreme oligarchs (including Antiphon himself, Peisander and Phrynichus) and the moderates (led by Theramenes and Aristocrates). Antiphon and Phrynichus were forced to go to Sparta for help, an embassy which outraged popular feeling at Athens. On their return Phrynichus was assassinated and the 400 were deposed. Most of the leading extremists fled to Decelea, but Antiphon, Archeptolemus and Onomacles stayed behind to face trial for treason (though Onomacles too seems later to have fled). Antiphon delivered what Thucydides regarded as the greatest defence speech by a man on a capital charge up to that time, entitled *On the Revolution* (*peri tēs metastaseōs*, frg. 1 Th), but he was nevertheless condemned. After his execution burial of his body was refused, his house was razed to the ground and he and his descendants were disgraced. See further on the revolution Lys. 12 *Erat.* 65-67, with notes.

In the Augustan age sixty speeches ascribed to Antiphon were extant, of which twenty-five were pronounced spurious by Caecilius. Fifteen survive today (including the three *Tetralogies* of four speeches each), as well as a number of fragments. All the remaining speeches relate to cases of homicide, but the titles of the fragments show either that this is a quirk of fate or that only homicide cases survived in the Antiphontean corpus, as representing the field in which Antiphon excelled (cf. the survival only of Isaeus' inheritance speeches). Our speech is the fifth one in the MSS. The other two complete surviving speeches are *Against a Stepmother* (1) and *On the Choreutes* (6).

Style

Dionysius (*Comp. Verb.* 22-24) took Antiphon as a representative of what he called the 'austere' or 'rugged' style (*austēra harmonia*). A feature of this style is its dignity and grandeur, relying on the weight of individual, pointed words and pregnant phrases (as in 94). The vocabulary is often rare or poetical (as *optēr* 27; *aeimnēstos* 79; see 10, a murderer shall pay with his life in requital); and there is frequent periphrasis, both substantival (definite article with neuter participle or adjective, i.e. synonyms for abstract nouns) and verbal (verbal noun with auxiliary, as in 94). Antiphon's sentence-structure is mainly periodic (*lexis katestrammenē*), though the brief narrative in the speech is in the more natural form of the running style (*lexis eiromenē*). But these periods are by no means carefully balanced (except in the proem and epilogue; n.b. the opening sections of the speech in particular, which contain several well-balanced, corresponding clauses), they are rather noticeable for their antithesis, a figure commonly brought out by the use of the particles *men* and *de*. But while many figures of language (*schēmata lexeōs*) occur, especially in the worked-up proem and epilogue sections, figures of thought (*schēmata dianoias*, such as irony and rhetorical questions) are rare.

The Murder of Herodes

Introduction

Antiphon composed this speech, which was recognised by ancient criticism as one of his best (cf. Caecilius in [Plut.] 833d), for a wealthy young Mytilenean defendant in a trial for homicide at Athens. Euxitheus[1] and an Athenian named Herodes (perhaps one of the cleruchs sent out to Lesbos after the revolt of 428-427) were among the passengers on a vessel sailing from Mytilene in Lesbos to Aenus in Thrace. Before rounding Lesbos they were forced by a storm to put in near Methymna, where they transferred from their undecked ship to a decked vessel bound for Mytilene and began drinking. During the evening Herodes left the vessel and was never seen again. After a search Euxitheus continued his voyage to Aenus, while the second vessel went on to Mytilene, where it was searched by Herodes' relatives. They also tortured two men, one of whom, a slave, incriminated Euxitheus. Additionally, a note was discovered during a second search of the vessel which purported to be a message to a certain Lycinus, informing him of the murder. Herodes' relatives then executed the slave and began proceedings against Euxitheus, lodging a writ of endictment (*endeixis*) with the Eleven at Athens. Euxitheus was imprisoned on his arrival there until his trial, which took place before a panel of heliasts in the court of the Eleven. The result is unknown. (For a good recent discussion see Schindel, *MH*, 29-41, who tends to believe Euxitheus' alibi but rightly draws attention to

23

the historical and political, as well as juridical, reasons why the long defence speech that has come down to us was necessary.)

Date
    The date of the speech is also uncertain. Scholars such as Blass, *AB* I, 126 and Jebb, *AO* I, 62 considered its style to be less developed than that of the *Choreutes* (speech 6) and guessed at 417–413, with c. 412 for the latter. B.D. Meritt, *The Athenian Calendar in the Fifth Century* (Harvard, 1928) 121–122 then contended that speech 6 is to be dated on internal evidence to 419–418, but Dover, *CAS*, 44–53 maintained the old dating of the *Herodes* by arguing that on points of style 5 is actually later than 6. Dover, however, is by no means fully convincing (e.g. the presence of poetic vocabulary in 5 and its absence in 6 is hardly an indication of stylistic development; similarly the archaic formula *touto men...touto de...* occurs several times in 5 but not in 6). Breuning 67–70 tried to find internal indications in the *Herodes*, taking 78 as referring to Lesbian exiles and traitors in Antandrus in the summer of 424 (cf. Thuc. 4.52.2). The common argument against such an early dating is that Euxitheus was still a child in 428 (cf. 75) and some time must therefore have passed before the trial, but Breuning rightly pointed out that when Euxitheus compares his age with that of his father (74, 75, 79) he does so in a rhetorical fashion, giving no indication as to what the ages ·actually were. So Euxitheus may have been about thirteen in 428, and this would not rule out the possibility that the trial took place in the late twenties. Nevertheless, Breuning's 424 does seem a little too early and 'your enemies' in 78, upon which he based his theory, need not necessarily refer to the exiles in Antandrus.[2] But if 78 reflects recent troubles in the area after the revolt, as befits the context of 76–78, we may still date the speech to c. 420.

The *Prokataskeuē* (8–19)
    The major difficulty presented by the *Herodes*, and the question which makes it so interesting and important in legal terms, is to what extent the objections Euxitheus raises in the *prokataskeuē* to the method of procedure adopted against him are valid. For he was tried under an *endeixis kakourgias*[3] (indictment for wrongdoing; cf. 9, *kakourgos endedeigmenos*) rather than the *dikē phonou* regular in homicide trials and this, he argues, was illegal. There has been much scholarly debate over the use of *endeixis* and the closely related *apagōgē* in homicide trials and arguments such as whether there are any parallels to our case, e.g. Lysias 13, *Against Agoratus*, continue to rage (see Hansen, *AEE*, 103–107; Gagarin (1979) 313–322; Hansen (1981) 21–30). The main considerations with regard to our speech are as follows:
i) did an alien accused of the murder of an Athenian citizen have the same rights as a citizen defendant (i.e. should Euxitheus have been tried as a murderer, *phoneus*, before the court of the Areopagus

rather than as a wrongdoer, *kakourgos*, before a heliastic court)? Maidment, *MAO* I, 151-152 argued that the *dikē phonou* was parochial in operation, being tied up with the concept of pollution of the community by one of its members with blood-guilt, and therefore it could not be applied to foreigners, for whom *apagōgē* was the regular procedure. But it is unwise to assume that a pollution doctrine was fundamental in the establishment of Athenian homicide law (see MacDowell, *AHL*, 141-150) and there is no other evidence that the position of foreigners in this respect was any different from that of Athenian citizens (though we might distinguish between citizens of a state which had a legal treaty with Athens, *sumbola*, and those whose state had no legal relations; see Schindel, *MH*, 11). Indeed, Euxitheus repeatedly argues that he was the first to suffer such harsh treatment: it was this new application of *endeixis*, not his nationality, that caused his loss of rights.[4]

ii) did homicide in any case fall within the range of crimes covered by the law on wrongdoers (*nomos tōn kakourgōn*)? *Kakourgēmata* were mainly offences against property and if thieves (*kleptai*), footpads (*lōpodutai*) and also kidnappers (*andrapodistai*) were mentioned in the law, murderers clearly were not (cf. 9; 10 shows that the prosecution had to justify their calling homicide a *kakourgēma*).[5] Perhaps, then, the prosecution were taking advantage of the loose wording of the law, while Antiphon saw this as another act of oppression by Athenians against a member of an allied state. Euxitheus should have been tried under a *dikē phonou* before the Areopagus[6] and he twice alludes to such a trial: in 16 he fears that on his acquittal in the present trial the prosecution will demand a second hearing and in the epilogue (85-96) he actually requests a retrial (although this was probably out of the question, on the principle of *ne bis in idem*; cf. Dem. 20 *Lept.* 147; Bonner & Smith, *AJHA* 2, 256; Harrison, *LA* 2, 119-120).

This is, of course, to take an anti-prosecution stance. It is also possible that they were in fact merely taking advantage of some recent legislation. Most scholars would interpret lines 74-75 of the Chalcis Decree (ML 52; c. 446-445) as meaning voluntary reference to Athens in the second instance by appeal; see De Ste Croix 271-272; Meiggs 224-226; MacDowell, *LCA*, 226-227. This decree probably reflects general Athenian practice in the early days of the empire with regard to trials involving major penalties. But between the Chalcis Decree and the *Herodes* such trials were compulsorily transferred to Athens, as is indicated both by 47, 'when it is not permitted even to an allied state to inflict the death penalty on anyone without the consent of the Athenian people', and by [Xen.] *Ath. Pol.* 1.16 (c. 424). Perhaps the beginning of the Archidamian War, with the revolt of Mytilene, had hardened Athens' attitude. The use of *endeixis* in Euxitheus' case was then an attempt to stop him defaulting, his right in a *dikē phonou* (below), and was possibly even what we would call a test case to find a more practical alternative to the regular procedure.

iii) was Euxitheus' imprisonment before the trial legal? In 17 he complains bitterly that no alien who had been willing to furnish the required sureties had ever been refused bail and that the relevant law applied to the Eleven as well as to other magistrates. Hansen, *AEE*, 13-17 countered that in truth it was up to the prosecution in an *endeixis* whether they wished to follow up the denunciation with an arrest and then grant bail or imprison their suspect. Another argument is that of Gauthier (1971) 53-55, that the right of bail for an alien such as Euxitheus must have been granted by the judicial treaty between Athens and Mytilene (all foreigners would not simply have been allowed this privilege) and now that cases involving the death penalty had been transferred to Athens this right probably no longer existed. Either way, one wonders whether the Eleven would have imprisoned Euxitheus if this was clearly illegal and Euxitheus' strong protest may be seen as another reflection of the ambiguity of Athenian laws: it was the regular practice to grant bail, but this was not in fact a legal requirement.

As a result of his imprisonment and the use of *endeixis* Euxitheus could neither default before the trial nor go into voluntary exile after his first defence speech in a *dikē phonou* (13). The common assumption of modern scholars has again been that the Athenians would not have allowed a foreigner the same rights as a citizen, especially since voluntary exile from Athens was hardly a penalty to many aliens. However, not only would the existence of a judicial treaty have given an alien defendant certain rights, but also Euxitheus was not imprisoned, it seems, until he reached Athens, whither he had gone of his own accord (13, cf. 93): if this was the case Euxitheus enjoyed similar rights to a citizen until he came to defend himself. In addition, we should expect that defaulting or self-imposed exile would have led to Euxitheus' debarment from Mytilene as well as from Athens, in that although the trial was now held in Athens as a matter of course the crime was still committed in Mytilene by a Mytilenean.[7] Indeed, in 62 Euxitheus contrasts what would have happened to himself and his alleged Athenian accomplice Lycinus if their plotting was discovered: Lycinus would have been deprived of all his rights, Euxitheus of his country.

iv) was the suit "estimable" (an *agōn timētos*) or "inestimable" (*atimētos*)? Euxitheus' statement in 10 that the prosecution had made a *timēsis* is perhaps the most difficult to deal with: the penalty for the deliberate murder of an Athenian citizen was death and normally the penalty in an *endeixis kakourgias* was also death (as Euxitheus envisages elsewhere, in 16, 59, 71, 90-92, 94-95); see Harrison, *LA* 2, 225-226, 231; Hansen, *AEE*, 21. Euxitheus' statement here, however, suggests that we have an estimable suit. If, as several scholars have been inclined to believe, the suit was in reality inestimable we probably have to read into this remark a deliberate attempt to confuse the jury. The novelty of the use of this procedure in a homicide case may have led to a certain amount of confusion and to a proposal of the death penalty by the prosecution, a slip with which Euxitheus is now making play. The Eleven would already have rejected their proposal at the *anakrisis* (preliminary hearing), but Euxitheus could still refer to it. Other scholars, however, think we must take Euxitheus' words at face value. In that case, it is unclear why an *endeixis kakourgias* for homicide should have been any different from other types of *endeixis kakourgias*. But the main question then is what the *timēsis* was and for this there are two options, the death penalty or some less severe punishment such as a fine. Euxitheus seems to imply the former in his speech, despite what he says in 10, but some scholars (such as Maidment and Hansen) have assumed from this passage that a monetary penalty was proposed by the prosecution.[8] However, it is almost unthinkable that the prosecution, having argued that Euxitheus killed Herodes, should then have proposed merely a fine. Rather, they probably proposed the death penalty, either according to correct procedure or by a technical error, and this provided Euxitheus with a ready opportunity to reproach them (since if, on his condemnation, his proposal for a less severe penalty was accepted Herodes would not be receiving his lawful due, *tōn en tōi nomōi keimenōn*).

In sum, Euxitheus does seem to have been the recipient of harsh treatment in this case, though it is doubtful whether we should believe all his contentions. But Antiphon had to use every means at his disposal if his Mytilenean client was to have any chance of success before a panel of Athenian heliasts, still mindful of the events on Lesbos in 428-427. Euxitheus' nationality was his greatest problem.

---

1. The name is given by Sopatros (ap. Walz, *Rhet. Graec.* IV, 316), a source whose value has been doubted more than once; see Blass, *AB* I, 645; Schindel, *MH*, 4.
2. E.g. Gomme, *HCT* 2, 331 n. 2 put the emigrants of 78 in the Persian Hellespont satrapy and, *pace* Breuning, the 'enemies' could well have been the Persians, even at a time when they were not actually at war with Athens.
3. Not under an *apagōgē kakourgias*, as many scholars have asserted. Hansen, *AEE*, 9-24 has brought out the differences between *endeixis* (denunciation), which was often followed by arrest (*apagōgē*, as in our case; cf. 9), and simple *apagōgē* (summary arrest). One relevant here is that *endeixis*, contrary to the traditional definition, did not preclude a summons (*prosklēsis*): for practical reasons Euxitheus could not be arrested until he came to Athens and so he was probably summoned to appear there on his return to Mytilene from Aenus. See further 13, even when summoned.
   We may at this point also dismiss the several attempts that have been made to show that, since *apagōgē* was used, the trial involved something more than just homicide, such as murder with robbery; see, e.g., H.J. Wolff, *Die attische Paragraphe* (Weimar, 1966) 112-119. All these theories have

serious defects, not least that throughout his speech Euxitheus treats his trial solely as one for homicide.
4. Although his nationality was probably the reason behind the use of *endeixis* and was a prominent factor in the case.
5. As Hansen, who then drew five parallels to support his view that homicide could nevertheless be classed as a *kakourgēma* (*AEE*, 10 3-107); *contra*, MacDowell, *AH L*, 135; Gagarin (1979) 320 n. 60; restated in Hansen (1981) 21-30.
6. Of the five homicide courts only the Palladium was specifically connected with foreigners ([Arist.] *Ath. Pol.* 57.3), hence Smith 358 thought that Euxitheus asks for a retrial there. But the *Ath. Pol.* only deals with the status of the victim and we should expect the killer of a citizen to have been tried before the Areopagus regardless of his nationality. Additionally, in 16 and 96 Euxitheus assumes that in a retrial he would be facing the death penalty, which was not imposed by the Palladium (see Schindel, *MH*, 10). Euxitheus never actually mentions the Areopagus by name, but he had to be careful not to give the impression that he thought he would receive a fairer hearing there than before a panel of heliasts.
7. And if a Mytilenean was found guilty of unintentional homicide, for which the penalty was exile, the Athenians would not have let him simply return to Mytilene.
8. *lusiteIountos* ('for their own benefit') does not, however, necessarily imply financial gain: Antiphon may be using the word to heighten the effect of the *ou...alla...* antithesis. It is also doubtful whether the prosecution would have had such a motive, as some scholars have inferred, since the fine in a public suit such as this went to the state.

ANTIPHON

ΠΕΡΙ ΤΟΥ ΗΡΩΙΔΟΥ ΦΟΝΟΥ

1   'Εβουλόμην μέν, ὦ ἄνδρες, τὴν δύναμιν τοῦ λέγειν καὶ
τὴν ἐμπειρίαν τῶν πραγμάτων ἐξ ἴσου μοι καθεστάναι τῇ τε
συμφορᾷ καὶ τοῖς κακοῖς τοῖς γεγενημένοις· νῦν δὲ τοῦ
μὲν πεπείραμαι πέρα τοῦ προσήκοντος, τοῦ δὲ ἐνδεής εἰμι
2   μᾶλλον τοῦ συμφέροντος. οὐ μὲν γάρ με ἔδει κακοπαθεῖν τῷ
σώματι μετὰ τῆς αἰτίας τῆς οὐ προσηκούσης, ἐνταυθοῖ οὐδέν με ὠφέλησεν ἡ ἐμπειρία· οὗ δέ με δεῖ σωθῆναι μετὰ
τῆς ἀληθείας εἰπόντα τὰ γενόμενα, ἐν τούτῳ με βλάπτει ἡ
3   τοῦ λέγειν ἀδυνασία. πολλοὶ μὲν γὰρ ἤδη τῶν οὐ δυναμένων
λέγειν, ἄπιστοι γενόμενοι τοῖς ἀληθέσιν, αὐτοῖς τούτοις
ἀπώλοντο, οὐ δυνάμενοι δηλῶσαι αὐτά· πολλοὶ δὲ τῶν <δυ-
ναμένων> λέγειν, πιστοὶ γενόμενοι τῷ ψεύδεσθαι, τούτῳ
ἐσώθησαν, διότι ἐψεύσαντο. ἀνάγκη οὖν, ὅταν τις ἄπειρος
ᾖ τοῦ ἀγωνίζεσθαι, ἐπὶ τοῖς τῶν κατηγόρων λόγοις εἶναι
μᾶλλον ἢ ἐπ' αὐτοῖς τοῖς ἔργοις καὶ τῇ ἀληθείᾳ τῶν πραγ-
4   μάτων. ἐγὼ οὖν, ὦ ἄνδρες, αἰτήσομαι ὑμᾶς οὐχ ἅπερ οἱ
πολλοὶ τῶν ἀγωνιζομένων ἀκροᾶσθαι σφῶν αὐτῶν αἰτοῦνται,
σφίσι μὲν αὐτοῖς ἀπιστοῦντες, ὑμῶν δὲ προκατεγνωκότες
ἄδικόν τι — εἰκὸς γὰρ ἐν ἀνδράσι γε ἀγαθοῖς καὶ ἄνευ τῆς
αἰτήσεως τὴν ἀκρόασιν ὑπάρχειν τοῖς φεύγουσιν, οὕπερ καὶ
5   οἱ διώκοντες ἔτυχον ἄνευ αἰτήσεως· — τάδε δὲ δέομαι ὑμῶν,
τοῦτο μὲν ἐάν τι τῇ γλώσσῃ ἁμάρτω, συγγνώμην ἔχειν μοι,
καὶ ἡγεῖσθαι ἀπειρίᾳ αὐτὸ μᾶλλον ἢ ἀδικίᾳ ἡμαρτῆσθαι,
τοῦτο δὲ ἐάν τι ὀρθῶς εἴπω, ἀληθείᾳ μᾶλλον ἢ δεινότητι
εἰρῆσθαι. οὐ γὰρ δίκαιον οὔτ' ἔργῳ ἁμαρτόντα διὰ ῥήματα
σωθῆναι, οὔτ' ἔργῳ ὀρθῶς πράξαντα διὰ ῥήματα ἀπολέσθαι·
τὸ μὲν γὰρ ῥῆμα τῆς γλώσσης ἁμάρτημά ἐστι, τὸ δ' ἔργον
6   τῆς γνώμης. ἀνάγκη δὲ κινδυνεύοντα περὶ αὐτῷ καί πού τι
καὶ ἐξαμαρτεῖν. οὐ γὰρ μόνον τῶν λεγομένων ἀνάγκη ἐνθυμεῖσθαι, ἀλλὰ καὶ τῶν ἐσομένων· ἅπαντα γὰρ τὰ ἐν ἀδήλῳ
ἔτ' ὄντα ἐπὶ τῇ τύχῃ μᾶλλον ἀνάκειται ἢ τῇ προνοίᾳ. ταῦτ'
οὖν ἔκπληξιν πολλὴν παρέχειν ἀνάγκη ἐστὶ τῷ κινδυνεύοντι.
7   ὁρῶ γὰρ ἔγωγε καὶ τοὺς πάνυ ἐμπείρους τοῦ ἀγωνίζεσθαι

---

2   ἀδυνασία Sauppe coll. Bekker an. I.345: ἀδυναμία
3   τῶν <δυναμένων> λέγειν Jernstedt: δυναμένων om. Apr. N,
     repos. A corr. 2 post λέγειν
4   post αἰτήσομαι add. δὲ N Jernstedt (qui — signum post
     ἄνδρες ponit), in A erasum
5   δὲ post τάδε om. N Apr., add. corr. 2   συγγνώμην
     ἔχειν μοι in libris ante τοῦτο μὲν tradita transp.
     Baiter   οὐ δίκαιον . . . γνώμης affert Stobaeus flor.
     46.65

Antiphon : On the Murder of Herodes

I could have wished, gentlemen, that my powers of speech and my experience of affairs were as great as the misfortune and the severities which have befallen me. But as it is, I have experienced far more of the last two than I should have and am more wanting in the first than is good for me. For when I had to submit to the physical suffering that accompanied this unwarranted charge I had no experience to help me; and now, when I have to win my safety by giving a truthful account of what happened, my cause is being damaged by my inability to speak. Many men poor at speaking have before now been disbelieved because they told the truth, and the truth itself ruined them because they could not establish it; while many able at speaking have been believed because they told lies and have been saved by this very fact, that they lied. Therefore it is inevitable that the fate of a man who is inexperienced in litigation depends more on his accusers' words than on the actual facts and the true account of the events. I shall therefore ask you, gentlemen, not for a hearing, as do the majority of those on trial, lacking confidence in themselves and prejudging you to be biased; for it is reasonable to assume that with an honest jury the same hearing will be granted to the defence even without its asking which the prosecution also received without asking. Rather, I request this of you, that if, on the one hand, I make some mistake in speaking, you will pardon me and attribute the error to inexperience and not to dishonesty; and if, on the other hand, I express something well, you will attribute this to truthfulness and not to skill. For it is not just either that a man who has transgressed in deed should be saved by words or that a man who has acted innocently should be undone by words : the tongue is to blame for a word, the will for an act. Moreover, it is inevitable that a man in personal danger will make some mistake : he must think not only of his argument but also of his fate, since anything which is still in doubt depends more on chance than foresight. Hence considerations such as these are bound to cause much consternation in the mind of a man in danger. I notice that even speakers with

1

2

3

4

5

6

7

πολλῷ χεῖρον ἑαυτῶν λέγοντας, ὅταν ἔν τινι κινδύνῳ ὦσιν·
ὅταν δ' ἄνευ κινδύνων τι διαπράσσωνται, μᾶλλον ὀρθουμέν-
ους. ἡ μὲν οὖν αἴτησις, ὦ ἄνδρες, καὶ νομίμως καὶ ὁσίως
ἔχουσα, καὶ ἐν τῷ ὑμετέρῳ δικαίῳ οὐχ ἧσσον ἢ ἐν τῷ ἐμῷ·
περὶ δὲ τῶν κατηγορημένων ἀπολογήσομαι καθ' ἕκαστον.

8   Πρῶτον μὲν οὖν, ὡς παρανομώτατα καὶ βιαιότατα εἰς
τόνδε τὸν ἀγῶνα καθέστηκα, τοῦτο ὑμᾶς διδάξω, οὐ τῷ φεύ-
γειν ἂν τὸ πλῆθος τὸ ὑμέτερον, ἐπεὶ κἂν ἀνωμότοις ὑμῖν
καὶ μὴ κατὰ νόμον μηδένα ἐπιτρέψαιμι περὶ τοῦ σώματος
τοῦ ἐμοῦ διαψηφίσασθαι, ἕνεκά γε τοῦ πιστεύειν ἐμοί τε
μηδὲν ἐξημαρτῆσθαι εἰς τόδε τὸ πρᾶγμα καὶ ὑμᾶς γνώσεσθαι
τὰ δίκαια, ἀλλ' ἵνα ᾖ τεκμήρια ὑμῖν καὶ τῶν ἄλλων πραγμάτων [καὶ] τῶν εἰς ἐμὲ ἡ τούτων βιαιότης καὶ παρανομία.

9   πρῶτον μὲν γὰρ κακοῦργος ἐνδεδειγμένος φόνου δίκην
φεύγω, ὃ οὐδεὶς πώποτ' ἔπαθε τῶν ἐν τῇ γῇ ταύτῃ. καὶ ὡς
μὲν οὐ κακοῦργός εἰμι οὐδ' ἔνοχος τῷ τῶν κακούργων νόμῳ,
αὐτοὶ οὗτοι τούτου γε μάρτυρες γεγένηνται. περὶ γὰρ τῶν
κλεπτῶν καὶ λωποδυτῶν ὁ νόμος κεῖται, ὧν οὐδὲν ἐμοὶ
προσὸν ἀπέδειξαν. οὕτως εἴς γε ταύτην τὴν ἀπαγωγὴν νομι-
10   μωτάτην καὶ δικαιοτάτην πεποιήκασιν ὑμῖν τὴν ἀποψήφισίν
μου. φασὶ δὲ αὖ τό τε ἀποκτείνειν μέγα κακούργημα εἶναι,
καὶ ἐγὼ ὁμολογῶ μέγιστόν γε. καὶ τὸ ἱεροσυλεῖν καὶ τὸ
προδιδόναι τὴν πόλιν· ἀλλὰ χωρὶς περὶ αὐτῶν ἑκάστου οἱ
νόμοι κεῖνται. ἐμοὶ δὲ πρῶτον μέν, οὗ τοῖς ἄλλοις εἴρ-
γεσθαι προαγορεύουσι τοῖς τοῦ φόνου φεύγουσι τὰς δίκας,
ἐνταυθοῖ πεποιήκασι τὴν κρίσιν, ἐν τῇ ἀγορᾷ· ἔπειτα τί-
μησίν μοι ἐποίησαν, ἀνταποθανεῖν τοῦ νόμου κειμένου τὸν
ἀποκτείναντα, οὐ τοῦ ἐμοὶ συμφέροντος ἕνεκα, ἀλλὰ τοῦ
σφίσιν αὐτοῖς λυσιτελοῦντος, καὶ ἐνταῦθα ἔλασσον ἔνειμαν
τῷ τεθνηκότι τῶν ἐν τῷ νόμῳ κειμένων· οὗ δ' ἕνεκα, γνώ-
11   σεσθε προϊόντος τοῦ λόγου. ἔπειτα δέ, ὃ πάντας οἶμαι
ὑμᾶς ἐπίστασθαι, ἅπαντα τὰ δικαστήρια ἐν ὑπαίθρῳ δικάζει
τὰς δίκας τοῦ φόνου, οὐδενὸς ἄλλου ἕνεκα ἢ ἵνα τοῦτο μὲν
οἱ δικασταὶ μὴ ἴωσιν εἰς τὸ αὐτὸ τοῖς μὴ καθαροῖς τὰς
χεῖρας, τοῦτο δὲ ὁ διώκων τὴν δίκην τοῦ φόνου ἵνα μὴ
ὁμωρόφιος γίγνηται τῷ αὐθέντῃ. σὺ δὲ τοῦτο μὲν παρελθὼν
τοῦτον τὸν νόμον τοὐναντίον τοῖς ἄλλοις πεποίηκας· τοῦτο
δὲ δέον σε διομόσασθαι ὅρκον τὸν μέγιστον καὶ ἰσχυρότατον,
ἐξώλειαν σαυτῷ καὶ γένει καὶ οἰκίᾳ τῇ σῇ ἐπαρώμενον, ἦ μὴν
μὴ ἄλλα κατηγορήσειν ἐμοῦ ἢ εἰς αὐτὸν τὸν φόνον, ὡς ἔκτεινα,
ἐν ᾧ οὔτ' ἂν κακὰ πολλὰ εἰργασμένος ἡλισκόμην ἄλλῳ ἢ
αὐτῷ τῷ πράγματι, οὔτ' ἂν πολλὰ ἀγαθὰ εἰργασμένος τού-
12   τοις ἂν ἐσῳζόμην τοῖς ἀγαθοῖς· ἃ σὺ παρελθών, αὐτὸς

---

8   καὶ del. Sauppe
10 αὖ τό γε Sauppe   μέγα Aldus: με   ἔνειμαν] ἔνειμαν
    ἂν N, ἂν ἔνειμαν ἂν Apr., in quo ἂν utrumque erasum,
    spiritus vocis ἔνειμαν a corr. 2 restitutus est
11 σαυτῷ N, αὐτῷ A
12 σὺ παρελθὼν A: συμπαρελθὼν N

32

considerable experience of litigation are far from being at their best when in any danger; they are more successful when seeking to effect some object without dangers. This, then, is my request, gentlemen, one made according to human and divine law and taking into account your duty no less than my right. As for the charges, I shall answer them one by one.

Firstly, I shall prove to you that I stand on trial here through highly illegal and violent methods. Not on the chance of eluding the judgment of your court, since I would commit my life to your decision even if you were not on oath and there were no law on the matter, having confidence in my innocence of this charge and the justice of your verdict. My object, rather, is that the violent and illegal behaviour of the prosecution may indicate to you also the nature of the rest of their case against me. 8

First, although an information has been laid against me as a malefactor I am being tried for murder, a thing which has never happened before to anyone in this country. Indeeed, the prosecution themselves have borne witness to the fact that I am not a malefactor nor liable to the law against malefactors. For this law is concerned with thieves and footpads and they have not shown me deserving of either title. Thus, as far as this arrest of mine is concerned, they have made my acquittal your most lawful and just course. They argue that murder is a grave malefaction – and I agree, a very grave one indeed – as are sacrilege and treason: but the laws which apply to each of them differ. In my case the prosecution have firstly caused the trial to be held in the very place from which others charged with murder are debarred by proclamation, the Agora; and secondly, although the law decrees that a murderer shall pay with his life in requital they made an assessment against me – not out of consideration for me, but for their own benefit – and by so doing assigned to the dead man less than his lawful due. Their motives for this you will learn in the course of my speech. 9 10

Secondly, as of course you all know, all the courts judge murder cases in the open air, for no other reason than that on the one hand the jurors may avoid entering the same building as those whose hands are unclean, and that on the other hand the one conducting the prosecution for murder may avoid being under the same roof as the murderer. But you on the one hand have evaded this law and done the opposite to the rest; and on the other., although you should have sworn the greatest and most binding oath known, on pain of bringing destruction on yourself, your kin and your house, that you would accuse me only in connection with the murder itself, to the effect that I committed it – whereby however many crimes I had carried out I could not have been condemned except for this one thing, and however many good deeds I had carried out I could not have been saved by these good deeds – this requirement you have evaded. You have invented laws to suit yourself, you are prosecuting me unsworn 11 12

σεαυτῷ νόμους ἐξευρών, ἀνώμοτος μὲν αὐτὸς ἐμοῦ κατηγορεῖς, ἀνώμοτοι δὲ οἱ μάρτυρες καταμαρτυροῦσι, δέον αὐτοὺς τὸν αὐτὸν ὅρκον σοὶ διομοσαμένους καὶ ἁπτομένους τῶν σφαγίων καταμαρτυρεῖν ἐμοῦ. ἔπειτα κελεύεις τοὺς δικαστὰς ἀνωμότοις πιστεύσαντας τοῖς μαρτυροῦσι φόνου δίκην καταγνῶναι, οὓς σὺ αὐτὸς ἀπίστους κατέστησας παρελθὼν τοὺς κειμένους νόμους, καὶ ἡγῇ χρῆναι αὐτοῖς τὴν σὴν παρανο-
13 μίαν κρείσσω γενέσθαι αὐτῶν τῶν νόμων. λέγεις δὲ ὡς οὐκ ἂν παρέμεινα εἰ ἐλελύμην, ἀλλ᾽ ᾠχόμην ἂν ἀπιών, ὡσπερεὶ ἄκοντά με ἀναγκάσας εἰσελθεῖν εἰς τὴν γῆν ταύτην. καίτοι ἐμοὶ εἰ μηδὲν διέφερε στέρεσθαι τῆσδε τῆς πόλεως, ἴσον ἦν μοι καὶ προσκληθέντι μὴ ἐλθεῖν, ἀλλ᾽ ἐρήμην ὀφλεῖν τὴν δίκην, τοῦτο δὲ ἀπολογησαμένῳ τὴν προτέραν ἐξεῖναι ἐξελθεῖν· ἅπασι γὰρ τοῦτο κοινόν ἐστι. σὺ δέ, ὃ τοῖς ἄλλοις Ἕλλησι κοινόν ἐστιν, ἰδίᾳ ζητεῖς με μόνον ἀπο-
14 στερεῖν, αὐτὸς σαυτῷ νόμον θέμενος. καίτοι τούς γε νόμους οἳ κεῖνται περὶ τῶν τοιούτων, πάντας ἂν οἶμαι ὁμολογῆσαι κάλλιστα νόμων ἁπάντων κεῖσθαι καὶ ὁσιώτατα. ὑπάρχει μέν γε αὐτοῖς ἀρχαιοτάτοις εἶναι ἐν τῇ γῇ ταύτῃ, ἔπειτα τοὺς αὐτοὺς ἀεὶ περὶ τῶν αὐτῶν, ὅπερ μέγιστόν ἐστι σημεῖον νόμων καλῶς κειμένων· ὁ γὰρ χρόνος καὶ ἡ ἐμπειρία τὰ μὴ καλῶς ἔχοντα ἐκδιδάσκει τοὺς ἀνθρώπους. ὥστε οὐ δεῖ ὑμᾶς ἐκ τῶν τοῦ κατηγόρου λόγων τοὺς νόμους καταμανθάνειν, εἰ καλῶς ὑμῖν κεῖνται ἢ μή, ἀλλ᾽ ἐκ τῶν νόμων τοὺς τοῦ κατηγόρου λόγους, εἰ ὀρθῶς καὶ νομίμως ὑμᾶς διδάσκουσι τὸ
15 πρᾶγμα ἢ οὔ. Οὕτως οἵ γε νόμοι κάλλιστα κεῖνται οἱ περὶ φόνου, οὓς οὐδεὶς πώποτε ἐτόλμησε κινῆσαι· σὺ δὲ μόνος δὴ τετόλμηκας γενέσθαι νομοθέτης ἐπὶ τὰ πονηρότερα, καὶ ταῦτα παρελθὼν ζητεῖς με ἀδίκως ἀπολέσαι. ἃ δὲ σὺ παρανομεῖς, αὐτὰ ταῦτά μοι μέγιστα μαρτύριά ἐστιν· εὖ γὰρ ᾔδεις ὅτι οὐδεὶς ἂν ἦν σοι ὃς ἐκεῖνον τὸν ὅρκον διομο-
16 σάμενος ἐμοῦ κατεμαρτύρησεν. Ἔπειτα δὲ οὐχ ὡς πιστεύων τῷ πράγματι ἀναμφισβητήτως ἕνα τὸν ἀγῶνα περὶ τοῦ πράγματος ἐποιήσω, ἀλλὰ ἀμφισβήτησιν καὶ λόγον ὑπελίπου ὡς καὶ τότε τοῖς δικασταῖς ἀπιστήσων. ὥστε μηδέν μοι ἐνθάδε [μηδὲ] πλέον εἶναι μηδ᾽ ἀποφυγόντι, ἀλλ᾽ ἐξεῖναί σοι λέγειν ὅτι κακοῦργος ἀπέφυγον, ἀλλ᾽ οὐ τοῦ φόνου τὴν δίκην· ἑλὼν δ᾽ αὖ ἀξιώσεις με ἀποκτεῖναι ὡς τοῦ φόνου

---

12 ἐξευρών A: εὑρών N
ἡγεῖ Dryander et P. Müller, ἡγῇ Blass: εὖ γε A, ἥ γε N
13 τὴν δίκην om. N
14 ὑμᾶς (post δεῖ) A: ἡμᾶς N   διδάσκουσι Reiske: διδάξ-ουσι A, διδάξει N
15 πονηρότερα N: πονηρότατα A   μαρτύρια A: μαρτυρία N
(μεγίστη corr. 2 N)
16 τότε τοὺς Denniston: τοῖς τότε AN, τοῖς ἐνθάδε vel τοῖσδε τοῖς Pahle   μηδὲ del. Reiske   αὖ ἀξιώσεις Bekker: ἂν ἀξιώσῃς NApr., ἂν ἀξιώσεις A corr. 2, ἂν ἀξιώσαις Sauppe

34

and your witnesses are giving evidence against me unsworn, although they should have given this evidence having sworn the same oath as you, with hand laid upon the sacrifice. Moreover, you bid the jurors believe your witnesses though unsworn and pass sentence for murder, witnesses whom you yourself have made untrustworthy by your evasion of the laws of the land – and you imagine that in the eyes of the jurors your illegal behaviour should have greater authority than the laws themselves. You reply that I would not have stayed to face   13 trial if I had been left at liberty but would have run away, as if you had forced me to come to this country against my will. Yet if it did not matter to me to be debarred from this city it would have been equally open to me not to come even when summoned, but lose the case by default, or alternatively to avail myself of the right of leaving the country after making my first defence speech: this is open to everyone. But you, for personal reasons, are trying to deprive me, and me alone, of a privilege accorded to every Greek by framing a law to suit yourself.

    Yet everyone would agree, I think, that the laws which deal with   14 such cases as this are the finest and most hallowed of all laws. They have the distinction of being the oldest in this country and also have always remained the same concerning the same matters; and this is the surest sign of laws well made, since time and experience show mankind what is imperfect. Hence you must not use the speech for the prosecution to discover whether your laws are good or bad, but you must use the laws to discover whether or not the speech for the prosecution is giving you a correct and lawful interpretation of the case.

    Thus the laws on homicide are excellent and no one has ever   15 before dared to change them. You alone have dared to turn legislator and make changes for the worse, and by this arbitrary behaviour you are seeking to destroy me unjustly. But your infringement of the law is itself very weighty evidence for me, because you well knew that you would find no one to testify against me once he had sworn that preliminary oath.

    Thirdly, instead of acting like a man confident in his case and   16 arranging that it be tried once and indisputably you left room for dispute and argument, as though even from the outset you were going to distrust the jurors. Hence I am no better off even if I am acquitted today, but you can say that I was acquitted as a malefactor, not on the charge of murder. On the other hand, if you win you will claim my life as being found guilty on the charge of

τὴν δίκην ὠφληκότα. καίτοι πῶς ἂν εἴη τούτων δεινότερα
μηχανήματα, εἰ ὑμῖν μὲν ἅπαξ τουτουσὶ πείσασι κατείργασ-
ται ἃ βούλεσθε, ἐμοὶ δ᾽ ἅπαξ ἀποφυγόντι ὁ αὐτὸς κίνδυνος
17 ὑπολείπεται; Ἔτι δὲ μάλ᾽ ἐδέθην, ὦ ἄνδρες, παρανομώτατα
ἁπάντων ἀνθρώπων. ἐθέλοντος γάρ μου ἐγγυητὰς τρεῖς καθιστάναι κατὰ τὸν νόμον, οὕτως οὗτοι διεπράξαντο τοῦτο ὥστε
μὴ ἐγγενέσθαι μοι ποιῆσαι. τῶν δὲ ἄλλων ξένων ὅστις πώποτε ἠθέλησε καταστῆσαι ἐγγυητάς, οὐδεὶς πώποτ᾽ ἐδέθη.
καίτοι οἱ ἐπιμεληταὶ τῶν κακούργων τῷ αὐτῷ χρῶνται νόμῳ
τούτῳ. ὥστε καὶ οὗτος κοινὸς τοῖς ἄλλοις πᾶσιν ὢν ἐμοὶ
18 μόνῳ ἐπέλιπε μὴ ὠφελῆσαι. τούτοις γὰρ ἦν τοῦτο συμφέρον,
πρῶτον μὲν ἀπαρασκευότατον γενέσθαι με, μὴ δυνάμενον δια-
πράσσεσθαι αὐτὸν τἀμαυτοῦ πράγματα, ἔπειτα κακοπαθεῖν τῷ
σώματι, τούς τε φίλους προθυμοτέρους ἔχειν τοὺς ἐμαυτοῦ
τούτοις τὰ ψευδῆ μαρτυρεῖν ἢ ἐμοὶ τἀληθῆ λέγειν, διὰ τὴν
τοῦ σώματος κακοπάθειαν. ὄνειδός τε αὐτῷ τε ἐμοὶ περι-
έθεσαν καὶ τοῖς ἐμοῖς προσήκουσιν εἰς τὸν βίον ἅπαντα.
19   Οὑτωσὶ μὲν δὴ πολλοῖς ἐλασσωθεὶς τῶν νόμων τῶν ὑμετέρων καὶ τοῦ δικαίου καθέστηκα εἰς τὸν ἀγῶνα· ὅμως
μέντοι γε καὶ ἐκ τούτων πειράσομαι ἐμαυτὸν ἀναίτιον ἐπιδεῖξαι. καίτοι χαλεπόν γε τὰ ἐκ πολλοῦ κατεψευσμένα καὶ
ἐπιβεβουλευμένα, ταῦτα παραχρῆμα ἀπελέγχειν· ἃ γάρ τις
μὴ προσεδόκησεν, οὐδὲ φυλάξασθαι ἐγχωρεῖ.
20   Ἐγὼ δὲ τὸν μὲν πλοῦν ἐποιησάμην ἐκ τῆς Μυτιλήνης, ὦ
ἄνδρες, ἐν τῷ πλοίῳ πλέων ᾧ Ἡρώδης οὗτος, ὅν φασιν ὑπ᾽
ἐμοῦ ἀποθανεῖν· ἐπλέομεν δὲ εἰς τὴν Αἶνον, ἐγὼ μὲν ὡς
τὸν πατέρα — ἐτύγχανε γὰρ ἐκεῖ ὢν τότε —, ὁ δ᾽ Ἡρώδης
ἀνδράποδα Θραξὶν ἀνθρώποις ἀπολύσων. συνέπλει δὲ τά τε
ἀνδράποδα ἃ ἔδει αὐτὸν ἀπολῦσαι, καὶ οἱ Θρᾷκες οἱ λυσό-
μενοι. τούτων δ᾽ ὑμῖν τοὺς μάρτυρας παρέξομαι.

ΜΑΡΤΥΡΕΣ

21   Ἡ μὲν πρόφασις ἑκατέρῳ τοῦ πλοῦ αὕτη· ἐτύχομεν δὲ
χειμῶνί τινι χρησάμενοι, ὑφ᾽ οὗ ἠναγκάσθημεν κατασχεῖν
εἰς τῆς Μηθυμναίας τι χωρίον, οὗ τὸ πλοῖον ὥρμει τοῦτο
εἰς ὃ μετεκβάντα φασὶν ἀποθανεῖν αὐτὸν τὸν Ἡρώδην. καὶ
πρῶτον μὲν αὐτὰ ταῦτα σκοπεῖτε, ὅτι <οὐ τῇ ἐ>μῇ προνοίᾳ
μᾶλλον ἐγίγνετο ἢ τύχῃ. οὔτε γὰρ πείσας τὸν ἄνδρα οὐδαμοῦ ἀπελέγχομαι σύμπλουν μοι γενέσθαι, ἀλλ᾽ αὐτὸς καθ᾽
22 αὐτὸν τὸν πλοῦν πεποιημένος ἕνεκα πραγμάτων ἰδίων· οὔτ᾽

17 μοι A: με N   ὅστις πώποτε A: ὅστύς ποτε N   ὑπέλειπε
    Apr., ἐπέλειπε N A corr. 1, tertium ε in A erasum
    μὴ ὠφελῆσαι Gernet: ὠφελῆσαι τοῦδε κόσμου N Apr.,
    ὠφελῆσθαι τοῦδε τοῦ νόμου corr. 2
18 αὐτὸν Bekker: ἐμαυτὸν   αὐτῷ τε Reiske: αὐτῷ γε
19 ἐλασσωθεὶς N Apr., ἕλος σωθεὶς A corr., ἕλος σωθεὶς
    libr. deter.
21 μετεκβάντα A corr. N: μεταβάντα Apr.   ὅτι <οὐ τῇ
    ἐ>μῇ Jebb: ὅτι μὴ ΑΝ, ὅτι οὐ Mätzner   καθ᾽ αὐτὸν
    Stephanus: κατ᾽ αὐτὸν

murder. Could anything more unfair be contrived, if you achieve your purpose by once convincing these jurors, while I am left facing the same peril after one acquittal?

Then again, gentlemen, I was imprisoned by an act of 17 unparalleled illegality. I was ready to furnish three sureties according to the law, but the prosecution took steps to ensure that I could not do so. Yet no other alien who ever was willing to furnish sureties has ever been imprisoned; and the custodians of malefactors abide by this same law. Hence this law by which everyone benefits failed to be of help in my case, and in mine alone. The reason was that it was to 18 the prosecution's advantage firstly that I should be quite unprepared for my trial, being unable to look after my interests in person; and secondly that I should undergo bodily suffering, and by reason of that bodily suffering find my friends readier to tell lies as witnesses for the prosecution than speak the truth on my behalf. Additionally, they have brought lifelong disgrace on me and my family.

Such, then, are the manifold ways in which I suffered loss in 19 respect of your laws and justice before coming to trial. However, despite this I shall try to prove my innocence, although it is indeed difficult to refute offhand false charges so carefully framed: one cannot prepare oneself against the unexpected.

I sailed from Mytilene, gentlemen, as a passenger on the same 20 boat as this Herodes whom they say I murdered. We were bound for Aenus, I to visit my father, who happened to be there at the time, and Herodes to ransom some slaves to certain Thracians. The slaves whom he was to release were also passengers, so too the Thracians who were to pay the ransom. I will produce witnesses to prove these statements to you.

WITNESSES

Such were the respective purposes of our voyage. However, we 21 happened to meet with a storm which forced us to put in at a place in the territory of Methymna, where there lay at anchor the boat on to which Herodes transhipped and on which the prosecution allege he met his end.

Now firstly consider these circumstances in themselves, that they were due to chance, not to any design on my part. It has nowhere been shown that I persuaded Herodes to come on the voyage with me: rather, it has been shown that I made the voyage independently on private business. Nor again, as is clear, was I making the voyage to 22

αὖ ἐγὼ ἄνευ προφάσεως ἱκανῆς φαίνομαι τὸν πλοῦν ποιησά-
μενος εἰς τὴν Αἶνον, οὔτε κατασχόντες εἰς τὸ χωρίον
τοῦτο ἀπὸ παρασκευῆς οὐδεμιᾶς, ἀλλ' ἀνάγκη χρησάμενοι·
οὔτ' αὖ ἐπειδὴ ὡρμισάμεθα, ἡ μετέκβασις ἐγένετο εἰς τὸ
ἕτερον πλοῖον οὐδενὶ μηχανήματι οὐδ' ἀπάτῃ, ἀλλ' ἀνάγκῃ
καὶ τοῦτο ἐγίγνετο. ἐν ᾧ μὲν γὰρ ἐπλέομεν, ἀστέγαστον
ἦν τὸ πλοῖον, εἰς ὃ δὲ μετ<εξ>έβημεν, ἐστεγασμένον· τοῦ
δὲ ὑετοῦ ἕνεκα ταῦτ' ἦν. τούτων δ' ὑμῖν μάρτυρας παρέξομαι.

MAPTYPEΣ

23 Ἐπειδὴ δὲ μετεξέβημεν εἰς τὸ ἕτερον πλοῖον, ἐπίνομεν. καὶ ὁ μέν ἐστι φανερὸς ἐκβὰς ἐκ τοῦ πλοίου καὶ οὐκ
εἰσβὰς πάλιν· ἐγὼ δὲ τὸ παράπαν οὐκ ἐξέβην ἐκ τοῦ πλοίου
τῆς νυκτὸς ἐκείνης. τῇ δ' ὑστεραίᾳ, ἐπειδὴ ἀφανὴς ἦν ὁ
ἀνήρ, ἐζητεῖτο οὐδέν τι μᾶλλον ὑπὸ τῶν ἄλλων ἢ καὶ ὑπ'
ἐμοῦ· καὶ εἴ τῳ τῶν ἄλλων ἐδόκει δεινὸν εἶναι, καὶ ἐμοὶ
ὁμοίως. καὶ εἷς τε τὴν Μυτιλήνην ἐγὼ αἴτιος ἢ πεμφθῆναι
24 ἄγγελον, καὶ τῇ ἐμῇ γνώμῃ ἐπέμπετο· καὶ ἄλλου οὐδενὸς
ἐθέλοντος βαδίζειν, οὔτε τῶν ἀπὸ τοῦ πλοίου οὔτε τῶν αὐτῷ
τῷ Ἡρῴδῃ συμπλεόντων, ἐγὼ τὸν ἀκόλουθον τὸν ἐμαυτοῦ πέμπειν ἕτοιμος ἦ· καίτοι οὐ δήπου γε κατ' ἐμαυτοῦ μηνυτὴν
ἔπεμπον εἰδώς. ἐπειδὴ δὲ ὁ ἀνὴρ οὔτε ἐν τῇ Μυτιλήνῃ
ἐφαίνετο ζητούμενος οὔτ' ἄλλοθι οὐδαμοῦ, πλοῦς τε ἡμῖν
ἐγίγνετο, καὶ τἆλλ' ἀνήγετο πλοῖα ἅπαντα, ᾠχόμην κἀγὼ
πλέων. τούτων δ' ὑμῖν τοὺς μάρτυρας παρασχήσομαι.

MAPTYPEΣ

25 Τὰ μὲν γενόμενα ταῦτ' ἐστίν· ἐκ δὲ τούτων ἤδη σκοπεῖτε τὰ εἰκότα. πρῶτον μὲν γὰρ πρὶν ἀνάγεσθαί με εἰς
τὴν Αἶνον, ὅτε ἦν ἀφανὴς ὁ ἀνήρ, οὐδεὶς ἠτιάσατό με
ἀνθρώπων, ἤδη πεπυσμένων τούτων τὴν ἀγγελίαν· οὐ γὰρ ἂν
ποτε ᾠχόμην πλέων. ἀλλ' εἰς μὲν τὸ παραχρῆμα κρεῖσσον ἦν
τὸ ἀληθὲς καὶ τὸ γεγενημένον τῆς τούτων αἰτιάσεως, καὶ
ἅμα ἐγὼ ἔτι ἐπεδήμουν· ἐπειδὴ δὲ ἐγώ τε ᾠχόμην πλέων καὶ
οὗτοι ἐξ ἐπιβουλῆς συνέθεσαν ταῦτα καὶ ἐμηχανήσαντο κατ'
26 ἐμοῦ, τότε ἠτιάσαντο. λέγουσι δὲ ὡς ἐν μὲν τῇ γῇ ἀπέθανεν
ὁ ἀνήρ, κἀγὼ λίθον αὐτῷ ἐνέβαλον εἰς τὴν κεφαλήν, ὃς οὐκ
ἐξέβην τὸ παράπαν ἐκ τοῦ πλοίου. καὶ τοῦτο μὲν ἀκριβῶς
οὗτοι ἴσασιν· ὅπως δ' ἠφανίσθη ὁ ἀνήρ, οὐδενὶ λόγῳ εἰκότι
δύνανται ἀποφαίνειν. δῆλον γὰρ ὅτι ἐγγύς που τοῦ λιμένος
εἰκὸς ἦν τοῦτο γίγνεσθαι, τοῦτο μὲν μεθύοντος τοῦ ἀνδρός,
τοῦτο δὲ νύκτωρ ἐκβάντος ἐκ τοῦ πλοίου· οὔτε γὰρ αὐτοῦ

---

22 μετέκβασις A corr. N: μετάβασις Apr.   μετ<εξ>έβημεν
    Pahle: μετέβημεν   μάρτυρας Reiske (sic semper Anti-
    pho): μαρτυρίας
23 μετεξέβημεν A: μετέβημεν N   ἐκ post ἐκβὰς om. N, ἐκ
    post ἐξέβην om. A   ἢ (post αἴτιος) Jernstedt: ἦν,
    item 24, 29
26 αὐτῷ ἐνέβαλον N: ἐνέβαλον αὐτῷ A   τοῦτο (post ἦν) A:
    αὐτὸ N   αὐτοῦ Taylor: αὐτοῦ

Aenus without good reason, nor did we put in at this place by any prearrangement; we were forced to do so. Nor again, when we had anchored, did the transhipment take place through any plan or ruse, but this too followed of necessity. For the boat on which we were sailing had no deck, whereas that onto which we transhipped had a deck; and the rain was the reason for this exchange. I will produce witnesses to prove these statements to you.

WITNESSES

After crossing to the other boat we began drinking. Now it is 23 clear that Herodes left the boat and did not board it again, but I did not leave the boat at all that night. Next day, when Herodes was missing, I joined in the search just as anxiously as any, and if anyone thought it was a serious matter I did. Not only was I responsible for a messenger being sent to Mytilene, that is, it was decided to send one on my suggestion, but also, when no one else 24 was willing to go, neither one of the passengers nor one of Herodes' companions, I offered to send my own attendant; and I hardly think I was deliberately proposing to send someone who would inform against me. When finally the search failed to reveal any trace of Herodes either in Mytilene or anywhere else, and fair sailing-weather returned and the rest of the boats began putting out to sea, I too took my departure. I will bring forward witnesses to prove these statements to you.

WITNESSES

Those are the facts; from them consider the probabilities. First, 25 before I put to sea for Aenus, when Herodes was missing, nobody at all accused me, although the prosecution had already heard the news; otherwise I should never have taken my departure. For the moment the true facts of the matter were more powerful than any accusation they could make and, besides, I was still on the island. It was when I had taken my departure and the prosecution had conspired to form this plot against me that they made their accusation.

They allege that Herodes died on shore and I, who did not leave 26 the boat at all, hit him on the head with a stone. Of this they have detailed information, but they cannot give any plausible account of how Herodes came to disappear. Clearly, the probabilities suggest that the crime was committed somewhere near the harbour, since on the one hand Herodes was drunk, and on the other it was at night that he left the boat. He would probably have been in no condition to

κρατεῖν ἴσως ἂν ἐδύνατο, οὔτε τῷ ἀπάγοντι νύκτωρ μακρὰν
27 ὁδὸν ἡ πρόφασις ἂν εἰκότως ἐγίγνετο· ζητουμένου δὲ τοῦ
ἀνδρὸς δύο ἡμέρας καὶ ἐν τῷ λιμένι καὶ ἄπωθεν τοῦ λιμένος, οὔτε ὀπτὴρ οὐδεὶς ἐφάνη οὔθ' αἷμα οὔτ' ἄλλο σημεῖον
οὐδέν. κᾆτ' ἐγὼ συγχωρῶ τῷ τούτων λόγῳ, παρεχόμενος μὲν
τοὺς μάρτυρας ὡς οὐκ ἐξέβην ἐκ τοῦ πλοίου· εἰ δὲ καὶ
ὡς μάλιστα ἐξέβην ἐκ τοῦ πλοίου, οὐδενὶ τρόπῳ εἰκὸς ἦν
ἀφανισθέντα λαθεῖν τὸν ἄνθρωπον, εἴπερ γε μὴ πάνυ πόρρω
28 ἀπῆλθεν ἀπὸ τῆς θαλάσσης. Ἀλλ' ὡς κατεποντώθη λέγουσιν.
ἐν τίνι πλοίῳ; δῆλον γὰρ ὅτι ἐξ αὐτοῦ τοῦ λιμένος ἦν τὸ
πλοῖον. πῶς ἂν οὖν οὐκ ἐξηυρέθη; καὶ μὴν εἰκός γε ἦν καὶ
σημεῖόν τι γενέσθαι ἐν τῷ πλοίῳ ἀνδρὸς τεθνεῶτος καὶ
ἐκβαλλομένου νύκτωρ. νῦν δὲ ἐν ᾧ μὲν ἔπινε πλοίῳ καὶ
ἐξ οὗ ἐξέβαινεν, ἐν τούτῳ φασὶν εὑρεῖν σημεῖα, ἐν ᾧ
αὐτοὶ μὴ ὁμολογοῦσιν ἀποθανεῖν τὸν ἄνδρα· ἐν ᾧ δὲ κατεποντώθη, οὐχ ηὗρον οὔτ' αὐτὸ τὸ πλοῖον οὔτε σημεῖον οὐδέν.
τούτων δ' ὑμῖν τοὺς μάρτυρας παρασχήσομαι.

ΜΑΡΤΥΡΕΣ

29   Ἐπειδὴ δὲ ἐγὼ μὲν φροῦδος ἦ πλέων εἰς τὴν Αἶνον, τὸ
δὲ πλοῖον ἧκεν εἰς τὴν Μυτιλήνην ἐν ᾧ ἐγὼ καὶ ὁ Ἡρῴδης
ἐπίνομεν, πρῶτον μὲν εἰσβάντες εἰς τὸ πλοῖον ἠρεύνων, καὶ
ἐπειδὴ τὸ αἷμα ηὗρον, ἐνταῦθα ἔφασαν τεθνάναι τὸν ἄνδρα·
ἐπειδὴ δὲ αὐτοῖς τοῦτο οὐκ ἐνεχώρει, ἀλλ' ἐφαίνετο τῶν
προβάτων ὂν αἷμα, ἀποτραπόμενοι τούτου τοῦ λόγου συλ-
30 λαβόντες ἐβασάνιζον τοὺς ἀνθρώπους. καὶ ὃν μὲν τότε
παραχρῆμα ἐβασάνισαν, οὗτος μὲν οὐδὲν εἶπε περὶ ἐμοῦ
φλαῦρον· ὃν δ' ἡμέραις ὕστερον πολλαῖς ἐβασάνισαν, ἔχοντες παρὰ σφίσιν αὐτοῖς τὸν πρόσθεν χρόνον, οὗτος ἦν ὁ
πεισθεὶς ὑπὸ τούτων καὶ καταψευσάμενος ἐμοῦ. παρέξομαι
δὲ τούτων τοὺς μάρτυρας.

ΜΑΡΤΥΡΕΣ

31   Ὡς μὲν ὕστερον τούτῳ τῷ χρόνῳ ὁ ἀνὴρ ἐβασανίσθη,
μεμαρτύρηται ὑμῖν· προσέχετε δὲ τὸν νοῦν αὐτῇ τῇ βασάνῳ,
οἷα γεγένηται. ὁ μὲν γὰρ δοῦλος, ᾧ ἴσως οὗτοι τοῦτο μὲν
ἐλευθερίαν ὑπέσχοντο, τοῦτο δ' ἐπὶ τούτοις ἦν παύσασθαι
κακούμενον αὐτόν, ἴσως ὑπ' ἀμφοῖν πεισθεὶς κατεψεύσατό
μου, τὴν μὲν ἐλευθερίαν ἐλπίσας οἴσεσθαι, τῆς δὲ βασάνου
32 εἰς τὸ παραχρῆμα βουλόμενος ἀπαλλάχθαι. οἶμαι δ' ὑμᾶς
ἐπίστασθαι τοῦτο, ὅτι ἐφ' οἷς ἂν τὸ πλεῖστον μέρος τῆς
βασάνου, πρὸς τούτων εἰσὶν οἱ βασανιζόμενοι λέγειν ὅσ'
ἂν ἐκείνοις μέλλωσι χαριεῖσθαι· ἐν τούτοις γὰρ αὐτοῖς
ἐστιν ἡ ὠφέλεια, ἄλλως τε κἂν μὴ παρόντες τυγχάνωσιν ὧν
ἂν καταψεύδωνται. εἰ μὲν γὰρ ἐγὼ ἐκέλευον αὐτὸν στρεβλοῦν

---

27 καὶ ἐν N: ἐν A   γε om. A
28 δὲ ἐν ᾧ μὲν A corr. 2: δὲ μὲν ᾧ Apr., δὲ ἐν μὲν ᾧ N
    παρασχήσομαι Bekker: παραστήσομαι
29 ὁ om. A   ἐπίνομεν Weil: ἐπλέομεν
32 ὅσ' ἂν Thalheim: ὅταν   εἰ μὲν γὰρ ἐγὼ Gebauer: εἰ
    γὰρ ἐγὼ μὲν N Apr., in quo μὲν erasum

control his movements, nor could anyone who wished to take him a long way away by night have found any plausible excuse for doing so. Yet in spite of two days' search, both in the harbour and at a distance from it, no eyewitness, no bloodstain and no clue of any other kind was found. Nevertheless, I will accept the prosecution's story, although I can produce witnesses to the fact that I did not leave the boat. But suppose as much as you please that I did leave the boat, it is in no way likely that the man should have remained undiscovered after his disappearance if he did not go very far from the sea. 27

But they allege that he was thrown into the sea. From what boat? 28 Clearly, the boat came from the harbour itself. In that case, how could it have not been identified? Indeed, it was probable that at least some clue should have been found in the boat of a dead man thrown overboard in the dark. Now the prosecution do claim to have found traces, in the boat on which he was drinking and which he left - the boat on which they themselves agree Herodes was not murdered. But the boat from which he was thrown into the sea they have not discovered, neither the boat itself nor any trace of it. I will bring forward witnesses to prove these statements to you.

WITNESSES

After I had departed on my voyage to Aenus and the boat on 29 which Herodes and I had been drinking had reached Mytilene, the prosecution firstly went on board and conducted a search. On finding the bloodstains they claimed that this was where Herodes had been killed. But when this did not turn out well for them, the blood turning out to be that of the sheep, they abandoned this line and, seizing the men, examined them under torture. The first, whom they 30 tortured there and then, said nothing compromising about me. The second they tortured several days later, after keeping him under their own control throughout the interval, and it was he who was induced by them falsely to incriminate me. I will produce witnesses to confirm these statements.

WITNESSES

You have heard the evidence that the man was tortured after this 31 length of time; now notice the nature of the examination itself. On the one hand the prosecution had doubtless promised the slave his freedom, on the other hand it was to the prosecution alone that he could look for release from his sufferings. Probably, the slave was induced by both these considerations to make his false charges against me: he hoped to gain his freedom and his immediate desire was to be released from the torture. I think you know that those who 32 are being examined under torture are biased in favour of those who do most of the torturing, so that they say anything with which they are likely to gratify them. Their salvation rests in these alone, especially when the victims of their lies happen not to be present. If I had myself ordered him to be racked for not telling the truth,

ὡς οὐ τἀληθῆ λέγοντα, ἴσως ἂν ἐν αὐτῷ τούτῳ ἀπετρέπετο μηδὲν
κατ' ἐμοῦ καταψεύδεσθαι· νῦν δὲ αὐτοῦ ἦσαν καὶ βασανισταὶ
33 καὶ ἐπιτιμηταὶ τῶν σφίσιν αὐτοῖς συμφερόντων. ἕως μὲν οὖν
μετὰ χρηστῆς τῆς ἐλπίδος ἐγίγνωσκέ μου καταψευσάμενος,
τούτῳ διισχυρίζετο τῷ λόγῳ· ἐπειδὴ δὲ ἐγίγνωσκεν ἀπο-
θανούμενος, ἐνταῦθ' ἤδη τῇ ἀληθείᾳ ἐχρῆτο, καὶ ἔλεγεν
34 ὅτι πεισθείη ὑπὸ τούτων ἐμοῦ καταψεύδεσθαι. διαπειραθέντα
δ' αὐτὸν τὰ ψευδῆ λέγειν, ὕστερον δὲ τἀληθῆ λέγοντα,
οὐδέτερα ὠφέλησεν, ἀλλ' ἀπέκτειναν ἄγοντες τὸν ἄνδρα,
τὸν μηνυτήν, ᾧ πιστεύοντες ἐμὲ διώκουσι, τοὐναντίον ποι-
ήσαντες ἢ οἱ ἄλλοι ἄνθρωποι. οἱ μὲν γὰρ ἄλλοι τοῖς μηνυ-
ταῖς τοῖς μὲν ἐλευθέροις χρήματα διδόασι, τοὺς δὲ δούλους
ἐλευθεροῦσιν· οὗτοι δὲ θάνατον τῷ μηνυτῇ τὴν δωρεὰν ἀπέδοσαν, ἀπαγορευόντων τῶν φίλων τῶν ἐμῶν μὴ ἀποκτείνειν
35 τὸν ἄνδρα πρὶν [ἂν] ἐγὼ ἔλθοιμι. δῆλον οὖν ὅτι οὐ τοῦ
σώματος αὐτοῦ χρεία ἦν αὐτοῖς, ἀλλὰ τῶν λόγων· ζῶν μὲν
γὰρ ὁ ἀνὴρ διὰ τῆς αὐτῆς βασάνου ἰὼν ὑπ' ἐμοῦ κατήγορος
ἂν ἐγίγνετο τῆς τούτων ἐπιβουλῆς, τεθνεὼς δὲ τὸν μὲν
ἔλεγχον τῆς ἀληθείας ἀπεστέρει δι' αὐτοῦ τοῦ σώματος
ἀπολλυμένου, τοῖς δὲ λόγοις τοῖς ἐψευσμένοις ὑπ' ἐκείνου
ὡς ἀληθέσιν οὖσιν ἐγὼ ἀπόλλυμαι. τούτων δὲ μάρτυράς μοι
κάλει.

<ΜΑΡΤΥΡΕΣ>

36   Ἐχρῆν μὲν γὰρ αὐτούς, ὡς ἐγὼ νομίζω, ἐνθάδε παρέχοντας τὸν μηνυτὴν αὐτὸν ἀπελέγχειν ἐμέ, καὶ αὐτῷ τούτῳ
χρῆσθαι ἀγωνίσματι, ἐμφανῆ παρέχοντας τὸν ἄνδρα καὶ
κελεύοντας βασανίζειν, ἀλλὰ μὴ ἀποκτεῖναι. φέρε γὰρ δὴ
ποτέρῳ νῦν χρήσονται τῶν λόγων; πότερα ᾧ πρῶτον εἶπεν ἢ
ᾧ ὕστερον; καὶ πότερ' ἀληθῆ ἐστιν, ὅτ' ἔφη με εἰργάσθαι
37 τὸ ἔργον ἢ ὅτ' οὐκ ἔφη; εἰ μὲν γὰρ ἐκ τοῦ εἰκότος ἐξ-
ετασθῆναι δεῖ τὸ πρᾶγμα, οἱ ὕστεροι λόγοι ἀληθέστεροι
φαίνονται. ἐψεύδετο μὲν γὰρ ἐπ' ὠφελείᾳ τῇ ἑαυτοῦ, ἐπειδὴ δὲ τῷ ψεύδεσθαι ἀπώλλυτο, ἡγήσατο τἀληθῆ κατειπὼν διὰ
τοῦτο σωθῆναι ἄν. τῆς μὲν οὖν ἀληθείας οὐκ ἦν αὐτῷ τιμω-
ρὸς οὐδείς· οὐ γὰρ παρὼν ἐγὼ ἐτύγχανον, ᾧπερ σύμμαχος ἦν
ἡ ἀλήθεια τῶν ὑστέρων λόγων· τοὺς δὲ προτέρους λόγους
τοὺς κατεψευσμένους ἦσαν οἱ ἀφανιοῦντες, ὥστε μηδέποτε
38 εἰς τὸ ἀληθὲς καταστῆναι. καὶ οἱ μὲν ἄλλοι, καθ' ὧν ἂν
μηνύῃ τις, οὗτοι κλέπτουσι τοὺς μηνύοντας κᾆτ' ἀφανί-
ζουσιν· αὐτοὶ δὲ οὗτοι οἱ ἀπάγοντες καὶ ζητοῦντες τὸ
πρᾶγμα τὸν κατ' ἐμοῦ μηνυτὴν ἠφάνισαν. καὶ εἰ μὲν ἐγὼ
τὸν ἄνδρα ἠφάνισα ἢ μὴ ἤθελον ἐκδοῦναι τούτοις ἢ ἄλλον

---

33 χρηστῆς τῆς A: χρηστῆς N
34 ὠφέλησεν Reiske: ὠφέλησαν   ἂν del. Dobree
35 titulum add. Reiske
36 μὲν om. N
37 τῷ A corr. 2: τὸ N Apr., <διὰ> τὸ Jernstedt
38 ὧν ἂν μηνύῃ N: ὧν μηνύῃ ἂν A   οὗτοι (ante κλέπτουσι)
    Reiske: αὐτοὶ

42

doubtless he would have been dissuaded by this very action from falsely accusing me. As it was, they were both torturers and assessors of what concerned their own interests.

Now as long as he believed he had something to hope for by falsely incriminating me he persisted in his statement; but when he found he was doomed he at once reverted to the truth and admitted that he had been induced by the prosecution to lie about me. However, neither his persistent attempts at telling lies nor his subsequent telling of the truth helped him. They took the man, the informer on whose evidence they rely to prosecute me, and put him to death, doing the exact opposite of what other men do. For other men reward informers with money if they are free and with freedom if they are slaves. The prosecution repaid their informer with the gift of death, in spite of a protest by my friends that they should not put the man to death until my return. Clearly, it was not his person they required but his evidence: if the man had remained alive and been tortured by me in the same way he would have denounced the prosecution's plot; but once he was dead not only did he, by the loss of his person, deprive me of my chance of proving the truth, but also I am being ruined by his false statements, which are assumed to be true. Call me witnesses to confirm these statements.

<WITNESSES>

In my opinion, they should have produced the informer himself here to prove me guilty and should have used this very action as the basis of their case, producing the man openly and challenging me to examine him under torture. They should not have put him to death. As it is, which of his statements will they use, may I ask? His first or his second? Which is true, the statement that I did the deed or the one that I did not? If we are to judge from probability the second statement is evidently the truer: he was lying for his own benefit, but when he was in danger of being ruined by his lies he thought he would be saved by telling the truth. However, he had no one to stand up for the truth, as I, whom the truth of his second statement defended, happened not to be present, while there were those who were ready to hide away the slave after his first, false statement so that it could never be corrected. Others against whom anyone lays information quietly seize and make away with the informer; but in this case it is the very persons who arrested the slave to discover the truth who have made away with their informer against me. If I had made away with the man or were refusing to surrender him to the

43

τινὰ ἔφευγον ἔλεγχον, αὐτοῖς ἂν τούτοις ἰσχυροτάτοις εἰς
τὰ πράγματα ἐχρῶντο, καὶ ἦν ταῦτα αὐτοῖς μέγιστα τεκμήρια κατ᾽ ἐμοῦ· νῦν δέ, ὁπότε αὐτοὶ οὗτοι προκαλουμένων
τῶν φίλων τῶν ἐμῶν ταῦτ᾽ ἔφυγον, ἐμοὶ δήπου κατὰ τούτων
εἶναι χρὴ ταὐτὰ ταῦτα τεκμήρια, ὡς οὐκ ἀληθῆ τὴν αἰτίαν
ἐπέφερον ἣν ᾐτιῶντο.
39   Ἔτι δὲ καὶ τάδε λέγουσιν, ὡς ὡμολόγει ὁ ἄνθρωπος
βασανιζόμενος συναποκτεῖναι τὸν ἄνδρα. ἐγὼ δέ φημι ταῦτα
μὲν οὐ λέγειν αὐτόν, ὅτι δὲ ἐξαγάγοι ἐμὲ καὶ τὸν ἄνδρα
ἐκ τοῦ πλοίου, καὶ ὅτι ἤδη τεθνεῶτα αὐτὸν ὑπ᾽ ἐμοῦ συν-
40   ανελὼν καὶ ἐνθεὶς εἰς τὸ πλοῖον καταποντώσειε. καίτοι
σκέψασθε ὅτι πρῶτον μέν, πρὶν ἐπὶ τὸν τροχὸν ἀναβῆναι, ὁ
ἀνὴρ μέχρι τῆς ἐσχάτης ἀνάγκης τῇ ἀληθείᾳ ἐχρῆτο καὶ
ἀπέλυέ με τῆς αἰτίας· ἐπειδὴ δὲ ἐπὶ τὸν τροχὸν ἀνέβη, τῇ
ἀνάγκῃ χρώμενος ἤδη κατεψεύδετό μου, βουλόμενος ἀπηλλάχ-
41   θαι τῆς βασάνου· ἐπειδὴ δὲ ἐπαύσατο βασανιζόμενος, οὐκέτι
ἔφη με τούτων εἰργάσθαι οὐδέν, ἀλλὰ τὸ τελευταῖον ἀπώμω-
ξεν ἐμέ τε καὶ αὐτὸν ὡς ἀδίκως ἀπολλυμένους, οὐ χάριτι
τῇ ἐμῇ — πῶς γάρ; ὅς γε κατεψεύσατο —, ἀλλ᾽ ἀναγκαζόμενος
ὑπὸ τοῦ ἀληθοῦς καὶ βεβαιῶν τοὺς πρώτους λόγους ὡς ἀλη-
42   θεῖς εἰρημένους. ἔπειτα δὲ ὁ ἕτερος ἄνθρωπος, ὁ ἐν τῷ
αὐτῷ πλοίῳ πλέων καὶ παρὼν διὰ τέλους καὶ συνών μοι, τῇ
αὐτῇ βασάνῳ βασανιζόμενος τοῖς μὲν πρώτοις καὶ τοῖς ὕστερον λόγοις τοῖς τοῦ ἀνθρώπου συνεφέρετο ὡς ἀληθέσιν
οὖσι, διὰ τέλους γάρ με ἀπέλυε, τοῖς δ᾽ ἐπὶ τοῦ τροχοῦ
λεγομένοις, οὓς ἐκεῖνος ἀνάγκῃ μᾶλλον ἢ ἀληθείᾳ ἔλεγε,
τούτοις δὲ διεφέρετο. ὁ μὲν γὰρ ἐκβάντα μ᾽ ἔφη ἐκ τοῦ
πλοίου ἀποκτεῖναι τὸν ἄνδρα, καὶ αὐτὸς ἤδη τεθνεῶτα συν-
ανελεῖν μοι· ὁ δὲ τὸ παράπαν ἔφη οὐκ ἐκβῆναί με ἐκ τοῦ
43   πλοίου. Καίτοι τὸ εἰκὸς σύμμαχόν μού ἐστιν. οὐ γὰρ δήπου
οὕτω κακοδαίμων ἐγώ, ὥστε τὸ μὲν ἀποκτεῖναι τὸν ἄνδρα
προὐνοησάμην μόνος, ἵνα μοι μηδεὶς συνειδείη, ἐν ᾧ μοι ὁ
πᾶς κίνδυνος ἦν, ἤδη δὲ πεπραγμένου μοι τοῦ ἔργου μάρ-
44   τυρας καὶ συμβούλους ἐποιούμην. καὶ ἀπέθανε μὲν ὁ ἀνὴρ
οὑτωσὶ ἐγγὺς τῆς θαλάσσης καὶ τῶν πλοίων, ὡς ὁ τούτων
λόγος ἐστίν· ὑπὸ δὲ ἑνὸς ἀνδρὸς ἀποθνῄσκων οὔτε ἀνέκρα-
γεν οὔτ᾽ αἴσθησιν οὐδεμίαν ἐποίησεν οὔτε τοῖς ἐν τῇ γῇ

---

38   αὐτοῖς ἂν Spengel: αὐτοὶ δὴ   ταῦτὰ ταῦτα Fuhr coll.
     6.27: ταῦτα τὰ   ᾐτιῶντο Dobree: ᾤοντο
39   ὡμολόγει A: ὁμολογεῖ N   ἐξαγάγοι Baiter: ἐξάγει N
     Apr., ἐξάγοι ras. corr.   συνανελὼν καὶ Mätzner:
     συνελὼν καὶ N, om. A
41   ἀδίκως A: ἀδίκους N
42   ὁ (ante ἐν) om. A   οὖσι A corr. 1, ...σι Apr. (ᾦσι
     vid. Thalheim), εἰρημένοις N   συνανελεῖν A: συνελεῖν
     N   ἔφη οὐκ ἐκβῆναί με A: οὐδ᾽ ἐκβῆναι μ᾽ ἔφη N
44   ὁ (ante ἀνὴρ) om. A   οὑτωσὶ Blass: οὗτοσὶ

prosecution or were evading any other enquiry they would be treating that very fact as most significant in the case, and this would be their strongest evidence against me. But as it is, since they themselves evaded an enquiry, in spite of a challenge being made by my friends, that same fact should be evidence for me against them that the charge which they were bringing against me was a false one.

They further allege that the slave admitted under torture to being 39 my accomplice in the murder. I maintain that he did not say this, but that he conducted Herodes and myself off the boat, and that after I had murdered him he helped me pick him up and put him in the boat, and then he threw him into the sea. Yet consider that at first, before 40 being placed on the wheel and until extreme pressure was brought to bear, the man adhered to the truth and declared me innocent. It was only when he was placed on the wheel and was driven to it that he falsely incriminated me, in order to be released from the torture. When the torture was over he no longer affirmed that I had done any 41 of this, but in the end bemoaned the injustice with which both I and he were being killed: not that he was trying to do me a favour – how could he, when he had falsely incriminated me? – rather, he was being compelled by the truth and was confirming as true the first statement he had made.

Then there was the second man, who had travelled on the same 42 boat, had been present throughout and had been my companion. When tortured in the same way he confirmed as true the first and last statements of the slave, for he declared me innocent throughout. But the statement made on the wheel, which the slave had made under compulsion, not because it was true, he contradicted. For the one said that I left the boat and killed Herodes, and that he himself had helped me remove the body after the murder, while the other maintained that I did not leave the boat at all. And indeed, 43 probability supports me. I would hardly have been so crazy as to plan the murder of Herodes on my own to ensure that no one was privy to it – wherein lay my whole danger – and then, with the crime committed, proceed to furnish myself with witnesses and confederates. Furthermore, Herodes was murdered very close to the sea and the 44 boats, according to the story of the prosecution. Was a man who was being murdered by but one assailant not going to shout out or attract the attention of those on shore or on board? Moreover, it is possible

45

οὔτε τοῖς ἐν τῷ πλοίῳ; καὶ μὴν πολλῷ <ἐπὶ> πλέον γε ἀκούειν ἔστι νύκτωρ ἢ μεθ' ἡμέραν, ἐπ' ἀκτῆς ἢ κατὰ πόλιν·
καὶ μὴν ἔτι ἐγρηγορότων φασὶν ἐκβῆναι τὸν ἄνδρα ἐκ τοῦ
45 πλοίου. ἔπειτα ἐν τῇ γῇ μὲν ἀποθανόντος, ἐντιθεμένου δὲ
εἰς τὸ πλοῖον, οὔτε ἐν τῇ γῇ σημεῖον οὐδὲ αἷμα ἐφάνη
οὔτε ἐν τῷ πλοίῳ, νύκτωρ μὲν ἀναιρεθέντος, νύκτωρ δ' ἐντιθεμένου εἰς τὸ πλοῖον. ἢ δοκεῖ ἂν ὑμῖν ἄνθρωπος δύνασθαι ἐν τοιούτῳ πράγματι ὢν τά τ' ἐν τῇ γῇ ὄντα ἀναξύσαι
καὶ τὰ ἐν τῷ πλοίῳ ἀποσπογγίσαι, ἃ οὐδὲ μεθ' ἡμέραν <ἂν>
τις οἷός τε ἐγένετο, ἔνδον ὢν αὐτοῦ καὶ μὴ πεφοβημένος,
τὸ παράπαν ἀφανίσαι; ταῦτα, ὦ ἄνδρες, πῶς εἰκότα ἐστίν;
46 "Ο δὲ <δεῖ> καὶ μάλιστα ἐνθυμεῖσθαι – καὶ μή μοι ἄχθεσθε,
ἂν ὑμᾶς πολλάκις ταὐτὰ διδάξω· μέγας γὰρ ὁ κίνδυνός ἐστι,
καθ' ὅ τι δ' ἂν ὑμεῖς ὀρθῶς γνῶτε, κατὰ τοῦτο σῴζομαι,
καθ' ὅ τι δ' ἂν ψευσθῆτε τἀληθοῦς, κατὰ τοῦτο ἀπόλλυμαι
– μὴ οὖν ἐξέληται τοῦτο ὑμῶν μηδείς, ὅτι τὸν μηνυτὴν
ἀπέκτειναν, καὶ διετείναντο αὐτὸν μὴ εἰσελθεῖν εἰς ὑμᾶς,
μηδ' ἐμοὶ ἐγγενέσθαι παρόντι ἄξαι τὸν ἄνδρα καὶ βασανί-
47 σαι αὐτόν· καίτοι πρὸς τούτων ἦν τοῦτο. νῦν δὲ πριάμενοι
τὸν ἄνδρα, ἰδίᾳ ἐπὶ σφῶν αὐτῶν ἀπέκτειναν, τὸν μηνυτήν,
οὔτε τῆς πόλεως ψηφισαμένης, οὔτε αὐτόχειρα ὄντα τοῦ
ἀνδρός. ὃν ἐχρῆν δεδεμένον αὐτοὺς φυλάσσειν, ἢ τοῖς φίλοις τοῖς ἐμοῖς ἐξεγγυῆσαι, ἢ τοῖς ἄρχουσι τοῖς ὑμετέροις
παραδοῦναι, καὶ ψῆφον περὶ αὐτοῦ γενέσθαι. νῦν δὲ αὐτοὶ
καταγνόντες τὸν θάνατον τοῦ ἀνδρὸς ἀπεκτείνατε· ὃ οὐδὲ
πόλει ἔξεστιν, ἄνευ Ἀθηναίων οὐδένα θανάτῳ ζημιῶσαι.
καὶ τῶν μὲν ἄλλων λόγων τῶν ἐκείνου τουτουσὶ κριτὰς ἠξι-
ώσατε γενέσθαι, τῶν δὲ ἔργων αὐτοὶ δικασταὶ γίγνεσθε.
48 καίτοι οὐδὲ οἱ τοὺς δεσπότας ἀποκτείναντες, ἐὰν ἐπ' αὐτοφώρῳ ληφθῶσιν, οὐδ' οὗτοι ἀποθνήσκουσιν ὑπ' αὐτῶν τῶν
προσηκόντων, ἀλλὰ παραδιδόασιν αὐτοὺς τῇ ἀρχῇ κατὰ νόμους
ὑμετέρους πατρίους. εἴπερ γὰρ καὶ μαρτυρεῖν ἔξεστι δούλῳ
κατὰ τοῦ ἐλευθέρου τὸν φόνον, καὶ τῷ δεσπότῃ, ἂν δοκῇ,
ἐπεξελθεῖν ὑπὲρ τοῦ δούλου, καὶ ἡ ψῆφος ἴσον δύναται τῷ
δοῦλον ἀποκτείναντι καὶ τῷ ἐλεύθερον, εἰκός τοι καὶ ψῆφον
γενέσθαι περὶ αὐτοῦ ἦν, καὶ μὴ ἄκριτον ἀποθανεῖν αὐτὸν
ὑφ' ὑμῶν. ὥστε πολλῷ ἂν ὑμεῖς δικαιότερον κρίνοισθε ἢ
ἐγὼ νῦν φεύγω ὑφ' ὑμῶν ἀδίκως.
49 Σκοπεῖτε δή, ὦ ἄνδρες, καὶ ἐκ τοῖν λόγοιν τοῖν ἀνδροῖν
ἑκατέροιν τοῖν βασανισθέντοιν τὸ δίκαιον καὶ τὸ εἰκός. ὁ

---

44 <ἐπὶ> πλέον γε ἀκούειν Schömann: πλέον γε ἀγνοεῖν
45 ἀποσπογγίσαι A: ἀνασπογγίσαι N   ἂν add. Baiter
46 δεῖ hic add. Thalheim, post μάλιστα add. A corr. 2
    ἐνθυμεῖσθαι Apr. (supra αι erasum ε), ἐνθυμεῖσθε N
    ταὐτὰ Reiske: ταῦτα   ἐξέληται A corr. 2: ἐξελεῖται N
    Apr.
48 ἀποθνήσκουσιν N: θνήσκουσιν A   τῷ ἐλεύθερον Reiske:
    τὸν ἐλεύθερον   ὑμεῖς δικαιότερον A: δικαιότερον
    ὑμεῖς N   κρίνοισθε vulg.: κρίνεσθε

46

to hear over a far greater distance by night than by day, on a beach than in a city. Moreover, they admit that the passengers were still awake when Herodes left the boat.

Again, although he was murdered on shore and placed in the boat 45 no trace or bloodstain was found either on shore or in the boat, despite the fact that it was at night that he was picked up and at night that he was placed in the boat. Do you think that any man in such circumstances would have been able to smooth out the traces on shore and wipe away the marks in the boat, clues which a calm and collected man could not have completely removed even by day? How probable is this, gentlemen?

There is one thing which you must indeed consider above all – and 46 I hope you will forgive me if I repeatedly tell you the same thing. For my danger is great and my safety depends on how far you come to the right decision, while my ruin depends on how far you are defrauded of the truth – let no one, then, cause you to forget that the prosecution put the informer to death and that they used every effort to prevent him coming to you and to make it impossible for me to take him and examine him under torture on my return. Yet it was to their own advantage to allow me to do so. Instead, they bought 47 the slave and put him to death entirely on their own initiative, their informer, although the state did not decree it nor was he the man's murderer. What they should have done was to keep him in custody, or to surrender him to my friends on security, or to hand him over to your magistrates, so that his fate might be decided by a court. As it was, you sentenced the slave to death on your own authority and executed him, when it is not permitted even to an allied state to inflict the death penalty on anyone without the consent of the Athenian people. You thought fit to let the present court be judges of his statements, but you pass judgment on his acts yourselves. Yet 48 even slaves who have murdered their masters and been caught in the act are not put to death by the victim's own relatives: they are handed over to the authorities according to the ancient laws of your country. If it is indeed permissible to give evidence for a slave against a free man of his being murdered, and for a master, if he thinks fit, to seek vengeance for the murder of his slave, and for a court to sentence the murderer of a slave as effectively as it can the murderer of a free man, it was surely reasonable that this slave should have had a public trial instead of being put to death by you without a hearing. Thus you deserve to be standing trial far more than I, who am now being prosecuted by you so unjustly.

Consider also, gentlemen, from the statements of the two men who 49 were tortured, which is supported by justice and probability. The

μὲν γὰρ δοῦλος δύο λόγω ἔλεγε· τοτὲ μὲν ἔφη με εἰργάσθαι τὸ
ἔργον, τοτὲ δὲ οὐκ ἔφη· ὁ δὲ ἐλεύθερος οὐδέπω νῦν εἴρηκε
περὶ ἐμοῦ φλαῦρον οὐδέν, τῇ αὐτῇ βασάνῳ βασανιζόμενος.
50 τοῦτο μὲν γὰρ οὐκ ἦν αὐτῷ ἐλευθερίαν προτείναντας ὥσπερ
τὸν ἕτερον πεῖσαι· τοῦτο δὲ μετὰ τοῦ ἀληθοῦς ἐβούλετο
κινδυνεύων πάσχειν ὅ τι δέοι, ἐπεὶ τό γε συμφέρον καὶ
οὗτος ἠπίστατο, ὅτι τότε παύσοιτο στρεβλούμενος, ὁπότε
εἴποι τὰ τούτοις δοκοῦντα. ποτέρῳ οὖν εἰκός ἐστι πιστεῦσαι, τῷ διὰ τέλους τὸν αὐτὸν ἀεὶ λόγον λέγοντι, ἢ τῷ
τοτὲ μὲν φάσκοντι τοτὲ δ᾽ οὔ; ἀλλὰ καὶ ἄνευ βασάνου τοι-
αύτης οἱ τοὺς αὐτοὺς αἰεὶ περὶ τῶν αὐτῶν λόγους λέγοντες
51 πιστότεροί εἰσι τῶν διαφερομένων σφίσιν αὐτοῖς. ἔπειτα
δὲ καὶ ἐκ τῶν λόγων τῶν τοῦ ἀνθρώπου μερὶς ἑκατέρῳ ἴση
ἐστί, τούτοις μὲν τὸ φάσκειν, ἐμοὶ δὲ τὸ μὴ φάσκειν· [ἔκ
τε ἀμφοῖν τοῖν ἀνδροῖν τοῖν βασανισθέντοιν· ὁ μὲν γὰρ
ἔφησεν, ὁ δὲ διὰ τέλους ἔξαρνος ἦν.] καὶ μὲν δὴ τὰ ἐξ
ἴσου γενόμενα τοῦ φεύγοντός ἐστι μᾶλλον ἢ τοῦ διώκοντος,
εἴπερ γε καὶ τῶν ψήφων ὁ ἀριθμὸς ἐξ ἴσου γενόμενος τὸν
φεύγοντα μᾶλλον ὠφελεῖ ἢ τὸν διώκοντα.
52 Ἡ μὲν βάσανος, ὦ ἄνδρες, τοιαύτη γεγένηται, ᾗ οὗτοι
πιστεύοντες εὖ εἰδέναι φασὶν ὑπ᾽ ἐμοῦ ἀποθανόντα τὸν
ἄνδρα. καίτοι τὸ παράπαν ἔγωγ᾽ ἂν εἴ τι συνῄδη ἐμαυτῷ
καὶ εἴ τί μοι τοιοῦτον εἴργαστο, ἠφάνισ᾽ ἂν τὼ ἀνθρώπω,
ὅτε ἐπ᾽ ἐμοὶ ἦν τοῦτο μὲν εἰς τὴν Αἶνον ἀπάγειν ἅμα ἐμοί,
τοῦτο δὲ εἰς τὴν ἤπειρον διαβιβάσαι, καὶ μὴ ὑπολείπεσθαι
53 μηνυτὰς κατ᾽ ἐμαυτοῦ τοὺς συνειδότας. φασὶ δὲ γραμματείδιον εὑρεῖν ἐν τῷ πλοίῳ, ὃ ἔπεμπον ἐγὼ Λυκίνῳ, ὡς ἀπο-
κτείναιμι τὸν ἄνδρα. καίτοι τί ἔδει με γραμματείδιον
πέμπειν, αὐτοῦ συνειδότος τοῦ τὸ γραμματείδιον φέροντος;
ὥστε τοῦτο μὲν σαφέστερον αὐτὸς ἔμελλεν ἐρεῖν ὁ εἰργασμένος, τοῦτο δὲ οὐδὲν ἔδει κρύπτειν αὐτόν· ἃ γὰρ μὴ οἷόν
τε εἰδέναι τὸν φέροντα, ταῦτ᾽ ἄν τις μάλιστα συγγράψας
54 πέμψειεν. ἔπειτα δὲ ὅ τι μὲν μακρὸν εἴη πρᾶγμα, τοῦτο

---

49 δύο N: δύω A
50 προτείναντας Reiske: προτείνοντας   παύσοιτο Madvig:
    παύσαιτο
51 ἴση ἐστὶ A corr. 2: ἴσο. (ν vel σ) εἰ. (η vel σ) Apr.,
    ἴσον εἰ N, ἴση ἂν εἴη Thalheim   τούτοις μὲν τὸ A
    corr. 2: τοῦτον μέντοι N Apr.   ἔκ τε . . . ἦν del.
    Hirschig   γενόμενος A: γιγνόμενος N
52 γεγένηται N: ἐγένετο A   συνῄδη Jernstedt: συνῄδειν
    εἴ τί μοι] εἴ τ᾽ ἐμοὶ N Apr., εἴ τι ἐμοὶ corr. 2
    ἀπάγειν A corr. 2: ἀπάγων N Apr.
53 γραμματείδιον Bekker: γραμματίδιον libri ubique
    post φέροντος in libris insunt: τίνος γε δὴ ἕνεκα
    . . . ἐμοὶ κἀκείνῳ; quae verba (57 init.) transp.
    Aldus   αὐτὸς Reiske: αὐτοῖς   ἐρεῖν A: εὑρεῖν N
    αὐτόν Aldus: αὐτά
54 τοῦτο (ante μὲν) A corr. 2: τούτου N Apr.

slave gave two accounts: at one time he said that I did the deed, at another that I did not. But the free man has not even yet said anything compromising about me, though he was subjected to the same torture. For on the one hand he could not be influenced by offers of 50 freedom, like the other one, and on the other hand he was willing, with truth on his side, to risk suffering whatever he must. Yet he too knew what was advantageous to him, that he would put an end to his torture just as soon as he said what the prosecution wanted. Which of the two, then, have we reason to believe, the one who firmly adhered to the same statement throughout, or the one who at one moment made a statement and at the next denied it? Why, even without such torture, those who consistently keep to one statement about one set of facts are more to be trusted than those who contradict themselves. Then again, of the slave's statements half are 51 in favour of one side, half in favour of the other: his affirmations support the prosecution, his denials support me. [Similarly with the combined statements of both men tortured: the one affirmed, the other consistently denied.] And, of course, an equal division is to the advantage of the defence rather than the prosecution, in view of the fact that an equal division of the votes of a jury benefits the defence rather than the prosecution.

Such was the examination under torture, gentlemen, relying on 52 which the prosecution say they are convinced that I murdered Herodes. Yet if I had had anything at all on my conscience, if I had committed such a crime, I would have got rid of the two men when it was in my power either to take them with me to Aenus or to ship them to the mainland, instead of leaving behind men who knew the facts to inform against me.

The prosecution also allege that they found on board a note which 53 I was going to send to Lycinus, stating that I had killed Herodes. But why did I need to send a note when the bearer was himself my accomplice? Not only was the man who did the deed likely to tell the story more clearly himself, but also there was no need to conceal the message from him. It is generally messages which cannot be disclosed to the bearer that are sent in writing. Then again, a man would be 54 compelled to write down a long message, as its length would prevent

μὲν ἄν τις ἀναγκασθείη γράψαι τῷ μὴ διαμνημονεύειν τὸν
ἀπαγγέλλοντα ὑπὸ πλήθους. τοῦτο δὲ βραχὺ ἦν ἀπαγγεῖλαι,
ὅτι τέθνηκεν ὁ ἀνήρ. ἔπειτα ἐνθυμεῖσθε ὅτι διάφορον ἦν
τὸ γραμματείδιον τῷ βασανισθέντι, διάφορος δ᾽ ὁ ἄνθρωπος
τῷ γραμματειδίῳ· ὁ μὲν γὰρ βασανιζόμενος αὐτὸς ἔφη ἀποκτεῖναι, τὸ δὲ γραμματείδιον ἀνοιχθὲν ἐμὲ τὸν ἀποκτεύ-
55 ναντα ἐμήνυεν. καίτοι ποτέρῳ χρὴ πιστεῦσαι; τὸ μὲν γὰρ
πρῶτον οὐχ ηὗρον ἐν τῷ πλοίῳ ζητοῦντες τὸ γραμματείδιον,
ὕστερον δέ. τότε μὲν γὰρ οὔπω οὕτως ἐμεμηχάνητο αὐτοῖς·
ἐπειδὴ δὲ ὁ ἄνθρωπος ὁ πρότερος βασανισθεὶς οὐδὲν ἔλεγε
κατ᾽ ἐμοῦ, τότε εἰσβάλλουσιν εἰς τὸ πλοῖον τὸ γραμματείδιον, ἵνα ταύτην ἔχοιεν ἐμοὶ τὴν αἰτίαν ἐπιφέρειν·
56 ἐπειδὴ δὲ ἀνεγνώσθη τὸ γραμματείδιον καὶ ὁ ὕστερος βασανιζόμενος οὐ συνεφέρετο τῷ γραμματειδίῳ, οὐκέτι οἷόν τ᾽
ἦν ἀφανίσαι τὰ ἀναγνωσθέντα. εἰ γὰρ ἡγήσαντο τὸν ἄνδρα
πείσειν ἀπὸ πρώτης καταψεύδεσθαί μου, οὐκ ἄν ποτ᾽ ἐμηχανήσαντο τὰ ἐν τῷ γραμματειδίῳ. καί μοι μάρτυρας τούτων
κάλει.

ΜΑΡΤΥΡΕΣ

57 Τίνος γε δὴ ἕνεκα τὸν ἄνδρα ἔκτεινα; οὐδὲ γὰρ ἔχθρα
οὐδεμία ἦν ἐμοὶ κἀκείνῳ. λέγειν δὲ τολμῶσιν ὡς ἐγὼ χάριτι
τὸν ἄνδρα ἀπέκτεινα. καὶ τίς πώποτε χαριζόμενος ἑτέρῳ
τοῦτο εἰργάσατο; οἶμαι μὲν γὰρ οὐδένα, ἀλλὰ δεῖ μεγάλην
τὴν ἔχθραν ὑπάρχειν τῷ τοῦτο μέλλοντι ποιήσειν, καὶ τὴν
πρόνοιαν ἐκ πολλῶν εἶναι φανερὰν ἐπιβουλευομένην. ἐμοὶ
58 δὲ κἀκείνῳ οὐκ ἦν ἔχθρα οὐδεμία. εἶεν, ἀλλὰ δεύσας περὶ
ἐμαυτοῦ μὴ αὐτὸς παρ᾽ ἐκείνου τοῦτο πάθοιμι; καὶ γὰρ ἂν
τῶν τοιούτων ἕνεκά τις ἀναγκασθείη τοῦτο ἐργάσασθαι. ἀλλ᾽
οὐδέν μοι τοιοῦτον ὑπῆρκτο εἰς αὐτόν. ἀλλὰ χρήματα ἔμελ-
59 λον λήψεσθαι ἀποκτείνας αὐτόν; ἀλλ᾽ οὐκ ἦν αὐτῷ. ἀλλὰ
σοὶ μᾶλλον ἐγὼ τὴν πρόφασιν ταύτην ἔχοιμ᾽ ἂν εἰκότως
μετὰ τῆς ἀληθείας ἀναθεῖναι, ὅτι χρημάτων ἕνεκα ζητεῖς
ἐμὲ ἀποκτεῖναι, μᾶλλον ἢ σὺ ἐμοὶ ἐκεῖνον· καὶ πολὺ ἂν
δικαιότερον ἁλοίης <σὺ> τοῦ φόνου ἐμὲ ἀποκτείνας ὑπὸ τῶν
ἐμοὶ προσηκόντων, ἢ ἐγὼ ὑπὸ σοῦ καὶ τῶν ἐκείνου ἀναγκαίων. ἐγὼ μὲν γὰρ σοῦ φανερὰν τὴν πρόνοιαν εἰς ἐμὲ ἀπο-
δείκνυμι, σὺ δ᾽ ἐμὲ ἐν ἀφανεῖ λόγῳ ζητεῖς ἀπολέσαι.

54 μὲν (ante ἄν) om. A   τῷ μὴ A corr. 2: τοῦ μὴ N Apr.
διάφορον Reiske: διαφέρον   γραμματιδίῳ Reiske:
γραμματείῳ N, γραμματίῳ A   γραμματίδιον N, γραμμά-
τιον A
55 ηὗρον Jernstedt: εὗρον   οὔπω A: οὕτω N   πρότερος
N: πρότερον A
57 Τίνος . . . κἀκείνῳ] cf. ad 53   οὐδὲ Aldus: οὔτε
εἶναι φανερὰν A: φανερὰν εἶναι N
58 ἀλλὰ χρήματα . . . αὐτῷ, quae in libris ante εἶεν
leguntur, huc transp. Dobree
59 σὺ ἐμοὶ A corr.: σὺν ἐμοὶ N Apr.   σὺ add. Aldus
σοῦ (post γὰρ) Blass: σοι   δ᾽ ἐμὲ Blass: δέ με

the bearer remembering it. But this one was brief enough to deliver:
"The man is dead". Moreover, bear in mind that the note contradicted
the slave who was tortured, and the slave the note. The slave stated
under torture that he had committed the murder himself, but the note
when opened declared that I was the murderer. Which are we to
believe? The prosecution did not find the note on board during the   55
first search, but during a later one – they had not yet then devised
this scheme. It was not until the man who was tortured first said
nothing against me that they dropped the note on board, in order to
have this charge to bring against me. But when the note had been   56
read and the second witness, under torture, persisted in disagreeing
with the note, it was no longer possible to suppress the message that
had been read in it. If they had thought that they would induce the
slave to lie about me from the first they would never have devised
the message in the note. Call me witnesses to confirm these facts.

WITNESSES

Now what was my motive in murdering Herodes? For there was not   57
even any bad feeling between him and me. The prosecution have the
audacity to suggest that I murdered him as a favour. But who has
ever done this to oblige another? No one, I am sure. Bitter feeling
must exist in the man who intends to do this and it must be clear
from many indications that the design is growing. But between
Herodes and myself there was no bad feeling. Very well. Then was it   58
that I was afraid of being murdered by him myself? For a man might
well be driven to do this for such a motive. No, I had no such fears
with regard to him. Then was I going to enrich myself by murdering
him? No, he had no money. Indeed, I could more reasonably and with   59
truth assign this motive to you, that you are attempting to secure my
death for money, than you could assign it to me in murdering
Herodes. You might much more justly be convicted of murder by my
relatives for killing me than I by you and the family of Herodes. For
I can show clear proof of your scheme against me, whereas you are
seeking to make an end of me by a tale which cannot be proved.

60　Ταῦτα μὲν ὑμῖν λέγω, ὡς αὐτῷ μοι πρόφασιν οὐδεμίαν
εἶχεν ἀποκτεῖναι τὸν ἄνδρα· δεῖ δέ με καὶ ὑπὲρ Λυκίνου
ἀπολογήσασθαι, ὡς ἔοικεν, ἀλλ' οὐχ ὑπὲρ αὐτοῦ μόνον, ὡς
οὐδ' ἐκεῖνον εἰκότως αἰτιῶνται. λέγω τοίνυν ὑμῖν ὅτι
ταὐτὰ ὑπῆρχεν αὐτῷ εἰς ἐκεῖνον ἅπερ ἐμοί· οὔτε γὰρ χρήματα ἦν αὐτῷ ὁπόθεν ἂν ἔλαβεν ἀποκτείνας ἐκεῖνον, οὔτε
κίνδυνος αὐτῷ ὑπῆρχεν οὐδεὶς ὅντινα διέφευγεν ἀποθανόντος
61　ἐκείνου. τεκμήριον δὲ μέγιστον ὡς οὐκ ἐβούλετο αὐτὸν
ἀπολέσαι· ἐξὸν γὰρ αὐτῷ ἐν ἀγῶνι καὶ κινδύνῳ μεγάλῳ κατα-
στήσαντι μετὰ τῶν νόμων τῶν ὑμετέρων ἀπολέσαι ἐκεῖνον,
εἴπερ προωφείλετο αὐτῷ κακόν, καὶ τό τε ἴδιον τὸ αὐτοῦ
διαπράξασθαι καὶ τῇ πόλει τῇ ὑμετέρᾳ χάριν καταθέσθαι,
εἰ ἐπέδειξεν ἀδικοῦντα ἐκεῖνον, οὐκ ἠξίωσεν, ἀλλ' οὐδ'
ἦλθεν ἐπὶ τοῦτον. καίτοι καλλίων γε ἦν ὁ κίνδυνος αὐτῷ...

ΜΑΡΤΥΡΕΣ

62　'Αλλὰ γὰρ ἐνταῦθα μὲν ἀφῆκεν αὐτόν· οὗ δὲ ἔδει κινδυνεύειν αὐτὸν περί τε αὐτοῦ καὶ περὶ ἐμοῦ, ἐνταῦθα δ'
ἐπεβούλευεν, ἐν ᾧ γνωσθεὶς ἂν ἀπεστέρει μὲν ἐμὲ τῆς
πατρίδος, ἀπεστέρει δὲ αὐτὸν ἱερῶν καὶ ὁσίων καὶ τῶν
ἄλλων ἅπερ μέγιστα καὶ περὶ πλείστου ἐστὶν ἀνθρώποις.
῎Επειτα δ' εἰ καὶ ὡς μάλιστα ἐβούλετο αὐτὸν ὁ Λυκῖνος
τεθνάναι — εἶμι γὰρ καὶ ἐπὶ τὸν τῶν κατηγόρων λόγον —,
οὗ αὐτὸς οὐκ ἠξίου αὐτόχειρ γενέσθαι, τοῦτο τὸ ἔργον ἐγὼ
63　ποτ' ἂν ἐπείσθην ἀντ' ἐκείνου ποιῆσαι; πότερα ὡς ἐγὼ μὲν
ἢ τῷ σώματι ἐπιτήδειος διακινδυνεύειν, ἐκεῖνος δὲ χρήμασι
τὸν ἐμὸν κίνδυνον ἐκπρίασθαι; οὐ δῆτα· τῷ μὲν γὰρ οὐκ ἦν
χρήματα, ἐμοὶ δὲ ἦν· ἀλλ' αὐτὸ τούτου τὸ ἐναντίον ἐκεῖνος
τοῦτο θᾶσσον ἂν ὑπ' ἐμοῦ ἐπείσθη κατά γε τὸ εἰκὸς ἢ ἐγὼ
ὑπὸ τούτου, ἐπεὶ ἐκεῖνός γ' ἑαυτὸν οὐδ' ὑπερήμερον γενόμενον ἑπτὰ μνῶν δυνατὸς ἦν λύσασθαι, ἀλλ' οἱ φίλοι αὐτὸν
ἐλύσαντο. καὶ μὲν δὴ καὶ τῆς χρείας τῆς ἐμῆς καὶ τῆς
Λυκίνου τοῦτο ὑμῖν μέγιστον τεκμήριόν ἐστιν, ὅτι οὐ σφόδρα ἐχρώμην ἐγὼ Λυκίνῳ φίλῳ, ὡς πάντα ποιῆσαι ἂν τὰ
ἐκείνῳ δοκοῦντα· οὐ γὰρ δήπου ἑπτὰ μὲν μνᾶς οὐκ ἀπέτεισα
ὑπὲρ αὐτοῦ δεδεμένου καὶ λυμαινομένου, κίνδυνον δὲ τοσοῦτον ἀράμενος ἄνδρα ἀπέκτεινα δι' ἐκεῖνον.

───────────────────────────────

60　εἶχεν ἀποκτεῖναι scripsi: ἔχει ἀποκτεῖναι AN, εἶχε
τἀποκτεῖναι Kayser　　δὲ om. N
61　post ὁ κίνδυνος αὐτῷ lacunam ind. Blass, cum putaret
deesse παρέξομαι δὲ τούτων τοὺς μάρτυρας vel simile;
ft. plura desunt (Thalheim)
62　οὗ δὲ Blass: οὐδὲ N, οὐ γὰρ A　　περὶ (ante ἐμοῦ) om. A
63　ἢ Jernstedt: ἦν　　αὐτὸ τούτου τὸ ἐναντίον scripsi
(cf. Lys. 6.36): αὐτὸ τοῦτο ἐναντίον N Apr., αὐτὸ τὸ
ἐναντίον corr. 2　　ἀπέτεισα Blass: ἀπέτισα A, ἐπέτισα
N　　ὑπὲρ Meier: περὶ

52

This I can assure you, I personally can have had no motive for 60
murdering Herodes. But I must also, it seems, clear Lycinus as well
as myself, by showing that in his case too their charge is
unreasonable. I assure you, then, that his position with regard to
Herodes was the same as mine. Neither had he any means of enriching
himself by murdering Herodes, nor was there any danger threatening
him from which he hoped to escape by Herodes' death. But here is 61
the greatest proof that he did not desire to make an end of Herodes:
though it was possible for Lycinus to put Herodes on trial and in
great danger, and with the help of your laws make an end of the
man, had redress for some injury been owing to him, thereby
obtaining his own revenge and winning favour with your city by
proving him a criminal, this he did not wish to do. He did not even
take legal proceedings against him, even though he was running a
more honourable risk <by bringing Herodes into court than by
engaging me to murder him. Call me witnesses to confirm these
facts.>

WITNESSES

So we are to understand that on this count he left Herodes 62
alone, whereas in the matter in which he was bound to endanger both
himself and me he plotted against Herodes, even though if discovered
he would have deprived me of my country and himself of all divine
and human rights and all that men hold most sacred and precious.
Then again, even if Lycinus was as eager as could be for Herodes to
die – I am now actually adopting the standpoint of the prosecution –
should I ever have been persuaded to do on his behalf this deed of
which he himself refused to be the perpetrator? Was it that I was 63
physically capable of running all the risks and he financially capable
of paying for the risks I ran? No, I had money and he had none. On
the contrary, according to probability he would sooner have been
induced by me to commit this crime than I by him, since he could not
even obtain his own release when imprisoned for arrears of debt of
seven minae: his friends procured his release. In fact, this is the
clearest indication for you of the relationship between Lycinus and
myself, that my friendship with him was hardly close enough to make
me do everything he wanted. For surely I did not refuse to pay
seven minae for him when he was suffering hardships in prison, and
then run so great a risk and kill a man to oblige him.

64   Ὡς μὲν οὖν οὐκ αὐτὸς αἴτιός εἰμι τοῦ πράγματος οὐδὲ
ἐκεῖνος, ἀποδέδεικται καθ᾽ ὅσον ἐγὼ δύναμαι μάλιστα. τούτῳ δὲ χρῶνται πλείστῳ <τῷ> λόγῳ οἱ κατήγοροι, ὅτι ἀφανής
ἐστιν ὁ ἀνήρ, καὶ ὑμεῖς ἴσως περὶ τούτου αὐτοῦ ποθεῖτε
ἀκοῦσαι. εἰ μὲν οὖν τοῦτο εἰκάζειν με δεῖ, ἐξ ἴσου τοῦτό
ἐστι καὶ ὑμῖν καὶ ἐμοί· οὔτε γὰρ ὑμεῖς αἴτιοι τοῦ ἔργου
ἐστὲ οὔτε ἐγώ· εἰ δὲ δεῖ τοῖς ἀληθέσι χρῆσθαι, τῶν εἰρ-
γασμένων τινὰ ἐρωτώντων· ἐκείνου γὰρ ἄριστ᾽ ἂν πύθοιντο.
65 ἐμοὶ μὲν γὰρ τῷ μὴ εἰργασμένῳ τοσοῦτον τὸ μακρότατον τῆς
ἀποκρίσεώς ἐστιν, ὅτι οὐκ εἴργασμαι· τῷ δὲ ποιήσαντι
ῥᾳδία ἐστὶν ἡ ἀπόδειξις, καὶ μὴ ἀποδείξαντι εὖ εἰκάσαι.
οἱ μὲν γὰρ πανουργοῦντες ἅμα τε πανουργοῦσι καὶ πρόφασιν
εὑρίσκουσι τοῦ ἀδικήματος· τῷ δὲ μὴ εἰργασμένῳ χαλεπὸν
περὶ τῶν ἀφανῶν εἰκάζειν. οἶμαι δ᾽ ἂν καὶ ὑμῶν ἕκαστον,
εἴ τίς τινα ἔροιτο ὅ τι μὴ τύχοι εἰδώς, τοσοῦτον ἂν εἰπεῖν, ὅτι οὐκ οἶδεν· εἰ δέ τις περαιτέρω τι κελεύοι λέγειν,
66 ἐν πολλῇ ἂν ἔχεσθαι ὑμᾶς ἀπορίᾳ δοκῶ. μὴ τοίνυν ἐμοὶ
νεύμητε τὸ ἄπορον τοῦτο, ἐν ᾧ μηδ᾽ ἂν αὐτοὶ εὐποροῖτε·
μηδὲ ἐὰν εὖ εἰκάζω, ἐν τούτῳ μοι ἀξιοῦτε τὴν ἀπόφευξιν
εἶναι, ἀλλ᾽ ἐξαρκείτω μοι ἐμαυτὸν ἀναίτιον ἀποδεῖξαι τοῦ
πράγματος. ἐν τούτῳ οὖν ἀναίτιός εἰμι, οὐκ ἐὰν [μὴ] ἐξ-
εύρω ὅτῳ τρόπῳ ἀφανής ἐστιν ἢ ἀπόλωλεν ἀνήρ, ἀλλ᾽ εἰ μὴ
67 προσήκει μοι μηδὲν ὥστ᾽ ἀποκτεῖναι αὐτόν. Ἤδη δ᾽ ἔγωγε
καὶ πρότερον ἀκοῇ ἐπίσταμαι γεγονός, τοῦτο μὲν τοὺς ἀπο-
θανόντας, τοῦτο δὲ τοὺς ἀποκτείναντας οὐχ εὑρεθέντας·
οὔκουν ἂν καλῶς ἔχοι, εἰ τούτων δέοι τὰς αἰτίας ὑποσχεῖν
τοὺς συγγενομένους. πολλοὶ δέ γ᾽ ἤδη σχόντες ἑτέρων πραγμάτων αἰτίας, πρὶν τὸ σαφὲς αὐτῶν γνωσθῆναι, προαπώλοντο.
68 αὐτίκα Ἐφιάλτην τὸν ὑμέτερον πολίτην οὐδέπω νῦν ηὕρηνται
οἱ ἀποκτείναντες· εἰ οὖν τις ἠξίου τοὺς συνόντας ἐκείνῳ
εἰκάζειν οἵτινες ἦσαν οἱ ἀποκτείναντες Ἐφιάλτην, εἰ δὲ
μή, ἐνόχους εἶναι τῷ φόνῳ, οὐκ ἂν καλῶς εἶχε τοῖς συν-
οῦσιν. ἔπειτα οἵ γε Ἐφιάλτην ἀποκτείναντες οὐκ ἐζήτησαν
τὸν νεκρὸν ἀφανίσαι, οὐδ᾽ ἐν τούτῳ κινδυνεύειν μηνῦσαι
τὸ πρᾶγμα, ὥσπερ οὐδὲ φασὶν ἐμὲ τῆς μὲν ἐπιβουλῆς οὐδένα
κοινωνὸν ποιήσασθαι τοῦ θανάτου, τῆς δ᾽ ἀναιρέσεως.
69 τοῦτο δ᾽ ἐντὸς οὐ πολλοῦ χρόνου παῖς ἐζήτησεν οὐδὲ δώ-
δεκα ἔτη γεγονὼς τὸν δεσπότην ἀποκτεῖναι· καὶ εἰ μὴ

---

64 τῷ add. Frohberger   με δεῖ N: δεῖ με A   ἄριστ᾽ ἂν
    Hirschig: ἄριστα
65 μακρότατον N: μακρότερον A   εἰργασμένῳ (ante χαλεπὸν)
    A: ἐργασαμένῳ N   εἰπεῖν A corr. 2: εἶπεν N Apr.
    τι (ante κελεύοι) om. A   κελεύοι Reiske: κελεύει
    ἔχεσθαι ὑμᾶς N: ὑμᾶς ἔχεσθαι A
66 εὐποροῖτε A: εὐπορῆτε N   μὴ del. Reiske   ἀνὴρ
    Sauppe: ἀνὴρ   προσήκει A: προσήσκει N
67 οὔκουν A corr. 2: οὐκοῦν N Apr.
68 ηὕρηνται Jernstedt: εὕρηνται

I have proved, then, to the best of my ability that both Lycinus   64
and I are innocent. However, the prosecution rely very heavily on
this argument that Herodes has disappeared and doubtless you are
desirous of hearing an explanation of this very point. Now if I must
conjecture about this your guess is as good as mine, for neither are
you guilty of the crime nor am I. But if it is necessary to get at the
truth let the prosecution ask one of the criminals, for they would
learn it best from him. The utmost that I who am not guilty can reply   65
is that I am not guilty; whereas a full revelation of the facts is easy
for the criminal, or if not a full revelation at least a good guess.
Criminals no sooner commit a crime than they invent an explanation of
it; but it is difficult for an innocent man to conjecture about unknown
circumstances. I am sure that each one of you also, if asked
something which he did not happen to know, would say as much, that
he did not know. But if you were then told to say more I think you
would find yourselves in a serious difficulty. So do not present me   66
with this difficulty in which not even you yourselves would come off
well and do not make my acquittal depend on my making a good
guess. Let it be enough for me to prove my innocence of the crime,
which depends on this point, not on my discovering how Herodes
disappeared or met his end, but on my having no motive whatever for
murdering him.

   I know from report that it has already happened in the past that   67
sometimes the victim, sometimes the murderer, has not been found; it
would be unfair if those who had been in their company had to bear
the blame for their murder. Many, again, have already been accused
of the crimes of others and have lost their lives before the truth
about them became known. For example, the murderers of one of your   68
own citizens, Ephialtes, have never to this day been discovered, and
it would therefore have been unfair to his companions if anyone had
required them to conjecture who his assassins were under pain of
being held guilty of the murder themselves. Moreover, the murderers
of Ephialtes made no attempt to get rid of the body, for fear of the
accompanying risk of publicity, whereas they say I made no one my
accomplice in planning the death of Herodes, but did so in the
disposing of the body.

   Once more, a slave, not twelve years old, recently tried to   69
murder his master. If, when his master cried out, he had not been

φοβηθείς, ὡς ἀνεβόησεν, ἐγκαταλιπὼν τὴν μάχαιραν ἐν τῇ
σφαγῇ ᾤχετο φεύγων, ἀλλ' ἐτόλμησε μεῖναι, ἀπώλοντ' ἂν οἱ
ἔνδον ἅπαντες· οὐδεὶς γὰρ ἂν ᾤετο τὸν παῖδα τολμῆσαί
ποτε τοῦτο· νῦν δὲ συλληφθεὶς αὐτὸς ὕστερον κατεῖπεν
αὐτοῦ. τοῦτο δὲ περὶ χρημάτων αἰτίαν ποτὲ σχόντες οὐκ
οὔσαν, ὥσπερ ἐγὼ νῦν, οἱ Ἑλληνοταμίαι οἱ ὑμέτεροι,
ἐκεῖνοι μὲν ἅπαντες ἀπέθανον ὀργῇ μᾶλλον ἢ γνώμῃ, πλὴν
70 ἑνός, τὸ δὲ πρᾶγμά ὕστερον καταφανὲς ἐγένετο. τοῦ δ'
ἑνὸς τούτου — Σωσίαν ὄνομά φασιν αὐτῷ εἶναι — κατέγνωστο
μὲν ἤδη θάνατος, ἐτεθνήκει δὲ οὔπω· καὶ ἐν τούτῳ ἐδηλώθη
ὅτῳ τρόπῳ ἀπωλώλει τὰ χρήματα, καὶ ὁ ἀνὴρ ἀπελύθη ὑπὸ
τοῦ δήμου τοῦ ὑμετέρου παραδεδομένος ἤδη τοῖς ἕνδεκα, οἱ
71 δ' ἄλλοι ἐτέθνασαν οὐδὲν αἴτιοι ὄντες. ταῦθ' ὑμῶν αὐτῶν
ἐγὼ οἶμαι μεμνῆσθαι τοὺς πρεσβυτέρους, τοὺς δὲ νεωτέρους
πυνθάνεσθαι ὥσπερ ἐμέ. οὕτως ἀγαθόν ἐστι μετὰ τοῦ χρόνου
βασανίζειν τὰ πράγματα. καὶ τοῦτ' ἴσως ἂν φανερὸν γένοιτ'
ἂν ὕστερον, ὅτῳ τρόπῳ τέθνηκεν ὁ ἄνθρωπος. μὴ οὖν ὕστερον
τοῦτο γνῶτε, ἀναίτιόν με ὄντα ἀπολέσαντες, ἀλλὰ πρότερόν
γ' εὖ βουλεύσασθε, καὶ μὴ μετ' ὀργῆς καὶ διαβολῆς, ὡς
72 τούτων οὐκ ἂν γένοιντο ἕτεροι πονηρότεροι σύμβουλοι. οὐ
γὰρ ἔστιν ὅ τι ἂν ὀργιζόμενος ἄνθρωπος εὖ γνοίη· αὐτὸ
γὰρ ᾧ βουλεύεται, τὴν γνώμην διαφθείρει τοῦ ἀνθρώπου.
μέγα τοι ἡμέρα παρ' ἡμέραν γιγνομένη γνώμην, ὦ ἄνδρες,
ἐξ ὀργῆς μεταστῆσαι καὶ τὴν ἀλήθειαν εὑρεῖν τῶν γεγενη-
73 μένων. Εὖ δὲ ἴστε ὅτι ἐλεηθῆναι ὑφ' ὑμῶν ἄξιός εἰμι μᾶλλον ἢ δίκην δοῦναι· δίκην μὲν γὰρ εἰκός ἐστι διδόναι τοὺς
ἀδικοῦντας, ἐλεεῖσθαι δὲ τοὺς ἀδίκως κινδυνεύοντας.
κρεῖσσον δὲ χρὴ γίγνεσθαι ἀεὶ τὸ ὑμέτερον δυνάμενον ἐμὲ
δικαίως σῴζειν ἢ τὸ τῶν ἐχθρῶν βουλόμενον ἀδίκως με ἀπολλύναι. ἐν μὲν γὰρ τῷ ἐπισχεῖν ἔστι καὶ τὰ δεινὰ ταῦτα
ποιῆσαι ἃ οὗτοι κελεύουσιν· ἐν δὲ τῷ παραχρῆμα οὐκ ἔστιν
ἀρχὴν ὀρθῶς βουλεύεσθαι.
74   Δεῖ δέ με καὶ ὑπὲρ τοῦ πατρὸς ἀπολογήσασθαι. καίτοι

---

69 ἐν om. A   ἔνδον ἅπαντες A: ἔνδον ὄντες ἅπαντες N
τολμῆσαί ποτε τοῦτο N: ποτε τοῦτο τολμῆσαι A
ἀπέθανον A corr. 2: ἀποθανόντες N Apr.
70 ὅτῳ Hirschig: τῷ   ἀπωλώλει A: ἀπολώλει N   ἀπελύθη
Kayser (cf. Poll. 8.68): ἀπήχθη NA, ἀπήγχθη Apr.
71 ἂν (post ἴσως) om. N   ὅτῳ τρόπῳ N: καὶ ὅτῳ τρόπῳ A
μὴ μετ' vulg.: μήτε μετ'
72 οὐ γὰρ . . . ἀνθρώπου affert Stobaeus flor. 20.44
ἂν add. Stobaeus, om. AN   εὖ Stobaeus: ἂν
ᾧ] ὃ Stobaeus   τοι N: τι A   ἡμέρα Stephanus:
ἡμέραν   γιγνομένη Stephanus: γιγνομένην
μεταστῆσαι Stephanus: μεταστήσειν
73 δὲ χρὴ A: δὴ χρή N   γίγνεσθαι ἀεὶ N: ἀεὶ γίγνεσθαι A
ἀρχὴν Aldus: ἀρχὴ ἢ

afraid and taken to his heels, leaving the knife in the wound, but had had the courage to stay where he was, the entire household would have perished – for no one would ever have thought him capable of such audacity. As it was, he was caught and later confessed his own guilt.

Then again, your Hellenotamiae were once accused of embezzlement, a charge as groundless as the one against me today. Through anger rather than reason they were all put to death save one, and later the true facts became known. This one, whose name is said to have been Sosias, had already been sentenced to death but had not yet been executed. Meanwhile it was shown how the money had been lost and Sosias was rescued by your people from the very hands of the Eleven – while the rest had died entirely innocent. I expect the older ones among you remember this yourselves and the younger ones have heard of it like myself.

Thus it is wise to test the truth of a matter with the help of time. Perhaps the circumstances of Herodes' death will similarly come to light hereafter. So do not discover when it is too late that you have put me to death though innocent, but come to the right decision while there is still time, without anger and without prejudice. For there could not be any worse counsellors than these. It is impossible for an angry man to make a right decision, as anger destroys his one instrument of decision, his judgment. Day succeeding day is a great force, gentlemen, for turning aside judgment from anger and bringing the truth of events to light.

Be assured that I deserve pity from you, not punishment. Wrongdoers should be punished, those wrongfully imperilled should be pitied. Your ability to save my life justly ought always to be more powerful than my enemies' desire to destroy my unjustly. By delaying it is still possible for you to do those terrible things which the prosecution bid you, by immediate action it is impossible to deliberate fairly at all.

I must also defend my father, although, as my father, it would

γε πολλῷ μᾶλλον εἰκὸς ἦν ἐκεῖνον ὑπὲρ ἐμοῦ ἀπολογήσασθαι,
πατέρα ὄντα· ὁ μὲν γὰρ πολλῷ πρεσβύτερός ἐστι τῶν ἐμῶν
πραγμάτων, ἐγὼ δὲ πολλῷ νεώτερος τῶν ἐκείνῳ πεπραγμένων.
καὶ εἰ μὲν ἐγὼ τούτου ἀγωνιζομένου κατεμαρτύρουν ἃ μὴ
σαφῶς ᾔδη, ἀκοῇ δὲ ἠπιστάμην, δεινὰ ἂν ἔφη πάσχειν ὑπ᾽
75 ἐμοῦ· νῦν δὲ ἀναγκάζων ἐμὲ ἀπολογεῖσθαι ὧν ἐγὼ πολλῷ
νεώτερός εἰμι καὶ λόγῳ οἶδα, ταῦτα οὐ δεινὰ ἡγεῖται εἰργάσθαι. ὅμως μέντοι καθ᾽ ὅσον ἐγὼ οἶδα, οὐ προδώσω τὸν
πατέρα κακῶς ἀκούοντα ἐν ὑμῖν ἀδίκως. καίτοι τάχ᾽ ἂν
σφαλείην, ἃ ἐκεῖνος ὀρθῶς ἔργῳ ἔπραξε, ταῦτ᾽ ἐγὼ λόγῳ μὴ
76 ὀρθῶς εἰπών· ὅμως δ᾽ οὖν κεκινδυνεύσεται. Πρὶν μὲν γὰρ
τὴν ἀπόστασιν τὴν Μυτιληναίων γενέσθαι, ἔργῳ τὴν εὔνοιαν
ἐδείκνυε τὴν εἰς ὑμᾶς· ἐπειδὴ δὲ ἡ πόλις ὅλη κακῶς ἐβου-
λεύσατο ἀποστᾶσα καὶ ἥμαρτε τῆς ὑμετέρας γνώμης, μετὰ
τῆς πόλεως ὅλης ἠναγκάσθη συνεξαμαρτεῖν. τὴν μὲν οὖν
γνώμην ἔτι καὶ ἐν ἐκείνοις ὅμοιος ἦν εἰς ὑμᾶς, τὴν δ᾽
εὔνοιαν οὐκέτι ἦν ἐπ᾽ ἐκείνῳ τὴν αὐτὴν εἰς ὑμᾶς παρέχειν.
οὔτε γὰρ ἐκλιπεῖν τὴν πόλιν εὐπόρως εἶχεν αὐτῷ· ἱκανὰ γὰρ
ἦν τὰ ἐνέχυρα ἃ εἴχετο αὐτοῦ, οἵ τε παῖδες καὶ τὰ χρήμα-
τα· τοῦτο δ᾽ αὖ μένοντι πρὸς τὴν πόλιν αὐτῷ ἀδυνάτως
77 εἶχεν ἰσχυρίζεσθαι. ἐπεὶ δ᾽ ὑμεῖς τοὺς αἰτίους τούτων
ἐκολάσατε, ἐν οἷς οὐκ ἐφαίνετο ὢν ὁ ἐμὸς πατήρ, τοῖς δ᾽
ἄλλοις Μυτιληναίοις ἄδειαν ἐδώκατε οἰκεῖν τὴν σφετέραν
αὐτῶν, οὐκ ἔστιν ὅ τι ὕστερον αὐτῷ ἡμάρτηται τῷ ἐμῷ πα-
τρί, οὐδ᾽ ὅ τι οὐ πεποίηται τῶν δεόντων, οὐδ᾽ ἧς τινος
λῃτουργίας ἡ πόλις ἐνδεὴς γεγένηται, οὔτε ἡ ὑμετέρα οὔτε
ἡ Μυτιληναίων, ἀλλὰ καὶ χορηγίας χορηγεῖ καὶ τέλη κατα-
78 τίθησιν. εἰ δ᾽ ἐν Αἴνῳ χωροφιλεῖ, τοῦτο <ποιεῖ> οὐκ ἀποστερῶν γε τῶν εἰς τὴν πόλιν ἑαυτὸν οὐδενὸς οὐδ᾽ ἑτέρας
πόλεως πολίτης γεγενημένος, ὥσπερ ἑτέρους ὁρῶ, τοὺς μὲν
εἰς τὴν ἤπειρον ἰόντας καὶ οἰκοῦντας ἐν τοῖς πολεμίοις
τοῖς ὑμετέροις καὶ δίκας ἀπὸ ξυμβόλων ὑμῖν δικαζομένους,
οὐδὲ φεύγων τὸ πλῆθος τὸ ὑμέτερον, τοὺς δ᾽ οἵους ὑμεῖς
79 μισῶν συκοφάντας. ἃ μὲν οὖν μετὰ τῆς πόλεως ὅλης ἀνάγκῃ
μᾶλλον ἢ γνώμῃ ἔπραξεν, τούτων οὐ δίκαιός ἐστιν ὁ ἐμὸς
πατὴρ ἰδίᾳ δίκην διδόναι. ἅπασι γὰρ Μυτιληναίοις ἀεί-
μνηστος ἡ τότε ἁμαρτία γεγένηται· ἠλλάξαντο μὲν γὰρ
πολλῆς εὐδαιμονίας πολλὴν κακοδαιμονίαν, ἐπεῖδον δὲ τὴν
ἑαυτῶν πατρίδα ἀνάστατον γενομένην. ἃ δὲ ἰδίᾳ οὗτοι δια-
βάλλουσι τὸν ἐμὸν πατέρα, μὴ πείθεσθε· χρημάτων γὰρ ἕνεκα
ἡ πᾶσα παρασκευὴ γεγένηται ἐπ᾽ ἐμοὶ κἀκείνῳ. πολλὰ δ᾽

---

74 ᾔδη Jernsteat: ᾔδειν
75 κεκινδυνεύσεται A corr. 2: καὶ κινδυνεύσεται N Apr.
76 τὴν Μυτιληναίων Blass: τῶν Μιτυληναίων   εὐπόρως A
     corr. 2: εὖρ᾽ ὅπως N Apr.
77 λῃτουργίας Blass: λειτουργίας   χορηγεῖ Blass:
     ἐχορήγει   κατατίθησιν N: κατετίθει A
78 ποιεῖ add. Reiske
79 ἐπ᾽ ἐμοὶ A: ὑπ᾽ ἐμοὶ N

have been far more fitting for him to be defending me. He is far older than I and knows my affairs, whereas I am far younger than he and do not know his past activities. If my accuser were on trial and I were giving evidence against him which I did not know for certain but had gathered from hearsay, he would protest that he was being treated terribly by me. But as it is, he sees nothing terrible in 75 forcing me to explain events which I am far too young to know of except from hearsay. Nevertheless, I will use what knowledge I have and not betray my father, whom you have heard being subjected to unwarranted abuse. Possibly, indeed, I may fail, explaining faultily his faultless conduct. Still, this risk will be run.

Before the Mytilenean revolt my father proved his devotion to 76 your interests by his actions. But when the whole city ill-advisedly revolted and failed in what you expected of it he was forced to join the whole city in that failure. His feelings towards you even then remained the same, but he could no longer display the same devotion towards you. It was not easy for him to leave the city, as the ties which bound him, his children and his property, were strong ones; on the other hand he could not set himself against the city while he remained there. But since the time when you punished the authors of 77 the revolt, of whom my father was not found to be one, and granted the other Mytileneans an amnesty allowing them to live on their own land, my father has not been guilty of a single fault or of a single lapse from duty. He has failed neither your city nor that of the Mytileneans in any public service, but he furnishes choruses and pays his taxes. If his favourite haunt is Aenus this does not mean he 78 is evading any of his public obligations or has become the citizen of another city, like those others I see, crossing to the mainland, living among your enemies and litigating with you under treaty; nor does it mean he desires to avoid your courts. It means he shares your own hatred of informers.

It is not just, then, that my father should be punished 79 individually for the act which he joined his whole city in committing, under compulsion and not from choice. The mistake made then has become an everlasting memory for every Mytilenean. They exchanged great prosperity for great misery and saw their country ruined. Nor must you be influenced by the prosecution's slanderous attack on my father's individual conduct: this whole intrigue against my father and myself has been fabricated for the sake of money. Many, indeed, are

ἐστὶ τὰ συμβαλλόμενα τοῖς βουλομένοις τῶν ἀλλοτρίων ἐφί-
εσθαι. γέρων μὲν ἐκεῖνος ὥστ' ἐμοὶ βοηθεῖν, νεώτερος δ'
80 ἐγὼ πολλῷ ἢ ὥστε δύνασθαι ἐμαυτῷ τιμωρεῖν ἱκανῶς. ἀλλ'
ὑμεῖς βοηθήσατέ μοι, καὶ μὴ διδάσκετε τοὺς συκοφάντας
μεῖζον ὑμῶν αὐτῶν δύνασθαι. ἐὰν μὲν γὰρ εἰσιόντες εἰς
ὑμᾶς ἃ βούλονται πράσσωσι, δεδειγμένον ἔσται τούτους μὲν
πείθειν, τὸ δ' ὑμέτερον πλῆθος φεύγειν· ἐὰν δὲ εἰσιόντες
εἰς ὑμᾶς πονηροὶ μὲν αὐτοὶ δοκῶσιν εἶναι, πλέον δ' αὐτοῖς
μηδὲν γένηται, ὑμετέρα ἡ τιμὴ καὶ ἡ δύναμις ἔσται, ὥσπερ
καὶ τὸ δίκαιον ἔχει. ὑμεῖς οὖν ἐμοί τε βοηθεῖτε καὶ τῷ
δικαίῳ.
81   Ὅσα μὲν οὖν ἐκ τῶν ἀνθρωπίνων τεκμηρίων καὶ μαρ-
τυριῶν οἷά τε ἦν ἀποδειχθῆναι, ἀκηκόατε· χρὴ δὲ καὶ τοῖς
ἀπὸ τῶν θεῶν σημείοις γενομένοις εἰς τὰ τοιαῦτα οὐχ
ἥκιστα τεκμηραμένους ψηφίζεσθαι. καὶ γὰρ τὰ τῆς πόλεως
κοινὰ τούτοις μάλιστα πιστεύοντες ἀσφαλῶς διαπράσσεσθε,
τοῦτο μὲν τὰ εἰς τοὺς κινδύνους ἥκοντα, τοῦτο δὲ [εἰς]
82 τὰ ἔξω τῶν κινδύνων. χρὴ δὲ καὶ εἰς τὰ ἴδια ταῦτα μέγιστα
καὶ πιστότατα ἡγεῖσθαι. οἶμαι γὰρ ὑμᾶς ἐπίστασθαι ὅτι
πολλοὶ ἤδη ἄνθρωποι μὴ καθαροὶ <τὰς> χεῖρας ἢ ἄλλο τι
μίασμα ἔχοντες συνεισβάντες εἰς τὸ πλοῖον συναπώλεσαν
μετὰ τῆς αὐτῶν ψυχῆς τοὺς ὁσίως διακειμένους τὰ πρὸς τοὺς
θεούς· τοῦτο δὲ ἤδη ἑτέρους ἀπολομένους μὲν οὔ, κινδυνεύσαντας δὲ τοὺς ἐσχάτους κινδύνους διὰ τοὺς τοιούτους ἀν-
θρώπους· τοῦτο δὲ ἱεροῖς παραστάντες πολλοὶ ἤδη καταφα-
νεῖς ἐγένοντο οὐχ ὅσιοι ὄντες, [καὶ] διακωλύοντες τὰ ἱερὰ
83 μὴ γίγνεσθαι τὰ νομιζόμενα. ἐμοὶ τοίνυν ἐν πᾶσι τούτοις
τὰ ἐναντία ἐγένετο. τοῦτο μὲν γὰρ ὅσοις συνέπλευσα, καλ-
λίστοις ἐχρήσαντο πλοῖς· τοῦτο δὲ ὅπου ἱεροῖς παρέστην,
οὐκ ἔστιν ὅπου οὐχὶ κάλλιστα τὰ ἱερὰ ἐγένετο. ἃ ἐγὼ ἀξιῶ
μεγάλα μοι τεκμήρια εἶναι τῆς αἰτίας, ὅτι οὐκ ἀληθῆ μου
οὗτοι κατηγοροῦσι. <παρέξομαι δὲ > τούτων μάρτυρας.

ΜΑΡΤΥΡΕΣ

84   Ἐπίσταμαι δὲ καὶ τάδε, ὦ ἄνδρες δικασταί, ὅτι εἰ μὲν
ἐμοῦ κατεμαρτύρουν οἱ μάρτυρες, ὥς τι ἀνόσιον γεγένηται
ἐμοῦ παρόντος ἐν πλοίῳ ἢ ἐν ἱεροῖς, αὐτοῖς γε τούτοις
ἰσχυροτάτοις ἂν ἐχρῶντο, καὶ πίστιν τῆς αἰτίας ταύτην
σαφεστάτην ἀπέφαινον, τὰ σημεῖα τὰ ἀπὸ τῶν θεῶν· νῦν δὲ

---

79 ὥστ' ἐμοὶ Bekker: ὥστε μοι
81 εἰς del. Bekker
82 τὰς add. Fuhr   μὲν οὔ, κινδυνεύσαντας A corr. 2:
    μὲν, οὐ κινδυνεύσαντας N Apr.   τοῦτο δὲ (ante
    ἱεροῖς) A: τοῦ δὲ N   ἤδη (ante καταφανεῖς) Ignatius:
    δὴ   καὶ del. Sauppe
83 παρέξομαι δὲ τούτων μάρτυρας scripsi: τούτων μάρτυρες

the circumstances which favour those seeking to lay their hands on the goods of others. My father is too old to help me, while I am far too young to be able to avenge myself as I should. You must help 80 me, then, and refuse to teach informers to become more powerful than yourselves. If when they come to you they achieve their purpose it will be shown that one compromises with them and avoids your court. But if when they come to you they achieve no more than being shown up as scoundrels you will enjoy the honour and the power which it is right that you should. So give me and give justice your support.

You have heard all that can be shown my human proof and 81 evidence. But in cases of this kind you should also be influenced in your verdict not least by the signs furnished by heaven. For you depend chiefly on these for your safe conduct of state affairs, both those involving danger and those that do not. So you should also 82 consider them most important and trustworthy in private affairs. I am sure you know that in the past many men with unclean hands or some other form of defilement have embarked on ship with the righteous and involved them in their own destruction. Others have escaped death but risked extreme danger through such men. Many, too, have been proved to be defiled while standing beside sacrifices, because they prevented the proper performance of the rites. With me the 83 opposite has happened in every case. Not only have those with whom I have sailed enjoyed the calmest of voyages, but whenever I have attended a sacrifice that sacrifice has never been anything but successful. These facts, I claim, are strong proof for me that the charge the prosecution are bringing is unfounded. I will produce witnesses to confirm these statements.

WITNESSES

I also know this, gentlemen of the jury, that if the witnesses 84 were testifying against me that with my presence on ship or at a sacrifice some unholy manifestation had occurred, the prosecution would be treating that as highly significant and would be showing that here was the clearest confirmation of their charge, in the signs

τῶν τε σημείων ἐναντίων τοῖς τούτων λόγοις γιγνομένων,
τῶν τε μαρτύρων ἃ μὲν ἐγὼ λέγω μαρτυρούντων ἀληθῆ εἶναι,
ἃ δ᾽ οὗτοι κατηγοροῦσι ψευδῆ, τοῖς μὲν μαρτυροῦσιν ἀπιστεῖν ὑμᾶς κελεύουσι, τοῖς δὲ λόγοις οὓς αὐτοὶ λέγουσι
πιστεύειν ὑμᾶς φασι χρῆναι. καὶ οἱ μὲν ἄλλοι ἄνθρωποι
τοῖς ἔργοις τοὺς λόγους ἐλέγχουσιν, οὗτοι δὲ τοῖς λόγοις
τὰ ἔργα ζητοῦσιν ἄπιστα καθιστάναι.

85   Ὅσα μὲν οὖν ἐκ τῶν κατηγορηθέντων μέμνημαι, ὦ ἄνδρες, ἀπολελόγημαι· οἶμαι δὲ καὶ <πρὸς> ὑμῶν <εἶναι μου>
ἀποψηφίσασθαι. ταὐτὰ γὰρ ἐμέ τε σῴζει, καὶ ὑμῖν νόμιμα
καὶ εὔορκα γίγνεται. κατὰ γὰρ τοὺς νόμους ὠμόσατε δικάσειν· ἐγὼ δὲ καθ᾽ οὓς μὲν ἀπήχθην, οὐκ ἔνοχός εἰμι τοῖς
νόμοις, ὧν δ᾽ ἔχω τὴν αἰτίαν, ἀγών μοι νόμιμος ὑπολείπεται. εἰ δὲ δύο ἐξ ἑνὸς ἀγῶνος γεγένησθον, οὐκ ἐγὼ αἴτιος,
ἀλλ᾽ οἱ κατήγοροι. καίτοι οὐ δήπου οἱ μὲν ἔχθιστοι οἱ
ἐμοὶ δύο ἀγῶνας περὶ ἐμοῦ πεποιήκασιν, ὑμεῖς δὲ οἱ τῶν
δικαίων ἴσοι κριταὶ προκαταγνώσεσθέ μου ἐν τῷδε τῷ ἀγῶνι

86 τὸν φόνον. μὴ ὑμεῖς γε, ὦ ἄνδρες· ἀλλὰ δότε τι καὶ τῷ
χρόνῳ, μεθ᾽ οὗ ὀρθότατα εὑρίσκουσιν οἱ τὴν ἀκρίβειαν
ζητοῦντες τῶν πραγμάτων. ἠξίουν μὲν γὰρ ἔγωγε περὶ τῶν
τοιούτων, ὦ ἄνδρες, εἶναι τὴν δίκην κατὰ τοὺς νόμους,
κατὰ μέντοι τὸ δίκαιον ὡς πλειστάκις ἐλέγχεσθαι. τοσούτῳ
γὰρ ἄμεινον ἂν ἐγιγνώσκετο· οἱ γὰρ πολλοὶ ἀγῶνες τῇ μὲν

87 ἀληθείᾳ σύμμαχοί εἰσι, τῇ δὲ διαβολῇ πολεμιώτατοι. φόνου
γὰρ δίκη καὶ μὴ ὀρθῶς γνωσθεῖσα ἰσχυρότερον τοῦ δικαίου
καὶ τοῦ ἀληθοῦς ἐστιν· ἀνάγκη γάρ, ἐὰν ὑμεῖς μου καταψηφίσησθε, καὶ μὴ ὄντα φονέα μηδ᾽ ἔνοχον τῷ ἔργῳ χρῆσθαι
τῇ δίκῃ καὶ τῷ νόμῳ· καὶ οὐδεὶς ἂν τολμήσειεν οὔτε τὴν
δίκην τὴν δεδικασμένην παραβαίνειν, πιστεύσας αὐτῷ ὅτι
οὐκ ἔνοχός ἐστιν, οὔτε ξυνειδὼς αὐτῷ τοιοῦτον ἔργον
εἰργασμένῳ μὴ οὐ χρῆσθαι τῷ νόμῳ· ἀνάγκη δὲ τῆς δίκης
νικᾶσθαι παρὰ τὸ ἀληθές, αὐτοῦ τε τοῦ ἀληθοῦς, ἄλλως τε

88 καὶ ἐὰν μὴ ᾖ ὁ τιμωρήσων. αὐτῶν δὲ τούτων ἕνεκα οἵ τε
νόμοι καὶ αἱ διωμοσίαι καὶ τὰ τόμια καὶ αἱ προρρήσεις,
καὶ τἆλλ᾽ ὁπόσα γίγνεται τῶν δικῶν ἕνεκα τοῦ φόνου, πολὺ
διαφέροντά ἐστιν ἢ [καὶ]ἐπὶ τοῖς ἄλλοις, ὅτι καὶ αὐτὰ τὰ
πράγματα, περὶ ὧν οἱ κίνδυνοι, περὶ πλείστου ἐστὶν ὀρθῶς
γιγνώσκεσθαι· ὀρθῶς μὲν γὰρ γνωσθέντα τιμωρία ἐστὶ τῷ
ἀδικηθέντι, φονέα δὲ τὸν μὴ αἴτιον ψηφισθῆναι ἁμαρτία

84 ἐναντίων A corr. 2 N: ἐναντίον Apr.   γιγνομένων A
corr. 2 N: γιγνομένοις Apr.   φασι χρῆναι N: χρῆναί
φασι A   τὰ ἔργα ζητοῦσιν N: ζητοῦσι τὰ ἔργα A
85 καὶ (post δὲ) om. N   πρὸς ὑμῶν εἶναι μου ἀποψηφίσασθαι scripsi: ὑμῶν ἀποψηφίσασθαι   ταὐτὰ Bekker: ταῦτα
μου (post προκαταγνώσεσθε) A: με N   ἀγῶνι Mätzner:
λόγῳ
86 γὰρ ἄμεινον ἂν N: γὰρ ἂν ἄμεινον A
88 ἕνεκα (post τούτων) A: εἵνεκα N   τἆλλ᾽ ὁπόσα A:
τἆλλα ὅσα N   καὶ del. Mätzner

from heaven. But as it is, since the signs are contradicting their assertions and the witnesses are testifying that what I say is true and what the prosecution accuse me of is false, they bid you disbelieve the witnesses and say you should believe the statements they are making themselves. Other men prove statements with facts, but the prosecution seek to discredit the facts by statements.

I have answered all the charges that I can remember, gentlemen; and I think it is to your own advantage to acquit me. For this same verdict will both save my life and be in accordance with the law and with your oath. You have sworn to give a verdict according to the laws; and I am not liable to the laws under which I was arrested, though the crime with which I am charged can still be tried legally. If two trials have been made out of one it is not I who am to blame but my accusers. Nor can I suppose that if my bitterest enemies have instituted two trials against me you who are impartial ministers of justice will prematurely find me guilty of murder in the present one. Do not do this, gentlemen. Give a chance to time also, with whose help those who seek the exact truth of events find it with most certainty. I would have thought it right, gentlemen, that in such matters as this the trial should be held according to the law, but that according to justice the case should be tested as many times as possible. For in this way it would be better understood, since repeated trials are the ally of the truth and the deadly foe of misrepresentation. In a trial for murder even a wrong judgment prevails over justice and the truth. If you condemn me I must of necessity submit to your verdict and the law even though I am not a murderer nor liable for the crime. No one would dare either to disregard the sentence passed upon him because he believed in his own mind that he was not liable, or to disobey the law if he knew in his heart that he had done such a deed. He must submit to the verdict in defiance of the facts, or to the facts themselves, especially if his victim has no one to avenge him. For these very reasons, the laws, the oaths, the sacrifices, the proclamations and everything else that takes place in connection with trials for murder are very different from what happens at other trials, because it is of supreme importance that the facts themselves, which concern danger to life, should be rightly understood. Facts rightly understood mean vengeance for the injured party, but for an innocent man to be condemned as a murderer is a mistake and a sinful error against the

85

86

87

88

καὶ ἀσέβειά ἐστιν εἴς τε τοὺς θεοὺς καὶ εἰς τοὺς νόμους.
89 καὶ οὐκ ἴσον ἐστὶ τόν τε διώκοντα μὴ ὀρθῶς αἰτιάσασθαι
καὶ ὑμᾶς τοὺς δικαστὰς μὴ ὀρθῶς γνῶναι. ἡ μὲν γὰρ τούτων
αἰτίασις οὐκ ἔχει τέλος, ἀλλ' ἐν ὑμῖν ἐστι καὶ τῇ δίκῃ·
ὅ τι δ' ἂν ὑμεῖς ἐν αὐτῇ τῇ δίκῃ μὴ ὀρθῶς γνῶτε, τοῦτο
οὐκ ἔστιν ὅποι ἄν τις ἀνενεγκὼν τὴν ἁμαρτίαν ἀπολύσαιτο.
90 πῶς ἂν οὖν ὀρθῶς δικάσαιτε περὶ αὐτῶν; εἰ τούτους τε
ἐάσετε τὸν νομιζόμενον ὅρκον διομοσαμένους κατηγορῆσαι,
κἀμὲ περὶ αὐτοῦ τοῦ πράγματος ἀπολογήσασθαι. πῶς δὲ
ἐάσετε; ἐὰν νυνὶ ἀποψηφίσησθέ μου. διαφεύγω γὰρ οὐδ'
οὕτω τὰς ὑμετέρας γνώμας, ἀλλ' ὑμεῖς ἔσεσθε οἱ κἀκεῖ
περὶ ἐμοῦ διαψηφιζόμενοι. καὶ ἀποψηφισαμένοις μὲν ὑμῖν
ἐμοῦ νῦν ἔξεστι τότε χρῆσθαι ὅ τι ἂν δὴ βούλησθε, ἀπολέ-
91 σασι δὲ οὐδὲ βουλεύσασθαι ἔτι περὶ ἐμοῦ ἐγχωρεῖ. καὶ μὴν
εἰ δέοι ἁμαρτεῖν τι, τὸ ἀδίκως ἀπολῦσαι ὁσιώτερον ἂν εἴη
τοῦ μὴ δικαίως ἀπολέσαι· τὸ μὲν γὰρ ἁμάρτημα μόνον ἐστί,
τὸ δὲ ἕτερον καὶ ἀσέβημα. ἐν ᾧ χρὴ πολλὴν πρόνοιαν ἔχειν,
μέλλοντας ἀνήκεστον ἔργον ἐργάζεσθαι. ἐν μὲν γὰρ ἀκεστῷ
πράγματι καὶ ὀργῇ χρησαμένους καὶ διαβολῇ πιθομένους
ἔλασσόν ἐστιν ἐξαμαρτεῖν· μεταγνοὺς γάρ <τις> ἔτι ἂν ὀρθῶς βουλεύσαιτο· ἐν δὲ τοῖς ἀνηκέστοις πλέον βλάβος τὸ
μετανοεῖν καὶ γνῶναι ἐξημαρτηκότας. ἤδη δέ τισιν ὑμῶν
καὶ μετεμέλησεν ἀπολωλεκόσι. καίτοι ὅπου ὑμῖν τοῖς ἐξ-
απατηθεῖσι μετεμέλησεν, ἦ καὶ πάνυ τοι χρῆν τούς γε ἐξ-
92 απατῶντας ἀπολωλέναι. ἔπειτα δὲ τὰ μὲν ἀκούσια τῶν ἁμαρτημάτων ἔχει συγγνώμην, τὰ δὲ ἑκούσια οὐκ ἔχει. τὸ μὲν
γὰρ ἀκούσιον ἁμάρτημα, ὦ ἄνδρες, τῆς τύχης ἐστί, τὸ δὲ
ἑκούσιον τῆς γνώμης. ἑκούσιον δὲ πῶς ἂν εἴη μᾶλλον ἢ εἴ
τις, ὧν βουλὴν ποιοῖτο, ταῦτα παραχρῆμα ἐξεργάζοιτο; καὶ
μὴν τὴν ἴσην γε δύναμιν ἔχει, ὅστις τε ἂν τῇ χειρὶ ἀπο-
93 κτείνῃ ἀδίκως καὶ ὅστις τῇ ψήφῳ. εὖ δ' ἴστε ὅτι οὐκ ἂν

89 ὅποι ἄν] ὁποίαν A, ὁπόιάν N
90 δικάσαιτε Bekker: δικάσητε   διομοσαμένους A:
διομοσομένους N   κἀκεῖ Aldus: κακοὶ   ἀποψηφισαμένοις
Aldus: ψηφισαμένοις A, φεισαμένοις N   ἂν δὴ βούλησθε
Jebb: ἃ δὴ βούλεσθαι N A corr. 1 (βούλεσθε pr.)
ἀπολέσασι δὲ Dobree: ἀπολογήσασθαι
91 εἰ δέοι . . . ἀσέβημα affert Stobaeus flor. 46.19
τι, τὸ Mätzner: ἐπὶ τῷ AN, τι ἁμαρτεῖν τὸ Stobaeus
ἂν εἴη Dobree: ἂν ἦ AN, om. Stobaeus   τοῦ Stobaeus,
Aldus: τὸ   γὰρ ἁμάρτημα μόνον N: γὰρ μόνον ἁμάρτημα
A, μόνον om. Stobaeus   ἀνήκεστον Stephanus:
ἀνηκέστερον   ἀκεστῷ Stephanus: ἑκάστῳ   πιθομένους
Cobet: πειθομένους   ἔλασσον Blass: ἔλαττον   τις
post γὰρ add. Bohlmann   ἀπολωλεκόσι A: ἀπολελωκόσι
N   ὅπου Leo: οὔπω   ἦ Leo: εἰ   χρῆν Blass: χρὴ
92 γὰρ om. N   post γνώμης N add. ἐστίν   ἐξεργάζοιτο
N: ἐργάζοιτο A

gods and the laws. Nor is it the same for the prosecutor to make a 89
wrongful accusation as it is for you jurors to pass a wrongful
verdict. The charge brought by the prosecution is not in itself
effective, but depends on you and your judgment. If you give a
wrongful verdict in your actual judgment there is no higher authority
to which you can refer this and rid yourselves of the responsibility
for the mistake.

How, then, can you make a correct judgment of the case? By 90
allowing the prosecution to bring their charge after swearing the
customary oath and by allowing me to make my defence on the actual
question before the court. How will you do this? By acquitting me
today. For I do not escape your judgment even so, but you will be
my judges in the other court too. If you spare me now you can treat
me as you wish then, but if you put me to death you cannot even
consider my case further.

Indeed, if you had to make some mistake, to acquit me unjustly 91
would be a more righteous act than to put me to death contrary to
justice: the one thing is merely a mistake, but the other is also a
sin. In this situation you must exercise the greatest caution, because
you are about to perform an irremediable action. For in a remediable
matter it is less serious to make a mistake, whether it be made
through giving way to anger or through believing a false accusation:
it is still possible to change one's mind and come to a right decision.
But in irremediable matters it is a greater wrong to change one's
mind and acknowledge one's mistake. Some of you have in fact
repented before now of having condemned men to death; and when
you, who had been misled, felt repentance most assuredly did those
who had misled you deserve death.

Then again, involuntary mistakes are excusable, voluntary 92
mistakes are not. An involuntary mistake, gentlemen, is due to
chance, a voluntary one to choice; and what could be more voluntary
than when a man immediately puts into effect what he has carefully
considered? Furthermore, the wrongful taking of life by one's vote is
just as criminal as the wrongful taking of life by one's hand.

ποτ' ἦλθον εἰς τὴν πόλιν, εἴ τι ξυνήδη ἐμαυτῷ τοιοῦτον·
νῦν δὲ πιστεύων τῷ δικαίῳ, οὗ πλέονος οὐδέν ἐστιν ἄξιον
ἀνδρὶ συναγωνίζεσθαι, μηδὲν αὐτῷ συνειδότι ἀνόσιον εἰργασμένῳ μήτ' εἰς τοὺς θεοὺς ἠσεβηκότι· ἐν γὰρ τῷ τοιούτῳ
ἤδη καὶ τὸ σῶμα ἀπειρηκὸς ἡ ψυχὴ συνεξέσωσεν, ἐθέλουσα
ταλαιπωρεῖν διὰ τὸ μὴ ξυνειδέναι ἑαυτῇ· τῷ δὲ ξυνειδότι
τοῦτο αὐτὸ πρῶτον πολέμιόν ἐστιν· ἔτι γὰρ καὶ τοῦ σώματος
ἰσχύοντος ἡ ψυχὴ προαπολείπει, ἡγουμένη τὴν τιμωρίαν οἱ
ἥκειν ταύτην τῶν ἀσεβημάτων· ἐγὼ δ' ἐμαυτῷ τοιοῦτον οὐδὲν
94   ξυνειδὼς ἥκω εἰς ὑμᾶς. τὸ δὲ τοὺς κατηγόρους διαβάλλειν
οὐδέν ἐστι θαυμαστόν. τούτων γὰρ ἔργον τοῦτο, ὑμῶν δὲ τὸ
μὴ πείθεσθαι τὰ μὴ δίκαια. τοῦτο μὲν γὰρ ἐμοὶ πειθομένοις
ὑμῖν μεταμελῆσαι ἔστιν, καὶ τούτου φάρμακον τὸ αὖθις
κολάσαι, τοῦ δὲ τούτοις πειθομένους ἐξεργάσασθαι ἃ οὗτοι
βούλονται οὐκ ἔστιν ἴασις. οὐδὲ χρόνος πολὺς ὁ διαφέρων,
ἐν ᾧ ταῦτα νομίμως πράξεθ' ἃ νῦν ὑμᾶς παρανόμως πείθουσιν
οἱ κατήγοροι ψηφίσασθαι. οὔ τοι τῶν ἐπειγομένων ἐστὶ τὰ
πράγματα, ἀλλὰ τῶν εὖ βουλευομένων. νῦν μὲν οὖν γνωρισταὶ
γίγνεσθε τῆς δίκης, τότε δὲ δικασταὶ [τῶν μαρτύρων]· νῦν
95   μὲν δοξασταί, τότε δὲ κριταὶ τῶν ἀληθῶν. Ῥᾷστον δέ τοί
ἐστιν ἀνδρὸς περὶ θανάτου φεύγοντος τὰ ψευδῆ καταμαρτυ-
ρῆσαι. ἐὰν γὰρ τὸ παραχρῆμα μόνον πείσωσιν ὥστε ἀποκτεῖναι, ἅμα τῷ σώματι καὶ ἡ τιμωρία ἀπόλωλεν. οὔτε γὰρ οἱ
φίλοι ἔτι θελήσουσιν ὑπὲρ ἀπολωλότος τιμωρεῖν. ἐὰν δὲ
96   καὶ βουληθῶσιν, τί ἔσται πλέον τῷ γε ἀποθανόντι; νῦν μὲν
οὖν ἀποψηφίσασθέ μου· ἐν δὲ τῇ τοῦ φόνου δίκῃ οὗτοί τε
τὸν νομιζόμενον ὅρκον διομοσάμενοι ἐμοῦ κατηγορήσουσι,
καὶ ὑμεῖς περὶ ἐμοῦ κατὰ τοὺς κειμένους νόμους διαγνώ-
σεσθε, καὶ ἐμοὶ οὐδεὶς λόγος ἔσται ἔτι, ἐάν τι πάσχω, ὡς
παρανόμως ἀπωλόμην. ταῦτά τοι δέομαι ὑμῶν, οὔτε τὸ ὑμέτερον εὐσεβὲς παριεὶς οὔτε ἐμαυτὸν ἀποστερῶν τὸ δίκαιον·
ἐν δὲ τῷ ὑμετέρῳ ὅρκῳ καὶ ἡ ἐμὴ σωτηρία ἔνεστι. πειθό-
μενοι δὲ τούτων ὅτῳ βούλεσθε, ἀποψηφίσασθέ μου.

---

93 ξυνήδη Jernstedt: ξυνήδειν   εἰργασμένῳ Ν: εἰργασμέ-
    νον Α   συνεξέσωσεν Α: συνεξέωσεν Ν   ἀσεβημάτων Ν:
    ἀσεβηκότων Α
94 τὸ δὲ Aldus: τῷ Ν, τῶ Α   ὑμῖν Ν: ἡμῖν Α   πράξεθ'
    Apr.: πράξεσθ' Ν Α corr.   ἃ Α: ἂν Ν   τῶν μαρτύρων
    del. Jernstedt
95 ῥᾷστον δέ τοι Dobree: ἀραῖς τῶν δετοι Α, om. Ν, qui
    lacunam hic habet
96 ἔσται Α: ἐστὶ Ν   ἐάν τι Bekker: ἐάν τε   παρανόμως
    Reiske: παράνομος   παριεὶς Fuhr: παρεὶς

66

Be assured that I should never have come to Athens if I had 93
had such a crime on my conscience. As it is, I am here because I
have faith in justice, than which there is nothing more valuable to aid
a man when he is conscious in his own mind that he has done nothing
sinful nor has been impious towards the gods. Often at such a time,
even when the body has given up, the spirit has come to its aid,
ready to endure hardship in the conscience that it is innocent. But
for the man whose conscience is guilty this very conscience is his
greatest enemy, for while his body is still strong his spirit fails him,
thinking that this guilty conscience has come upon it as the
punishment for his iniquities. But I come before you with no such
guilty conscience.

There is nothing remarkable in the fact that the prosecution are 94
maligning me. This is their duty, as it is your duty not to be
persuaded to do what is unjust. For on the one hand, if you listen to
me it is still possible for you to change your mind and the remedy for
this is to punish me at the second trial; but there is no remedy for
your being persuaded by the prosecution and carrying out what they
wish. Nor is the time interval long before you will do lawfully what
the prosecution are today urging you to vote for unlawfully. This is
not a matter for haste but for careful consideration. So learn the
facts of the case today, sit in judgment on it later; form an opinion
on the truth today, give your decision about it later.

It is easy, remember, to give false evidence against a man on a 95
capital charge. If you are persuaded only for a moment to put him to
death his chance of obtaining requital is lost together with his life.
Not even his friends will still be willing to seek requital for him once
he is dead; and even if they are willing what good will it be to the
dead man? Acquit me, then, today; and in the trial for murder the 96
prosecution shall swear the customary oath before accusing me, you
shall decide my case according to the laws of the land and I, if the
worst happens to me, shall have no grounds left for complaining that
I was sentenced to death illegally. That is my request of you, neither
asking you to set aside your sacred duty nor depriving myself of my
rights; for my salvation too depends on your oath. Respect whichever
of these you will and acquit me.

The Murder of Herodes: Commentary

1-7 **PROOEMIUM**: A noticeable feature of the speeches of both Antiphon and Andocides is the length of their introductory remarks (e.g. Ant. 6 *Chor.* 1-6; And. 1 *Myst.* 1-10) and in all three of the extant speeches which were written for delivery in court Antiphon adds a further section, the *prokataskeuē*, to the proem (1 *Stepmother* 5-13; 5 *Her.* 8-19; 6 *Chor.* 7-10). Thus in the *Herodes* the narrative does not begin until 20. Later orators preferred much shorter proems, omitting many of the well-worn commonplace elements which abound in Antiphon (*topoi*; see n. below), and they tended to avoid the *prokataskeuē*, beginning their narratives much earlier. This may be due in part to the later practice of editing speeches for publication, Antiphon's being distributed more or less in their original form; see 74-80, heading n.; Due 72-75. But Antiphon clearly attached great importance to the beginnings and also the endings of his speeches (the *epilogos* occupies 85-96 in the *Herodes*) as a means of winning the goodwill of the jury (*captatio benevolentiae*). This is further indicated both by the collection of such passages attributed to him (cf. Suidas, s.v. *aisthesthai*; Photius and Suidas, s.v. *mochthēros*; Cic. *Brut.* 46-47) and by their polished style: in the proem of the *Herodes*, for instance, the clauses are more balanced than in other parts of the speech, with parison in 1 (*tou men...tou de...*; n.b. the homoeoteleuton), more complex, though slightly less balanced correspondence in 2 (*hou men...entauthoi.../hou de...en toutōi...*; again with homoeoteleuton) and parallelism in 5 (*out'ergōi...out'ergōi...*).

1 **I could have wished...But as it is...**: the antithetical opening to the speech is familiar from other orators, e.g. And. 2 *Return*; Lys. 7 *Sac.Ol.* 31 *Phil.*; Isoc. 19 *Aeg.*; Is. 10 *Arist.*; cf. further Lys. 10 *Theomn.* 2 with comm. So too the plea of inexperience in litigation, which is the first of many commonplaces (*topoi*) in the speech; cf. Ant. 1 *Stepmother* 1, 3 *Second Tetralogy* b1-2; Lys. 12 *Erat.* 3 (with comm.); Dem. 27 *Aph. i* 2; D.H. *Is.* 10-11. Much of the proem is taken up by such *topoi* and other general reflections (e.g. 5, 'the tongue is to blame for a word, the will for an act'; 6, 'anything which is still in doubt depends more on chance than foresight') and these, enhanced by rhetorical effects such as repetition and amplification, form the basis of the *captatio benevolentiae*; see further Due 29-30. Antiphon makes much greater use of *topoi* in the proem and in connection with *atechnoi pisteis* (non-artificial proofs, such as torture-evidence and documents) than later orators (see above).

68

As Blass, *AB* I, 178 n.2 and Dover, *CAS*, 44 have pointed out, it is noticeable that Euxitheus, though protesting inexperience, makes no plea of youth as does the speaker of Ant. 1 *Stepmother*. This could have been dangerous for him, since he had been drinking on the night of Herodes' disappearance and the jury might well have held similar views on the effects of wine on young men to those expressed in Ant. 4 *Third Tetralogy* c2, but some would see in it an instance of a general absence of personal characterisation in Antiphon's speeches. This has often been remarked upon and criticised as revealing a lack of *ēthos* in them: for example, the very different defendants of the *Herodes* and the *Choreutes* speak in a similar fashion and Jebb, *AO* I, 29-31 concludes that Lysias would have made the Mytilenean Euxitheus show greater deference to the judges and avoid some of the rhetoric of the Athenian statesman. Now in individual characterisation Antiphon is indeed markedly inferior to Lysias (on whom see Usher (1965) 99-119) and the well-balanced style of the present proem may be regarded as conflicting with Euxitheus' professed inexperience in speaking. But this is not, it should be noted, a question of *ēthopoiia* (cf. D.H. *Lys.* 8), which is not a personal, but a generalising moral characterisation, designed to make the litigant's character appealing to the jury. Antiphon has to create an especially favourable impression for this Mytilenean defendant and so he puts into Euxitheus' mouth polished and refined sentences which he thinks will have this effect. If, then, personal characterisation is lacking here, an attempt at *ēthopoiia* is not.

For the omission of *an* with *eboulomēn*, expressing what one wishes were now true but which is not, cf. 86; Is. 10 *Arist.* 1 (with Wyse); *GMT* 425; and on the 'inceptive' *men* (ten out of the fifteen preserved speeches of Antiphon and all three of the genuine speeches of Andocides have *men* at the beginning, a tendency which decreases from Lysias onwards) see Denniston (1954) 382-384. The first section is also noteworthy for a number of stylistic features which recur in the speech, including
i) the use of abstract substantives, among which are several noticeable verbal substantives such as *apopsēphisis* (9), *metekbasis* (22) and *aitiasis* (25); see further 10, a murderer shall pay with his life in requital. The abstract nouns are frequently used periphrastically, especially those ending in *-sis* (cf. 4, 22, 65, 66, 76, 94); further on periphrasis in Antiphon see Cucuel 25-28; Dover, *CAS*, 50. To be noted in this context is the periphrastic use of *nomina agentium* in *-tēs*, emphasising individual words and a mark of the 'austere' style; cf. *nomothetēs* (15), *basanistēs*, *epitimētēs* (32), *kritēs* (47, 94), *dikastēs* (47, 94), *doxastēs*, *gnōristēs* (94). Other abstract expressions in the speech include those in which the definite article is joined with
a) a neuter adjective (a mainly poetical usage); see Cucuel 61-63; Denniston (1952) 20;

b) a neuter participle (again mainly poetical); see Cucuel 119-120; GMT 829 (a). Both usages are frequent in Thucydides, the latter almost confined in prose to these two authors;
c) the infinitive (very common); see Cucuel 115.
ii) metabole (*tou legein/tōn pragmatōn*), a characteristic figure of the 'austere' style and very common in both Antiphon and Thucydides.
iii) alliteration (n.b. *pepeiramai perai*).
Finally, note the chiastic arrangement of thought, *tou men* corresponding with *tēi te sumphorai...gegenēmenois, tou de* with *tēn dunamin...pragmatōn*.

my experience of affairs: especially the workings of the law.
am more wanting in the first: a similar lack of rhetorical ability was protested by Socrates in Plato, *Ap.* 17a-d.

2   submit to the physical suffering: referring to Euxitheus' imprisonment (17-18). Elsewhere in the proem Euxitheus speaks in more general terms applicable to most lawsuits.

    kakopathein reflects Antiphon's fondness for compounds (see Dover, *CAS*, 46), other instances of which are found in 11 (*homōrophios*), 18 (*kakopathein, kakopatheia*), 43 (*kakodaimōn*), 78 (*chōrophilein*), 79 (*aeimnēstos, eudaimonia, kakodaimonia*), 93 (*talaipōrein*) and throughout the speech. The *dipla* almost perforce have a poetical colour.

I had no experience to help me: legal experience would not, in fact, have helped prevent his confinement, on which see P. 26.

3   Many men poor at speaking...: reminiscent of this passage is Eur. frg. 56 (Nauck), lines 2-3, 'often a man seized by want of eloquence, though speaking justly, wins less than a clever speaker'. *Hipp.* 986-989 reveal further thoughts of Euripides on poor speakers and his source for these ideas may have been the orators' *topoi*.
his accusers' words...the actual facts: the antithesis of word (*logos*) and deed (*ergon*), recurring in 5 (*rhēma* for *logos*), 47, 75, 84 and in the *Tetralogies* (3 *Second Tetralogy* c1, c3), is well-known from the Sophists and from Thucydides; cf. Epicharm. frg. 39 (Diels); Democr. frg. 55, 145 (D); Gorg. *Pal.* 34; Thuc. 1.128.3, 3.38.4.

4   not for a hearing: appeals to the judges for a fair hearing were naturally a commonplace element of proems, especially those spoken by litigants professing inexperience; cf. Ant. 3 *Second Tetralogy* b2, c3; And. 4 *Alc.* 7; Lys. 19 *Arist.* 2; Is. 8 *Cir.* 5; Dem. 18 *Cor.* 6-7, 57 *Euboul.* 1. But in 4-5 Antiphon cleverly adapts this *topos*. With some amount of flattery Euxitheus says he will not make such an appeal and professes confidence in the fairness of the jury (which serves well as a *captatio benevolentiae*; the heliastic oath naturally demanded that jurors be impartial; cf. Dem. 18 *Cor.* 2, 24 *Tim.* 151). Euxitheus' request (5) is that the jury pardon errors in his speaking and

consider points well-made as spoken truthfully rather than skilfully (the request being made in just such a skilful manner) – which is really only asking for a hearing in a different way.

for it is reasonable to assume that...: the first of several parenthetical remarks in the speech, which help give it an extemporaneous character; see Dorjahn & Fairchild 29-30. Other instances occur in 10, 20, 41, 46, 62, 70, 77 and (a somewhat longer parenthesis) 93.

without asking: note the repetition, another very common feature of Antiphon's style.

5   I request this of you...: Andocides (1 *Myst*.9) similarly requested 'do not view my story with suspicion nor watch for faults of expression'. But Antiphon was also well aware that, in a case of murder where there were no witnesses, the speeches of both prosecution and defence had to be closely scrutinised and suspected on the slightest grounds (cf. 6 *Chor*.18, where there are verbal similarities with And. 1 *Myst*.9). Despite the commonplace nature of Euxitheus' request we should remember that correct diction was considered to be of great importance by the Athenians; see Bonner, *LL*, 165. A noticeable feature of the diction here and in 21-22 is the frequency of hiatus, which has the effect of emphasing each important point or word; see L. Pearson, 'Hiatus and its Effect in the Attic Speech-writers', *TAPA* 108 (1978) 137.

on the one hand...on the other hand: the formula *touto men/touto de* is an old-fashioned idiom frequent in the *Herodes* but not found in the *Choreutes* or the *Tetralogies*, or in Lysias.

For it is not just...: similarly Eur. *Hec*. 1187-88, 'Agamemnon, the tongue should never prevail over the actions of a man'. Note the parallelism in the Greek here.

6   The thought of 6-7 is part of the general *topos* (as And. 1 *Myst*.6; Lys. 19 *Arist*.3) that the defence is always at a disadvantage, which leads to appeals for a fair hearing (see 4, not for a hearing) and here to emphasis on how personal danger causes errors in speaking (cf. Eur. frg. 67 N).

depends more on chance than foresight: *tuchē* (chance) is again contrasted with *pronoia* (foresight) in 21 (where *pronoia* = design), and with *gnōmē* (choice) in 92. *Tuchē* also appears in the proems of speeches 1 and 6, a fact which Due 54 finds important as evidence for the way people of this time looked on responsibility, destiny and crime.

cause much consternation: note the emphatic alliteration in the Greek (sim. Thuc. 4.112.1).

7   I notice that...: note the fine example of chiasmus in the Greek in *pollōi cheiron...orthoumenos*.

according to human and divine law: Antiphon, like other orators, was fond of such amplified expressions, whose force is often heightened by the use of the superlative; cf. 8, 9, 11, 14, 19, 62, 82, 1 *Stepmother* 3, 6 *Chor*. 10.

taking into account your duty: i.e. Euxitheus' request is compatible with the heliastic oath.

8-19 PROKATASKEUE: It may be felt that the insertion of this section leads to a certain imbalance in the speech, the narrative not beginning until 20. Later oratory on the whole dispensed with the prokataskeuē, but for Antiphon structural aesthetics came second to practical purposes. He saw the prokataskeuē as the most effective place in which to attack his opponent's behaviour and as an extra opportunity for making an impression on the jury. In the Herodes, however, there was an additional factor involved. For the argument here is that the trial was being conducted under the wrong process and it seems clear that Antiphon would have entered a paragraphic plea before the trial had one been available at this time. Paragraphē, however, was a later innovation (see Harrison, LA 2, 106-124; D.M. MacDowell, 'The Chronology of Athenian Speeches and Legal Innovations in 401-398 B.C.', RIDA 18 (1971) 267-273), hence Antiphon is forced to insert these procedural arguments into the speech to be made at the trial itself. For the legal points arising in this section of the speech see the Introduction.

8 Firstly, I shall prove: the prothesis, or explanatory introduction, usually to the narrative but here to the prokataskeuē.
Not on the chance of eluding the judgment of your court: this is precisely what Euxitheus did want - he would have a much fairer hearing in a regular dikē phonou before the Areopagus. Plēthos refers to the court, the representative of the people (cf. 78, 80; And. 1 Myst. 135 with MacDowell; likewise the use of humeis in 90, see you will be my judges in the other court too), not to the people as a whole (as Ant. 6 Chor. 9; And. 1 Myst. 136, 150).
        On the art. inf. with an, as in Thuc. 7.62.2, see Kühner-Gerth I, 241. This construction helps to heighten the effect of flattery desired, i.e. 'not by way of possibly escaping', and changes in the alla clause below to hina ēi (metabole).
even if you were not on oath: at the start of every year all the heliasts swore the heliastic oath, on which cf. And. 1 Myst. 31; Isoc. 15 Ant. 21; Dem. 24 Tim. 149-151; Harrison, LA 2, 48. Among the provisions of the oath were
i) the jurors should be impartial (see 4, not for a hearing);
ii) they should judge 'according to the laws' (85).
having confidence in...the justice of your verdict: for various expressions of confidence in judges and justice cf. 4, 2 First Tetralogy d1, 6 Chor. 10, 51; And. 1 Myst. 2, 9; Lys. 3 Sim. 2; Isoc. 15 Ant. 169-170; Aesch. 2 Fals.Leg. 24.
may indicate: note the singular verb with a plural subject in the Greek (sim. 14, 20, 64, 80); see Cucuel 33-34; Kühner-Gerth I, 79; Goodwin (1976) 901.

9 an information has been laid against me as a malefactor: in the Greek kakourgos endedeigmenos, i.e. Euxitheus is being accused

under the legal process *endeixis* as a *kakourgos*, his *kakourgia* (malefaction) being that he murdered Herodes. His argument in 9-10 is that homicide did not fall within the compass of the law concerning malefactors (*nomos tōn kakourgōn*).

a thing which has never happened before to anyone in this country: there is no ambiguity here, as being true of citizens but not of those who happened to be in Attica (as Maidment, *MAO* I, 164 n.b). Rather, the separation of *oudeis* from *tōn en tēi gēi tautēi* and the alliteration are designed to emphasise that this was a new procedure. Even less is it correct to say that throughout the *prokataskeuē* Euxitheus was trying to trick the jury by concealing the fact that he was not an Athenian, when the law prohibiting the use of *apagōgē* in homicide cases only applied to citizens (as Due 31-33). The jury would have been in no doubt as to Euxitheus' nationality.

this arrest: i.e. Herodes' relatives arrested Euxitheus after lodging the *endeixis* and on his arrival in Athens. For this two-part procedure see Hansen, *AEE*, 13-17.

my acquittal: *apopsēphisis* is a rare word later used by Demosthenes in the sense of 'disfranchisement' (57 *Euboul.* 2, 4, 6; cf. Harpoc. s.v. *apopsēphizontai*; Bekker, *An.* I, 186, lines 7-11). For such verbal substantives in Antiphon see 1, I could have wished...But as it is....

10   the laws which apply to each of them differ: there was, in fact, a law covering both sacrilege and treason (in the sense of betrayal of one's country); cf. Xen. *Hell.* 1.7.22; Harrison, *LA* 2, 59; MacDowell, *LCA*, 176.

debarred by proclamation: on the *prorrēsis* in homicide trials see 88, the proclamations.

the Agora: the precise location of the dicasteries in the fifth century and later has been a matter of great controversy, but their general situation is attested by this statement and by Lys. 19 *Arist.* 55.

a murderer shall pay with his life in requital: on the concept of vengeance for a victim of homicide cf. 88; MacDowell, *AHL*, 1-5, 141-148.

In the Greek 'pay with his life in requital' is *antapothanein*, a compound only elsewhere found in Philo 1.94. This and other rare words such as *metekbasis* (22), *aitiasis* (25), *gnōristēs* and *doxastēs* (94) were perhaps instrumental in gaining Antiphon the reputation of one who liked 'to form new words' (*poiein onomata kaina*, frg. 76 Th). Also reflected here is Antiphon's fondness for compound vocabulary, on which see 2, submit to the physical suffering.

they made an assessment against me: see P. 26-27.

for their own benefit: the use of *lusitelountos* is not certain evidence that Herodes' relatives proposed a fine; see P. 28, n.8. But it casts doubt on their motives and Euxitheus' promise

73

to reveal these motives during the course of his speech is only partially fulfilled by veiled accusations in 59 and 79 that money was at the bottom of the prosecution.

11 all the courts: there were five regular homicide courts, on the Areopagus, at the Palladium, Delphinium and Prytaneium and in Phreatto; for their different functions see MacDowell, *AHL*.

in the open air: cf. [Arist.] *Ath.Pol.* 57.4; Pollux 8.118; MacDowell, *AHL*, 145-146.

being under the same roof: *homōrophios* is another rare word, though it is used by Demosthenes (18 *Cor.* 287, 21 *Meid.* 118, 120); cf. also Pollux 1.80, 6.155; 2, submit to the physical suffering.

But you: the repeated employment of *su* in the following sections (12 *bis*, 13, 15 *bis*), in conjunction with the ideas reiterated from 8 of evasion and breaking of the law (*parelthōn ton nomon* 11, cf. 12 *bis*, 15; *paranomian* 12; *paranomeis* 15) and of personal framing of new laws (*autos seautōi nomous exeurōn* 12, 13; *nomothetēs* 15), helps emphasise Euxitheus' indignation at the methods of his accusers. For other instances of apostrophe in the speech cf. 16, 47-48, 59. Note also the repetition of the *touto men*/*touto de* formula in this section, a fitting use of this archaism in the grave context of the homicide law.

the greatest and most binding oath known: the *diōmosia* sworn by the parties in homicide trials, on which cf. Ant. 6 *Chor.* 16; Lys. 10 *Theomn.* 11; Dem. 23 *Aristoc.* 67-69; MacDowell, *AHL*, 90-98. Here and in 90 Euxitheus emphasises that part of the oath dealing with irrelevant evidence, the rules on which seem to have been rather more strictly observed in the court of the Areopagus than elsewhere (see MacDowell, *id.*, 43-44). Hence an advantage accrued to the prosecution in this case by their avoidance of a regular homicide trial.

bringing destruction on yourself, your kin and your house: a form of oath appearing in other contexts; cf. And. 1 *Myst.* 98; Lys. 12 *Erat.* 10; Aesch. 2 *Fals.Leg.* 87, 3 *Ctes.* 111; Dem. 24 *Tim.* 151; ML 40, lines 16-17; Glotz 477 n.4; MacDowell, *AHL*, 92.

whereby however many crimes...by these good deeds: Euxitheus objects to the common practice of the insertion in speeches of character evidence, both good and bad; see Bonner, *EAC*, 18-19; Lofberg 13. Instances of this are found even in trials before the Areopagus (cf. Kys. 3 *Sim.* 47, 7 *Sac.Ol.* 31; no doubt it was the same in Antiphon's day as later).

this requirement you have evaded: there is anacolouthon in the Greek resulting from the length of this sentence (*ha* following the colon instead of *tauta*, a usage more familiar in the 'middle' style; see S. Usher, 'The Style of Isocrates', *BICS* 20 (1973) 45). Other instances of this figure are found in 46, 82 and 93.

12 you are prosecuting me unsworn: probably a rhetorical statement referring to the solemn oath of the *dikē phonou*. Euxitheus may, however, be speaking the truth if there was no *anakrisis* (on

74

which see Harrison, *LA* 2, 223), at which the oath was normally sworn (*id.*, 99–100).

your witnesses are giving evidence against me unsworn: again, probably rhetorical. But the question of witnesses' oaths in trials other than for homicide is much disputed and it seems that they did not swear oaths as a matter of course; see Bonner & Smith, *AJHA* 2, 172–174; Harrison, *LA* 2, 150. So, once more, Euxitheus may be speaking the truth. On witnesses' oaths in regular homicide trials see MacDowell, *AHL*, 98–100.

Note the anaphora here (*anōmotos men...anōmotoi de...*), a figure on the whole sparingly used by Antiphon and Thucydides; cf. further instances in 45, 54, 62; Denniston (1952) 84–86.

with hand laid upon the sacrifice: the essential parts of the sacrifice were 'the cut pieces' (*ta tomia*; cf. 88; Dem. 23 *Aristoc.* 68; also Aesch. 2 *Fals.Leg.* 87; Paus. 5.24.9), by which Demosthenes simply says one stood.

13   On Euxitheus' contentions in 13 see P. 26. Here he argues from a practical point of view and from his rights as a free Greek; in 93 he resumes the theme of his voluntary appearance in a *topos* concerning conscience; see Be assured...on my conscience.

You reply: such apparent references to the opponent's speech (as in 21, 26, 28, 39, 44, 53, 57, 64, 74–75, 85) and expressions like 'you have heard the evidence' (31, also 21, 'it has nowhere been shown', and 84, 'the witnesses are testifying') are a second way of giving the speech an extemporaneous character, after the parenthesis in 4 (see n. there). It is reasonably certain that there is no true extemporisation in the speech as we have it (see 74–80, heading n.), but by skilfully anticipating the opponent's arguments Antiphon makes the words seem to be Euxitheus' own rather than his; see further Bonner, *LL*, 209–210, 212.

would have run away: those who fled before their trial were naturally presumed guilty; cf. And. 1 *Myst.* 3; [Lys.] 20 *Polystr.* 21; Aesch. 2 *Fals.Leg.* 6.

equally open to me: or possibly 'right and fair for me'.

even when summoned: the phrase *kai prosklēthenti* cannot be used as evidence that *endeixis* did not preclude a summons, as it is by Hansen, *AEE*, 21–22, since it forms part of an unreal condition: Euxitheus has suddenly started talking about what his rights would have been in a *dikē phonou*. One of these was 'the right of leaving the country after making my first defence speech', for which cf. Ant. 4 *Third Tetralogy* d1; Dem. 23 *Aristoc.* 69; MacDowell, *AHL*, 114–115 (the traditional view); Gagarin (1981) 112–113 (a new interpretation). In homicide and private suits each side would make two speeches; see Harrison, *LA* 2, 160–161; MacDowell, *LCA*, 249.

The participle *apologēsamenōi* is the Attic form of the aorist, recurring in 60, 74 *bis*, 90, 6 *Chor.* 8, whereas the passive form *apelogēthēn* is found in the *Tetralogies* (2 *First Tetralogy* c1, d3, 3 *Second Tetralogy* c2, 4 *Third Tetralogy* c1); cf. Pollux 2.119; Bekker, *An*. I, 82, lines 5-6. But this is not a conclusive indication that the latter were written neither by Antiphon nor by an Attic author, since Antiphon has *prounoēsamēn* in 43 for the regular Attic form *prounoēthēn*; see further F.D. Caizzi, *Antiphontis Tetralogiae* (Milano, 1969) 194.

14 **14** and 87-89 reappear in Ant. 6 *Chor*. 2-4, where they are more outwardly to the point, the case there being a *dikē phonou*. But they are also well-suited to our speech: in the *prokataskeuē* Euxitheus protests that he is being tried under the wrong process, although (*kaitoi*, 14) the homicide laws are the finest of all. (For 87-89 see 86, Give a chance to time also.) Hence we should not bracket 14 as Sauppe desired. Additionally, the numerous differences in language between the passages as they stand (see, e.g., Dover, *CAS*, 45-46) should rule out mere interpolation (as well as comparative textual emendations).

The passage, finally, was perhaps drawn from a collection of *topoi* which Antiphon may have employed in addition to his book of proems and epilogues; see Radermacher, *AS*, 78. The laws, indeed, were a favourite topic of the orators, giving rise to a great range of arguments, (e.g. And. 1 *Myst*. 81-105; Lys. 1 *Caed.Erat*. 34-36; Aesch. 3 *Ctes*. 2; Dem. 18 *Cor*. 6-7, 23 *Aristoc*. 22-87), and Antiphon was noted in antiquity for his references to them (cf. [Plut.] 832e). He particularly stressed the venerable age of the homicide laws (see below).

the finest and most hallowed of all laws: the religious foundation of the homicide laws gave them a special place in the body of legislation. Killing not only is an offence against human laws, but also takes away the life given to men by the gods (cf. Ant. 4 *Third Tetralogy* a2-3, b7). Additionally, these laws were believed to have had a divine origin (see next n.). For further praise of the homicide laws cf. Ant. 3 *Second Tetralogy* d8; Isoc. 4 *Paneg*. 40; Dem. 23 *Aristoc*. 70, 72-73; and of the law-giver (Draco) *id*. 23 *Aristoc*. 29, 24 *Tim*. 211 (though on Draco's legendary severity cf. Lyc. 1 *Leocr*. 65; Arist. *Rhet*. 2.23.29; Plut. *Sol*. 17; Aulus Gellius, *Attic Nights* 11.18. This tradition has been challenged by modern scholars; see Gagarin (1981) 116-125).

the oldest in this country: the homicide laws were said to go back to Draco in the seventh century and to be the only ones left unaltered by Solon; cf. Dem. 23 *Aristoc*. 51; [Arist.] *Ath.Pol*. 7.1; Plut. *Sol*. 17; Bonner & Smith, *AJHA* I, 110-111; R.S. Stroud, *Drakon's Law on Homicide* (Berkeley, 1968) 76 n. 44; Gagarin (1981) 21-29. But their great age tended to obscure their origin, so that they would often be referred to rather as ancestral or divine; cf. 48, 1 *Stepmother* 3, frg. 78 (Th); Dem. 23 *Aristoc*. 70.

have always remained the same concerning the same matters: i.e. the provisions present in Draco's laws had remained unaltered, while new provisions were added when necessary (see Gagarin (1981) 22-23). Antiphon does not mean that the laws had remained completely unaltered until his day, which would indeed be highly improbable.

this is the surest sign of laws well made: the Athenians and the Greeks in general were loath to alter laws; cf. Thuc. 1.71.3, 3.37.3; Xen. *Mem*. 4.4.14; Arist. *Polit*. 2.5.10-13; and the especially conservative Locrians in Dem. 24 *Tim*. 139-141. Hence the *topos* that the oldest and unchanged laws were the best, as here; Isoc. 15 *Ant*. 82; Hes. frg. 322 (Merkelbach-West, = 221 Rzach); Cic. *de Leg*. 2.40; Bonner & Smith, *AJHA* I, 75.

time and experience show mankind what is imperfect: a gnomic statement, but with the well-worn *topos* in Greek literature of time as the great teacher of men; cf. 71, 86, 4 *Third Tetralogy* d11, frg. 79 (Th); Lys. 19 *Arist*. 61; Dem. *pr*.49.3; Gorg. *Pal*. 34-35; Aeschyl. *Prom*. 981; Soph. *OC* 7-8; and other examples adduced by H.M. ten Berge, *Antiphon's Zesde Rede* (Nijmegen, 1948) 78-79.

Hence you must not...interpretation of the case: though within a *topos* a most fitting demand in the context of the *prokataskeuē*, where Euxitheus is trying to show how the prosecution are framing new laws for their own purposes. A similar thought appears in Aesch. 3 *Ctes*. 16.

The antithesis in this sentence ('not use the speech...to discover whether your laws/use the laws to discover whether or not the speech...') takes the form of antimetabole, a figure recurring in 54 and 84 (cf. also Lys. 10 *Theomn*. 7; Dem. 19 *Fals. Leg*. 97; Thuc. 1.143.5). Note the change from *ē mē* to *ē ou*, perhaps reflecting the change from abstract speculation on the laws to practical decision on the speech of the prosecution (rather than through a simple desire to avoid monotony, as Wyse 596).

15   no one has ever before dared to change them: not even Solon (see 14, the oldest in this country), nor Cleisthenes (see Bonner & Smith, *AJHA* I, 193), Ephialtes (*id*., 257-258) or Pericles (see MacDowell, *AHL*, 52-56, followed by Harrison, *LA* 2, 40-42, against Smith 353-358, followed by Bonner & Smith, *id*., 270-275). (On Lys. 1 *Caed. Erat*. 30 see MacDowell, *id*., 43).

to turn legislator: for the periphrasis *genesthai nomothetēs* see 1, I could have wished...But as it is....

by this arbitrary behaviour: lit. 'by evading these (laws, *tauta*)'. Though neuter *tauta* refers to the laws (*nomoi*, masc.); sim. 1 (*tēn dunamin...tēn empeirian...tou men...tou de*), 4 (*tēn akroasin...houper*), 22 (*hē metekbasis...touto*), 72 (*auto...gnōmēn; mega...hēmera*), 87 (*dikē...ischuroteron*).

you well knew...preliminary oath: mainly rhetorical, but perhaps reflecting a degree of success in the restrictions in homicide cases (as Bonner, *EAC*, 15).

16   In 16 Euxitheus suggests that even if he is acquitted in this trial he might still be prosecuted under a *dikē phonou* (an argument in the form of a dilemma, *dilēmmaton*). In the *epilogos* he resumes this idea, but there he turns this possibility to his advantage and actually requests a retrial, employing *topoi* about haste and the finality of the *dikē phonou* to show how repeated trials are desirable. On the legality of a retrial see P. 25. Euxitheus' dire position is underlined by the rhetoric employed here: note, for example, the chiastic word-order of the first sentence (*hōs pisteuōn...epoiēsō* X *hupelipou hōs...apistēsōn*), its alliteration et. fig. (*pisteuōn/apistēsōn; anamphisbētētōs/amphisbētēsin*, the latter with metabole) and repetition (*pragmati/pragmatos*; note also the repetition of *hapax* below).

as though even from the outset: reading *kai tote tois* with J.D. Denniston, 'Varia II', *CR* 47 (1933) 216. The MSS. have *kai tois tote*, but for the meaning '(you left grounds for dispute) as though you were going to distrust even the present jurors' the very difficult *tois tote* has generally been altered (after Pahle) to *toisde tois* or *tois enthade*. Denniston's simple emendation, which has the advantage of keeping more closely to the MSS., is perhaps preferable (and for similar transpositions in A see Wyse xxxvii).

you will claim my life: possibly a reference to the *timēsis* (as MacDowell, *AHL*, 136), but more readily to be taken in the antithesis here as a general remark, emphasising the danger Euxitheus was in whether he won the case or not.

Could anything more unfair be contrived: to Euxitheus the whole charge was carefully framed, from its details (see 25, before I put to sea) to the type of trial to be faced.

17   I was imprisoned: see P. 26.

the custodians of malefactors: the Eleven, who are named in a different context in 70. Further on these officials (one appointed from each of the ten tribes, plus a secretary) cf. Lys. 10 *Theomn.* 10; Isoc. 15 *Ant.* 237; Dem. 24 *Tim.* 113; Hyp. 4 *Eux.* 6; [Arist.] *Ath.Pol.* 52.1; Pollux 8.102; ML 45 (section 8); Harrison, *LA* 2, 17-18: Hansen, *AEE*, 20, 36-37.

failed to be of help: reading *mē ōphelēsai* with Gernet. The text is corrupt here: N and Apr. have *ōphelēsai toude kosmou* (*ōphelēsthai toude tou nomou* A corr. 2), *kosmou* probably being a corruption of *nomou*, as the corrector of A thought. This in turn may have been the remains of further corruption, of a gloss or possibly of *desmou* (hence *aphelesthai tou desmou* Blass, *apolusai tou desmou* Thalheim, 'release me from prison').

18   18 is noticeable for its pathos, a figure which, although well-suited to the 'austere' style (see Jebb, *AO* I, 29-31), only occurs here and in 79 (the sole instance admitted by Jebb, *id.*, 61). Albini 61 rightly rejects other supposed instances in the *epilogos*, especially in 85 and 91, noting that even there Antiphon

is more concerned with logical argument than with arousing feeling.

I should be quite unprepared for my trial: sim. Dem. 24 *Tim.* 145.

by reason of that bodily suffering...: for the rats will leave a sinking ship (as Maidment, *MAO* I, 173 n. b); i.e. the prosecution inspired fear by imprisoning Euxitheus and this fear would cause even his friends to desert him (sim. [Lys.] 20 *Polystr.* 18). But this is a rhetorical statement (note, for example, the well-balanced antithesis *toutois...legein*, with homoeoteleuton) and does not necessarily imply that Euxitheus' friends *did* give evidence against him (as Palau 207–208).

On *kakopathein* and *kakopatheian* see 2, submit to the physical suffering; and for the single connecting *te* here and below, also [51], 87, 1 *Stepmother* 9, 26, see Denniston (1954) 497–500.

they have brought lifelong disgrace on me and my family: for the idea of disgrace accompanying imprisonment cf. also Dem. 24 *Tim.* 115, *Ep.* 2.17.

19   I suffered loss: in the Greek *elassōtheis*, the reading of N and Apr. which was corrected in A to *elos sōtheis* and thence in the inferior MSS. to *helos sōtheis*. This in turn led the author of a hypothesis prefixed to the speech in A and N to name the defendant Helos.

it is indeed difficult...: compare similar arguments over the length of time an opponent has been preparing his case in And. 1 *Myst.* 1, 6; Lys. 7 *Sac.Ol.* 3; Aesch. 2 *Fals. Leg.* 1; Dem. 30 *Onetor i* 3; and the inverted *paraskeuē-topos* in Lys. 12 *Erat.* 81 (with comm.). Euxitheus' topical remarks here are also designed to have an extemporaneous character (see Dorjahn & Fairchild 30) and his comment that 'one cannot prepare oneself against the unexpected' should not be pressed to mean that he came to Athens expecting to face a *dikē phonou* (as Palau, 208; Palau similarly misinterprets *aparaskeuotaton* in 18 – Euxitheus was 'totally unprepared' because of his imprisonment). Rather, this epigrammatic remark is designed to bring the *prokataskeuē* to a forceful climax.

'To refute' is *apelegchein*, another rare word recurring in 21 and 36 and conjectured in Lys. 7 *Sac.Ol.* 2.

20–24   NARRATIVE (*diēgēsis*): We have noticed how Antiphon's proems and epilogues are of a much greater length than those of Lysias. Now, in the narrative, we can see how Antiphon is so markedly inferior in technique to Lysias, whose vivid descriptions of the backgrounds to his cases contrast with the dull brevity of the earlier orator. Antiphon's strength and interests lay rather in his argumentation, elements of which creep into the narrative (as in 21 and 22; see below). Note also the change to a free-running style (*lexis eiromenē*), indicated, for example, by the two relatives in 20 (*hōi, hon*); the singular *suneplei* (perhaps influenced by the proximity of the neuter plural *andrapoda*) with its two subjects connected by *te/kai*; the change of number in the participles of 22 (*poiēsamenos/kataschontes*, *chrēsamenoi*) in a long sentence strung together with *oute* clauses; the multitude of *kai*'s in 23.

I sailed: the beginning of the narrative is marked by *de*; later orators such as Lysias preferred *gar* (as 1 *Caed. Erat.* 6, 10 *Theomn.* 4).

Mytilene: Euxitheus' fatherland (cf. 76), the largest of the five states on Lesbos and leader of the revolt from Athens in 428-427 (Thuc. 3.2).

Herodes: it is usually accepted that Herodes was an Athenian, probably one of the cleruchs sent out by Athens after the revolt (Thuc. 3.50.2). Euxitheus' statement in 58 that Herodes had no money accords with this theory, for it seems to have been a policy of Athens to send out poorer citizens as cleruchs; cf. Plut. *Per.* 11.6; Meiggs 260-261; Schindel, *MH*, 14-22. Herodes' Athenian citizenship has only been seriously challenged by P. Roussel, 'Remarques sur un discours d'Antiphon', *Mélanges Glotz* II (1932) 813-822 (followed by Gauthier (1972) 196 n. 59; Cataldi 30 n. 57), against whom see Schindel, *id.*, 9-13.

Aenus: approx. 100 miles north of Lesbos on the Thracian coast, at the mouth of the Hebrus. Founded, according to Ephorus (in Harpoc. s.v. *Ainious*; see also Strabo, Bk. 7, frgg. 51, 51a Jones), by colonists from Alopeconnesus and later from Mytilene and Cyme, Aenus was a town in the tribute-paying class and fought for Athens both at Pylos (Thuc. 4.28.4) and in Sicily (*id.* 7.57.5); cf. further Hdt. 4.90.2, 7.58.3; Steph. Byz. s.v.; J.M.F. May, *Ainos, its History and Coinage 474-341 B.C.* (Oxford, 1950) 1 n.2; Cataldi 21 n. 14.

my father: see 74 n.

who happened to be there at the time: probably an understatement; see 78, **If his favourite haunt is Aenus.**

to ransom some slaves to certain Thracians: Gernet 114 n. 1 (see Maidment, *MAO* I, 175 n. a; Schindel, *MH*, 15-16) suggests that these slaves were prisoners of war being ransomed by their relatives or friends (or by agents, Schindel), and the vocabulary employed seems to support this view. Although *andrapoda* by itself is not conclusive (it seems to be 'slaves' in Ant. 1 *Stepmother* 7-12, and in Thucydides both 'slaves' – 7.27.5 – and 'prisoners of war' – 8.28.4), its use in conjunction with *apolusōn* and especially *lusomenoi* (cf. Isoc. 15 *Ant.* 288; Dem. 53 *Nicostr.* 7, 11) leaves little doubt. For other examples of this practice cf. Is. 7 *Apoll.* 8; Dem. 53 *Nicostr.* 6-13 (cf. also Thuc. 5.3.4). But due to the brevity of the narrative we can only speculate as to how and when Herodes came to be in control of these captives. Schindel notes the existence of inscriptions for Thracian campaigns in 418-417, 417-416 and 414-412 and contends that Herodes took part in operations there as a hoplite. The theory is attractive, however the speech may have been earlier than this (see P. 24) and we do not even know that the slaves belonged to Herodes.

Several other questions are left unanswered by the brief narrative. For instance, it is suprising that Euxitheus does not try to cast suspicion on the Thracians. Scheidweiler 330 points out that it is strange that the ransoming was to have taken place in Aenus rather than Mytilene. Possibly the Thracians had made an especially attractive offer to a man in financial need, but whatever the reason they now had the opportunity as well as the motive for murdering Herodes. Why, then, does Euxitheus not question their whereabouts and activities on the night of the murder? Scheidweiler thinks that the slaves must have gone on to Aenus with Euxitheus and the Thracians since there is no mention of their being tortured, and that Euxitheus did not have a clear conscience. Further, the loss of the slaves may have prompted the prosecution to use *apagōgē* against Euxitheus in an attempt to recover their money – but Euxitheus confines his defence to the murder aspect. This idea was expanded by Schindel, *MH*, 23–29, but such interpretations are highly fanciful. Rather, there may have been some obvious reason why the Thracians were not implicated (see Palau 200–201) or Antiphon may simply have felt the jury would not take kindly to such tactics – and therefore Euxitheus will not conjecture (64; see further on this 23, we began drinking). Nor do we know what happened to the Thracians and the slaves, and it is quite possible that they remained on Lesbos to complete the deal with Herodes' relatives (and the slaves were not tortured because they had been firmly under lock and key on the night in question).

21   As with 5, a noticeable feature of 21 and 22 is the frequency of hiatus; see I request this of you....
purposes: in the Greek *prophasis*, a cause truly alleged (as in 22; And. 4 *Alc.* 17; 'motive' rather than 'purpose' in 59, 60), whereas in 26 and 65 (and cf. 6 *Chor.* 14, 26; Lys. 12 *Erat.* 6; Thuc. 3.86.4) *prophasis* is a cause falsely alleged, an excuse. See further L. Pearson, *'Prophasis* and *Aitia'*, *TAPA* 83 (1952) 205–223.
a place: perhaps Limanion (as Palau 199), but more likely Skala Sikamineas; see P.M. Green, 'Longus, Antiphon, and the Topography of Lesbos', *JHS* 102 (1982) 213–214.
Methymna: situated in the extreme north-west of Lesbos, Methymna was the one Lesbian state that did not revolt in 428; cf. Thuc. 3.2.1. Hence her land was not confiscated (*id*. 3.50.2) and only she and Chios still provided ships instead of money in 415 (*id*. 6.85.2, 7.57.5). Nevertheless, both were to revolt in 412 (*id*. 8.22).
the boat: this vessel was on its way to Mytilene (29).
transhipped: for the rare compound *metekbanta* cf. 23; Hdt. 7.41.1, 100.2; Plato, *Laws* 1.642b, 11.935a; Anth. Pal. 12.187.2.

on which the prosecution allege he met his end: they did not actually maintain that Herodes died on the boat (taking the sentence literally). This may therefore be an allusion to the prosecution's first version of the events which they subsequently modified (as Gernet thought, 114 n. 2, comparing 29), or more simply may be a general, imprecise remark.

The MSS. reading *auton ton Heroiden* has been suspected by most editors, who generally delete *ton Heroiden* as a gloss. But the repetition of the name is to be expected at this early stage of the narrative and after the break for witnesses, and the difficult use of the intensive pronoun is perhaps similarly explicable as adding emphasis at the start of the narrative. Likewise, the repetition *toi emoi patri* in 77, though awkward after *autoi*, may be aimed at gaining extra emphasis, the effect being heightened by the hyperbaton (another very common figure in Antiphon). Repetition, we may add, is also common in Antiphon and there is therefore no need to delete the second 'Ephialtes' in 68, as some have desired. Another approach to these passages is to see *ton Heroiden* and *toi emoi patri* as being in apposition, and Wyse 709, noting several possible parallels in the orators, placed a comma after *auton* in 21 and after *hemartetai* in 77.

Now firstly consider these circumstances: Antiphon now inserts a section of recapitulation into the narrative (to the end of 22) which is virtually a proof (n.b. *skopeite,* which introduces the proof in 25).

not to any design on my part: following Jebb's reading ⟨*ou tei e*⟩*mei pronoiai* for the MSS. *me pronoiai.* This is perhaps preferable to the simple alteration of *me* to *ou,* with the explanation of the error as deriving from the common such use of *me* in late Greek (see H. Richards, 'Notes on Greek Orators I, Antiphon', *CR* 20 (1906) 152).

The crux of 21 and 22 is that no design (*pronoia*) can be imputed to Euxitheus in his encountering Herodes. Antiphon may have thought that the prosecution would attempt to prove premeditation on Euxitheus' part and so he i) emphasises the role of chance (*tuche*) in these events (see further 6, depends more on chance than foresight); ii) gives the passage an extemporaneous character with 'it has nowhere been shown' (see 13, You reply). But it may be significant that Euxitheus does not deny that he knew Herodes before the voyage either here or in 57-59.

22 we were forced to do so: emphasis on the compulsion is gained by the repetition below of *anagkei*, both times joined with *alla* in chiastic word-order.

the transhipment: the substantival is even rarer than the verbal form; cf. Adam. *Vent.* 32 (= Rose, *An. Graec.* 32, line 12); 10, a murderer shall pay with his life in requital. Antiphon here places emphasis on the act of transhipment, by means of periphrasis and the use of the aorist (*egeneto;* the crossing as a consequence of *anagkē* is then given in the imperfect *egigneto*).

had no deck: more rare vocabulary in *astegaston*; cf. Thuc. 7.87.1; schol. Soph. *Phil.* 1327; Galen vol. 17 (2), 153 (ed. Kühn); Apollod. *Poliorc.* 185.10.

had a deck: on the participle in periphrasis with *einai* cf. 88 (= 6 *Chor.* 6), 90, 1 *Stepmother* 11 and frequently in the *Tetralogies* (as 2 *First Tetralogy* a9, 3 *Second Tetralogy* d5); Kühner-Gerth I, 38 n.3.

witnesses: the MSS. have *marturias* ('evidence'), not *marturas* ('witnesses'), but evidence was given orally at this time (and *MARTURES* follows in the MSS.); see Bonner, *EAC*, 46-47. Reiske long ago made the correction.

23   **we began drinking:** a dangerous assertion in view of Euxitheus' age and the Greek attitude to young men and drinking as expressed in Ant. 4 *Third Tetralogy* c2.

    The imperfect tense of *epinomen* is ingressive and does not in itself indicate a heavy drinking-bout, though Herodes at least was drunk (26). Nevertheless, suspicion is raised by this statement that the influence of drink may have been a direct factor in Herodes' disappearance. Thus A. Reuter, 'Beobachtungen zur Technik des Antiphon I', *Hermes* 38 (1903) 495 suggested that Euxitheus led the drunk Herodes to a place in the harbour and threw him into the sea; Breuning, 68n. 6 that Herodes was accidentally drowned under the influence of too much wine. However, Scheidweiler 323-324 attacked Reuter's theory, questioning whether there was a suitable place in the harbour from which to throw Herodes into the sea without the risk of the body reappearing on the surface (it could, of course, have been weighted, though Palau 200 notes that the waters in this region are clear). Additionally, such theories clash with the prosecution's story, wrung from the tortured slave (39), that Herodes was thrown into the sea from a boat (28, 45); see 28, they allege that he was thrown into the sea. Reuter complained that Euxitheus only considers this possibility and does not put forward any alternative explanation of Herodes' disappearance. But Scheidweiler rightly saw that Euxitheus had no need to conjecture, as he says himself in 64-66, for conjectures expressly contradicting the prosecution's story, which was well thought out and backed by the slave's evidence, would not have seemed very credible. Euxitheus needed, rather, to undermine the prosecution's reconstruction. See further Due 46-47, who concludes that Euxitheus' attitude was juridically quite correct. But if drink was not a direct factor we may at least feel that Herodes' murderers would have found their task the easier as a result of his condition.

I did not leave the boat at all that night: sim. 26, 27, 42, but we should have expected Euxitheus to make much more of this alibi. Hence we wonder how many witnesses he could in fact produce to support this claim at the end of 24 (and note 'I can produce witnesses' in 27). Thus Thür 50 thinks there were none at all, while Maidment, *MAO* I, 178 n. a suspects that Euxitheus is merely alluding to the free man who exonerated him (42). On the other hand Schindel, *MH*, 37-39 (v. Thür) doubts that Euxitheus could have said 'I can produce witnesses' if no such witnesses existed, though his attempt to prove that the free man was produced is not conclusive (see 49, has not even yet said anything compromising about me). Nevertheless, it does seem difficult to reject this alibi out of hand as mere rhetoric and we do not know how many passengers there were on the decked vessel that night. Euxitheus' brevity in this matter is perhaps to be seen in the light of the tendency towards 'artificial proofs' (*entechnoi pisteis*, as opposed to 'non-artificial proofs', *atechnoi pisteis*) during the second half of the fifth century (see Solmsen 44-47) and as due to the prejudice the Athenian court probably felt against him. He must prove conclusively that he did not kill Herodes, but it was not enough simply to bring forward witnesses for an alibi whose evidence the jurors might well disbelieve. He must question the likelihood of the prosecution's story and examine their evidence by employing argument from probability, the *entechnos pistis* which plays a great part in Antiphon's argumentation (see 25, consider the probabilities). Similarly with the favourable evidence of the free man who was tortured (see 30, The first): Euxitheus uses this in antithetical argumentation with the slave's evidence (42, 49) rather than as the basis of his defence.

I joined in the search just as anxiously as any: Euxitheus' keen part in the search and readiness to help in any way he could (thus suggesting his innocence) is brought out by the use of the passive *ezēteito* with *hup'emou* and below by *kai emoi homoiōs*, *egō*, *tēi emēi gnōmēi* (with repetition of the verb *pempein*). Then in 24 a tricolon (the failure of the search, the return of fair weather and the departure of the other boats) emphasises how Euxitheus' departure from Methymna followed a perfectly innocent chain of events.

24 nor one of Herodes' companions: we are only informed about the slaves and the Thracians, and it is understandable why the Thracians, 'who were to pay the ransom' (20), should decline to volunteer.

my own attendant: see 29, the men.

I was...proposing to send: the imperfect of attempted action, commonly employed with *edidoun* and *epeithon*; cf. 53; *GMT*, 36.

When finally the search failed: it lasted for two days (27).

5-84 PROOFS (*pisteis*): Euxitheus turns now to his proofs, beginning in 25-28 with a refutation of his opponents' version of the murder on the basis of probability.

25 consider the probabilities: this *entechnos pistis*, the argument from probability (*to eikos*), formed the basis of the rhetorical handbook (*technē*) of Corax, according to Arist. *Rhet.* 2.24.11

(but Aristotle attributed the same example of the argument from probability to Corax as Plato had done to Tisias, in *Phaedr.* 273a-c). It features prominently in the early oratory of Antiphon, especially in the *Herodes* (as 37, 43, 45, 49-50, 63) and the *Tetralogies*. Bonner, *LL*, 227-228 suggests that Antiphon's use of this argument was one of the reasons for his reputation for cleverness which earned him the distrust of the people (Thuc. 8.68.1).

before I put to sea: Albini 142 simply remarks that, unlike in Antiphon's sixth speech, little is made of the delay before the charge was brought. Closer consideration is required. Firstly, we must remember that Herodes' relatives were informed of his disappearance at Mytilene. Thus the messenger would have taken about a day to reach Mytilene from the harbour and probably would not have returned until the second day of the search – and Euxitheus and the others possibly left on the next day, after the search was completed. So Herodes' relatives hardly had time to come to the harbour, make a search and charge Euxitheus, and in any case we are told that they conducted their investigations after the second, decked boat had reached Mytilene (29). The rhetorical nature of the argumentation here, then, stands revealed. But there is more to it than this, for Euxitheus' contention that the time-lapse (which seems outwardly from his account to be longer than it probably was) reveals the plotting of the prosecution is the first instance of a recurrent theme in the speech. Thus the slave and the free man were tortured only after no traces of the murder could be found (29); and the slave was tortured several days after the free man (30) and in Euxitheus' absence, so that the prosecution were able to induce him to lie about Euxitheus. He also changed his story, which again allegedly reveals the plot and includes the temporal theme – first the slave said Euxitheus was innocent, then that he was guilty and finally once more that he was innocent. Further, the note was found during the second search of the boat, after the free man had refused to incriminate Euxitheus and before the slave was induced to lie (55-56), and the evidence of the note and of the slave was contradictory. Hence it was forged by the prosecution in case the slave would not cooperate. So the whole prosecution was a carefully devised plot against Euxitheus in which time played an important part.

For the moment...they could make: but once the charge was made the verdict of the jurors was final, even if against the true facts (87).

'Accusation' in the Greek is *aitiasis*, another rare word (see 10, a murderer shall pay with his life in requital) recurring in 89 (= 6 *Chor.* 6); Arist. *Poet.* 18.3; Dio Cass. 52.26.5; Pollux 3.138; Theodor, *Metoch.* 317 (ed. Müller). Note also the hendiadys *to alēthes kai to gegenēmenon* ('the true facts of the matter') and contrast 72, *tēn aletheian...tōn gegenēmenōn*.

26   **hit him on the head with a stone**: the core of the prosecution's reconstruction and presumably part of the slave's evidence (n.b. 'of this they have detailed information'). Euxitheus himself may have known the details of the slave's confession through the existence of minutes of the torture, but he speaks here and in 28 in extemporaneous fashion (see 13, You reply).

    Even in the unlikely event of the stone being found it would not have been produced in court as 'real' evidence; see Bonner, *EAC*, 81; and further on 'real' evidence see Harrison, *LA* 2, 153-154.

Of this they have detailed information, but...: slightly ironical. Further instances of irony are found in 45 and 47, but such figures of thought are rare in Antiphon; see Blass, *AB* I, 146-147; Jebb, *AO* I, 28-29.

Clearly, the probabilities suggest: according to 44 this was in fact what the prosecution alleged.

He would probably have been in no condition: the imperfect with *an* expresses Herodes' state at the time in question, not merely his ability to do something at that time (the aorist); see further Kühner-Gerth I, 212-213.

have found any plausible excuse: is it not, in truth, often easier to find an excuse to persuade a person to do something when he is not sober? For 'excuse' (*prophasis*) see 21, purposes.

27   **two days' search**: the diligence of the search is reflected in the Greek by correspondence (*kai...kai..., oute...outh'...out'...*), antithesis (*en/apōthen*) and a tricolon (*optēr - haima - allo sēmeion*).

eyewitness: *optēr* is a poetic word (cf. Hom. *Od.* 14.261; Aeschyl. *Supp*. 185; Soph. *Aj*. 29, *Ich*. 77), but is also used in this sense by Xenophon (*Cyr*. 4.5.17); see also Pollux 2.57; Hesych. s.v.; Suidas, s.v. *optēras*.

no bloodstain: expanded in 45. On bloodstains as a clue cf. Anon. Seg. 153 (in Spengel-Hammer I^2. 379).

clue: here and in 28 and 45 *sēmeion* is a physical 'clue' or 'trace', and in 81 and 84 a 'sign' from the gods. Finally, in 14 it is similar to *tekmērion* ('proof', which occurs in 8, 38 *bis*, 61, 63, 81 'human proof' as opposed to 'the signs furnished by heaven', 83), and this reflects the frequent difficulty encountered in distinguishing between the two terms. Antiphon's own definition, that 'what has happened is confirmed by signs, what will happen by presumptions' (frg. 72 Th), is hardly observed by him in practice, nor was Aristotle's distinction (*Rhet*. 1.2.16-18) between the conclusive *tekmērion* and the fallible *sēmeion* clearly drawn by earlier authors. See further Lys. 25 *Def.Sub.Dem*. 5 with comm.

I will accept the prosecution's story: this figure of thought, whereby an opponent's argument is allowed (*consensio*), recurs in 62 (also with *ei kai hōs malista*); cf. further Lys. 12 *Erat*. 34 with comm.

I can produce witnesses: see 23, **I did not leave the boat at all that night**.

    For the change from participial to finite construction (*parechomenos men...ei de...eikos ēn*) see Denniston (1954) 369 n. 1.

28   **they allege that he was thrown into the sea**: a further part of the opponents' reconstruction, based on the confession of the slave. It seems probable that the slave would have given details of the alleged sinking of the body and that these would have been recorded in the minutes made of the torture. Hence it is doubtful whether Euxitheus here deliberately misrepresents the meaning of *katapontō*, as Due 36 contends (i.e. 'sunk from a boat' instead of 'drowned from the shore').

    We may briefly consider at this point how and when Herodes would have been thrown into the sea. Some scholars have thought that one of the large boats which took shelter in the harbour would have been used, and that the body was firstly hidden and then disposed of either during the crossing to Aenus or on the voyage to Mytilene. But we should remember both that one of these boats was undecked (22) and that a search was made (24). So it is more likely that a smaller boat would have been employed (and this is what Euxitheus questions) and it is perhaps not too surprising that this craft remained undiscovered. This assumes, of course, that there was some basis of truth in the slave's confession and it could be that Herodes was in fact done away with somewhere on the land.

of a dead man thrown overboard: lit. 'of a man dead and thrown overboard'. Some scholars have needlessly suspected the phrase (e.g. Blass, who added *entithemenou* after *tethneōtos*, i.e. 'of a dead man placed in the boat and thrown overboard').

the prosecution do claim to have found traces: referring to the bloodstains mentioned in 29, which the prosecution at first took as traces of the murder.

on which they themselves agree Herodes was not murdered: note the word-order (*mē* going with *apothanein*), the hyperbaton helping to stress the negative; sim. Thuc. 6.18.2, *alla kai mē hopōs epeisi* (both passages have been suspected by editors).

29   **I had departed on my voyage**: a noticeable expression in the Greek, with the poetic *phroudos ē* replacing the more regular *ōichomēn*. Indeed, *phroudos* is not found elsewhere in classical prose (sim. *apōimōxen* in 41).

had been drinking: reading *epinomen* for the MSS. *epleomen* ('had been sailing') with H. Weil, 'Antiphon, Meurtre d'Hérode, 29, 5, et 49', *Rev. de Phil.* 4 (1880), 150. Euxitheus and Herodes crossed to the decked boat on the night of the storm and after Herodes' disappearance Euxitheus would have continued on his way to Aenus on the original, undecked vessel, while the decked one completed its voyage to Mytilene.

the bloodstains: presumably those involved in the sacrifice confirmed that these were sheep's blood, though Erbse (1977) 210 n. 2 still has his doubts. The stains were probably mentioned in the evidence given after 28 and so there is no need to alter the MSS. *to haima* to *ti haima* ('some bloodstains'), as did Aldus. Similarly below with 'the sheep' (the article was deleted by Reiske) and also 'the men', who would already have been referred to by the prosecution. Note the chronological argument again here; see 25, before I put to sea.

the men: these were two in number, one a slave, the other a free man (49). Maidment's statement, *MAO* I, 180 n. c, that the latter cannot have been a Greek, as he was tortured, has been challenged by Bushala 61-63. Bushala notes that Antiphon clearly states this person was a free man and that no objection is raised in the speech to his being tortured, and he therefore contends that homicide investigations may have been an exception to the general rule. He supports this with the torture of the Plataean Theodotus in Lys. 3 *Sim.* 33 (in a case of wounding with intent to kill, *dikē traumatos ek pronoias*), arguing against the assumption of most scholars that Theodotus was a slave. His view was rejected by Thür 22 n. 43, but Thür's own theory that the torturing of the free man was justified because it was part of a public, not the normal private, investigation is very doubtful (see Schindel, *MH*, 32 n. 172). C. Lacombrade, 'Un problème de droit attique', *Pallas* 20 (1973) 19-23 rather differently considers that the free man of Antiphon 5 was Euxitheus' attendant (24; see below) and the Plataean of Lysias 3 was virtually a prostitute: since, therefore, neither Antiphon nor Lysias denounces the torture it must have taken place according to a customary practice and was due to the almost servile status of the two men. They were 'déclassés', under a kind of moral dishonour tacitly admitted by all: an interesting theory which is perhaps supported by the use of *anthrōpos* in connection with the free man (see 39, the slave). But the free man's status is most uncertain.

Other difficulties involved with these two men are who they were exactly and on which vessel each was travelling. Maidment, *loc. cit.*, detected an inconsistency within the speech over the free man. It has been assumed from 29 and 52 that he was a passenger on, or a member of the crew of, the vessel bound for Mytilene, or even that he was the boat's owner. But these inferences contradict Euxitheus' words in 42, 'then there was the second man, who had travelled on the same boat, had been present throughout and had been my companion'. This statement suggests at first sight that the free man went all the way to Aenus, but since we know he was tortured we may assume that the alliteration and tricolon in the Greek indicate rhetorical exaggeration, designed to show that Euxitheus and the free man were well acquainted and that Euxitheus had an alibi. In other words, 'throughout' (*dia telous*) only in fact refers to the time up to the night of Herodes' disappearance or to the night itself. Nevertheless, the statement does seem to be an assertion that the two men were travelling companions. Maidment explains the inconsistency by theorising that the free man was in Euxitheus' pay, perhaps being the attendant of 24, and Euxitheus must have been intentionally misrepresenting the facts in 42 for the sake of his alibi. But he was playing a dangerous game in actually emphasising that the free man was travelling with him and it may seem preferable to accept his words in 42. But if so, why should the free man have started out for Aenus, reached Methymna and then returned to Mytilene? Or why, if he was the attendant and was sent to Mytilene, should he not have returned with the news that Herodes was nowhere to be found and continued with Euxitheus to Aenus? If Herodes' relatives detained him we might have expected Euxitheus to complain about this before leaving the island. However, we should note that in 24 Euxitheus does not actually say that he did send his attendant to Mytilene, only that he was ready to do so, and so the identification of the free man as Euxitheus' attendant must be doubtful. The third limb of the tricolon in 42, 'had been my companion', is in the Greek *sunōn moi*, which need not mean anything more than that the free man was an independent voyager who was in Euxitheus' company. So it is possible that the free man was originally Herodes' companion on the trip (as was suggested by Palau 202), which both fits with 42 and provides a reason why he remained on Lesbos and was seized for torture by Herodes' relatives. But his whole situation is obscure, as, indeed, is that of the slave. We know that at some stage he was bought by the prosecution (47), therefore he was neither Herodes' nor Euxitheus' slave. Perhaps he was a member of the crew of the decked boat and was seized on arrival in Mytilene. But why did the prosecution wish to torture him in particular?

examined them under torture: the main section of the speech is the *basanos* (torture)-argumentation (29-52), which questions both the results of the torture and the methods used to obtain them. Both the slave and the free man were tortured, but only the former incriminated Euxitheus. The core of his confession, as far as we can glean it from the speech, is
i) Euxitheus left the boat and murdered Herodes;
ii) the slave was his accomplice in the crime, though to what degree (whether he helped in the actual killing or merely in the disposal of the body) is unclear.
Euxitheus counters by
a) disputing the legality of the prosecution's actions in gaining this confession (which leads to commonplace arguments over the value of *basanos* evidence). Also, and very importantly, Euxitheus contends that their putting to death of the slave before he had a chance to question him himself both was illegal and

showed how the slave was not trusted even by the prosecution to give consistent and true evidence (34-35; 47-48);
b) emphasising the alleged contradictory nature of the slave's evidence, saying he changed his story for personal advantages (as 37) and under the compulsion of truth (41). In addition, the slave's confession was itself contradicted by the testimony of the free man, who consistently exonerated Euxitheus (30, 42).

We must briefly consider two legal points arising in connection with the torturing of a slave which are relevant to our speech. Firstly, a slave's evidence could normally only be produced in court if it had been given under torture, since it was strongly believed that a slave would only speak the truth under torture; see Harrison, *LA* I, 170. Hence there was a *topos* that such evidence was more reliable than that given by a free man; cf. Is. 8 *Cir.* 12; Dem. 30 *Onetor i* 37; also Ant. 1 *Stepmother* 10, 6 *Chor.* 25; Isoc. 17 *Trapez.* 54; Lyc. 1 *Leocr.* 29; Dem. 47 *Euerg.* 8; Harrison, *id.* 2, 147. But the opposite argument, that slaves would lie in order to escape further pain and so evidence given under torture was suspect, was also employed, as by Antiphon below (31-35); cf. [Arist.] *Rhet. ad Alex.* 16.2; Arist. *Rhet.* 1.15.26; Harrison, *ibid.* So among the Athenians themselves the value of this *atechnos pistis* was in doubt and much of its real worth lay in the possibilities arising from it for *entechnoi pisteis*. To be mentioned in this context is the question of the challenge (*proklēsis*). A slave's evidence had to be given with the consent of both parties to be valid and so litigants would issue challenges to their opponents either to hand over or to accept a slave for torture; see 36, challenging me to examine him under torture. The refusal of a challenge could then be used against an opponent, as happens in a slightly unusual way (since the slave was put to death) in 36-38.

Secondly, the vexed question as to whether a slave could appear in court in homicide trials as a witness for the prosecution. Two passages from our speech (36, 48) have been adduced as evidence, the former against, the latter for the possibility. In 36 Euxitheus says that the prosecution should have produced the slave for him to torture. Now if his words reflect the procedure in a *dikē phonou* they show almost conclusively that slaves could not appear - for why does Euxitheus not argue simply that the prosecution should have produced the slave in court? See Bonner & Smith, *AJHA* 2, 227-228. However, MacDowell, *AHL*, 103 notes that our speech was delivered in an *endeixis*, not a *dikē phonou*, and contends that this passage therefore cannot be used as evidence. 48, on the other hand, is the main passage brought forward in support of the theory that slaves could appear. The crucial clause is *eiper gar kai marturein exesti doulōi kata tou eleutherou ton phonon*, traditionally translated 'if it is permissible for a slave to give evidence against a free man about a killing'. But MacDowell, *id.*, 103-104 translates 'if it is permissible to give evidence for a slave against a free man of his being killed', and this is preferable. As he points out, Euxitheus is talking about the killing of a slave, arguing that it was illegal, and evidence given by a slave against a free man is irrelevant. Further, the sentence from *eiper* builds up to a climax through a tricolon with correspondence. The whole effect of this is ruined if the first limb refers to a different situation from the other two; and the juxtaposing of *douloi* with *kata tou eleutherou* is much more effective on MacDowell's rendering. MacDowell also dismisses other passages cited in connection with this matter and comes to the conclusion that we simply do not have the evidence to settle the question one way or the other. This approach, though not without its drawbacks (for example, as MacDowell is well aware, Euxitheus earlier in our speech argues that the procedure for a regular homicide trial ought to have been followed in his case and so he may likewise be thinking of this in 36), is perhaps to be adopted.

30   The first: the free man, who declared Euxitheus innocent throughout (42, 49). As with the alibi, we might have expected Euxitheus to make more of the free man's favourable evidence, though his approach is again understandable; see 23, I did not leave the boat at all that night. Additionally, he was probably unable to produce the free man at the trial; see 49, has not even yet said anything compromising about me.
The second they tortured several days later: we should have expected the torturings of the witnesses to have been conducted one after the other, their vessel having been thoroughly searched beforehand so that no evidence could be removed or the boat leave before examination. Therefore the interval between the torturings, during which the boat was searched for a second time (55), may arouse suspicions of foul play with regard to both the slave and the discovery of fresh 'evidence', the note (53-56). Scheidweiler 321 notes that the scene is Lesbos (although we should not perhaps place too much significance in this: Lesbian laws and procedure would probably have reflected Athenian practice, especially after the quelling of the revolt and setting up of the cleruchy) and suggests that the delay was made in order to soften up the slave after the free man had refused to incriminate Euxitheus. Against this is Erbse (1977) 211-212, asking why Euxitheus did not himself make this suggestion and pointing out that
i) the purchasing of the slave (47) may have taken a certain amount of time; and
ii) since the slave was allegedly involved in the crime the prosecution would naturally want to make thorough investigations before they tortured him, to have some other form of proof with which to check his assertions. But this does not fully deal with Scheidweiler's contention. We should not, for instance, expect the buying of the slave to have taken too much time, though

Euxitheus may be exaggerating the length of the delay with 'several days later' (see further on this transaction 47, they bought the slave). Then we must remember that the prosecution had conducted a search before they tortured the free man (29) – so while we may agree with Erbse that the prosecution desired some back-up evidence before they examined the slave it may still seem suspicious that they decided to make a second search when they had already suffered two setbacks (the unproductive first search and torture of the free man). Thus arguments can be adduced for either view and the delay can be interpreted in two ways. But whatever the truth is here Euxitheus has cleverly achieved a double attack on the prosecution. He has to be careful before an Athenian jury over making allegations and so he takes this opportunity of impugning the prosecution's actions by implication. He omits to mention the second search, which, whether undertaken from good or bad motives, is the immediate reason for the delay, and concentrates on the delay itself, with another temporal argument (see 25, before I put to sea). It is only in connection with the note, where the burdening weight of the document compels him to make an allegation, that Euxitheus tells us of the second search and explicitly suspects foul play.

31   You have heard the evidence: regular in such summarising expressions are i) the absence of a connecting particle after the witnesses; see Wyse 295 (*oun* is found when no witnesses precede, as 64, 4 *Third Tetralogy* b7); ii) the perfect tense (hence read *gegenētai* in 52 and cf. 64, 81, 85). Note also the extemporaneous character of the sentence; see 13, You reply.
the examination: *basanos* developed in meaning from 'touch-stone' (Theog. 1.417; Harpoc. s.v.), to the touch-stone as a 'means of testing' (Pi. *Pyth*. 10.67) and so to 'test' or 'trial' in general ([Simonid.] 175.1, ed. Bergk), then 'trial by torture' and finally the 'torture' itself. See further Thür 13-15.
doubtless: *isōs* indicates that the offer of freedom is a guess on Euxitheus' part, recalling the common practice with informers (see 34, other men reward informers...). If such an offer was actually made we might have expected Euxitheus' friends who were present at the torture (34) to have known this and informed him, and it is in any case unlikely that the prosecution would have promised freedom to a slave who was himself implicated in the murder (except to trick him into a confession). The point of this remark (and of the one concerning release from sufferings) is that it serves as the basis of Euxitheus' argument against the value of *basanos*-evidence in 31-35.

32   If I had myself ordered...As it was...: a shortened form of argumentation by 'hypothetical inversion', on which see 38, If I had made away with...But as it is.... This statement should not be taken as indicating that two tortures were regular; see Thür 199-200.

92

to be racked: on the use of the rack or wheel (40) and other tortures cf. Ar. *Frogs* 618-621; R. Turasiewicz, *De servis testibus in Atheniensium iudiciis saec. V et IV a. Chr. n. per tormenta cruciatis* (Wroclaw, 1963) 78-80.

torturers: it has generally been accepted that in private suits the torture resulting from a challenge was directed by a third party, an official *basanistēs*; cf. Isoc. 17 *Trapez.* 15-17; Dem. 37 *Pant.* 40, 42; Harrison, *LA* 2, 148. Thür 160-173 has more recently argued strongly that one of the parties involved (i.e. the one not in possession of the slave) in fact regulated the proceedings, although it is dangerous to press 32 ('if I had myself ordered him to be racked'), 35 ('been tortured by me in the same way'), 36 ('challenging me to examine him under torture') and 46 ('to make it impossible for me to take him and examine him under torture') for this meaning.

assessors: *epitimētēs*, especially in this sense, is another rare word; cf. IG i².75, ii².1176; and with other meanings Aeschyl. *Prom.* 77; Soph.frg. 533 (ed. Pearson, = Pollux 9.140); Eur. *Supp.* 255; Plato, *Phaedr.* 240a; Harpoc. s.v. *epitimētas* (= Lys. frg. 82 Sa). The periphrasis (see 1, I could have wished...But as it is...) helps make this a hard-hitting comment with which to end the section.

34   the informer: *mēnutēs* occurs several times in the speech (cf. below, 36, 38, 46, 47, 52, also 24; *mēnuein* twice in 38) and Bonner, *EAC*, 71 takes its frequency as indicating that the slave was properly an informer, in which capacity alone could he have been produced in court (36, 46, translating *enthade* in the former as 'in court'). The use of the word here in conjunction with the reference to the reward of freedom for slave informers (see n. below) could be seen to support this view. So too the employment of the slave's testimony as evidence by the prosecution though no challenge had been made to Euxitheus to torture him (and slave informers may have been tortured; see n. below). But could a slave give such voluntary information in a case of homicide (rather than in its regular cases of treason, sacrilege and theft of public money, Harrison, *LA* I, 171)? The idea that this was possible stems from the interpretation of *marturein* in 48 as equal to *mēnuein*, which is of doubtful validity (see Bonner & Smith, *AJHA* 2, 225-226; 29, examined them under torture, for a preferable interpretation of 48). Nor does Bonner interpret 36 and 46 correctly (see 36, here), and we should remember that in 36 Euxitheus argues that the slave should have been produced and a challenge made – which suggests that in his eyes at least the slave was a witness rather than an informer. So Antiphon may be using *mēnutēs* in a contemptuous manner and at the same time be indulging in a clever analogy, one which is continued in 46.

put him to death: see 47 n.

doing the exact opposite of what other men do: Antiphon similarly contrasts the opponents' behaviour with what normally happened in 38, 84 (= 6 *Chor.* 47), 6 *Chor.* 45.

other men reward informers...: these rewards are frequently mentioned; cf. And. 1 *Myst.* 27-28; Lys. 5 *Call.* 3-5, 7 *Sac. Ol.* 16; Gorg. *Pal.* 11; Thuc. 6.27.2; Plato, *Laws* 11.914a, 932d; Bonner, *EAC*, 39; Harrison, *LA* I, 171. Ant. 2 *First Tetralogy* c4 (if reflecting normal Attic procedure) suggests that the slave informer would not be tortured and this was accepted by Bonner for cases in which the information was freely given. But the opposite view, that a slave informer would be freed only if he kept to his story under torture, was taken by Thür 56 n. 33. Finally, MacDowell, *LCA*, 181 thinks the reward of freedom was not a legal requirement but a customary act (which would be supported by the killing of the slave by Herodes' relatives if he was an informer).

in spite of a protest by my friends: the brevity of the narrative leaves us in the dark over the identity of these friends and how they came to be present at the torture. For their request, and Euxitheus' employment of its refusal by the prosecution as an argument against them, see 36, challenging me to examine him under torture.

35 proving the truth...assumed to be true: in the Greek the verb *apollumai* ('be ruined') stands at the end of parallel clauses (antistrophe), which helps emphasise how the loss of the slave's life was causing the loss of Euxitheus'. A similar effect has been attempted in the translation with truth/true.

36 here: most obviously to be rendered 'in court', which should then make this sentence evidence for the disputed question as to whether a challenge could be delivered even at the start of the trial itself (for contrasting views on which see Bonner, *EAC*, 72-73 and Thür 190-193, v. Harrison, *LA* 2, 149 n. 4). However, should we take *enthade* so literally? If we remember that the torture of the slave took place in Euxitheus' absence and assume that Herodes' relatives had then gone to Athens to register the charge with the Eleven (perhaps soon after Euxitheus' return) it is clearly possible and logical for Euxitheus to argue that they should have produced the slave after his own arrival in Athens (even though we might rather have expected him to say that the slave should have been produced in Mytilene). So *enthade* may be 'in Athens'. Alternatively (and preferably), this may be little more than a rhetorical statement by Euxitheus, the point being that Herodes' relatives ought not to have put the slave to death but should have produced him for Euxitheus to examine, regardless of location (similarly, in Aesch. 2 *Fals. Leg.* 126 the offer made in court to hand over slaves for torture may be mere rhetoric; see Harrison, *ibid.*). For there appears to be no suggestion that the slave should have been produced in court either as a witness or as an informer – the emphasis lies rather on the idea that the slave should have been presented to Euxitheus and a challenge made. Therefore when Euxitheus says

in 46 that the prosecution put their informer to death and used every effort to prevent him from 'coming to you' and himself from torturing him he may simply be continuing the analogy with informers, who would come forward with their information to the Assembly or Council, and be reiterating his point here.

challenging me to examine him under torture: referring to the *proklēsis* made by a litigant to his opponent; for the procedure see Bonner, *EAC*, 67-69; Harrison, *LA* 2, 148-149; Thür *passim* (62-64 for *keleuein* in challenges). From this and from the statements in 34 and 38 that Euxitheus' friends made a vain challenge at the slave's torture it is clear that the prosecution themselves made no challenge to Euxitheus to torture their slave (nor, indeed, was Euxitheus on Lesbos at the time of the torture). Thus, if the prosecution actually used the slave's confession in court (and they seem to have based their case on this and on the note) and if the slave was not an informer his statement was strictly invalid as evidence, since a prosecutor could only use the evidence of his slave if his opponent had accepted the slave for torture. So Euxitheus seems to have a justifiable grievance (see also Harrison, *id.*, 150 n. 2) and he turns the prosecution's refusal to make him a challenge to his own advantage in 38.

They should not have put him to death: see 47 n.

37 If we are to judge from probability: for similar weighing of the alternatives with probability cf. 42-45, 49-51; Solmsen 37-38.

when he was in danger of being ruined: the imperfect (*apōlluto*) denotes likelihood, intention or danger, as in 60 (*diepheugen*); see *GMT* 38.

whom the truth of his second statement defended: lit. 'to whom the truth...was an ally'. Metaphor with *summachos* recurs in 43 and 86 and with *sunagōnizesthai* in 93, while the opposite metaphor with *polemios* appears in 86 and 93. For other instances of metaphor in the speech cf. 71, 91 and 94.

while there were those...corrected: the Greek is difficult here, in that *hoi aphaniountes* (lit. 'those hiding away') hardly fits with *tous proterous logous* ('the first statement') since the prosecution would not have wanted to hide away the words of the slave that were favourable to them. Hence editors have understood the participle in the sense of 'distort' or 'obscure', but obscuring the slave's words would not have made it impossible for them to have been corrected later (*hōste mēdepote eis to alēthes katastēnai*, lit. 'so as never to restore them to the truth'). Rather, the slave's removal would have this effect and Antiphon goes on to argue against just this in 38. So 'the first statement (of the slave)' is being used periphrastically for 'the slave, uttering his first statement'.

38 Others...but in this case: for this line of argument see 34, doing the exact opposite of what other men do. 'Quietly seize' is *kleptousi*, a usage of the simple verb paralleled in Eur. *Troad.* 958.

the very persons who arrested the slave: *hoi apagontes* is not to be taken as referring to the use of *apagōgē* against Euxitheus in the initiation of the suit, which would be a sudden change of thought quite out of context here.

If I had made away with...But as it is...: the argument of this sentence takes the form of a 'hypothetical inversion' (a phrase coined by Solmsen 10); sim. 32 (a much shortened version), 74-75, 84, 1 *Stepmother* 11, 12, 6 *Chor.* 27, 28, 29; And. 1 *Myst.* 24; Lys. 7 *Sac.Ol.* 36. Like the form the thought is commonplace (cf. especially Ant. 1 *Stepmother* 11, 6 *Chor.* 27; further Lys. 4 *Wound* 12, 7 *Sac.Ol.* 36; Isoc. 17 *Trapez.* 27-28; Is. 8 *Cir.* 11; Dem. 49 *Timoth.* 58), and note the rhetoric employed here, including a tricolon (*ēphanisa/ēthelon/epheugon*), alliteration (*tauta tauta tekmēria*) and amplification with et. fig. (*aitian epepheron hēn ēitiōnto*): Antiphon makes gain out of the prosecution's refusal to accept or offer the slave for torture.

in spite of a challenge being made by my friends: reiterating 34. The use of *prokaloumenōn* makes it clear that a *proklēsis* was being made; see Thür 61.

39 the slave: *anthrōpos* is used with a demeaning tone both of the slave (also 42, 51, 54) and of the free man (42, 55; the two together in 29, 52). This does not, against Gernet 122 n. 4, imply that the latter was in fact a slave, but it may reflect his low social standing (on which see 29, the men).

my accomplice in the murder: Euxitheus here argues that the slave admitted not to being an accomplice in the murder but to helping him remove the body. But in 54 he contradicts himself; see the slave stated...he had committed the murder himself.

  sunapokteinai is another rare word, occurring also in Aesch. 2 *Fals.Leg.* 148; Dio Cassius frg. 11.18.

but that he conducted: in the Greek *hoti de exagagoi*, a remarkable change from the regular infinitive (*legein*) after *phēmi* to *hoti* with the optative; compare possibly Plato, *Gorg.* 487d (with Dodds' note); further Lys. 7 *Sac.Ol.* 19; Dem. 4 *First Philippic* 48; Xen. *Anab.* 7.1.5; *GMT*, 753.2; Kühner-Gerth 2, 356. A vivid effect is produced, highlighting the antithesis, and the construction may be intended to reflect the slave's words.

helped me pick him up: *sunanelōn* simply means 'take up together with', in contrast with *sunapokteinai*, 'kill together with' (cf. further 42, *anairethentos* in 45 and *anaireseōs* in 68). But the active of *anairein* normally carries the sense of 'destroying', the middle form being used for 'taking up', and Antiphon may be playing on a double-meaning of *sunanairein*, which was in the minutes and which the prosecution understood as = *sunapokteinai*.

threw him into the sea: see 28 n.

40 the wheel: for torture on the wheel cf. Suidas, s.v. *trochistheisa*; Bekk. *An.* I, 306, lines 28-30; 32 to be racked.

in order to be released from the torture: reiterating the thought of 31.

41   bemoaned: like *phroudos* in 29 *apōimōxen* is a poetic word not found elsewhere in classical prose.

compelled by the truth: completing a circle of sophistic argumentation in 40–41 (truth – necessity – truth). Probably the slave altered his story when he realised he was about to be put to death, but equally his confession under torture may have been made under the compulsion of necessity – and we can understand why the prosecution may have been anxious to execute the unreliable slave.

42   the second man: the free man. On the difficulties involved with this sentence see 29, the men.

he confirmed: the free man, of course, was actually tortured before the slave, but his favourable evidence is rightly considered afterwards (see 30, The first).

I did not leave the boat at all: repeating the alibi of 23; see n. there.

43   probability supports me: more metaphor, recalling that of 37 (see whom the truth of his second statement defended).

I would hardly have been...witnesses and confederates: for the commonplace thought that murderers plan and commit their crimes in secret cf. Ant. 1 *Stepmother* 28, 2 *First Tetralogy* a2, c8; Lys. 1 *Caed.Erat.* 46. Secrecy naturally makes the solving of the crime more difficult; cf. Ant. 6 *Chor.* 18; Aesch. 1 *Tim.* 91. Two other topical themes are discernible here, both forms of *a fortiori* argument:

i) Theodorus' 'topos from errors committed' (*topos ek tōn hamartēthentōn*; cf. Arist. *Rhet.* 2.23.28), the argument that if Euxitheus had done one thing he would not have made the mistake of doing another; sim. 53–54, 61, 62;

ii) the 'topos of the more and less' (*topos tou mallon kai hētton*, Arist. *id.* 2.23.4–5) – if Euxitheus planned the murder by himself because of the danger so much the more would he not have told anyone after he had committed it; sim. 61–62.

crazy: lit. 'possessed by an evil genius', *kakodaimōn* is another of the noticeable compounds in Antiphon (see 2, submit to the physical suffering) and is very common in Aristophanes (as *Ach.* 105, *Knights* 7, *Clouds* 104, *Plutus* 386). The adjective is found once in Demosthenes (19 *Fals.Leg.* 115), who also uses the substantival (2 *Second Olynthiac* 20, *pr.* 24.3) and verbal forms (8 *Chers.* 16; cf. also Isoc. 7 *Areop.* 73; Din. 1 *Dem.* 91); while Lysias has *kakodaimonistēs* ('member of a 'Satanist' club' LSJ, frg. 53.2 Scheibe).

to plan: on *prounoēsamēn* see 13, even when summoned.

44   Was a man...on board?: a fully unconvincing argument since a swift blow from behind could have prevented any such cries. It was also a stormy night and the passengers were drinking.

by night...in a city: for arguments based on time and place cf. Ant. 2 *First Tetralogy* a4, 6 *Chor.* 45; Lys. 7 *Sac.Ol.* 15, 28; Gorg. *Pal.* 10. The text is corrupt here: Wyse 311 rejected the

97

combination *pollōi pleon* and *agnoein* ('not to hear') gives the opposite sense to that which is required. It is easiest, with Schömann, to add *epi* and simply alter *agnoein* to *akouein* (or *gegōnein*, with Cobet). See further Maidment, *MAO* I, 190 n. a (but against his interpretation of *kai mēn* see Denniston (1954) 358).

45   The argument here resumes and expands that of 27, a technique recurring in 46-48 (after 33-35) and 49-51 (after 42); see Due 39. As there, the structure is well-balanced: n.b. the chiastically arranged *en tēi gēi men apothanontos* X *entithemenou de eis to ploion* and the parallel *ta t'en tēi gēi...ta en tōi ploiōi* (with homoeoteleuton). This careful structure helps to bring out the difficulties involved in murdering a person without leaving clues, especially at night; and the possibility that these traces were removed is mentioned in question form, which contrasts with the statement that there were no traces and adds a certain amount of irony.

picked up: *anairethentos* could be 'killed' but compare *anaireseōs* in 68 and *sunanelōn* in 39 (see n. there). 'Picking up' is also a regular meaning of the verb in connection with bodies, as Thuc. 3.24.3; Eur. *Or.* 404. However, it is to be noted that in the second *nuktōr* phrase *entithemenou* is repeated from the antithesis above – and *anairethentos* may be a simple variation on *apothanontos*.

smooth out...wipe away: more rare vocabulary. For the former cf. Arist. *HA* 6.15, 8.20; Plut. *Mor.* 637f, *Public.* 15.4; for the latter (the reading of A) cf. schol. Hom. *Od.* 8.88; schol. Ar. *Frogs* 490; Antyll. ap. Orib. 6.9.1. N has *anaspoggisai*, also rare but used by Hippocrates (*Ulc.* 4; *Nat. Mul.* 32, 74).

46   I hope you will forgive me...: Antiphon apologises for his argumentation technique of repetition of a point. Speakers, as might be expected, often plead for the jurors' forgiveness over certain contentions and lines of argument; cf. And. 3 *Peace* 21; Lys. 21 *Brib. Def.* 16; Lyc. I *Leocr.* 128; Dem. 10 *Fourth Philippic* 54 (sim. 19 *Fals. Leg.* 227; Plato, *Ap.* 31e), 21 *Meid.* 58. For their part, the jurors in the popular courts would freely vent their disapproval; see Lofberg 12.

to prevent him coming to you: see 36, here. In the analogy with informers the judges (*humas*) represent the people; see 90, you will be my judges in the other court too.

to take him: *axai* is a very rare form of the aorist and has been suspected more than once. A parallel would be *prosēxan* in Thuc. 2.97.3 if that reading too were not doubtful (see Gomme's note).

it was to their own advantage: since, if he was telling the truth, the slave would keep to his story when tortured by Euxitheus and the prosecution would be able to make play with this in court (as Maidment, *MAO* I, 192 n. a). but the prosecution probably feared that the pain of the torture would make the slave change his story, whether or not it was true.

47   <u>they bought the slave</u>: this sentence suggests that the buying
took place after the torture, which goes against Erbse's
contention that the length of time involved was a factor in the
delay before the questioning (see 30, <u>The second they tortured</u>
<u>several days later</u>). In 47-48 Euxitheus tries to show the illegality
of killing one's slave, so he makes it clear from the outset that
the slave put to death in Mytilene belonged to the prosecution.
His implication, then, is that the prosecution bought the slave for
the very purpose of executing him (which may indeed have been
the case, whether from good or bad motives), but this does not
rule out the possibility that the transaction was in fact made
before the torture. However, some scholars (as Bonner, *EAC*, 71)
have been too ready to assume that the buying would have
preceded the torturing (though this was the regular practice).
<u>put him to death</u>: Harrison is emphatic on the position between
master and slave in this respect – there is no doubt that the act
of putting one's slave to death was illegal; see *LA* I, 171
(MacDowell, *AH L*, 21-22, *LCA*, 80 is more cautious). Also in little
doubt is Morrow 211-212 and we may note that it was one of the
functions of the Palladium to try those accused of killing a slave
(cf. [Arist.] *Ath.Pol.* 57.3). However, before we condemn the
prosecution with Euxitheus we should remember Morrow's own
valid comment that distinction must be made between legal
principles and legal remedies. The slave had confessed his part in
a murder, so the prosecution, whatever their motives, could have
said they were carrying out what was in their view his proper
punishment. Was this illegal? The scene was Lesbos and we may
wonder whether it was the law or general practice that a slave
who admitted his part in a murder in any corner of the Empire
whatsoever should be brought to Athens for trial. This is
doubted by De Ste Croix 271 and Antiphon may well, as he
suggests, have taken advantage of general wording in an
Athenian decree and applied it to a slave. Gernet 122 n. 3,
followed by Thür 52 n. 15, felt Antiphon's argument was a
sophism but Erbse (1977) 213-214 goes further and contends that the
killing was justified – and an Athenian authority was probably
present at the torture. He adduces as a parallel the killing of
Philoneus' *pallakē* in Ant. 1 *Stepmother* 20, but this is a much
disputed question; and he is perhaps too dogmatic in saying that
putting the slave to death was the regular punishment of an
unfree murderer. But he has indicated that this was not simply
the killing of a slave – it was his punishment for a crime.

    Nevertheless, if the killing of the slave was illegal how
should the slayer have been prosecuted? The law laid down that a
slave's killer should be brought to justice by a *dikē phonou*
before the Palladium (cf. the *Ath.Pol.* passage cited above), his
master conducting the prosecution (cf. 48; Dem. 47 *Euerg.* 70;
MacDowell, *AH L*, 20-21). But what happened when the master was
himself the killer, as in our case? The slave's relatives, if he had

any, would most likely be servile too and without competence to prosecute. MacDowell admits the possibility that any citizen could prosecute, but the whole concept of such a *graphē phonou* remains doubtful. Perhaps a preferable view is that of Gagarin (1979) 306-313 (esp. 312-313), who concludes that there was no explicit statement in the law that no one other than the relatives of the victim or the master of a slave could prosecute, and a prosecution by an outsider might be allowed in the absence of relatives (but see Hansen (1981) 11-13). Finally, Ant. 6 *Chor.* 4 may indicate that the master need only undergo purification (see Harrison, *LA* I, 172), but against this see Morrow 222; MacDowell, *id.*, 20.

their informer: see 34 n.

the state did not decree it: referring to a court at Athens. *psēphos* is used below and in 48 of a judicial procedure.

nor was he the man's murderer: see 54, the slave stated...he had committed the murder himself. Even if the slave admitted only to being an accomplice this would have seemed sufficient reason to the prosecution for putting him to death.

surrender him to my friends on security: *exegguēsai* is only found here in this sense. It more regularly bears the meaning 'release on payment of bail', as Dem. 24 *Timocr.* 73.

hand him over to your magistrates: to whom? There are two main alternatives:
i) Athenian overseas officials in Mytilene;
ii) officials in Athens (i.e. the Eleven, who were in charge of the city prison).
(That they would not have been local officials seems to be indicated by *tois humeterois*, and see Bonner & Smith, *AJHA* 2, 251-252.)
i) would seem the more likely, perhaps referring to Athenian officials who conducted a preliminary hearing of the case. The presence of such officials in Mytilene after the 'friendly' decree (on which see 77, granted the other Mytileneans an amnesty) would hardly have been an infringement of the Lesbians' new autonomy (as S. Cataldi, reviewing W. Schuller, *Die Herrschaft der Athener*, in *ASNP* 5 (1975) 1593) and an Athenian official may have been involved in the primary stages of trials which were transferred to Athens.

when it was not permitted...Athenian people: reflecting Athenian interference in allied jurisdiction, on which see P. 25.

judges...pass judgment: *kritēs* is a judge in general, an arbiter, *dikastēs* more specifically one who judges in court. Hence there is a certain amount of irony here, the roles being reversed by Euxitheus.

statements...acts: on the antithesis see 3, his accusers' words...the actual facts.

48 caught in the act: on arrest *in flagrante delicto* see Hansen, *AEE*, 48-53.

they are handed over to the authorities: in 47-48 Euxitheus argues that a slave should stand trial if suspected of murder. The reference here, then, is to the Eleven, who would keep the slave in custody until his trial. But it is hard to believe that a slave caught red-handed in a homicide or one, as in our case, who confessed to such a crime would have been granted this privilege, especially if the murder was committed abroad. So, in truth, the laws may have ordained that the slave caught *in flagrante* should be handed over to the Eleven not for confinement but for execution – and that private citizens should not perform the task.

according to the ancient laws of your country: i.e. those of Draco; see 14, the oldest in this country.

If it is indeed permissible...of his being murdered: see 29, examined them under torture.

for a court to sentence...of a free man: it appears that there was no fixed penalty for killing a slave but that it would have been less than that for killing a citizen; see Morrow 213-214; MacDowell, *AH L*, 126-127. So this statement seems to be a rhetorical exaggeration, but Antiphon may be comparing the punishment of slaves and free non-citizens. Alternatively, the clause may refer to the availability of legal procedure and *psēphos* in the next clause bears the idea more of 'judicial proceeding' than 'vote'.

you deserve to be standing trial...: a forceful conclusion to 46-48 (n.b. the et. fig. in *dikaioteron*/*adikōs*, the latter in emphatic position), with the accused becoming accuser, as in 59, 2 *First Tetralogy* b11, 4 *Third Tetralogy* b7; Lys. 3 *Sim.* 44, 21 *Brib.Def.* 16.

49   In 49-51 we see a third example of Antiphon's technique of repeating and expanding upon arguments.

the free man: the only explicit statement in the speech as to the status of the first person tortured.

has not even yet said anything compromising about me: why, then, did Euxitheus not produce him as a witness? Possibly because he had left Lesbos and Euxitheus could not now find him or could not get him to come to Athens. Schindel, *MH*, 38-39 thinks that this sentence shows the free man *was* produced, taking *oudepō nun* as 'even now still not'. However, this may simply be rhetorical exaggeration, since it was no lie to say the free man had not to that day denounced Euxitheus if he had disappeared.

50 like the other one: i.e., presumably, 'as they could have persuaded the other one', rather than 'as they persuaded', since the offer was Euxitheus' assumption (see 31, doubtless).

he was willing...: his loyalty would be the easier to understand if he was Euxitheus' attendant, but this is doubtful; see 29, the men.

those who consistently keep to one statement...: the credibility of witnesses is rarely attacked convincingly by the orators, but an effective method was to show that their accounts varied materially; see Bonner, *EAC*, 86-88.

51 [Similarly...denied]: the brackets were inserted by Thalheim after C.A. Hirschig, 'Selectae emendationes et observationes in Antiphonte', *Philologus* 9 (1854) 737. As Maidment notes, *MAO* I, 197 n. a, the syntax is harsh and the reasoning unsound: the slave altered his story, as has just been said, and so he cannot be set against the free man in this way.

an equal division...: an interesting, sophistic analogy, though Gernet 123 n. 1 sees it as perhaps retaining the unconscious recollection of an ancient procedure based on the counting of the witnesses. For the idea of *in dubio pro reo* cf. Aesch. 3 *Ctes.* 252; [Arist.] *Ath.Pol.* 69.1, *Rhet. ad Alex.* 18.7; Arist. *Prob.* 29.13, 15; Aeschyl. *Eum.* 741, 752-753; Harrison, *LA* 2, 47 (with n. 3). Note the antistrophe here (*diōkontos/diōkonta*).

52 I would have got rid of the two men: a surprisingly bald statement by Euxitheus, perhaps reflecting the real contemporary attitude to a problem such as an embarrassing slave; see Due 39. In this sentence Antiphon puts 'having something on one's conscience' before 'committing a crime' instead of in its correct temporal position after – the figure hysteron-proteron.

to the mainland: i.e. to Asia Minor.

to inform: *mēnutas* is here used in a general sense, with no legal connotations as possibly elsewhere; see 34, the informer.

53 Euxitheus now turns to the second *atechnos pistis*, the note which was found during the second search of the decked boat in Mytilene. This note must have formed the basis of the prosecution along with the slave's evidence since, if genuine, it was conclusive (and provided the motive for the murder). But genuine or not, such evidence was hard to refute without the aid of forensic science; and the burdening weight of the note is to some extent reflected by the much briefer treatment it receives from Antiphon in comparison with the *basanos* (though the opportunities for *eikos*-argument were greater with the latter). Euxitheus argues that

i) a note was unnecessary;

ii) the contents of the note were different from those of the slave's statement; and therefore

iii) the note was a forgery.

To secure this last point he once more in 55-56 employs a temporal/plot theme (see 25, before I put to sea), that the note was only discovered during the second search of the vessel – i.e. after the free man had refused to incriminate Euxitheus the prosecution decided to forge the note in case the slave was similarly obstinate. Thus Euxitheus is concerned not only with the contents of the *basanos* and the note, but also with the way in which the evidence was obtained. In addition, the argumentation over the note is delayed until after that over the *basanos*, since it is easier to believe in the forgery when the prosecution's behaviour with regard to the torture has been vilified.

Finally, the argument in 53-54 has a topical nature; see 43, I would hardly have been...witnesses and confederates.

a note: was the note forged? There was, we remember, a delay before it was found; and the forging of such a brief note would have presented few problems and could hardly have been proved. But, on the other hand, the note may have been hidden on the boat by the slave and when the prosecution discovered it they forced him to confess; or the slave may have revealed the hiding-place of the note. Again, while it does seem that there was no need for the note, the alleged contradiction between its contents and the slave's statement does not in fact exist; see 54, the slave stated...he had committed the murder himself. Clearly, the note was a great obstacle for Euxitheus to overcome.

Lycinus: the most mysterious figure in the case. On the basis of 61 ('though it was possible...this he did not wish to do') and especially 62 (see even though if discovered...sacred and precious) he is generally considered to have been, like Herodes, an Athenian living at Mytilene; see Blass, *AB* I, 175 n. 3; Jebb, *AO* I, 56 with n. 2; Gernet 123 n. 2. His poor financial condition (63) suggests that he was also a cleruch. If so, Lycinus probably knew Herodes, and he seems to have been an acquaintance of Euxitheus (n.b. 63, 'my friendship with him was hardly close enough'). The fact that he was implicated in the murder perhaps suggests either a closer friendship with Euxitheus than the defendant admits to in 63, or that Lycinus had some quarrel with Herodes or Herodes' relatives for which the latter were now trying to gain revenge. If, further, the prosecution even argued that Lycinus was behind the whole affair (as may be implied in 60, 'in his case too their charge is unreasonable', and by the defence of Lycinus in 60-63) we might well wonder whether he was proceeded against too. There seems to have been more to all this than meets the eye.

54   the note contradicted the slave...the slave the note: for the antimetabole see 14, Hence you must not...interpretation of the case.

the slave stated...he had committed the murder himself: this contradicts Euxitheus' words in 39, which are reiterated in 42 and implied in 47 ('nor was he the man's murderer'), and a close consideration of 39, 42, 54 and also 68 reveals a high degree of ingenuity in Antiphon's argumentation.

To begin with 39 and 42, where the crucial word is *sunanairein*. This word was presumably found in the minutes of the torture and represents the slave's confession of complicity in the murder. But Antiphon saw here a possibility of disputing what the slave was supposed to have said, upon a different interpretation of the wording of the minutes. He could then minimise the slave's alleged part in the crime and complain that Euxitheus was not afforded the opportunity of examining this witness personally, while protesting against the illegal killing of a man who had not been party to the deed itself. Now when it came to the note, Antiphon realised that this burdening piece of evidence could also be best dealt with by disputing its actual contents – but he could only do this by emphasising an apparent contrast between the note and the slave's evidence (the one saying that Euxitheus had performed the deed, the other that the slave had helped). The slave's mere complicity is, in this instance, not enough and Euxitheus has to insist upon a discrepancy in order to show that the whole business with the note was part of the prosecution's plot against him. So he contradicts his previous statement and says that the slave confessed to the murder.

Although Antiphon's clever manipulation of the evidence may be apparent to the leisurely reader of the speech, in the heat of the moment the contradiction could easily have escaped detection. So it is not too surprising when, in 68, Euxitheus reverts to his first version of the slave's evidence, but attributes it to the prosecution themselves. Again, this is an argument for the moment, necessary to complete the comparison with the Ephialtes affair, and Antiphon was taking a calculated risk that the jurors would not detect this further inconsistency.

55   but during a later one: on Antiphon's arguments from the delay see 53, heading n. Note also the simple joining of opposites here (not during the first search, but during a later one), a method Antiphon frequently employs in the *Tetralogies* (as 2 *First Tetralogy* b5 *bis*, c6, 3 *Second Tetralogy* a2, 4 *Third Tetralogy* d6) and one familiar from Herodotus (as 3.25.2, 4.161.1).

56   from the first: to *apo prōtēs* supply *archēs* (sim. Thuc. 1.77.3).

57   Euxitheus now changes from refutative to confirmative arguments, beginning with his motive for killing Herodes (57-59). In 60-61 Lycinus' motive is dealt with and in 62-63 Euxitheus discusses his relationship with Lycinus, to dispense with the idea that he was acting on his behalf. The different possible motives (not all of which would have been adduced by the prosecution) are:

i) a favour (57). This is combined with the motive of personal enmity, in that one will not simply kill as a favour, but must also have bad feelings towards the victim;

ii) a preventive measure (58);

iii) financial gain (58-59). This last motive prepares the way for a counter-charge against the prosecution's motive in bringing the case (59).

These motives, ii) and iii) being repeated in 60 for Lycinus, are naturally commonplace ones; cf. Ant. 2 *First Tetralogy* a5-6, c8, d9, *Ap*. Col. I-II (Antiphon's motives for desiring a revolution); Lys. 1 *Caed. Erat.* 43-46; Dem. 19 *Fals. Leg.* 221-223 (motives for a prosecution), 29 *Aphobus iii* 22-24 (motives for false testimony); Gorg. *Pal.* 13-19.

there was not even any bad feeling between him and me: the repetition in the Greek of the negative, and later of the whole sentence, helps disguise that we have no proof of this lack of enmity. In addition, it is noticeable that Euxitheus only considers motives applicable to a premeditated murder and so he does not deal with the possibility that enmity could have arisen as a result of, say, the drinking-bout.

as a favour: Euxitheus only asserts in a general manner that he cannot have murdered Herodes for a favour since there was no enmity between them. Then, in 58, he contends that there was no financial reward to be gained from the killing since Herodes was poor. Finally, in 62-63 he denies that he could have been hired by Lycinus to perform the murder since Lycinus was also poor. Thus he does not specifically mention what the prosecution may have claimed, that he killed Herodes as a favour for Lycinus, and this possibility is only indirectly refuted by the argument of 57. Whether or not this is significant we cannot, of course, be sure; but it is, perhaps, an example of the way in which Antiphon would enfeeble the prosecution's arguments, especially the ones most difficult to deal with, by separating them into different parts.

it must be clear...that the design is growing: recalling the contention of 21-22 that no design could be attributed to Euxitheus in his meeting Herodes.

58   Noticeable here is the hypophora in the questions, with repeated *alla*; for other examples of this figure, in which suggestions are made and rejected in succession, cf. 63, *Ap*. Col. I.15-II.14; And. 1 *Myst.* 148, 3 *Peace* 14-15; Lys. 10 *Theomn.* 23, 24 *Inv.* 24-25, 30 *Nicom.* 26-27; Isoc. 12 *Panath.* 23; Is. 5 *Dic.* 45-46; Dem. 14 *Navy Boards* 27; Gorg. *Pal.* 7-12.

I had no such fears with regard to him: lit. 'nothing of the kind had been begun by me with regard to him'. For a similar use of the passive *hupērkto* cf. Thuc. 1.93.3 (where it is impersonal).

was I going to enrich myself by murdering him?: some scholars, indeed, have seen the trial as being, in truth, one for murder with robbery; *contra* see P. 27 n. 3.

he had no money: suggesting that Herodes was a cleruch (see 20 n.). But note that he was travelling with some Thracian slaves in order to ransom them (20), and if these belonged to him he would have been wealthier than Euxitheus makes out (at least, after the deal was completed). The ransom money or possession of the slaves could then have been a motive for Euxitheus to kill Herodes. The possibility that the financial gain came in the form of money from a third person (i.e. Lycinus) is discussed in 62-63.

59   motive: on *prophasis* here and in 60 see 21, purposes.

that you are attempting to secure my death for money: an accusation repeated in 79. Erbse (1977) 219-220 detects a double function in the invective:
i) to suspect the prosecution's whole behaviour in the case. Neither Herodes (58) nor Lycinus (63) was wealthy, but Euxitheus was (*ibid*.), so he should have been the one murdered for his money;
ii) to fulfil the promise of 10 ('their motives for this you will learn in the course of my speech') over the *timēsis*.
But it has elsewhere been argued that money would not have been the object of the prosecution, unless Herodes' relatives made a mistake in thinking that by employing *endeixis* they would be able to propose a monetary penalty (see P. 27 with n. 8); and Erbse (1977) 225 is himself doubtful over this.

Another line of approach is to suspect the prosecution either of being bribed to bring the suit (of which we have no other indication) or of having demanded blood-money not to bring it (as Gernet 125 n. 1; it is hardly relevant in the context of the pre-trial scene of Lesbos whether this was legal or not). This would fit in with Euxitheus' defence of his father (74-80) and especially with 'this whole intrigue against my father and myself has been fabricated for the sake of money' (79): the wealthy Mytilenean, whose political stance was open to question, may have seemed an easy target, his son having travelled with Herodes. But deeper considerations of this kind may appear too speculative and there is, besides, another much simpler explanation of Euxitheus' invective, a development of i) above. For it became a commonplace method of argumentation in the orators, with the rise of sycophancy in Athens, to attempt to embarrass one's opponent with just such a charge of sycophantic intent; cf. Lys. 7 *Sac.Ol.* 1, 38-40; Aesch. 1 *Tim.* 1; Dem. 36 *For Phormion* 54; Lofberg 22; Bonner & Smith, *AJHA* 2, 46 (hence the denial of such intent, as Dem. 53 *Nicostr.* 1; Ar. *Peace* 191). The possibilities of this argument were, however, already evident to Antiphon (cf. 2 *First Tetralogy* b13) and, indeed, in 80 Euxitheus actually speaks at length of sycophants in a veiled but sure reference to the prosecution. Further, in 78 Euxitheus asserts that his father went to Aenus to escape the sycophants, perhaps implying that he himself had fallen victim to them. So it may be significant that in 59 the *hoti* clause follows a potential optative, which, like the subsequent *kai polu an dikaioteron haloiēs...*, suggests a rhetorical statement. The attack in 79 is made in a positive form, but after 59 this may be taken equally rhetorically. Further on sycophants cf. Lys. 21 *Brib.Def.* 1.
You might much more justly be convicted: the accused becomes the accuser once more; see 48, you deserve to be standing trial...; for the thought cf. 2 *First Tetralogy* b11. Euxitheus does not, of course, imply that an actual trial of the prosecution could have followed upon his wrongful condemnation – he

maintains the *justice* of such a trial.

<u>by you and the family of Herodes</u>: Hansen, *AEE*, 124 n. 7 infers from this that the prosecution speech was delivered by an advocate (*sunēgoros*). But *sunēgoroi* were normally supporting speakers, the main speech usually being delivered by the litigant himself; see Bonner, *EAC*, 82-84, *LL*, 200-209; Bonner & Smith, *AJHA* 2, 7-15; Harrison, *LA* 2, 158-159. Hence *sou* may simply be the relative who actually made the speech.

60   <u>I must also, it seems, clear Lycinus</u>: Euxitheus considers similar motives for Lycinus as for himself, but with 'redress for an injury' replacing 'favour'.

61   In 61-62 Antiphon employs two *topoi*; see 43, <u>I would hardly have been...witnesses and confederates.</u>

<u>winning favour with your city</u>: it was a *topos* in the orators that a prosecution might help the city (cf. Ant. 6 *Chor.* 9; Lys. 7 *Sac.Ol.* 20; Aesch. 1 *Tim.* 2; Lyc. 1 *Leocr.* 3) and prosecutors customarily would make out that their actions were for the city's benefit; see Lofberg 2.

⟨by bringing ...facts.⟩: Blass saw the need for the insertion of a witness-formula before the rubric *MARTURES*, while Thalheim and Maidment perhaps rightly suspected a larger lacuna (see Maidment's note *ad loc.*, whose suggested addition is followed in the translation).

62   <u>on this count he left Herodes alone</u>: of course, Lycinus' grievance need not have been actionable but may still have been serious enough for him to wish to kill Herodes.

<u>even though if discovered...sacred and precious</u>: this sentence has caused much difficulty and was bracketed by Gernet 107, on the ground that exile or exclusion from sacred and public places were too mild to be penalties for homicide (and there is no evidence for the latter as a separate penalty). But

i) the rhetoric being employed here must be recognised. Euxitheus wishes to bring home to the jury how ridiculous the idea was that Lycinus should not have taken any legal action against Herodes but would then have dared to murder him. So he puts extra emphasis on what Lycinus had to lose by means of a highly rhetorical (n.b. the anaphora, *apesterei men...apesterei de...*, and the tricolon in the latter clause) and false antithesis: both Euxitheus and Lycinus would have been deprived of their country, but see how much more Lycinus would have lost (this also suggests that Lycinus' nationality was different from Euxitheus', though perhaps not as strongly as many scholars have assumed);

ii) Euxitheus is talking about what would have happened if Lycinus had been discovered whilst *plotting* Herodes' death (*epebouleuen, en hōi gnōstheis*) – this is then, in fact, evidence for MacDowell's type E of *bouleusis* of homicide, *AH L*, 61, not a reference to a penalty for actual homicide.

I am now actually adopting the standpoint of the prosecution: for the second time (cf. 27 and n.).

63 Was it that...: more hypophora, on which see 58, heading n.
since he could not...: Lycinus was presumably imprisoned as a state debtor (for this form of imprisonment see Harrison, *LA* 2, 242-244), if Lesbian laws were similar to those of Athens in the matter of imprisonment. On *huperēmeros*, lit. 'over the day for payment', see Harrison, *id*. I, 282.
seven minae: paying for Lycinus' release would have been a true mark of friendship. Euxitheus minimises the size of the debt to prove his point and, below, to make a contrast with the serious crime of homicide. But seven minae was not a negligible sum.
was hardly close enough: this seems to imply at least some acquaintance with Lycinus; see 53 n.

64-73 In 64-66 Euxitheus argues that it is not up to him to explain Herodes' disappearance and in 67-71 he adduces three historical parallels to show the difficulties involved in doing so. The first two deal with the difficulty in discovering a murderer, while the third adds another theme, that care should be taken in judgments. This prepares the way for commonplace argumentation over haste and anger in 71-73.

64 if I must conjecture...: Euxitheus refuses to make simple conjectures which may well have seemed banal after his lengthy refutation of the prosecution's version of events; see 23, we began drinking. But such argument also smacks of a *topos* and the defendant in the *First Tetralogy* takes a similar stance (2d3) but feels he has to go further and reveal the true culprits (b2, 4). As Blass noted, *AB* I, 185, Euxitheus' refusal to conjecture has a slightly ironical tone.

65 Criminals no sooner commit a crime...: i.e. the one who commits a crime is the first to suggest that another is to blame. The effect of this remark is enhanced by the pi alliteration and the repetition of the forceful compound *panourgein*; while the effect of 'but if you were then told...' below is again increased by the pi sounds, this time with hyperbaton (*en pollēi...aporiai*).

67 I know from report...: Antiphon now adduces his three historical parallels (a commonplace form of argumentation; cf. And. 1 *Myst*. 106-109; Lys. 19 *Arist*. 45-52; Isoc. 15 *Ant*. 155-156; Dem. 21 *Meid*. 58-65; Arist. *Rhet*. 2.20.2-4) in order to show that
a) homicides might remain unexplained and it is therefore unfair simply to hold those in the victim's company responsible unless they can explain the crime;
b) the truth about a crime might, on the other hand, become known at a later date, when it is too late to save the person wrongly condemned for it. Hence the judges at Euxitheus' trial should not be over-hasty in condemning him.
a) is paralleled in the cases of Ephialtes, whose murderers were never discovered, and of the slave-boy, who was indeed caught

but only by chance – had he not been, a whole household of slaves would have suffered for his act. The case of the Hellenotamiae parallels b), only one of whom was saved after the whole board had been wrongly condemned to death for embezzlement. No doubt this example was also intended to remind the judges of what happened after the Mytilenean revolt a few years previously, how the hasty decision to put to death the entire adult male population and to enslave the women and children had been reversed when anger had subsided a little. Note, finally, that there is no example of a case where the victim was not found, as with Herodes.

68 Ephialtes: this radical democrat alienated the oligarchic faction at Athens by his attack on the Areopagus and his democratic reforms in 462; and after the oligarchic leader Cimon was ostracised in 461 he was assassinated. According to Antiphon and Diodorus (11.77.6) the assassins were never discovered, but [Arist.] *Ath.Pol.* (25.4; cf. Plut. *Per.* 10.8) states that the crime was committed by Aristodicus of Tanagra. Gernet 127 n. 2 therefore contends that Antiphon is here revealing his own oligarchic stance, because the murderer was well-known. But this would have been dangerous before a jury full of democrats. Equally, Maidment's suggestion, *MAO* I, 208 n. a that it suited Antiphon's requirements here to assume the mystery was never solved must be doubted, when many of the jurors could well have known the name of the murderer. Rather, it is the version in the *Ath.Pol.* that is to be suspected, one which was perhaps not current in Antiphon's day (and arose later from a confusion with another murder?). See further Rhodes *ad loc.* (pp.321-322).

   D. Stockton has recently argued that Ephialtes was not murdered at all, but died in bed of, say, a heart-attack; see 'The Death of Ephialtes', *CQ* N.S. 32 (1982) 227-228. However, while it is easy to see why the story that he was murdered should have been invented it is hardly 'clear enough' that Ephialtes was found dead in his bed; none of the above-mentioned sources indicates where he was found.

whereas they say I...: a further purpose of this parallel is to attack once more the prosecution's interpretation of the slave's statement. Euxitheus attributes his own version to his opponents and then compares Ephialtes' murderers, who did not try to get rid of the body, with himself, who allegedly committed the murder alone and afterwards sought help in the removal of the corpse.

69 the entire household: of slaves.

your Hellenotamiae: the Athenian financial officials, ten in number until 411, who administered the funds of the Delian League; cf. And. 3 *Peace* 38; Thuc. 1.96.2; [Arist.] *Ath.Pol.* 30.2; Meiggs 234-235. Nothing more is known of this incident, but the officials were possibly accused by an *eisangelia* before the Assembly (though see Hansen (1975) 67 n. 7).

Through anger rather than reason: on the antithesis between *orgē* and *gnōmē*, which recurs in 72 and in a similar expression in Thuc. 2.22.1, see P. Huart, *GNŌMĒ chez Thucydide et ses contemporains* (Paris, 1973) 46-49.

70 Sosias was rescued...from the very hands of the Eleven: Sosias and the others had been placed in the custody of the Eleven until their execution by the same (for this role of the Eleven cf. Lys. 22 *Corn.* 2; Aesch. 1 *Tim.* 16). On the pardoning power of the ecclesia see Bonner & Smith, *AJHA* 2, 253-254.

71 I expect the older ones...like myself: for similar calls on the judges' memories and experiences cf. Ant. 6 *Chor.* 36, 41; Lys. 10 *Theomn.* 1; Isoc. 16 *Chariot* 4; Dem. 19 *Fals. Leg.* 19, 21 *Meid.* 1-2, 24 *Tim.* 128, 49 *Timoth.* 13; Bonner, *EAC*, 84-85; and further, with this antithesis between old and young jurors, Isoc. 8 *Peace* 12; Lyc. 1 *Leocr.* 93; Thuc. 1.42.1.

test the truth of a matter: on metaphor in the speech see 37, whom the truth of his second statement defended.

with the help of time: for commonplace arguments over time see 14, time and experience show mankind what is imperfect. Taking one's time helps avoid judicial error; cf. 86, 91 (with you must exercise the greatest caution), 94.

without anger and without prejudice: anger and prejudice (or rather 'false accusation') reappear in 91. On a par with them is haste (as in 73, 94), and Diodotus warns against haste and anger in the Mytilenean Debate (Thuc. 3.42.1). He also uses *diabalōn* (*id.* 42.2) and this passage of Thucydides may have been influenced by Antiphon. However, such ideas must have been abundant in this sophistic age and Aristophanes had already attacked the Athenians' reckless decisions in the *Acharnians* (*tachuboulois* 630, *metaboulous* 632: he may well be referring here to the Mytilenean affair, which had taken place two years before this play was produced, but similar attacks were frequent in comedy, as *Clouds* 587-588, *Ecc.* 797-798; Eupol. I, 314, frg. 205 Kock). Thucydides, for his part, additionally praises Athenian deliberation (2.40.2-3, Pericles' speech), as well as Spartan slowness (1.84.1-2, through Archidamus); and the arguments over haste and delay in 73 and 94 have been compared with Ant. Soph. frg. 58 (Diels); see E. Bignone, *Antifonte oratore e Antifonte sofista* (Urbino, 1974) 55-56; cf. further Eur. *Phoen.* 452-453; Plato, *Laws* 6.766e.

Like Aristophanes in the *Acharnians* Antiphon appears to be alluding to the Mytilenean affair in 71-72 or, at least, this passage would have pricked the memories of many of the jurors, the more so since it was delivered by a Mytilenean. Its insertion in the speech might therefore seem something of a gamble on Antiphon's part, in that the jurors may not have taken kindly to being reminded of these events by the young defendant. But Antiphon may have counted on raising sympathy for his client among jurors who recalled their part in a near-atrocity and have hoped thereby to avert the very real danger that the heliastic court would condemn the Mytilenean without giving him a fair hearing.

72 **as anger destroys...his judgment:** for the *orgē/gnōmē* antithesis see 69, Through anger rather than reason.

73 **Be assured that I deserve pity:** the appeal for pity here is unique in the speech and is itself only made indirectly. Elsewhere Euxitheus adopts a very practical attitude, pathos is rare and in the *epilogos*, where we might expect appeals for pity, he rather reasserts his contention that he was being tried under the wrong process. Euxitheus makes no concessions to this stance and Antiphon may have felt that appeals for pity by a Mytilenean were wasted on an Athenian jury; see further 85-96, heading n. Nevertheless, 71-73 are full of rhetoric and form one of the high-points of the speech, preparing us for the emotional subject of Euxitheus' father.

Wrongdoers should be punished...pitied: naturally the argument that the innocent deserve pity, the guilty punishment, is a commonplace one; cf. Ant. 1 *Stepmother* 25; [Lys.] 6 *Andoc.* 55, 22 *Corn.* 21, 27 *Epicr.* 12; Dem. 27 *Aphobus i* 68, 45 *Stephanus i* 88, 54 *Con.* 43; Din. 1 *Dem.* 109. Equally, it is a circular argument, as his innocence is what Euxitheus is trying to prove.

save my life justly...destroy me unjustly: another topical antithesis; cf. And. 1 *Myst.* 2; Lys. 19 *Arist.* 54.

By delaying...by immediate action...: see 71, without anger and without prejudice.

74-80 The defence of Euxitheus' father. G. Vollmer, in his unpublished doctoral dissertation *Studien zum Beweis antiphontischer Reden* (Hamburg, 1958) 109-111, argues that this section has the character of an excursus, composed in case of an attack on Euxitheus' father and otherwise easily omitted. In this Vollmer is supported both by the subject-matter itself and by its arrangement. For the section is like a mini-speech and may be divided into a proem (74-75; n.b. the polished, antithetical style), narrative (76-77), proofs (78-79) and epilogue (80). Then 81 could simply have been joined to 73 if the defence was not required. As to the subject-matter, two themes are apparent, the revolt and the father's absences from Mytilene; and the immediate purpose is to show the father's loyalty to Athens in spite of his participation in the former and regular indulgence in the latter. His father's activities must have been a delicate topic for Euxitheus to raise before an Athenian jury and it does seem that if the prosecution had made no reference to his family background it was better for him to remain silent as well. Equally, this background must have seemed to the prosecution an obvious means of attacking Euxitheus and an opportunity for raising angry emotions against him too good to miss (and such attacks on the origins of one's adversary were commonplace; n.b. especially Demosthenes' attack on Aeschines in 18 *Cor.* 126-131). So

Antiphon probably had no difficulty in anticipating such an attack and the line of defence he adopts could well have been composed before the trial. Vollmer's theory is most attractive.

The theory also accords well with the idea that Antiphon presented his clients with complete speeches ready for delivery, a view expressed by Usher in his attack on Dover's theory of composite authorship in Lysias' speeches; see Usher (1976) 32 v. Dover, *LCL*, ch. VIII. Euxitheus was a young Mytilenean and may have been inexperienced in litigation and forensic speaking just as he maintains in the proem (though this was a commonplace opening). As a foreigner (and a Mytilenean at that) addressing an Athenian court he needed extra help which Antiphon was willing to provide, being concerned with the treatment of allies (cf. his speeches for the Lindians and Samothracians in the matter of their tribute). It is not unreasonable, then, to assume that Antiphon composed a whole speech for the young alien to learn, removing from his shoulders the double burden of finding out what were the right things to say and how to say them; see further Due 74. Hence there is no true extemporisation in the speech (see 13, You reply).

74 my father: a wealthy Mytilenean – cf. 76 ('as the ties which bound him, his children and his property, were strong ones') and 77 (' he furnishes choruses'), also Euxitheus' statement over his own wealth (63). Perhaps the payment of *telē* (77) and more certainly his second residence in Aenus (78) reveal that the father was landed, and this was possibly the source of his income. But he may also have had mercantile interests, as Aenus was in an important trading position at the mouth of the Hebrus.

Though wealthy, Euxitheus' father was not one of those oligarchs who led the revolt (as Euxitheus says in 77), for this would without doubt have cost him his life. Presumably, however, the prosecution argued that he was nevertheless a typical, untrustworthy Mytilenean who at least joined in the revolt (76) and this could well have raised the jurors' anger. Euxitheus replies that his father (and by implication he himself) was actually pro-Athenian, despite his part in the revolt. He stayed in Aenus because of the activities of sycophants, not because he wished to avoid the Athenian courts (78). Euxitheus then counter-attacks and reiterates his charge that money was at the bottom of the prosecution (79).

He is far older than I: on the comparison of the ages of father and son (repeated in 79; see also 'forcing me to explain events which I am far too young to know of' in 75) as a factor in the dating of the speech see P. 24.

Noticeable in the introduction to the defence of the father is the balanced, antithetical style, here with etymological figure, homoeoteleuton and metabole in *tōn emōn pragmatōn/tōn ekeinōi pepragmenōn*.

If my accuser were on trial...But as it is (75)...: another 'hypothetical inversion'; see 38, If I had made away with...But as it is....

from hearsay: hearsay evidence was forbidden by law; see Bonner, *EAC*, 20.

75 explaining faultily his faultless conduct: in the Greek we have another instance of the *logos/ergon* antithesis; see 3, his accusers' words...the actual facts.

76 Before the Mytilenean revolt: in 428.

my father proved his devotion...by his actions: the argument from past services to the state is commonplace; cf. Ant. 2 *First Tetralogy* b12, 6 *Chor.* 11; And. 4 *Alc.* 41; Lys. 7 *Sac.Ol.* 30-31, 12 *Erat.* 20, 18 *Nicias' Brother* 21, 19 *Arist.* 57, 21 *Brib.Def.* 23, 25 *Def.Sub.Dem.* 12; Dem. 18 *Cor.* 257-267, 36 *For Phormion* 41 (where the opponent's lack of services is used against him; sim. Is. 5 *Dic.* 45). However, Euxitheus does not specify what his father's 'actions' were (the furnishing of choruses in 77 refers to Mytilenean festivals) and they perhaps consisted of little more than regular payment of taxes (again cf. 77).

failed in what you expected of it: Due 48 perceptively notes that in this section of the speech Euxitheus is careful to describe the revolt as an 'error' (cf. *hēmarte, sunexamartein* 76, *hamartia* 79, alsc *ouk estin...hēmartētai* 77), as this was a delicate matter for him to handle in an Athenian court. No doubt the prosecution described the revolt in rather stronger terms. But we may expand on Due's observation and note that there is a further idea of *joint* error (cf. *hē polis holē* 76 *bis*, 79 in antithesis with *idiai; sun-examartein*), emphasising how Euxitheus' father could in no way be represented as a leading figure in the revolt, but had by necessity moved with the crowd.

easy: *europōs* is elsewhere found in Anth. Pal. 9.543.5 and compare *palirropon gonu* in Eur. *El.* 492.

the ties: *enechura* are 'ties' rather than 'pledges', the only meaning given by *LSJ*.

77 you punished the authors of the revolt: for the punishment cf. Thuc. 3.50.1-3; Diod. 12.55.10; Cataldi 23-25: the leaders were executed, the walls of Mytilene rased, her fleet confiscated and the whole island, except for the territory of Methymna, divided into lots which were assigned to Athenian cleruchs.

granted the other Mytileneans an amnesty: it has been argued, as by Meritt 363-364 and Cataldi, that both Antiphon (in *tois d'allois...autōn*) and Thucydides (in 3.50.2) condense their narratives and confuse the provisions of the decree punishing the rebels with those of a subsequent treaty restoring the cleruchs' lots to their previous owners (IG i². 60, = Hicks & Hill 61; Tod 63; ATL ii. D22; Lactor 1 (3rd. ed., 1984) 169). On this theory, the cleruchs at first took over their lots and the previous owners worked the land as lessees, then the land was restored by this 'friendly' decree to the original owners, who subsequently paid the cleruchs a rent of two minae p.a. (the sum recorded by Thucydides as part of the original settlement). The cleruchs remained on the island as a garrison (Cataldi 27-28) and additionally received compensation for the lots of either money ('as Gomme, *HCT* 2, 330) or land (Meritt 364; how the land would have been divided both for the lots and after the restoration is another question; see Gomme, *id.*, 328; Cataldi 24). The theory is, indeed, attractive, but it is not without its difficulties. For instance, the two minae rent is only recorded for certain in Thucydides, the text of lines 13-15 of the decree (where Cataldi follows Tod in reading *duo mnas*) being very fragmentary. So we do not know for sure that this was the rent paid to the cleruchs after the restoration. Nor does *spheteran* ('their own') in Antiphon necessarily indicate, with Cataldi, that the Mytileneans were living on land which they owned (i.e. which had been restored) – rather, it may simply mean that they were not moved to other land. So while Antiphon almost certainly omits to mention the restoration decree when he says that Euxitheus' father 'furnishes choruses and pays his taxes' – for this implies normal, free conditions in the state – it is not so sure that we should take *adeian* as referring to this decree. Either way, Antiphon can hardly be censured for historical inaccuracy in this brief reflection on events in a legal speech.

It is open to question whether *edōkate* is an acceptable form of the aorist (regularly *edote*) in an orator as early as Antiphon; see Wyse 447-448.

my father: the repetition *tōi emōi patri* has been suspected but is defensible; see 21, on which the prosecution allege he met his end.

He has failed...pays his taxes: for the use of one's public services in argumentation see 76, my father proved his devotion...by his actions: and on these services in general see Bonner, *LL*, 101-102; MacDowell, *LCA*, 161-164. The furnishing of choruses was one of the main liturgies at Athens and provides the background to Antiphon's sixth speech. Here local choruses in Mytilene are meant and so Antiphon is indulging in zeugma when he says that Euxitheus' father had performed services for Athens (*humetera*), i.e. by paying the *telē* (n.b. the chiastic arrangement of thought). This payment was not a service but a tax, although it is unclear what these *telē* were precisely. Breuning 68 n. 2 saw them as the rent on the confiscated land, but this had by now been restored. Hence Meritt 367 takes them as rent on the restored land, while rejecting Wade-Gery's theory that the *eikostē* of Thuc. 7.28.4 may be meant (see Maidment, *MAO* I, 214 n. b; Maidment himself suggests harbour-dues). This impost, indeed, did not replace the tribute until 413, not only a late date for the speech, but also contrary to the implication here of continuous payments since the revolt. Finally, Cataldi 26 n.

39 suggests the *telē* are either taxation after the restoration or the supposed two minae rent. With the omission of the article before *chorēgias* and *telē* perhaps a general range of payments is to be understood rather than specific taxes, including rent to the cleruchs (though *telē* need not necessarily refer to this rent at all); but *telē* would seem to imply that the father was landed.

78 if his favourite haunt is Aenus: *chorophilei* indicates an extended residence, so 'who happened to be there at the time' in 20 may well be an understatement. From Euxitheus' words in this section we can also infer that his father's residence in Aenus was possibly caused by actual or feared sycophantic attacks on him. He may, however, have had business interests there (see 74, my father). The prosecution were presumably expected to assail the father for his absences from Mytilene, as revealing an anti-Athenian stance.

On *chorophilei* cf. Pollux 9.13; D.H. *Comp. Verb.* 6; Diog. Laert. 1.44; P.S. Breuning, 'De voce *chorophilein* apud Antiphontem oratorem', *Donum Natalicium Schrijnen* (Nijmegen & Utrecht, 1929) 656-659; 2, submit to the physical suffering. evading any of his public obligations: lit. 'withdrawing himself from any of the things towards the city'; for similar constructions cf. Dem. 13 *Organisation* 22; Thuc. 1.40.2; Soph. *OT* 1381. *polin* is ambiguous but perhaps refers to Mytilene rather than Athens.

like those others I see...under treaty: most scholars have felt the need for textual emendation here, on the grounds that

i) *tous men* requires a corresponding *tous de*;

ii) *sumbola* (inter-state judicial agreements) cannot have existed between enemy states.

Reiske long ago inserted *tous de* before *kai dikas*, thus contrasting those Lesbians who resisted passively by settling on the Asiatic coast with those who remained on the island and actively resisted by these lawsuits. His addition has found the most favour and was adopted by Thalheim, Maidment (see *MAO I*, 215 n. d) and Gauthier (1972) 165-166.

Three objections may be raised. On the linguistic side, H.G. Robertson, 'Note on Antiphon v. 78', *CP* 19 (1924) 368-369 noted other examples from Antiphon of *men* with no following *de* (cf. 37, 1 *Stepmother* 9, 2 *First Tetralogy* d4, 4 *Third Tetralogy* a1, 6 *Chor.* 14). Secondly, a reference to those remaining on Lesbos does not logically follow from 'or has become the citizen of another city, like those others I see', upon which the three participles depend (unless they moved to Methymna). This is not conclusive, but it does lead one to consider whether the text as it stands is defensible and is thus a most forceful tricolon. So to the third objection, that the passage does not, in fact, have to be taken as referring to suits between members of enemy states, which would indeed seem out of the question. For Antiphon might well label as hostile (with some rhetorical exaggeration) a state or states on the Asia Minor continent which had a strong anti-Athenian party but which were still, or once again, within the Athenian alliance. These states would be ones in which Lesbian exiles had settled after the revolt and which had perhaps rebelled themselves, as Antandrus (cf. Thuc. 4.52). After the fall of Antandrus armed resistance may have ceased, but the struggle against Athens was continued by means of these lawsuits. Hence no emendation is necessary. (Breuning took these words as reflecting events in 424 before the fall of Antandrus, but this is probably too early a date for the speech; see P. 24.)

nor does it mean...informers: completing the tricolon *ouk...oud'...oude*. We might have expected the positive clause to have been connected with *alla*, not *de*, but see sim. 5; Thuc. 4.86.1; Kühner-Gerth 2, 262.

On *plēthos* see 8, Not on the chance of eluding the judgment of your court. The father's avoidance of the sycophants by extended absence from Mytilene was by no means unique; see Lofberg 23-24, 70-71; Bonner & Smith, *AJHA* 2, 247 n. 3. It is thus conceivable that, with the chance of attacking the father gone, the sycophants directed their assault on the son, and this statement may be seen as a variation on the commonplace charge of sycophantic intent in one's adversary (see 59, that you are attempting to secure my death for money).

79 the act which he joined his whole city in committing: on this and on 'the mistake' below see 76, failed in what you expected of it.

They exchanged great prosperity for great misery: the et. fig. and emotive vocabulary in the Greek help achieve pathos, on which see 18, heading n. For *aeimnēstos, eudaimonias* and *kakodaimonian* see 2, submit to the physical suffering.

saw their country ruined: compare similar uses of *anastatos* in And. 1 *Myst.* 108; Hdt. 7.220.3; Thuc. 8.24.3. Taken literally this is something of an exaggeration, since only the walls of Mytilene were in fact pulled down (Thuc. 3.50.1); see Gomme, *HCT* 2, 328.

this whole intrigue...for the sake of money: see 59, that you are attempting to secure my death for money. The attack is heightened by the pi alliteration and the use of *paraskeuē*, on which see Wyse 375.

Many, indeed, are the circumstances...: a general remark, but perhaps reflecting how speculators may have laid their hands on the property of the executed and exiled Mytilenean oligarchs.

My father is too old...I am far too young: for the comparison of ages see 74, He is far older than I.

80 You must help me...: for the commonplace principle of collective advantage for litigants and judges in the decisions of the latter cf. 85, 96, 6 *Chor.* 3; And. 1 *Myst.* 105; Lys. 14 *Alc.* A. 12. The reference to informers is no doubt aimed at the prosecution.

your court: see 8, Not on the chance of eluding the judgment of your court.

116

scoundrels: *ponēros* is frequently used in connection with sycophants, as in Lys. 7 *Sac.Ol.* 1; 12 *Erat.* 5; Aesch. 2 *Fals.Leg.* 99; Dem. 25 *Aristog. i* 45, 58 *Theoc.* 27. A reputation for losing would lessen the sycophant's chances of success; see Lofberg 94.

81-84   The 'signs from heaven'. The idea that pollution (*miasma*) reveals itself in voyages and religious ceremonies, and affects not only the defiled person but also those around him, is a *topos* very familiar from tragedy (see especially Aeschyl. *Seven* 597-614, also *Ag.* 397-398; Soph. *OT* 236-243; Eur. *El.* 1355, *HF* 1225, 1294-98), but common throughout ancient literature (cf. *Ant.* 2 *First Tetralogy* a10; Aesch. 2 *Fals.Leg.* 158; Xen. *Cyr.*8.1.25; Plato, *Laws* 9.866a; Theophrast. *Charact.* 25; Callim. *Hymn* 6.116-117; Dioq. Laert. 1.86; Cic. *de Nat. Deorum* 3.37; Hor. *Od.* 3.2.26-7 , and the story of Jonah in the Old Testament); see Glotz 228-231; MacDowell, *AHL*, 2-5. Antiphon employs the *topos* as an *atechnos pistis* for Euxitheus' innocence and a similar argument occurs in And. 1 *Myst.* 137-139 (cf. [Lys.] 6 *Andoc.* 19). But although supernatural signs were regarded as highly important in state affairs (as 81) this particular presumptive argument of divine favour must have been well-worn by Antiphon's day (and it does not appear in fourth century speeches). In this respect it is perhaps significant that neither Antiphon nor Andocides includes it in the main body of the proof – it seems the very last argument Antiphon can raise in support of Euxitheus. Nevertheless, it *is* still being used in court in the last quarter of the fifth century, which, along with the agitation over the mutilation of the Hermae, shows that the average Athenian at this time was no rationalist (as Maidment notes, *MAO I*, 218 n. a; cf. also Lys. 12 *Erat.* 59).

It is doubtful, finally, whether this argument reveals any deep religious feeling on the part of Antiphon himself, as Jebb sensed, *AO I*, 39-43 (comparing 2 *First Tetralogy* a10, 3 *Second Tetralogy* c8 and especially the opening of the *Third Tetralogy*). The Aeschylean tone of 82-83 may well, with Jebb, indicate his sympathies for the old democracy. But the religious scepticism of the time is reflected in Thucydides (as 2.54), with whom Antiphon was closely connected (in the tradition as his teacher; see P. 21). So did Antiphon hold similar views to the historian over the old religion? These would not have prevented him from including such a religious argument in the speech, for a logographer wrote what he thought the jury wanted to hear rather than what he believed himself; see further Dobson 33-34; Erbse (1977) 218.

81   you depend chiefly on these for your safe conduct of state affairs: coming from the mouth of a Mytilenean these words probably indicate that the Sicilian disaster and Ionian revolt had not yet occurred (as Blass, *AB I*, 178 with n. 3) and hence provide a *terminus ante quem* for the speech.

117

both those involving danger and those that do not: in Latin *res bellicae* and *res civiles* respectively.

82 have embarked on ship...in their own destruction: reminiscent of Aeschyl. *Seven* 602-604 (Aeschylus has *xuneisbas*), with the poetic *psuchē*.

Others have escaped death: the anacolouthon in this clause, with *heterous* and the participles depending on the idea of knowing to be supplied from *epistasthai* above, may be seen as reflecting that this second example is only a variation on the first – when we come to the third, different example the original construction after *hoti* is resumed.

because they prevented the proper performance of the rites: thus the pollution the Spartans incurred by their killing of Persian heralds prevented favourable sacrifices until the wrath of Talthybius had been appeased; cf. Hdt. 7.134.

84 Most of 84 reappears, with alterations in part due to the context, in 6 *Chor.* 28, while the last sentence recurs in 6.47. The main *topos* takes the form of a 'hypothetical inversion', on which see 38, If I had made away with...But as it is....

the witnesses are testifying: helping to give the speech an extemporaneous character; see 13, You reply.

Other men...by statements: another instance of the contrast between usual behaviour and what happened in this case (see 34, doing the exact opposite of what other men do), though in the form of a *topos* (that of the greater importance of facts than words; cf. Ant. 3 *Second Tetralogy* c3-4, d9, 6 *Chor.* 28-32; Lys. 7 *Sac.Ol.* 30, 12 *Erat.* 33; Gorg. *Pal.* 34). For the *logos/ergon* antithesis see 3, his accusers' words...the actual facts. Note also the antimetabolē, on which see 14, Hence you must not...interpretation of the case.

85-96 EPILOGUE(*epilogos*): The epilogue is remarkable both for its length (see 1-7, heading n.) and for its logical argument and lack of pathos (see 73, Be assured that I deserve pity). Due 49-50 makes the valid point that the argumentation of the epilogue presupposes that of the *prokataskeuē*, and to the end Antiphon maintains the plea that the wrong process had been used and Euxitheus should therefore be found not guilty and retried.

85 I have answered...: again the extemporaneous character (see 13, You reply).

this same verdict...with your oath: for the idea of joint interest see 80, You must help me....

You have sworn...according to the laws: on the heliastic oath see 8, even if you were not on oath.

the laws under which I was arrested: those concerning *kakourgia*. As with *hoi apagontes* in 38 *apēchthēn* is not to be taken as signifying that the case was one of *apagōgē*; it rather refers to the arrest which followed the *endeixis* (see 9, this arrest).

can still be tried legally: on the question of a retrial (requested in 90, 94, 96) see 16, heading n.
impartial ministers of justice: a striking phrase, serving well as a *captatio benevolentiae* and adapted by Thucydides to *kritai de ontes apo tou isou* (3.37.4).

86 Give a chance to time also: for the temporal *topos* see 14, time and experience show mankind what is imperfect. In 86-90 Antiphon argues that the truth can only be discovered and the correct judgment can only be made if the jurors take their time. He begins by contrasting the law, which prescribes one final trial, with his own concept of justice, that it may, in such cases as Euxitheus', only be done if the trial be repeated. This prepares the way for the *topos* in 87 over the *dikē phonou*, the supreme example of the dangers of a single trial since the defendant's life is at stake: yet even in a *dikē phonou* the wrong decision might be made (though no one had ever proved this according to Dem. 23 *Aristoc*. 66). But at least the proceedings in the court of the Areopagus were carefully devised to minimise the margin of error (88) and this is the whole point of the inclusion of the *topos*: Euxitheus was being tried for homicide but without the safeguards of a regular homicide trial. Antiphon therefore asks for a retrial (90), which would enable the jurors to take their time in their verdict, avoid error and judge Euxitheus under the proper rules of the *dikē phonou*.
     As to the construction here cf. Hor. *Sat*. 2.2.94, *das aliquid famae*.
I would have thought it right: *ēxioun*, like *eboulomēn* in 1; see I could have wished...But as it is....
the ally of the truth...: for the metaphor in this clause see 37, whom the truth of his second statement defended.

87 87-89 recur in 6 *Chor*. 3-6 (after the *topos* of 6.2, = 5.14). The linguistic differences between the two passages seem to go against the idea of mere interpolation from one speech into the other and the *topos* is in any case well-suited to our speech; see 86, Give a chance to time also.
If you condemn me: Euxitheus was not, of course, being tried under a *dikē phonou*, but this is no reason to suspect the authenticity of the passage: we merely have an example of how *topoi* might not be fully suited to every context. Alternatively, Euxitheus may be taken as assuming his acquittal now and asserting that he will obey the judges' verdict in a regular homicide trial.
to disregard the sentence passed upon him: not by going into voluntary exile (as Maidment, *MAO* I, 223 n. b) since this was a citizen's right and he would not have to 'dare' to disregard the sentence – on the contrary, if he felt he was going to be condemned this was precisely the course open to him. Rather, we should take this as referring to fleeing after the sentence had been passed (as Socrates' friends urged him to do). In the

Choreutes (where the homicide was *akousios*) the reference is to the refusal to go into exile as a punishment for unintentional homicide (on which see MacDowell, *AH L*, 117-125) and again the *topos* is more fitting there. The implication of the second *oute* clause, brought out in the *Choreutes*, is that a guilty man would also obey the law and admit his crime since not to do so would bring the wrath of the gods upon him. There an example is adduced, that of a master who has killed his slave and must purify himself even if the slave has no one to avenge him: *kan mē ho timōrēsōn ēi* is perfectly comprehensible, therefore, in 6.5, but *allōs te kai...timōrēsōn* in 5.87 seems a somewhat sudden addition.

He must submit to the verdict: for a similar expression cf. Isoc. 1 *Dem.* 26, but the use of the genitive with this verb is mainly poetical; see Kühner-Gerth I, 392 n. 8. After *tēs* most editors add *te* (as in 6 *Chor.* 5, not a fully convincing comparison in view of the many differences between the two passages), but for single *te* see 18, by reason of that bodily suffering....

88   the oaths: see 11, the greatest and most binding oath known.

the sacrifices: lit. 'the cut-pieces' of the sacrifice, on which see 12, with hand laid upon the sacrifice.

the proclamations: on these *prorrēseis* see MacDowell, *AH L*, 23-27, *LCA*, 111-113; M. Piérart, 'Note sur la "prorrhesis" en droit attique', *L'Ant. Class*. 42 (1973) 427-435.

everything else: such as the three *prodikasiai*, on which cf. Ant. 6 *Chor.* 42; MacDowell, *AH L*, 34-37.

are very different: thus the oath was 'the greatest and most binding known' (11) and other cases would be preceded by an *anakrisis* rather than by *prodikasiai*.

supreme importance: we might remember, however, that due to its being a matter for the family of the victim to handle homicide was not considered by the state the *most* heinous of crimes; see Bonner & Smith, *AJHA* 2, 207. Nevertheless, Antiphon heightens the importance of the homicide laws with *te...kai...kai...kai...kai...* and *peri pleistou*.

vengeance: see 10, a murderer shall pay with his life in requital.

a mistake and sinful error against the gods and the laws: cf. 91, 2 *First Tetralogy* b11, 4 *Third Tetralogy* b8. An accused will naturally try to impress upon the judges their responsibility for his wrongful condemnation (cf. 89). A prosecutor, on the other hand, will claim that the punishment for a wrongful condemnation will fall on him alone; cf. 2 *First Tetralogy* a3, 4 *Third Tetralogy* a4. Note also that a wrongful acquittal is only a *hamartēma*, not an *asebēma* (91; but cf. 2 *First Tetralogy* c10, 3 *Second Tetralogy* c11); and that wrongful killing by hand and by vote amount to the same thing (92).

For i) the idea of killing as a joint error against the gods and human law cf. 3 *Second Tetralogy* c12, 4 *Third Tetralogy* a2; ii) the conjunction of the divine and human in general cf. 7, 1

120

Stepmother 25, 3 *Second Tetralogy* b12, 4 *Third Tetralogy* b2, b7, d9. Every human law, indeed, 'is an invention and gift of the gods' (Dem. 25 *Aristog. i* 16).

Note, finally, the neat chiasmus here, *hamartia* referring to the laws, *asebeia* to the gods (sim. 1 *Stepmother* 25).

89 Nor is it the same...a wrongful verdict: cf. Gorg. *Pal.* 36.

The charge...is not in itself effective: lit. 'does not have end'; for this use of *telos* cf. esp. Gorg. *Pal.* 36, also Dem. 18 *Cor.* 193; Thuc. 4.118.10 with schol.; and in verse Hom. *Il.* 16.630; Hes. *Works* 669; Semonid. 1.1; Soph. *OC* 422; Eur. *Or.* 1545. On *aitiasis* see 25, For the moment...they could make.

but depends on you and your judgment: serving to impress the jurors with their own importance and hence a *captatio benevolentiae*.

there is no higher authority to which you can refer this: for a similar construction cf. Eur. *Ion* 253.

90 the customary oath: again the *diōmosia*, as also in 96.

you will be my judges in the other court too: in the *dikē phonou* envisaged the jury would consist of ex-archons sitting in the court of the Areopagus, hence *humeis* means 'you Athenians' (sim. 87, 96). Of course, our speaker was also a foreigner, but this was in any case a common form of address to a heliastic jury as representing the whole people; cf. 46; And. 1 *Myst.* 7 (with MacDowell); Lys. 13 *Agor.* 10; Is. 4 *Nic.* 17 (with Wyse); Dem. 43 *Macart.* 72, 47 *Euerg.* 73; also Ar. *Wasps* 917 (with MacDowell). Compare the use of *plēthos* in 8. This does not, therefore, indicate that the second trial would have been held before a heliastic jury (wrongly Hansen, *AEE*, 124 n. 16) or, more specifically, before a heliastic jury at the Palladium (as Smith 357-358): the statement is rather designed to avoid giving the impression that Euxitheus felt he would receive a fairer hearing before the Areopagus than before a heliastic jury.

91 to acquit me unjustly...contrary to justice: for this concept cf. 4 *Third Tetralogy* b8, d9. The sentence is remarkable for its paronomasia, in *adikōs apolusai/ mē dikaiōs apolesai* and *hamartēma/asebēma* below.

you must exercise the greatest caution: the thought that judicial error is avoided by *pronoia* is a variation on, and recalls that of 71-73 and 86, where the importance of taking one's time is emphasised. Such caution over an irreversible decision also helps avoid later regret should one change one's mind, and this second theme is resumed in 94 – an acquittal now enables future regret to be remedied, but a condemnation is final. See further on regret 2 *First Tetralogy* d12; and with 91 and 2d12 compare Gorg. *Pal.* 34, where *anēkesta, akestōi, pronoēsasi* (*pronoian* Antiphon) and *metanoēsasi* all appear (n.b. also Democr. frg. 66 Diels).

irremediable: *anēkeston* is a metaphor from medicine, which is continued below by *akestōi* and *anēkestois* and resumed in 94 by

pharmakon and *iasis*. See similar metaphor in 2 *First Tetralogy* b13, d12, 4 *Third Tetralogy* c7; Aeschyl. *Cho.* 699, *Prom.* 378, frgg. 73.6 (Mette, suppl.), 255.2-3 (Nauck); Soph. frgg. 198, 636 (Nauck). Further on Antiphon's metaphor see 37, whom the truth of his second statement defended.
remediable: *akestos* is a rare word which Dover, *CAS*, 47 lists as poetic (cf. Hom. *Il.* 13.115) and as not occurring elsewhere in prose - but cf. Hippoc. *Art.* 58; Gorg. *Pal.* 34; Plut. *Ages.* 28.4; further Hesych. s.v. *akestai*; Bekk. *An.* I, 202, line 18.
through giving way to anger or through believing a false accusation: again recalling 71; see without anger and without prejudice.
Some of you have in fact repented before now...: seemingly another allusion to the Mytilenean affair, in which Cleon's proposal of a massacre was carried and then rescinded. If so, 'those who had misled you' below may be directed against Cleon and his party (whether or not the speech was delivered before his death in 422), to whose policies the oligarch Antiphon was deeply opposed, especially with regard to the allies. On the other hand, Gernet 134 n. 2 sees in this a reference to sycophants, who could be prosecuted under the procedure *probolē* (cf. [Arist.] *Ath.Pol.* 43.5). However, the earliest known example of this is the much later charge against Callixenus and the others who attacked the Arginousae generals (Xen. *Hell.* 1.7.35; Harrison, *LA* 2, 61) and so Gernet is forced to conclude that this is perhaps a *desideratum* of Antiphon's.

Speakers naturally often refer to and complain about juries' unjust verdicts induced by litigant's deceptions; cf. And. 2 *Return* 27; Is. 5 *Dic.* 8; Dem. 45 *Steph. i* 7, 46 *Steph. ii* 9. Euxitheus is careful to emphasise that the jurors were misled (*exapatētheisi*), thus avoiding any suspicion of prejudice against the heliastic court by comparison with the Areopagus.

92 involuntary mistakes are excusable...: sim. 4 *Third Tetralogy* a6; Arist. *EN* 3.1; see also Ant. 1 *Stepmother* 27; Lys. 31 *Phil.* 10-11. In line with this thought the penalty for unintentional homicide was less severe than that for intentional killing.
An involuntary mistake...choice: the Greek construction recalls that of 5. As we have seen, *tuchē* is elsewhere in the speech contrasted with *pronoia* (6, 21); and for the *tuchē/gnōmē* antithesis in the orators cf. And. 1 *Myst.* 140; Lys. 34 *Subv. Const.* 2; Isoc. 2 *Nic.* 30, 3 *Cypr.* 47.
the wrongful taking of life by one's vote...: once more impressing on the jurors the importance of their decision.

93 Be assured...on my conscience: sim. [Lys.] 20 *Polystr.* 22; and further on conscience cf. Ant. 6 *Chor.* 1; Gorg. *Pal.* 5. A variation of the *topos* was that the guilty flee the places dangerous to them and avoid trial, so those who willingly submit to a trial must be innocent; cf. And. 1 *Myst.* 3; [Lys.] 20 *Polystr.* 21; Aesch. 2 *Fals.Leg.* 6. But the opposite was also

argued, that wrongdoers would dare anything (cf. Lys. 12 *Erat.*
84; further *id.* 26 *Euand.* 1); and Lycurgus demolishes the *topos*
(1 *Leocr.* 90). Euxitheus, then, employs a commonplace argument
here, but in 13 he contends from a practical/legal point of view
that he came to Athens voluntarily and hence would not have
defaulted if allowed his freedom before the trial.

As it is...: the construction is interrupted by a long parenthesis
beginning at *en gar* and is resumed by *egō d'emautōi* (recalling
the anacolouthon in 11–12); further on parenthesis see 4, for it is
reasonable to assume that....

to aid: for the metaphor in *sunagōnizesthai*, also with *polemion*
below, see 37, whom the truth of his second statement defended.

The combination *mēden...mēt'...* is rare in prose but is
defensible in Antiphon, whose style often has a poetical tinge (as
in the personification of *psuchē* below, for which cf. also 4 *Third
Tetralogy* a7; Isoc. 15 *Ant.* 189; Dem. 18 *Cor.* 309).

come to its aid: *sunexesōsen* is a rare double-compound; cf.
Soph. *OC* 566; Arrian, *Anab.* 6.30.2. 93 is noticeable for its
compound vocabulary, as *talaipōrein* (see 2, submit to the
physical suffering) and the rare *proapoleipei* (cf. Hippoc. *Mul.*
1.59; [Arist.] *Rhet. ad Alex.* 30.6; Arist. *Mete.* 1.14 (= 352
b11), *HA* 9.7; Plut. *Mor.* 789d, 1078f; Paus. 2.1.5). The latter is
similarly used intransitively in Plut. *Mor.* 558c (sim. *apoleipei* in
Isoc. 1 *Dem.* 19). In contrast to this passage compare the jocular
Ar. *Birds* 1556–64 (with *proulipe*).

94   For on the one hand...: repeating the request for a retrial in 85
and 90, and resuming the thought and medical metaphor of 91.
For *iasis* in connection with a wrong see also Arist. *Rhet.*
1.14.2.

before you will do lawfully...: the effect of the et. fig.
(*nomimōs/paranomōs*) is greatly enhanced by the pi alliteration.

This is not a matter for haste...: a weighty antithesis, recalling
the thought of 71–73.

learn the facts...form an opinion: more striking antithesis,
formed by periphrasis with nouns in -*tēs* (see 1, I could have
wished...But as it is...). Note also the rare vocabulary in
gnōristai (cf. 4 *Kings* 23.24) and *doxastai* (cf. Plato, *Tht.* 208e;
Antisthenes, *Ajax* 8; Sext. Emp. *adv. Dogmat.* 1.157; Hesych.
s.v.; also Bekk. *An.* 1, 242, lines 19–22, where the name
doxastēs is erroneously given to certain officers concerned with
oaths – see Harrison, *LA* 2, 99 n. 2); see further 10, a murderer
shall pay with his life in requital.

94   It is easy...capital charge: but the procedure in a *dikē phonou*,
with the evidence being given under a solemn oath, was designed
to prevent just such false evidence. Therefore no reopening of
the case on the ground of false evidence was allowed (*dikē
anadikos*; see Harrison, *LA* 2, 196) and Antiphon's argument
that 'not even his friends will still be willing to seek requital for
him once he is dead' would not legally apply in a regular homicide

123

trial. The redress available in other cases to a man's friends when false evidence was alleged would take the form of a *dikē pseudomarturiōn* (Harrison, *id.*, 192–197). There was, however, a *topos*, reflected in 'and even if they are willing what good will it be to the dead man?', that in cases carrying the death penalty such redress was too late to be of help to the victim of false witness (cf. And. 1 *Myst.* 7; Lys. 19 *Arist.* 4; cf. also *id.* 12 *Erat.* 88); and Antiphon is attempting here (as throughout the epilogue) to impress upon the jurors the gravity of their position.

96 **and in the trial for murder**: to the last Euxitheus maintains his request for acquittal in the present trial on the understanding that he will readily face a regular *dikē phonou*. So there is no real attempt to arouse pity even at the very end of the speech, despite *deomai* below.

you shall decide: see 90, **you will be my judges in the other court too.**

neither asking you...: it was in line with the judges' duty towards the gods to acquit Euxitheus because in the heliastic oath they swore to judge according to the laws (85) – and this they were not, in his view, doing at present. Euxitheus for his part had a right to ask for acquittal because he was not being tried according to the law on homicide. On the theme of joint interest see 80, **You must help me....**

Lysias

Contemporary sources, even the autobiographical speech *Against Eratosthenes*, furnish little information about Lysias' life. In that speech he says that his father Cephalus, who reappears as the aged host in Plato's *Republic*, 'was persuaded by Pericles' to move to Athens, where he lived for thirty years (4). Later biographical sources state that Cephalus was a Syracusan, and that Lysias was born at Athens and went to Thurii in South Italy at the age of fifteen (D.H. *Lys*.1; [Plut.] *Vit.X.Or*.835c-d). Stripped of the inferences to which they were prone, the accounts of the biographers yield only these bare facts; but they allow certain approximations to be deduced.

If Dionysius' statement *koinōnēsōn tēs apoikias* (*Lys*.1) is taken to mean that Lysias was present at the founding of the colony of Thurii in 444/3 B.C., the date of his birth is fixed at 459/8. This is the date accepted by most subsequent authorities, and it has been defended in recent times (See Schindel 1967). But its acceptance entails serious difficulties when confronted with other evidence. Lysias would have written his last extant speech (26, probable date 382 B.C.) at the age of 76/77, and most of his speeches between the ages of 54 and 76. More serious difficulties are presented by the speech *Against Neaira*, which is in the Demosthenic corpus and was made c. 343-340 B.C. In it Lysias' mother is described as still alive in 380 (22), while Lysias himself is keeping a young mistress, Metaneira. Imagination may perhaps be stretched to accommodate one or even two of these improbabilities, but it is more natural to consider whether the solution to the problem lies in a later date for Lysias' birth. To a historian like Dionysius, consideration of a period of Mediterranean history brought certain events to the forefront of his mind. Of such events surely the foundation of Thurii as a pan-Hellenic colony was one of the most important. His statement that Lysias went there in its foundation-year may be due purely to a desire to attach a known year to this important event in Lysias' life. The confused state of our information is made worse by [Plut.] *Vit.X.Or*. 835c, that Cephalus had died before this time. If he did, after living in Athens for thirty years, he must have arrived there around 474, and it is difficult to see Pericles as an effective sponsor at this early stage of his career. A later dating along the lines suggested by Dover (*LCL*,42) therefore seems desirable. He suggests that Lysias went to Thurii around 430/29, either to avoid the plague or for some reason connected with the family's status as foreigners at a sensitive time. This would make 445 or 444 the year of his birth. Much later than this would draw him too close to the birth-year of

Isocrates (436), thereby violating the tradition that he was an established literary figure when Isocrates was only 18 (Plato,*Phaedr*.278e – 279a).

Lysias may have returned to Athens at any time between about 422 and 412, after living in Thurii long enough to be instructed by the rhetorician Tisias, to come of age and acquire citizen– and property-rights there (*Vit.X.Or*.835d). He also needed time to build up the family's shield-making business in the Piraeus to the impressive size it had reached by the end of the Peloponnesian War, so the earlier of those two dates is perhaps to be preferred (so Dover,*LCL*,43 for political reasons and because it permits a dramatic date of 418-416 for Plato *Phaedrus*). The most important facts about this stage of Lysias' career are that the family's shield factory made them wealthy enough to perform all their civic duties by 404 (*Ag.Erat*.20), that the family property was valued at 70 talents at this time (P.Oxy.13,1606,I.30), and that this caused Lysias to be described as 'the richest of the metics' (id.I.153-4). It also caused the ruin of Lysias and the murder of his brother Polemarchus that followed the usurpation of power by the Thirty Tyrants. They needed money to pay for the Spartan garrison which propped up their regime, and rich metics (resident aliens) were their easiest victims because xenophobia was rife in the defeated city. Lysias himself describes what happened (*Ag.Erat*.6-20). The Thirty confiscated most of their property, including 700 shields and 120 slaves. On hearing of Polemarchus' death, Lysias fled to Megara.

When the democrats under Thrasybulus returned, Lysias aided them with a gift of 2000 drachmae, 200 shields and pay for 300 mercenaries (P.Oxy.13,1606,I.163-171). Grateful to him and to other foreigners who had supported the democratic cause, Thrasybulus proposed that they should be granted citizenship, and a decree to that effect was passed by the Assembly. But its revocation was secured by Archinus, a moderate politician whose motives were probably constitutional rather than personal, but whose apparent political association with Theramenes has caused much speculation (see Cloche,*RDA*, 319; Loening (1981); Lateiner (1971) 45ff). Lysias' disappointment may have been acute, but it was probably short-lived, since he decided to live out the rest of his life in Athens, earning his living as a writer of speeches for the law-courts and, to a lesser extent, of other forms of oratory, in the process of which he acquired an enviable literary reputation. His political status during this period was one of equality with Athenian citizens except for the vote and eligibility for state office (*isoteleia*) (See Loening 283-4). He lived beyond 380, but since the ancient biographers base their calculation of his age at death on a birth year of 459 or 458, their estimate of an age of 76 – 83 (D.H.*Lys*.12;[Plut.] *Vit.X.Or*. 836a) may be too high unless Lysias lived for some time after writing his last extant speech.

The hazards of searching for political affinities in the speeches of Lysias have been well demonstrated by Dover (*LCL*, 47-56). His family background, particularly the friendship of his father Cephalus with Pericles and his own support for the restored democracy, seem to provide clear indications. It might further be supposed that he would have regarded democratic politicians as potentially more favourable than oligarchs to the extension of Athenian citizenship, which would benefit himself and his family. Fragments of two of his speeches opposing exclusive measures against foreigners after the restoration, *Against Phormisius* and *Against Theozotides*, appear to affirm his support for a liberal approach to the question of citizenship and rewards for aliens who supported the democracy. But all this is hardly surprising in view of his own circumstances. A genuine ideological adherence to democracy is much less easy to isolate and identify in his speeches. In the first place, his choice of clients shows no bias in favour of those with democratic sympathies, and the fact that many of these were wealthy property-owners (see Lateiner 76) suggests that some, at least, were probably less than ardent supporters of popular government, whatever words Lysias has put in their mouths. For the speechwriter the only ineligible litigants were those who were unable to pay and those whose known views were so extreme that they were impossible to characterise convincingly without losing the case. These considerations as well as his own views prevented Lysias from accepting clients from among close associates of the Thirty and others who had injured the democracy. The main sentiments that emerge from the more political speeches are those of reconciliation and the admission to state offices of the ablest men, excepting only those of extreme views; and the abomination of all who make slanderous allegations against innocent men for personal gain. Clients in less political cases tend to lack strong political colouring, and Lysias did not actively propound democratic ideas independently of the cases he was pleading. His personal associations were with the wealthy and the moderately wealthy rather than with the poorer citizens who formed the backbone of the democratic electorate; and as a well-known literary figure he drew his readership mainly from the upper, literate classes. But as a foreigner in a city which had recently undergone traumatic upheavals, he served his own interests by continuing to support democracy, while quietly counselling moderation. It is this position, pragmatic and rational, that is broadly reflected in his oratory. To it may be added the intelligence which enabled him to gauge the shifting prejudices of jurors and to play on them.

The corpus of Lysianic speeches that has survived to modern times contains 35 speeches, of which only 23 are complete and several may be spurious (see Usher & Najock (1982): the strongest candidates are marked with asterisks(*) in the list below). There are also shorter fragments and notices of over fifty other speeches (see the Budé *Lysias*,Vol.2). All three of the Aristotelian oratorical forms – deliberative, forensic and epideictic (display or ceremonial) – are represented, but the great majority are forensic. Apart from the present selection, the most important are as follows (Oxford text numbering):

3. Defence against Simon.
7. Defence concerning the Sacred Olive.
13. Against Agoratus.
14. Against Alcibiades.
19. On the Estate of Aristophanes.
21. Defence against a charge of taking bribes.
30. Against Nicomachus.
31. Against Philon.
32. Against Diogeiton.
34. On the Constitution.

The titles of the remaining speeches are as follows:

2. Funeral Speech*.
4. Defence against a charge of malicious wounding.
5. For Callias.
6. Against Andocides*.
8. Reply to Associates, following Slander*.
9. For the Soldier.
11. Against Theomnestus B (an epitomised version of 10)*.
15. Against Alcibiades (relationship to 14 uncertain).
17. On the Property of Eraton.
18. For the Brother of Nicias.
20. For Polystratus*.
23. Against Pancleon*.
26. Against Euandros.
27. Against Epicrates.
28. Against Ergocles.
29. Against Philocrates.
33. Olympic Oration.
35. Eroticus.

Of the second list of speeches, 2, 6 and 20 are important historical documents, and 2 is of considerable literary merit as an example of epideictic oratory. But the weight of evidence is against their authenticity as works of Lysias.

Lysias' literary reputation both in his own time (see Plato *Phaedrus, passim*) and, to an even greater extent, in later antiquity was higher than that of Antiphon. He was regarded both as a pioneer and as an all-rounder in the new genre, and the esteem in which he was held was reflected in the large number of speeches published under his name and catalogued by librarians. In the first century B.C. Dionysius and Caecilius of Caleacte knew of 425, but pronounced only 233 genuine. He was widely read, quoted, plagiarised and imitated. In literary circles, after controversy over the virtues of style had polarised into the opposing factions of Atticism and Asianism, Lysias was made the model of Attic style. His admirers called attention to the purity and lucidity of his language, achieved by the use of current, not poetic vocabulary. They found his style vivid, persuasive and invested with a certain indefinable charm (*charis*) (D.H.*Lys*.10). These qualities fitted him for another part in the critic's scheme: they made him the model of the Plain Style (the other two styles being the Middle and the Grand). This choice has had a not wholly salutary influence on modern criticism, which has too frequently been content to endorse the ancient judgment without reference to the context in which it was reached. Much ancient criticism was concerned with identifying models for imitation, and for this reason was much given to comparison of authors and generalised opinions. As a result of this preoccupation, Lysias was found to be plain and simple when compared with Isocrates, who perfected the smooth, complex period, with its high concentration of parallelism, antithesis and subordination of clauses; and lacking in emotion when compared with the most colourful, stirring and brilliant of the Greek orators, Demosthenes. Such comparisons do less than full justice to Lysias' versatility and range of expression. The speeches contain many elaborately constructed periods, and in certain speeches the average length of sentences is higher than the Isocratean average (18,26,33,35). There are high concentrations of rhetorical devices in certain passages and in certain speeches (e.g. hyperbaton in 24, rhetorical question in 10,24,31,34, hypostasis in 3,16,30, Gorgianic figures in 13,31). In some speeches Lysias appears to make a special effort to avoid hiatus (e.g. 16), while in others passages may be found in which rhythmic effects have been sought (e.g. 3). Even the critic's claim that Lysias used only current words (*kuria onomata*) (D.H.*Lys*.3) needs qualification (see Blass, *AB* 1, 408-9), although in general it stands examination. Turning to subject-matter, it has been shown that Lysias' argumentation and his approach to legal problems can have great subtlety (Bateman 1958 and 1962), and it seems certain that Isaeus and his pupil Demosthenes could not have developed their techniques of argument if Lysias had not laid the foundations of these in his more difficult cases.

Two qualities, one of style, the other of content, deserve special notice. The stylistic quality may best be described as a certain looseness of structure which may leave antitheses uncompleted or the logical or grammatical sequences interrupted. Müller counted 43 examples of *men solitarium* (*men* not followed by *de*), and listed several passages containing *anacolouthon* or imprecise antithesis. Blass also remarks on this characteristic (*AB* 1, 418), noting that it occurs especially in narrative, and where the orator becomes involved in direct argument with his opponent. It undoubtedly contributes to the impression of natural artlessness.

The other quality concerns Lysias' presentation of character, mainly of his clients but occasionally of their opponents. There is room for argument as to what ancient critics meant when they used the word *ēthopoiia* and whether it accurately describes what Lysias actually did (see Usher 1965). For the present it is sufficient to point out that characterisation in Lysias rises far above the general moral tone which satisfied the critics' demands, and in some cases, notably those of Euphiletus in 1 and Mantitheus in 16, carries individualisation to the exent of admitting venial flaws of character which give the client a sympathetic human face and add to his credibility.

In his handling of the different parts of the speech Lysias set the standards which later orators were to follow. The great variety of material in his introductions shows the care he took to prepare his juries in the precise manner that each case required. He is the first orator to realise the full potential of narrative as a persuasive medium through which to present evidence clearly, characterise his client or opponent and, by means of stylistic techniques such as the use of historic tenses, to involve the jury in his story and carry them along with him, 'smuggling conviction unnoticed past the listener's senses' (D.H.*Lys*.18). In his proofs, Lysias uses probability-arguments with great skill, often pressing them vehemently, and linking them closely to the facts to which he has given prominence in the narrative and reinforcing them with examples and generalisations about human behaviour. The end of the proof section often has a tone of high moral indignation or conviction. The conclusions of his speeches are mostly brief, quiet and dignified, and sometimes contain solemn adjurations to the jury couched in striking language. With the speeches of Lysias the pattern of classical Attic oratory is set.

SIGLA

```
X = cod. Palatinus 88
    X¹ = scriptura ante correcturam factam
    Xᶜ = scriptura correctura illata
    Xᶜ(1) = scriptura correctura manus primae illata
    Xʳ = scriptura correctura manus recentioris illata
    Xˢ = scriptura manu prima suprascripta
C = cod. Laurentianus lvii, 4
H = cod. Marcianus 422
M = cod. Vaticanus 66
N = cod. Vaticanus 1366
O = cod. Urbinas 117
P = cod. Vaticanus Palatinus 117
Aldus = editio Aldina
marg. ed. Ald. = marg. exempli Leidensis editionis Aldinae
Turr. = editores Turicenses (Baiter et Sauppe)
```

LYSIAS

ΥΠΕΡ ΤΟΥ ΕΡΑΤΟΣΘΕΝΟΥΣ ΦΟΝΟΥ ΑΠΟΛΟΓΙΑ

1   Περὶ πολλοῦ ἂν ποιησαίμην, ὦ ἄνδρες, τὸ τοιούτους ὑμᾶς
ἐμοὶ δικαστὰς περὶ τούτου τοῦ πράγματος γενέσθαι, οἷοίπερ
ἂν ὑμῖν αὐτοῖς εἴητε τοιαῦτα πεπονθότες· εὖ γὰρ οἶδ' ὅτι,
εἰ τὴν αὐτὴν γνώμην περὶ τῶν ἄλλων ἔχοιτε, ἥνπερ περὶ ὑμῶν
αὐτῶν, οὐκ ἂν εἴη ὅστις οὐκ ἐπὶ τοῖς γεγενημένοις ἀγανακ-
τοίη, ἀλλὰ πάντες ἂν περὶ τῶν τὰ τοιαῦτα ἐπιτηδευόντων τὰς
2   ζημίας μικρὰς ἡγοῖσθε. καὶ ταῦτα οὐκ ἂν εἴη μόνον παρ' ὑμῖν
οὕτως ἐγνωσμένα, ἀλλ' ἐν ἁπάσῃ τῇ Ἑλλάδι· περὶ τούτου γὰρ
μόνου τοῦ ἀδικήματος καὶ ἐν δημοκρατίᾳ καὶ ὀλιγαρχίᾳ ἡ αὐτὴ
τιμωρία τοῖς ἀσθενεστάτοις πρὸς τοὺς τὰ μέγιστα δυναμένους
ἀποδέδοται, ὥστε τὸν χείριστον τῶν αὐτῶν τυγχάνειν τῷ βελ-
τίστῳ· οὕτως, ὦ ἄνδρες, ταύτην τὴν ὕβριν ἅπαντες ἄνθρωποι
3   δεινοτάτην ἡγοῦνται. περὶ μὲν οὖν τοῦ μεγέθους τῆς ζημίας
ἅπαντας ὑμᾶς νομίζω τὴν αὐτὴν διάνοιαν ἔχειν, καὶ οὐδένα
οὕτως ὀλιγώρως διακεῖσθαι, ὅστις οἴεται δεῖν συγγνώμης τυγχάνειν ἢ μικρᾶς ζημίας ἀξίους ἡγεῖται τοὺς τῶν τοιούτων
4   ἔργων αἰτίους· ἡγοῦμαι δέ, ὦ ἄνδρες, τοῦτό με δεῖν ἐπιδεῖξαι, ὡς ἐμοίχευεν Ἐρατοσθένης τὴν γυναῖκα τὴν ἐμὴν καὶ
ἐκείνην τε διέφθειρε καὶ τοὺς παῖδας τοὺς ἐμοὺς ᾔσχυνε καὶ
ἐμὲ αὐτὸν ὕβρισεν εἰς τὴν οἰκίαν τὴν ἐμὴν εἰσιών, καὶ οὔτε
ἔχθρα ἐμοὶ καὶ ἐκείνῳ οὐδεμία ἦν πλὴν ταύτης, οὔτε χρημάτων
ἕνεκα ἔπραξα ταῦτα, ἵνα πλούσιος ἐκ πένητος γένωμαι, οὔτε
ἄλλου κέρδους οὐδενὸς πλὴν τῆς κατὰ τοὺς νόμους τιμωρίας.
5   ἐγὼ τοίνυν ἐξ ἀρχῆς ὑμῖν ἅπαντα ἐπιδείξω τὰ ἐμαυτοῦ πράγματα, οὐδὲν παραλείπων, ἀλλὰ λέγων τἀληθῆ· ταύτην γὰρ ἐμαυτῷ
μόνην ἡγοῦμαι σωτηρίαν, ἐὰν ὑμῖν εἰπεῖν ἅπαντα δυνηθῶ τὰ
πεπραγμένα.
6   Ἐγὼ γάρ, ὦ Ἀθηναῖοι, ἐπειδὴ ἔδοξέ μοι γῆμαι καὶ γυναῖκα ἠγαγόμην εἰς τὴν οἰκίαν, τὸν μὲν ἄλλον χρόνον οὕτω
διεκείμην ὥστε μήτε λυπεῖν μήτε λίαν ἐπ' ἐκείνῃ εἶναι ὅ τι
ἂν ἐθέλῃ ποιεῖν, ἐφύλαττόν τε ὡς οἷόν τε ἦν, καὶ προσεῖχον
τὸν νοῦν ὥσπερ εἰκὸς ἦν· ἐπειδὴ δέ μοι παιδίον γίγνεται,
ἐπίστευον ἤδη καὶ πάντα τὰ ἐμαυτοῦ ἐκείνῃ παρέδωκα, ἡγούμε-
7   νος ταύτην οἰκειότητα μεγίστην εἶναι. ἐν μὲν οὖν τῷ πρώτῳ
χρόνῳ, ὦ Ἀθηναῖοι, πασῶν ἦν βελτίστη, καὶ γὰρ οἰκονόμος
δεινὴ καὶ φειδωλὸς [ἀγαθὴ] καὶ ἀκριβῶς πάντα διοικοῦσα·
ἐπειδὴ δέ μοι ἡ μήτηρ ἐτελεύτησε, πάντων τῶν κακῶν ἀπο-
8   θανοῦσα αἰτία μοι γεγένηται. ἐπ' ἐκφορὰν γὰρ αὐτῇ ἀκολου-

---

1   εἴητε marg. ed. Ald.: εἰ ἦτε CHX   μικρὰς X^c(1):

4   οὔτε ex οὕτως corr. X^r

7   ἀγαθὴ del. Dobree

SPEECH 1 : THE KILLING OF ERATOSTHENES

I should much appreciate it, gentlemen, if you would adopt the same attitude to me as jurymen in this case as you would towards yourselves if you had faced a similar experience; for I am sure that if you were to hold the same view about other people as you do about yourselves, not one of you could fail to feel indignation at what has happened, but all of you would regard as small the penalties imposed upon men who engage in such practices. And you would not be alone in this opinion : the whole of Greece would agree with you, since this is the one crime for which, under both democracy and oligarchy, the weakest citizens are accorded the same redress as the most powerful, so that the humblest receives the same treatment as the most eminent. Such is the feeling of outrage, gentlemen, that the whole human race has about this violation. I think, then, that concerning the magnitude of the penalty you are all of the same mind, and none of you regards the matter so lightly as to think that those responsible for such actions should receive pardon or deserve small penalties. But I consider, gentlemen, that my task is to show that Eratosthenes seduced my wife and corrupted her, and also brought disgrace upon my children and insulted me by entering my house; that no enmity existed between him and me except over this; that I did not do it for money, to raise myself from rags to riches, nor for any gain except the right of punishment accorded by the laws. I shall now describe to you from the beginning all my actions, omitting nothing but telling the whole truth, for I see that my sole chance of a safe outcome lies in my ability to give you a complete account of events.

Now when I decided to marry, Athenians, and brought a wife into my house, during the whole of that time my attitude was that I should neither harass her nor leave her too free to do whatever she wished. I watched her as far as possible, and paid as much attention to her as was reasonable. But when a child was born to me, I then came to trust her and placed all my affairs in her keeping, thinking that we were now in the closest intimacy. And indeed in the earliest days, Athenians, she was the best wife in the world, an efficient, thrifty housekeeper who managed everything to a nicety. But when my

θήσασα ἡ ἐμὴ γυνὴ ὑπὸ τούτου τοῦ ἀνθρώπου ὀφθεῖσα, χρόνῳ
διαφθείρεται· ἐπιτηρῶν γὰρ τὴν θεράπαιναν τὴν εἰς τὴν
ἀγορὰν βαδίζουσαν καὶ λόγους προσφέρων ἀπώλεσεν αὐτήν.

9 Πρῶτον μὲν οὖν, ὦ ἄνδρες, (δεῖ γὰρ καὶ ταῦθ᾽ ὑμῖν διηγήσασθαι) οἰκίδιον ἔστι μοι διπλοῦν, ἴσα ἔχον τὰ ἄνω τοῖς κάτω
κατὰ τὴν γυναικωνῖτιν καὶ κατὰ τὴν ἀνδρωνῖτιν. ἐπειδὴ δὲ
τὸ παιδίον ἐγένετο ἡμῖν, ἡ μήτηρ αὐτὸ ἐθήλαζεν· ἵνα δὲ μή,
ὁπότε λούεσθαι δέοι, κινδυνεύῃ κατὰ τῆς κλίμακος καταβαί-
10 νουσα, ἐγὼ μὲν ἄνω διῃτώμην, αἱ δὲ γυναῖκες κάτω. καὶ οὕτως
ἤδη συνειθισμένον ἦν, ὥστε πολλάκις ἡ γυνὴ ἀπῄει κάτω
καθευδήσουσα ὡς τὸ παιδίον, ἵνα τὸν τιτθὸν αὐτῷ διδῷ καὶ μὴ
βοᾷ. καὶ ταῦτα πολὺν χρόνον οὕτως ἐγίγνετο, καὶ ἐγὼ οὐδέποτε ὑπώπτευσα, ἀλλ᾽ οὕτως ἠλιθίως διεκείμην, ὥστε ᾤμην
τὴν ἐμαυτοῦ γυναῖκα πασῶν σωφρονεστάτην εἶναι τῶν ἐν τῇ
11 πόλει. Προϊόντος δὲ τοῦ χρόνου, ὦ ἄνδρες, ἧκον μὲν ἀπροσ-
δοκήτως ἐξ ἀγροῦ, μετὰ δὲ τὸ δεῖπνον τὸ παιδίον ἐβόα καὶ
ἐδυσκόλαινεν ὑπὸ τῆς θεραπαίνης ἐπίτηδες λυπούμενον, ἵνα
ταῦτα ποιῇ· ὁ γὰρ ἄνθρωπος ἔνδον ἦν· ὕστερον γὰρ ἅπαντα
12 ἐπυθόμην. καὶ ἐγὼ τὴν γυναῖκα ἀπιέναι ἐκέλευον καὶ δοῦναι
τῷ παιδίῳ τὸν τιτθόν, ἵνα παύσηται κλᾶον. ἡ δὲ τὸ μὲν
πρῶτον οὐκ ἤθελεν, ὡς ἂν ἀσμένη με ἑορακυῖα ἥκοντα διὰ
χρόνου· ἐπειδὴ δὲ ἐγὼ ὠργιζόμην καὶ ἐκέλευον αὐτὴν ἀπιέναι,
'ἵνα σύ γε' ἔφη 'πειρᾷς ἐνταῦθα τὴν παιδίσκην· καὶ πρότερον
13 δὲ μεθύων εἷλκες αὐτήν.' κἀγὼ μὲν ἐγέλων, ἐκείνη δὲ ἀνα-
στᾶσα καὶ ἀπιοῦσα προστίθησι τὴν θύραν, προσποιουμένη
παίζειν, καὶ τὴν κλεῖν ἐφέλκεται. κἀγὼ τούτων οὐδὲν ἐνθυμούμενος οὐδ᾽ ὑπονοῶν ἐκάθευδον ἄσμενος, ἥκων ἐξ ἀγροῦ.
14 ἐπειδὴ δὲ ἦν πρὸς ἡμέραν, ἧκεν ἐκείνη καὶ τὴν θύραν
ἀνέῳξεν. ἐρομένου δέ μου τί αἱ θύραι νύκτωρ ψοφοῖεν, ἔφασκε
τὸν λύχνον ἀποσβεσθῆναι τὸν παρὰ τῷ παιδίῳ, εἶτα ἐκ τῶν
γειτόνων ἐνάψασθαι. ἐσιώπων ἐγὼ καὶ ταῦτα οὕτως ἔχειν
ἡγούμην. ἔδοξε δέ μοι, ὦ ἄνδρες, τὸ πρόσωπον ἐψιμυθιῶσθαι,
τοῦ ἀδελφοῦ τεθνεῶτος οὔπω τριάκονθ᾽ ἡμέρας· ὅμως δ᾽ οὐδ᾽
οὕτως οὐδὲν εἰπὼν περὶ τοῦ πράγματος ἐξελθὼν ᾠχόμην ἔξω
15 σιωπῇ. Μετὰ δὲ ταῦτα, ὦ ἄνδρες, χρόνου μεταξὺ διαγενομένου
καὶ ἐμοῦ πολὺ ἀπολελειμμένου τῶν ἐμαυτοῦ κακῶν, προσέρχεταί
μοί τις πρεσβῦτις ἄνθρωπος, ὑπὸ γυναικὸς ὑποπεμφθεῖσα ἣν
ἐκεῖνος ἐμοίχευεν, ὡς ἐγὼ ὕστερον ἤκουον· αὕτη δὲ ὀργιζο-
μένη καὶ ἀδικεῖσθαι νομίζουσα, ὅτι οὐκέτι ὁμοίως ἐφοίτα
παρ᾽ αὐτήν, ἐφύλαττεν ἕως ἐξηῦρεν ὅ τι εἴη τὸ αἴτιον.
16 προσελθοῦσα οὖν μοι ἐγγὺς ἡ ἄνθρωπος τῆς οἰκίας τῆς ἐμῆς
ἐπιτηροῦσα, 'Εὐφίλητε' ἔφη 'μηδεμιᾷ πολυπραγμοσύνῃ προσ-
εληλυθέναι με νόμιζε πρὸς σέ· ὁ γὰρ ἀνὴρ ὁ ὑβρίζων εἰς σὲ
καὶ τὴν σὴν γυναῖκα ἐχθρὸς ὢν ἡμῖν τυγχάνει. ἐὰν οὖν λάβῃς

---

9 λούεσθαι] λοῦσθαι Thalheim, Hude
10 ἐμαυτοῦ CXʳ: ἑαυτοῦ NPX1
12 κλᾶον Thalheim, Hude: κλαῖον
15 ὑποπεμφθεῖσα NX: ἐπιπεμφθεῖσα CHPXˢ   αὕτη Taylor:
   αὐτή

134

mother passed away, her death became the cause of all my troubles, 8
for it was when my wife attended her funeral that she was seen by
this man, and was eventually corrupted by him. He did this by
looking out for the servant-girl who does our shopping in the market,
and passing on the proposals by which he ruined her. Now firstly, 9
gentlemen (for I must tell you these details), my home is on two
levels, the upper and lower floors being equal in area, with the
women's quarters upstairs and the men's downstairs. When our child
was born, its mother nursed it. To avoid the risk of a fall as she
came downstairs when the child needed to be washed, I used to live
upstairs, and the women below. This had now become such a routine 10
procedure that my wife would often go below to sleep with the child
to give it the breast and prevent its crying. And this was how things
were for a long time, and I never had any suspicion, but was so
naïve as to think my wife the most virtuous in the city. Time passed, 11
and one day I returned unexpectedly from the estate. After dinner,
the child was crying and fretting. The servant-girl was deliberately
annoying it so that it would do this, for the seducer was in the
house: I found all this out later. I told my wife to go and give the 12
child the breast, so that it would stop crying. At first she was
unwilling, as if she were pleased to see me back after such a time.
But when I became angry and told her to go, she said, "So that you
can try your hand here with the little maid: once before, when you
were drunk, you made a grab at her." And I laughed, while she got 13
up and shut the door as she left, pretending it as a joke; and she
turned the key. Now I thought nothing of this and had no suspicion,
but went to sleep readily after my day on the estate. Towards 14
daybreak she came and opened the door. When I asked why the doors
had banged in the night, she told me that the lamp by the baby had
gone out, so she had got a light from the neighbours. I made no
comment and supposed her story to be true. But I noticed her face
was powdered, though her brother had died not thirty days before.
Yet I said nothing about the matter in spite of this but left the house
and went away in silence. After this, gentlemen, some time elapsed 15
and I remained quite unaware of the wrongs being done to me. Then
some old crone came up to me, covertly sent, as I heard later, by a
woman with whom that man was having an affair. This woman was
angry, and felt she was being mistreated because his visits were
becoming less frequent, so she kept watch on him until she found the
reason. The old crone, then, waited near my house, came up to me 16
and said, "Euphiletus, do not think that it is from any meddlesome
motive that I have approached you, for the man who is dishonouring
both yourself and your wife happens to be our enemy. So if you take

135

τὴν θεράπαιναν τὴν εἰς ἀγορὰν βαδίζουσαν καὶ διακονοῦσαν
ὑμῖν καὶ βασανίσῃς, ἅπαντα πεύσει. ἔστι δ'' ἔφη ''Ἐρατοσθένης Ὀῆθεν ὁ ταῦτα πράττων, ὃς οὐ μόνον τὴν σὴν γυναῖκα
διέφθαρκεν ἀλλὰ καὶ ἄλλας πολλάς· ταύτην γὰρ [τὴν] τέχνην
17 ἔχει.' ταῦτα εἰποῦσα, ὦ ἄνδρες, ἐκείνη μὲν ἀπηλλάγη, ἐγὼ δ'
εὐθέως ἐταραττόμην, καὶ πάντα μου εἰς τὴν γνώμην εἰσῄει,
καὶ μεστὸς ἦ ὑποψίας, ἐνθυμούμενος μὲν ὡς ἀπεκλῄσθην ἐν τῷ
δωματίῳ, ἀναμιμνησκόμενος δὲ ὅτι ἐν ἐκείνῃ τῇ νυκτὶ ἐψόφει
ἡ μέταυλος θύρα καὶ ἡ αὔλειος, ὃ οὐδέποτε ἐγένετο, ἔδοξέ τέ
μοι ἡ γυνὴ ἐψιμυθιῶσθαι. ταῦτά μου πάντα εἰς τὴν γνώμην
18 εἰσῄει, καὶ μεστὸς ἦ ὑποψίας. ἐλθὼν δὲ οἴκαδε ἐκέλευον
ἀκολουθεῖν μοι τὴν θεράπαιναν εἰς τὴν ἀγοράν, ἀγαγὼν δ'
αὐτὴν ὡς τῶν ἐπιτηδείων τινὰ ἔλεγον ὅτι ἐγὼ πάντα εἴην πεπυσμένος τὰ γιγνόμενα ἐν τῇ οἰκίᾳ· 'σοὶ οὖν' ἔφην 'ἔξεστι
δυοῖν ὁπότερον βούλει ἐλέσθαι, ἢ μαστιγωθεῖσαν εἰς μύλωνα
ἐμπεσεῖν καὶ μηδέποτε παύσασθαι κακοῖς τοιούτοις συνεχομέ-
νην, ἢ κατειποῦσαν ἅπαντα τἀληθῆ μηδὲν παθεῖν κακόν, ἀλλὰ
συγγνώμης παρ' ἐμοῦ τυχεῖν τῶν ἡμαρτημένων. ψεύσῃ δὲ μηδέν,
19 ἀλλὰ πάντα τἀληθῆ λέγε.' κἀκείνη τὸ μὲν πρῶτον ἔξαρνος ἦν,
καὶ ποιεῖν ἐκέλευεν ὅ τι βούλομαι· οὐδὲν γὰρ εἰδέναι· ἐπειδὴ
δὲ ἐγὼ ἐμνήσθην Ἐρατοσθένους πρὸς αὐτήν, καὶ εἶπον ὅτι
οὗτος ὁ φοιτῶν εἴη πρὸς τὴν γυναῖκα, ἐξεπλάγη ἡγησαμένη με
πάντα ἀκριβῶς ἐγνωκέναι. καὶ τότε ἤδη πρὸς τὰ γόνατά μου
πεσοῦσα, καὶ πίστιν παρ' ἐμοῦ λαβοῦσα μηδὲν πείσεσθαι
20 κακόν, κατηγόρει πρῶτον μὲν ὡς μετὰ τὴν ἐκφορὰν αὐτῇ προσίοι, ἔπειτα ὡς αὐτὴ τελευτῶσα εἰσαγγείλειε καὶ ὡς ἐκείνη
τῷ χρόνῳ πεισθείη, καὶ τὰς εἰσόδους οἷς τρόποις προσίοιτο,
καὶ ὡς Θεσμοφορίοις ἐμοῦ ἐν ἀγρῷ ὄντος ᾤχετο εἰς τὸ ἱερὸν
μετὰ τῆς μητρὸς τῆς ἐκείνου· καὶ τἆλλα τὰ γενόμενα πάντα
21 ἀκριβῶς διηγήσατο. ἐπειδὴ δὲ πάντα εἴρητο αὐτῇ, εἶπον ἐγώ,
'ὅπως τοίνυν ταῦτα μηδεὶς ἀνθρώπων πεύσεται· εἰ δὲ μή,
οὐδέν σοι κύριον ἔσται τῶν πρὸς ἔμ' ὡμολογημένων. ἀξιῶ δέ
σε ἐπ' αὐτοφώρῳ ταῦτά μοι ἐπιδεῖξαι· ἐγὼ γὰρ οὐδὲν δέομαι
λόγων, ἀλλὰ τὸ ἔργον φανερὸν γενέσθαι, εἴπερ οὕτως ἔχει.'
22 ὡμολόγει ταῦτα ποιήσειν. καὶ μετὰ ταῦτα διεγένοντο ἡμέραι
τέτταρες ἢ πέντε, . . . ὡς ἐγὼ μεγάλοις ὑμῖν τεκμηρίοις
ἐπιδείξω. πρῶτον δὲ διηγήσασθαι βούλομαι τὰ πραχθέντα τῇ
τελευταίᾳ ἡμέρᾳ. Σώστρατος ἦν μοι ἐπιτήδειος καὶ φίλος.
τούτῳ ἡλίου δεδυκότος ἰόντι ἐξ ἀγροῦ ἀπήντησα. εἰδὼς δ'
ἐγὼ ὅτι τηνικαῦτα ἀφιγμένος οὐδένα καταλήψοιτο οἴκοι τῶν
ἐπιτηδείων, ἐκέλευον συνδειπνεῖν· καὶ ἐλθόντες οἴκαδε ὡς
23 ἐμέ, ἀναβάντες εἰς τὸ ὑπερῷον ἐδειπνοῦμεν. ἐπειδὴ δὲ καλῶς
αὐτῷ εἶχεν, ἐκεῖνος μὲν ἀπιὼν ᾤχετο, ἐγὼ δ' ἐκάθευδον. ὁ
δ' Ἐρατοσθένης, ὦ ἄνδρες, εἰσέρχεται, καὶ ἡ θεράπαινα

16 τὴν del. Bekker
19 ὁ φοιτῶν Xᶜ(1): σοι φοιτῶν HP
20 προσίοιτο Kayser: προσίοι
21 πεύσεται OPW: πεύσηται rell.
22 οὐδένα Bekker: οὐδὲν ἂν

the servant-girl who does your shopping and housework, and question her, you will find out everything. The man doing this," she said, "is Eratosthenes of Oe, who has corrupted not only your wife but many others besides, for he practises seduction as a profession". With these words she was gone, gentlemen; but I was at once thrown 17 into confusion, and every detail came into my mind, and I was full of suspicion as I recalled how I had been shut in the room, and I remembered the inner and outer doors banging during that night, which had never happened before, and I had thought my wife was wearing make-up. All these things came into my mind, and I was full 18 of suspicion. I went home and ordered the servant-girl to follow me to the market, where I took her to a friend's house and told her that I had full knowledge of what was going on in the house. And I said "So you can take your choice from two alternatives, either to be whipped and sent to the mill, where you will suffer the unrelieved miseries of that work, or to reveal the whole truth and suffer no harm, but obtain indulgence from me for your sins. Do not lie at all, but tell the whole truth". At first she denied it and told me to do as 19 I wished, as she knew nothing. But when I mentioned Eratosthenes' name to her and said that this was the man who was visiting my wife, she panicked, thinking that I knew everything in detail. So now she threw herself down at my knees, and after obtaining from me a pledge that she would suffer no harm, accused him, firstly, of 20 approaching her after the funeral, and described how she eventually carried his message and how my wife was in time persuaded. She told too of the arrangements they made to effect his entry, and how she went off to the temple with his mother to attend the Thesmophoria while I was at the farm; and she gave a detailed account of everything else that had happened. When she had completed her 21 story, I said, "Now see to it that no other human being hears of this: if they do, no part of the agreement you have with me will be valid. And I expect you to show me their guilty act as they commit it, for I have no use for mere words, but want a clear exposure of the deed, if it is really happening". She agreed to do this. Four or 22 five days passed after this......as I shall prove to you with strong evidence. But first I want to describe what happened on the last day. Sostratus was a close friend of mine. I met him after sunset as he was coming from the farm. Knowing that he would find none of his family at home when he arrived there at that time, I invited him to dine with me. And we came to my house, went upstairs and had dinner. After he had dined well, he went away and I went to sleep. 23 But Eratosthenes entered, gentlemen, and the servant-girl aroused me

ἐπεγείρασά με εὐθὺς φράζει ὅτι ἔνδον ἐστί. κἀγὼ εἰπὼν
ἐκείνῃ ἐπιμελεῖσθαι τῆς θύρας, καταβὰς σιωπῇ ἐξέρχομαι,
καὶ ἀφικνοῦμαι ὡς τὸν καὶ τόν, καὶ τοὺς μὲν <οὐκ> ἔνδον
24 κατέλαβον, τοὺς δὲ οὐδ' ἐπιδημοῦντας ηὗρον. παραλαβὼν δ'
ὡς οἷόν τε ἦν πλείστους ἐκ τῶν παρόντων ἐβάδιζον. καὶ δᾷδας
λαβόντες ἐκ τοῦ ἐγγύτατα καπηλείου εἰσερχόμεθα, ἀνεῳγμένης
τῆς θύρας καὶ ὑπὸ τῆς ἀνθρώπου παρεσκευασμένης. ὤσαντες δὲ
τὴν θύραν τοῦ δωματίου οἱ μὲν πρῶτοι εἰσιόντες ἔτι εὔδομεν
αὐτὸν κατακείμενον παρὰ τῇ γυναικί, οἱ δ' ὕστερον ἐν τῇ
25 κλίνῃ γυμνὸν ἑστηκότα. ἐγὼ δ', ὦ ἄνδρες, πατάξας καταβάλλω
αὐτόν, καὶ τὼ χεῖρε περιαγαγὼν εἰς τοὔπισθεν καὶ δήσας
ἠρώτων διὰ τί ὑβρίζει εἰς τὴν οἰκίαν τὴν ἐμὴν εἰσιών. κά-
κεῖνος ἀδικεῖν μὲν ὡμολόγει, ἠντεβόλει δὲ καὶ ἱκέτευε μὴ
26 ἀποκτεῖναι ἀλλ' ἀργύριον πράξασθαι. ἐγὼ δ' εἶπον ὅτι 'οὐκ
ἐγώ σε ἀποκτενῶ, ἀλλ' ὁ τῆς πόλεως νόμος, ὃν σὺ παραβαίνων
περὶ ἐλάττονος τῶν ἡδονῶν ἐποιήσω, καὶ μᾶλλον εἵλου τοιοῦτον ἁμάρτημα ἐξαμαρτάνειν εἰς τὴν γυναῖκα τὴν ἐμὴν καὶ
εἰς τοὺς παῖδας τοὺς ἐμοὺς ἢ τοῖς νόμοις πείθεσθαι καὶ
27 κόσμιος εἶναι.' οὕτως, ὦ ἄνδρες, ἐκεῖνος τούτων ἔτυχεν ὧνπερ οἱ νόμοι κελεύουσι τοὺς τὰ τοιαῦτα πράττοντας, οὐκ
εἰσαρπασθεὶς ἐκ τῆς ὁδοῦ, οὐδ' ἐπὶ τὴν ἑστίαν καταφυγών,
ὥσπερ οὗτοι λέγουσι· πῶς γὰρ ἄν, ὅστις ἐν τῷ δωματίῳ πλη-
γεὶς κατέπεσεν εὐθύς, περιέστρεφα δ' αὐτοῦ τὼ χεῖρε, ἔνδον
δὲ ἦσαν ἄνθρωποι τοσοῦτοι, οὓς διαφυγεῖν οὐκ ἐδύνατο, οὔτε
σίδηρον οὔτε ξύλον οὔτε ἄλλο οὐδὲν ἔχων, ᾧ τοὺς εἰσελθόντας
28 ἂν ἠμύνατο; ἀλλ', ὦ ἄνδρες, οἶμαι καὶ ὑμᾶς εἰδέναι ὅτι οἱ
μὴ τὰ δίκαια πράττοντες οὐχ ὁμολογοῦσι τοὺς ἐχθροὺς λέγειν
ἀληθῆ, ἀλλ' αὐτοὶ ψευδόμενοι καὶ τὰ τοιαῦτα μηχανώμενοι
ὀργὰς τοῖς ἀκούουσι κατὰ τῶν τὰ δίκαια πραττόντων παρα-
σκευάζουσι. Πρῶτον μὲν οὖν ἀνάγνωθι τὸν νόμον.

ΝΟΜΟΣ

29 Οὐκ ἠμφεσβήτει, ὦ ἄνδρες, ἀλλ' ὡμολόγει ἀδικεῖν, καὶ
ὅπως μὲν μὴ ἀποθάνῃ ἠντεβόλει καὶ ἱκέτευεν, ἀποτίνειν δ'
ἕτοιμος ἦν χρήματα. ἐγὼ δὲ τῷ μὲν ἐκείνου τιμήματι οὐ συν-
εχώρουν, τὸν δὲ τῆς πόλεως νόμον ἠξίουν εἶναι κυριώτερον,
καὶ ταύτην ἔλαβον τὴν δίκην, ἣν ὑμεῖς δικαιοτάτην εἶναι
ἡγησάμενοι τοῖς τὰ τοιαῦτα ἐπιτηδεύουσιν ἐτάξατε. Καί μοι
ἀνάβητε τούτων μάρτυρες.

ΜΑΡΤΥΡΕΣ

30 Ἀνάγνωθι δέ μοι καὶ τοῦτον τὸν νόμον <τὸν> ἐκ τῆς

---

23 οὐκ add. Reiske cf. 41   οὐδ' Reiske: οὐκ
25 ἀποκτεῖναι Hertlein: αὐτὸν κτεῖναι
26 ἐποιήσω P: ἐποίησας rell.
27 ξύλον . . . ἔχων] ὅπλον ἄλλο οὐδὲν ἔχων Schenkl
30 τὸν add. Westermann

at once and told me that he was in the house. Telling her to watch the door, I silently went downstairs and out of the house. I called at the houses of several neighbours, but found some not at home and others not even in town. Taking with me as many as I could in the circumstances, I made my way back. We got torches from the nearest shop, and went in, the door having been kept open by the maid. Pushing the bedroom door open, those of us who entered first saw him still lying beside my wife, and those following saw him standing naked on the bed. I struck him and knocked him down, gentlemen, and pulling his hands behind his back, tied them and asked him why he was committing the outrage of entering my house. And he admitted his crime, but begged and beseeched me not to kill him but to negotiate a monetary settlement. But I replied: "It is not I who shall be killing you, but the law of the city, which you are flouting: you thought it less important than your pleasures, and chose to commit this crime against my wife and my children rather than obey the laws and behave decently". Thus that man, gentlemen, met the fate which the laws enjoin for such malefactors. He was neither seized from the street and taken in, nor had he taken refuge at the hearth, as these men allege. For how could that be, when he was struck in the bedroom and fell at once, and I tied his hands behind his back; and there were so many men in the house that he could not escape them, and he had no iron or wooden weapon with which he could have warded off the incomers? But, gentlemen, I think you know as well as I that wrongdoers do not admit when their enemies are speaking the truth, but lie themselves and devise stories designed to arouse anger in their audience against those who are acting justly. Firstly, then, read the law.

24

25

26

27

28

LAW

He did not argue, gentlemen, but admitted his guilt, and begged and pleaded not to be killed; and he was ready to compensate me with money. But I would not agree to his valuation, and demanded that the city's law should take precedence. I exacted the penalty which you considered the most just when you prescribed it for those who engage in such practices. Now let the witnesses to this evidence come forward.

29

WITNESSES

Please read out also that law from the pillar on the Areopagus.

30

στήλης τῆς ἐξ Ἀρείου πάγου.

ΝΟΜΟΣ

Ἀκούετε, ὦ ἄνδρες, ὅτι αὐτῷ τῷ δικαστηρίῳ τῷ ἐξ
Ἀρείου πάγου, ᾧ καὶ πάτριόν ἐστι καὶ ἐφ' ἡμῶν ἀποδέδοται
τοῦ φόνου τὰς δίκας δικάζειν, διαρρήδην εἴρηται τούτου μὴ
καταγιγνώσκειν φόνον, ὃς ἂν ἐπὶ δάμαρτι τῇ ἑαυτοῦ μοιχὸν
31 λαβὼν ταύτην τὴν τιμωρίαν ποιήσηται. καὶ οὕτω σφόδρα ὁ
νομοθέτης ἐπὶ ταῖς γαμεταῖς γυναιξὶ δίκαια ταῦτα ἡγήσατο
εἶναι, ὥστε καὶ ἐπὶ ταῖς παλλακαῖς ταῖς ἐλάττονος ἀξίαις
τὴν αὐτὴν δίκην ἐπέθηκε. καίτοι δῆλον ὅτι, εἴ τινα εἶχε
ταύτης μείζω τιμωρίαν ἐπὶ ταῖς γαμεταῖς, ἐποίησεν ἄν· νῦν
δὲ οὐχ οἷός τε ὢν ταύτης ἰσχυροτέραν ἐπ' ἐκείναις ἐξευρεῖν,
τὴν αὐτὴν καὶ ἐπὶ ταῖς παλλακαῖς ἠξίωσε γίγνεσθαι. Ἀνάγνωθι δέ μοι καὶ τοῦτον τὸν νόμον.

ΝΟΜΟΣ

32 Ἀκούετε, ὦ ἄνδρες, ὅτι κελεύει, ἐάν τις ἄνθρωπον
ἐλεύθερον ἢ παῖδα αἰσχύνῃ βίᾳ, διπλῆν τὴν βλάβην ὀφείλειν·
ἐὰν δὲ γυναῖκα, ἐφ' αἶσπερ ἀποκτείνειν ἔξεστιν, ἐν τοῖς
αὐτοῖς ἐνέχεσθαι· οὕτως, ὦ ἄνδρες, τοὺς βιαζομένους ἐλάττονος ζημίας ἀξίους ἡγήσατο εἶναι ἢ τοὺς πείθοντας· τῶν
μὲν γὰρ θάνατον κατέγνω, τοῖς δὲ διπλῆν ἐποίησε τὴν βλάβην,
33 ἡγούμενος τοὺς μὲν διαπραττομένους βίᾳ ὑπὸ τῶν βιασθέντων
μισεῖσθαι, τοὺς δὲ πείσαντας οὕτως αὐτῶν τὰς ψυχὰς δια-
φθείρειν, ὥστ' οἰκειοτέρας αὐτοῖς ποιεῖν τὰς ἀλλοτρίας
γυναῖκας ἢ τοῖς ἀνδράσι, καὶ πᾶσαν ἐπ' ἐκείνοις τὴν οἰκίαν
γεγονέναι, καὶ τοὺς παῖδας ἀδήλους εἶναι ὁποτέρων τυγχάνουσιν ὄντες, τῶν ἀνδρῶν ἢ τῶν μοιχῶν. ἀνθ' ὧν ὁ τὸν νόμον
34 τιθεὶς θάνατον αὐτοῖς ἐποίησε τὴν ζημίαν. Ἐμοῦ τοίνυν, ὦ
ἄνδρες, οἱ μὲν νόμοι οὐ μόνον ἀπεγνωκότες εἰσὶ μὴ ἀδικεῖν,
ἀλλὰ καὶ κεκελευκότες ταύτην τὴν δίκην λαμβάνειν· ἐν ὑμῖν
δ' ἐστὶ πότερον χρὴ τούτους ἰσχυροὺς ἢ μηδενὸς ἀξίους
35 εἶναι. ἐγὼ μὲν γὰρ οἶμαι πάσας τὰς πόλεις διὰ τοῦτο τοὺς
νόμους τίθεσθαι, ἵνα περὶ ὧν ἂν πραγμάτων ἀπορῶμεν, παρὰ
τούτους ἐλθόντες σκεψώμεθα ὅ τι ἡμῖν ποιητέον ἐστίν. οὗτοι
τοίνυν περὶ τῶν τοιούτων τοῖς ἀδικουμένοις τοιαύτην δίκην
36 λαμβάνειν παρακελεύονται. οἷς ὑμᾶς ἀξιῶ τὴν αὐτὴν γνώμην
ἔχειν· εἰ δὲ μή, τοιαύτην ἄδειαν τοῖς μοιχοῖς ποιήσετε,
ὥστε καὶ τοὺς κλέπτας ἐπαρεῖτε φάσκειν μοιχοὺς εἶναι, εὖ
εἰδότας ὅτι, ἐὰν ταύτην τὴν αἰτίαν περὶ ἑαυτῶν λέγωσι καὶ
ἐπὶ τούτῳ φάσκωσιν εἰς τὰς ἀλλοτρίας οἰκίας εἰσιέναι,
οὐδεὶς αὐτῶν ἅψεται. πάντες γὰρ εἴσονται ὅτι τοὺς μὲν
νόμους τῆς μοιχείας χαίρειν ἐᾶν δεῖ, τὴν δὲ ψῆφον τὴν
ὑμετέραν δεδιέναι· αὕτη γάρ ἐστι πάντων τῶν ἐν τῇ πόλει
κυριωτάτη.

---

30 ἡμῶν Reiske: ὑμῶν   τούτου . . . φόνον Reiske:
τοῦτον μὴ κατ. φόνου
36 ὥστε Turr.: ὡς

LAW

You hear it stated categorically by the Areopagus itself, the court to which, both in our fathers' and our own time, cases of homicide have been assigned, that any man who exacts this penalty when he has caught an adulterer in the act with his wife should not be convicted of murder. And so strongly did the lawgiver feel the justice of this punishment in the case of married women that he imposed the same penalty in the case of mistresses, who are worthy of less consideration. And yet it is clear that if any greater punishment than this had been available to him in the case of married women, he would have imposed it; but as things were, being unable to discover a more severe one in their case, he decided that it should be the same for mistresses also. Please read this law also.

31

LAW

You hear, gentlemen, how it prescribes double the damages if anyone rapes a free adult or child, while if a woman is the victim, for whose seduction the penalty of death is allowed, he is subject to the same scale of damages. Thus, gentlemen, the law found rapists to deserve less severe penalties than seducers: the latter it condemned to death, but for the former it merely doubled the damages [for free victims], believing that those who gain their ends by force are hated by those violated, whereas those who have persuaded them corrupt their souls, and thereby make others' wives more devoted to themselves than to their husbands. Thus the whole family comes under their control, and it becomes uncertain whether the children's father is the husband or the seducer. For these reasons the legislator made death the penalty for them. Therefore, gentlemen, the laws not only acquit me of any crime, but actually command me to exact this punishment. It is in your power to decide whether these laws are to carry force or to be worthless. For I think all cities make their laws for this reason: so that we may consult them in matters we find difficult to settle, and inquire what we should do. Now it is these laws that urge the wronged parties in cases like this to exact this kind of punishment. I demand that you take the same view as they. If you do not, the immunity you grant will be such as to encourage burglars also to allege that they are adulterers, because they will know well that if they give this as their reason and allege that it is for this purpose that they are entering other men's houses, nobody will touch them. For everyone will know that the laws on adultery must be discounted, and that it is your vote that is to be feared, because this has supreme power in all state matters. Consider,

32

33

34

35

36

37

37   Σκέψασθε δέ, ὦ ἄνδρες· κατηγοροῦσι γάρ μου ὡς ἐγὼ τὴν
θεράπαιναν ἐν ἐκείνῃ τῇ ἡμέρᾳ μετελθεῖν ἐκέλευσα τὸν νεανί-
σκον. ἐγὼ δέ, ὦ ἄνδρες, δίκαιον μὲν ἂν ποιεῖν ἡγούμην ὡτινιοῦν τρόπῳ τὸν τὴν γυναῖκα τὴν ἐμὴν διαφθείραντα λαμβάνων
38   (εἰ μὲν γὰρ λόγων εἰρημένων ἔργου δὲ μηδενὸς γεγενημένου
μετελθεῖν ἐκέλευον ἐκεῖνον, ἠδίκουν ἄν· εἰ δὲ ἤδη πάντων
διαπεπραγμένων καὶ πολλάκις εἰσεληλυθότος εἰς τὴν οἰκίαν
τὴν ἐμὴν ὡτινιοῦν τρόπῳ ἐλάμβανον αὐτόν, σωφρονεῖν <ἂν>
39   ἐμαυτὸν ἡγούμην)· σκέψασθε δὲ ὅτι καὶ ταῦτα ψεύδονται·
ῥᾳδίως δὲ ἐκ τῶνδε γνώσεσθε. ἐμοὶ γάρ, ὦ ἄνδρες, ὅπερ καὶ
πρότερον εἶπον, φίλος ὢν Σώστρατος καὶ οἰκείως διακείμενος
ἀπαντήσας ἐξ ἀγροῦ περὶ ἡλίου δυσμὰς συνεδείπνει, καὶ
40   ἐπειδὴ καλῶς εἶχεν αὐτῷ, ἀπιὼν ᾤχετο. καίτοι πρῶτον μέν, ὦ
ἄνδρες, ἐνθυμήθητε· [ὅτι] εἰ ἐν ἐκείνῃ τῇ νυκτὶ ἐγὼ ἐπε-
βούλευον Ἐρατοσθένει, πότερον ἦν μοι κρεῖττον αὐτῷ ἑτέρωθι
δειπνεῖν ἢ τὸν συνδειπνήσοντά μοι εἰσαγαγεῖν; οὕτω γὰρ ἂν
ἧττον ἐτόλμησεν ἐκεῖνος εἰσελθεῖν εἰς τὴν οἰκίαν. εἶτα δοκῶ
ἂν ὑμῖν τὸν συνδειπνοῦντα ἀφεὶς μόνος καταλειφθῆναι καὶ
ἔρημος γενέσθαι, ἢ κελεύειν ἐκεῖνον μεῖναι, ἵνα μετ' ἐμοῦ
41   τὸν μοιχὸν ἐτιμωρεῖτο; ἔπειτα, ὦ ἄνδρες, οὐκ ἂν δοκῶ ὑμῖν
τοῖς ἐπιτηδείοις μεθ' ἡμέραν παραγγεῖλαι, καὶ κελεῦσαι
αὐτοὺς συλλεγῆναι εἰς οἰκίαν τῶν φίλων τὴν ἐγγυτάτω, μᾶλλον
ἢ ἐπειδὴ τάχιστα ᾐσθόμην τῆς νυκτὸς περιτρέχειν, οὐκ εἰδὼς
ὅντινα οἴκοι καταλήψομαι καὶ ὅντινα ἔξω; καὶ ὡς Ἁρμόδιον
μὲν καὶ τὸν δεῖνα ἦλθον οὐκ ἐπιδημοῦντας (οὐ γὰρ ᾔδη),
ἑτέρους δὲ οὐκ ἔνδον ὄντας κατέλαβον, οὓς δ' οἷός τε ἦ
42   λαβὼν ἐβάδιζον. καίτοι γε εἰ προῄδη, οὐκ ἂν δοκῶ ὑμῖν καὶ
θεράποντας παρασκευάσασθαι καὶ τοῖς φίλοις παραγγεῖλαι,
ἵν' ὡς ἀσφαλέστατα μὲν αὐτὸς εἰσῇα (τί γὰρ ἤδη εἴ τι
κἀκεῖνος εἶχε σιδήριον;), ὡς μετὰ πλείστων δὲ μαρτύρων τὴν
τιμωρίαν ἐποιούμην; νῦν δ' οὐδὲν εἰδὼς τῶν ἐσομένων ἐκείνῃ
τῇ νυκτί, οὓς οἷός τε ἦ παρέλαβον. Καί μοι ἀνάβητε τούτων
μάρτυρες.

ΜΑΡΤΥΡΕΣ

43   Τῶν μὲν μαρτύρων ἀκηκόατε, ὦ ἄνδρες· σκέψασθε δὲ παρ'
ὑμῖν αὐτοῖς οὕτως περὶ τούτου τοῦ πράγματος, ζητοῦντες εἴ
τις ἐμοὶ καὶ Ἐρατοσθένει ἔχθρα πώποτε γεγένηται πλὴν ταύ-
44   της. οὐδεμίαν γὰρ εὑρήσετε. οὔτε γὰρ συκοφαντῶν γραφάς με
ἐγράψατο, οὔτε ἐκβάλλειν ἐκ τῆς πόλεως ἐπεχείρησεν, οὔτε ἰδί-
ας δίκας ἐδικάζετο, οὔτε συνῄδει κακὸν οὐδὲν ὃ ἐγὼ δεδιὼς μή
τις πύθηται ἐπεθύμουν αὐτὸν ἀπολέσαι, οὔτε εἰ ταῦτα διαπραξαίμην, ἤλπιζόν ποθεν χρήματα λήψεσθαι· ἔνιοι γὰρ
τοιούτων πραγμάτων ἕνεκα θάνατον ἀλλήλοις ἐπιβουλεύουσι.

38 ἂν add. Taylor
40 ὅτι del. Reiske   μεῖναι Fuhr: μὲν εἶναι HPX¹: μένειν
    CXᶜ(1)
41 τὴν Bergk: τιν' Weidner: τῶν
44 διαπραξαίμην Lipsius: διεπραξάμην   ποθεν Emperius: μὲν

gentlemen, their allegation that I told the servant-girl to seek the 37
fellow out on that day. Now I could have felt myself justified,
gentlemen, in using any means in apprehending the man who had
corrupted my wife. If I had told her to fetch him after we had merely 38
exchanged words and no act had been committed, I should be in the
wrong; but if, when once he had achieved all his objectives and
entered my house many times, I sought to catch him by any means
available, I should consider I was behaving reasonably. But notice 39
that they are lying in this matter also, as you will easily realise from
these facts. My close friend Sostratus met up with me, gentlemen, as
I said before, at sunset and had dinner with me, and after he had
dined well he went away. Now you should consider this point first, 40
gentlemen: if I was setting a trap for Eratosthenes on that night, was
it to my own greater advantage to dine somewhere else or to bring my
guest home to dine? For in the latter case that man was less likely to
dare to enter the house. Then again, does it seem likely to you that
I would let my guest go, leaving me alone and unaided, or that I
would ask him to stay so that he could help me punish the seducer?
And finally, would I not have called upon my close friends by day 41
and asked them to foregather in the house of my nearest neighbour,
rather than running around at night as soon as I had made the
discovery, not knowing whom I should find at home and whom away?
In fact I went to the houses of Harmodius and someone else, and they
were not even in town (for I did not know); and I found others not
at home, but I took with me those that I could. Yet if I had had 42
prior knowledge, does it not seem likely to you that I would have
arranged for servants to be at hand, and passed the word to my
friends, so that I should make my own entrance in the greatest
possible safety (for how was I to know whether he too had some
weapon?) and take my revenge on him with as many witnesses present
as possible? But as it was, knowing nothing of what was going to
happen on that night, I took with me those I could. Let the witnesses
to these facts come up.

WITNESSES

You have heard the witnesses, gentlemen. Think about this case 43
in your own minds asking this question, whether there has ever been
any enmity between me and Eratosthenes except that arising from this
affair. You will find none, for he had neither filed false charges 44
against me, nor had he tried to have me exiled, nor was he engaged
in any private suits against me; nor did he know of any crime for which
I was so afraid of being found out that I desired to destroy him; nor
did I have hopes of acquiring money from anywhere if I was
successful. Such are the motives from which some men plot one

45 τοσούτου τοίνυν δεῖ ἢ λοιδορία ἢ παροινία ἢ ἄλλη τις διαφορὰ ἡμῖν γεγονέναι, ὥστε οὐδὲ ἑορακὼς ἦ τὸν ἄνθρωπον πώποτε πλὴν ἐν ἐκείνῃ τῇ νυκτί. τί ἂν οὖν βουλόμενος ἐγὼ τοιοῦτον κίνδυνον ἐκινδύνευον, εἰ μὴ τὸ μέγιστον τῶν
46 ἀδικημάτων ἦ ὑπ' αὐτοῦ ἠδικημένος; ἔπειτα παρακαλέσας αὐτὸς μάρτυρας ἠσέβουν, ἐξόν μοι, εἴπερ ἀδίκως ἐπεθύμουν αὐτὸν ἀπολέσαι, μηδένα μοι τούτων συνειδέναι;
47 Ἐγὼ μὲν οὖν, ὦ ἄνδρες, οὐκ ἰδίαν ὑπὲρ ἐμαυτοῦ νομίζω ταύτην γενέσθαι τὴν τιμωρίαν, ἀλλ' ὑπὲρ τῆς πόλεως ἁπάσης· οἱ γὰρ τοιαῦτα πράττοντες, ὁρῶντες οἷα τὰ ἆθλα πρόκειται τῶν τοιούτων ἁμαρτημάτων, ἧττον εἰς τοὺς ἄλλους ἐξαμαρτή-
48 σονται, ἐὰν καὶ ὑμᾶς ὁρῶσι τὴν αὐτὴν γνώμην ἔχοντας. εἰ δὲ μή, πολὺ κάλλιον τοὺς μὲν κειμένους νόμους ἐξαλεῖψαι, ἑτέρους δὲ θεῖναι, οἵτινες τοὺς μὲν φυλάττοντας τὰς ἑαυτῶν γυναῖκας ταῖς ζημίαις ζημιώσουσι, τοῖς δὲ βουλομένοις εἰς
49 αὐτὰς ἁμαρτάνειν πολλὴν ἄδειαν ποιήσουσι. πολὺ γὰρ οὕτω δικαιότερον ἢ ὑπὸ τῶν νόμων τοὺς πολίτας ἐνεδρεύεσθαι, οἳ κελεύουσι μέν, ἐάν τις μοιχὸν λάβῃ, ὅ τι ἂν οὖν βούληται χρῆσθαι, οἱ δ' ἀγῶνες δεινότεροι τοῖς ἀδικουμένοις καθεστήκασιν ἢ τοῖς παρὰ τοὺς νόμους τὰς ἀλλοτρίας καταισχύ-
50 νουσι γυναῖκας. ἐγὼ γὰρ νῦν καὶ περὶ τοῦ σώματος καὶ περὶ τῶν χρημάτων καὶ περὶ τῶν ἄλλων ἁπάντων κινδυνεύω, ὅτι τοῖς τῆς πόλεως νόμοις ἐπιθόμην.

---

45 τοσούτου M corr.: τοσοῦτον H: τοσοῦτο M¹PX¹
50 ἐπιθόμην C: ἐπειθόμην rell.

another's death. Indeed, far from there having been any abusive or drunken exchanges between us or any other quarrel, I had never even seen the fellow before that night. So what could have been my aim in risking so great a danger if I had not suffered the most grievous wrong at his hands? And finally, would I have committed an impious act myself after calling witnesses when it was open to me, if I desired to destroy him unjustly, to have none of these sharing my knowledge? 45 46

Therefore, gentlemen, I consider this punishment not to have been a private one exacted on my own behalf, but on behalf of the whole city. For men who commit such acts, when they see the kind of prizes offered for such crimes, will less readily sin against others if they see you also taking the same view. Otherwise it would be much better to erase the established laws and make others which impose penalties upon men who guard their wives and accord a high degree of immunity to those who wish to commit offences against them. This would be much fairer than to let the citizens be entrapped by the laws, when these say that anyone who catches an adulterer may deal with him however he wishes, but the actual trials are made more hazardous for the wronged parties than for those who break the laws by dishonouring other men's wives. For I am now in danger of losing my life, my property and everything else because I obeyed the city's laws. 47 48 49 50

ΚΑΤΑ ΘΕΟΜΝΗΣΤΟΥ

1   Μαρτύρων μὲν οὐκ ἀπορίαν μοι ἔσεσθαι δοκῶ, ὦ ἄνδρες
δικασταί· πολλοὺς γὰρ ὑμῶν ὁρῶ δικάζοντας τῶν τότε παρόντων, ὅτε Λυσίθεος Θεόμνηστον εἰσήγγελλε τὰ ὅπλα ἀποβεβλη-
κότα, οὐκ ἐξὸν αὐτῷ, δημηγορεῖν· ἐν ἐκείνῳ γὰρ τῷ ἀγῶνι
2   τὸν πατέρα μ' ἔφασκεν ἀπεκτονέναι τὸν ἐμαυτοῦ. ἐγὼ δ', εἰ
μὲν τὸν ἑαυτοῦ με ἀπεκτονέναι ᾐτιᾶτο, συγγνώμην ἂν εἶχον
αὐτῷ τῶν εἰρημένων (φαῦλον γὰρ αὐτὸν καὶ οὐδενὸς ἄξιον
ἡγούμην)· οὐδ' εἴ τι ἄλλο τῶν ἀπορρήτων ἤκουσα, οὐκ ἂν
ἐπεξῆλθον αὐτῷ (ἀνελεύθερον γὰρ καὶ λίαν φιλόδικον εἶναι
3   νομίζω κακηγορίας δικάζεσθαι)· νυνὶ δὲ αἰσχρόν μοι εἶναι
δοκεῖ περὶ τοῦ πατρός, οὕτω πολλοῦ ἀξίου γεγενημένου καὶ
ὑμῖν καὶ τῇ πόλει, μὴ τιμωρήσασθαι τὸν ταῦτ' εἰρηκότα, καὶ
παρ' ὑμῶν εἰδέναι βούλομαι πότερον δώσει δίκην, ἢ τούτῳ
μόνῳ 'Αθηναίων ἐξαίρετόν ἐστι καὶ ποιεῖν καὶ λέγειν παρὰ
τοὺς νόμους ὅ τι ἂν βούληται.
4   'Εμοὶ γάρ, ὦ ἄνδρες δικασταί, ἔτη ἐστὶ <δύο καὶ> τριάκοντα, ἐξ ὅτου <δ'> ὑμεῖς κατεληλύθατε, εἰκοστὸν τουτί.
φαίνομαι οὖν τρισκαιδεκέτης ὢν ὅτε ὁ πατὴρ ὑπὸ τῶν τριάκοντα ἀπέθνῃσκε. ταύτην δὲ ἔχων τὴν ἡλικίαν οὔτε τί ἐστιν
ὀλιγαρχία ἠπιστάμην, οὔτε ἂν ἐκείνῳ ἀδικουμένῳ ἐδυνάμην
5   βοηθῆσαι. καὶ μὲν δὴ οὐκ ὀρθῶς τῶν χρημάτων ἕνεκα ἐπεβού-
λευσα <ἂν> αὐτῷ· ὁ γὰρ πρεσβύτερος ἀδελφὸς Πανταλέων ἅπαντα
παρέλαβε, καὶ ἐπιτροπεύσας ἡμᾶς τῶν πατρῴων ἀπεστέρησεν,
ὥστε πολλῶν ἕνεκα, ὦ ἄνδρες δικασταί, προσῆκέ μοι αὐτὸν
βούλεσθαι ζῆν. ἀνάγκη μὲν οὖν περὶ αὐτῶν μνησθῆναι, οὐδὲν
δὲ δεῖ πολλῶν λόγων· σχεδὸν <γὰρ> ἐπίστασθε ἅπαντες ὅτι
ἀληθῆ λέγω. ὅμως δὲ μάρτυρας αὐτῶν παρέξομαι.

ΜΑΡΤΥΡΕΣ

6   "Ισως τοίνυν, ὦ ἄνδρες δικασταί, περὶ τούτων μὲν οὐδὲν
ἀπολογήσεται, ἐρεῖ δὲ πρὸς ὑμᾶς ἅπερ ἐτόλμα λέγειν καὶ πρὸς
τὸν διαιτητήν, ὡς οὐκ ἔστι τῶν ἀπορρήτων, ἐάν τις εἴπῃ τὸν
πατέρα ἀπεκτονέναι· τὸν γὰρ νόμον οὐ ταῦτ' ἀπαγορεύειν,
7   ἀλλ' ἀνδροφόνον οὐκ ἐᾶν λέγειν. ἐγὼ δὲ οἶμαι <δεῖν> ὑμᾶς,
ὦ ἄνδρες δικασταί, οὐ περὶ τῶν ὀνομάτων διαφέρεσθαι ἀλλὰ
τῆς τούτων διανοίας, καὶ πάντας εἰδέναι ὅτι, ὅσοι <ἀπεκτό-
νασί τινας, καὶ ἀνδροφόνοι εἰσί, καὶ ὅσοι> ἀνδροφόνοι εἰσί,

---

4   ἐστὶ Contius: εἰσὶ   δύο καὶ add. Contius   δ' add.
Markland   τί Ziel, Madvig: εἰ
5   ἂν add. Markland   προσῆκε Frohberger, Hude: προσῆκει
γὰρ add. Reiske
7   δεῖν add. Scheibe coll. 11.3   ἀπεκτόνασί . . . ὅσοι
add. Auger

SPEECH 10 : AGAINST THEOMNESTUS

I do not think I shall have any shortage of witnesses, gentlemen   1
of the jury, for I see many of you serving on the jury who were
present when Lysitheus prosecuted Theomnestus for addressing the
people after being disqualified through casting away his armour. It
was during that trial that he alleged that I had killed my own father.
Now if he had accused me of killing his own father I should have   2
found his statement excusable, since I regarded him as a sorry and
worthless individual. Nor if I had been called any of the other
forbidden names should I have prosecuted him, for I consider legal
action for slander to be a mean and excessively litigious business.
But in the present case I see it as shameful not to exact revenge   3
from the man who has said these things about my father, who has
deserved such esteem from both you and the city. And I wish to
know from you whether he is going to pay the penalty, or whether he
is to enjoy the privilege, uniquely among Athenians, of doing and
saying whatever he likes contrary to the laws.

I am thirty-two years old, gentlemen of the jury, and it is   4
nineteen years since you returned to the city. I was therefore
obviously thirteen when my father was murdered by the Thirty. At
that age I neither knew what an oligarchy was nor could I have
rescued him from the wrong he suffered. And again, there was no   5
point in my plotting against him for financial reasons, as my elder
brother Pantaleon took over everything, and on being appointed our
guardian deprived us of our patrimony. So I had many reasons,
gentlemen of the jury, for wishing him alive. Now it was necessary to
mention these facts, but there is no need to dwell on them, for you
all know quite well that I am telling the truth. Nevertheless I shall
provide witnesses to those facts.

WITNESSES

Now perhaps he will not attempt a defence in these matters,   6
gentlemen of the jury, but will make the same statement to you that
he rashly made before the arbitrator, that to say someone "killed his
father" is not to use one of the forbidden words, since the law does
not forbid this, but does not allow one to say "murderer". But I   7
think, gentlemen of the jury, that you should make this an argument
not about words, but about their meaning; and everyone knows that
all those who have killed people are also murderers, and all those who

καὶ ἀπεκτόνασί τινας. πολὺ γὰρ ἔργον ἦν τῷ νομοθέτῃ ἅπαντα
τὰ ὀνόματα γράφειν ὅσα τὴν αὐτὴν δύναμιν ἔχει· ἀλλὰ περὶ
8 ἑνὸς εἰπὼν περὶ πάντων ἐδήλωσεν. οὐ γὰρ δήπου, ὦ Θεόμνηστε,
εἰ μέν τίς σε εἴποι πατραλοίαν ἢ μητραλοίαν, ἠξίους ἂν
αὐτὸν ὄφλειν σοι δίκην, εἰ δέ τις εἴποι ὡς τὴν τεκοῦσαν ἢ
τὸν φύσαντα ἔτυπτες, ᾤου ἂν αὐτὸν ἀζήμιον δεῖν εἶναι ὡς
9 οὐδὲν τῶν ἀπορρήτων εἰρηκότα. ἡδέως γὰρ ἄν σου πυθοίμην
(περὶ τοῦτο γὰρ δεινὸς εἶ καὶ μεμελέτηκας καὶ ποιεῖν καὶ
λέγειν)· εἴ τίς σε εἴποι ῥῖψαι τὴν ἀσπίδα (ἐν δὲ τῷ νόμῳ
εἴρηται, 'ἐάν τις φάσκῃ ἀποβεβληκέναι, ὑπόδικον εἶναι'),
οὐκ ἂν ἐδικάζου αὐτῷ, ἀλλ' ἐξήρκει ἄν σοι ἐρριφέναι τὴν
ἀσπίδα, λέγοντι οὐδέν σοι μέλειν; οὐδὲ γὰρ τὸ αὐτό ἐστι
10 ῥῖψαι καὶ ἀποβεβληκέναι· ἀλλ' οὐδ' ἂν τῶν ἕνδεκα γενόμενος
ἀποδέξαιο, εἴ τις ἀπάγοι τινὰ φάσκων θοἰμάτιον ἀποδεδύσθαι
ἢ τὸν χιτωνίσκον ἐκδεδύσθαι, ἀλλ' ἀφείης ἂν τὸν αὐτὸν τρό-
πον, ὅτι οὐ λωποδύτης ὀνομάζεται. οὐδ' εἴ τις παῖδα ἐξαγαγὼν
ληφθείη, οὐκ ἂν φάσκοις αὐτὸν ἀνδραποδιστὴν εἶναι, εἴπερ
μαχεῖ τοῖς ὀνόμασιν, ἀλλὰ μὴ τοῖς ἔργοις τὸν νοῦν προσέξεις,
11 ὧν ἕνεκα τὰ ὀνόματα πάντες τίθενται. Ἔτι τοίνυν σκέψασθε,
ὦ ἄνδρες δικασταί· οὑτοσὶ γάρ μοι δοκεῖ ὑπὸ ῥᾳθυμίας καὶ
μαλακίας οὐδ' εἰς Ἄρειον πάγον ἀναβεβηκέναι. πάντες γὰρ
ἐπίστασθε ὅτι ἐν ἐκείνῳ τῷ χωρίῳ, ὅταν τὰς τοῦ φόνου δίκας
δικάζωνται, οὐ διὰ τούτου τοῦ ὀνόματος τὰς διωμοσίας ποιοῦνται, ἀλλὰ δι' οὗπερ ἐγὼ κακῶς ἀκήκοα· ὁ μὲν γὰρ διώκων
12 ὡς ἔκτεινε διόμνυται, ὁ δὲ φεύγων ὡς οὐκ ἔκτεινεν. οὐκ οὖν
ἄτοπον ἂν εἴη τὸν δράσαντ' ἀφεῖναι φάσκοντα ἀνδροφόνον
εἶναι, ὅτι ὁ διώκων, ὡς ἔκτεινε, τὸν φεύγοντα διωμόσατο; τί
γὰρ ταῦτα, ὧν οὗτος ἐρεῖ, διαφέρει; καὶ αὐτὸς μὲν Λυσιθέῳ
κακηγορίας ἐδικάσω εἰπόντι σε ἐρριφέναι τὴν ἀσπίδα. καίτοι
περὶ μὲν τοῦ ῥῖψαι οὐδὲν <ἐν> τῷ νόμῳ εἴρηται, ἐὰν δέ τις
εἴπῃ ἀποβεβληκέναι τὴν ἀσπίδα, πεντακοσίας δραχμὰς ὀφείλειν
13 κελεύει. οὐκ οὖν δεινόν, εἰ ὅταν μὲν δέῃ σὲ κακῶς ἀκούσαντα
τοὺς ἐχθροὺς τιμωρεῖσθαι, οὕτω τοὺς νόμους ὥσπερ ἐγὼ νῦν
λαμβάνεις, ὅταν δ' ἕτερον παρὰ τοὺς νόμους εἴπῃς κακῶς, οὐκ
ἀξιοῖς δοῦναι δίκην; πότερον οὕτως σὺ δεινὸς εἶ ὥστε, ὅπως
ἂν βούλῃ, οἷός τ' εἶ χρῆσθαι τοῖς νόμοις, ἢ τοσοῦτον δύνα-
σαι ὥστε οὐδέποτε οἴει τοὺς ἀδικουμένους ὑπὸ σοῦ τιμωρίας
14 τεύξεσθαι; εἶτ' οὐκ αἰσχύνει οὕτως ἀνοήτως διακείμενος,
ὥστε οὐκ ἐξ ὧν εὖ πεποίηκας τὴν πόλιν, ἀλλ' ἐξ ὧν ἀδικῶν

---

9 εἴρηται Dobree: εἴρητο   μέλειν Stephanus: μέλει C:
μέλλει X
10 ἀφείης Thalheim: ἀφίεις
11 κακῶς Contius: καλῶς
12 δράσαντ' ἀφεῖναι Dobson coll. Dem. 37.59: δείξαντα
κτεῖναι   Λυσιθέῳ Frohberger: Θέωνι   εἰπόντι σε Taylor: εἰπέ τίς σε X: ὅτι σε εἶπεν C   ἐν add. Markland
13 δέῃ σὲ Contius: δεήσῃ   λαμβάνεις Taylor: λαμβάνειν

148

are murderers have also killed people. It would have been a major task for the lawgiver to write all the words that have the same meaning, but by mentioning one he indicated his intention regarding all of them. For I do not suppose, Theomnestus, that whereas you 8 would expect someone to pay you the penalty after he had called you a father-beater or a mother-beater, you would think he ought to go unpunished when he has said that you struck your female or male parent, because he has used none of the forbidden words. I should 9 like to ask you this (since you are a practical expert in this matter, both in action and words): if anyone were to say that you had flung away your shield (the text of the law says "if anyone alleges that he has thrown it away, he is liable to prosecution"), you would not proceed against him, but acquiesce in the term "flung his shield away", saying you were unconcerned because "flinging" and "throwing" are not the same thing? And, if you were one of the 10 Eleven, you would not accept an arrest by a citizen alleging that he had been stripped of his cloak or divested of his tunic, but you would release the prisoner on the same principle, because he is not called a "clothes-stealer". Or if someone were arrested for abducting a child, you would not say he was a slave-dealer, if indeed you intend to fight your case on words, and pay no attention to the deeds to which all men apply the words. Now consider the matter 11 further, gentlemen of the jury, for I think this man, through idleness and remissness, has never mounted the Hill of Ares. For you all know that when homicide trials are being held in that place, in taking the oath they do not use that name, but the one with which I was slandered. The accuser swears that the defendant has "killed", and the defendant swears that he has not "killed". So would it not be 12 absurd to release the perpetrator when he described himself as a "murderer" because the prosecutor has sworn in his oath that the defendant has "killed"? What difference is there between this and what this man will claim? And you have yourself taken Lysitheus to court for slander when he said that you "flung your shield away". Yet there is no reference in the law to "flinging": it says that "if anyone says that a man has thrown his shield away, the penalty is five hundred drachmae." Therefore is it not shocking that, when you 13 need to punish your enemies for slandering you, you interpret the laws in the sense I do now, but when you slander someone else contrary to the laws you expect to escape punishment? Are you so clever that you can use the laws to suit your purposes, or are you so influential that you imagine that people wronged by you will never obtain revenge? And then, are you not ashamed at your senselessness 14 in thinking you should prosper not from benefits you have bestowed upon the city but from misdeeds for which you have escaped

οὐ δέδωκας δίκην, οἴει δεῖν πλεονεκτεῖν; Καί μοι ἀνάγνωθι
τὸν νόμον.

ΝΟΜΟΣ

15 Ἐγὼ τοίνυν, ὦ ἄνδρες δικασταί, ὑμᾶς μὲν πάντας εἰδέναι
ἡγοῦμαι ὅτι ἐγὼ μὲν ὀρθῶς λέγω, τοῦτον δὲ οὕτω σκαιὸν εἶναι
ὥστε οὐ δύνασθαι μαθεῖν τὰ λεγόμενα. βούλομαι οὖν αὐτὸν καὶ
ἐξ ἑτέρων νόμων περὶ τούτων διδάξαι, ἄν πως ἀλλὰ νῦν ἐπὶ
τοῦ βήματος παιδευθῇ καὶ τὸ λοιπὸν ἡμῖν μὴ παρέχῃ πράγματα.
Καί μοι ἀνάγνωθι τούτους τοὺς νόμους τοὺς Σόλωνος τοὺς
παλαιούς.
16   ΝΟΜΟΣ. Δεδέσθαι δ᾽ ἐν τῇ ποδοκάκκῃ ἡμέρας πέντε τὸν
πόδα, ἐὰν [μὴ] προστιμήσῃ ἡ ἡλιαία.
ꞌΗ ποδοκάκκη αὕτη ἐστίν, ὦ θεόμνηστε, ὃ νῦν καλεῖται ἐν
τῷ ξύλῳ δεδέσθαι. εἰ οὖν ὁ δεθεὶς ἐξελθὼν ἐν ταῖς εὐθύναις
τῶν ἕνδεκα κατηγοροίη ὅτι οὐκ ἐν τῇ ποδοκάκκῃ ἐδέδετο ἀλλ᾽
ἐν τῷ ξύλῳ, οὐκ ἄν ἠλίθιον αὐτὸν νομίζοιεν; Λέγε ἕτερον
νόμον.
17   ΝΟΜΟΣ. Ἐπεγγυᾶν δ᾽ ἐπιορκήσαντα τὸν Ἀπόλλω. δεδιότα
δὲ δίκης ἕνεκα δρασκάζειν.
Τοῦτο τὸ ἐπιορκήσαντα ὀμόσαντά ἐστι, τὸ δὲ δρασκάζειν,
ὃ νῦν ἀποδιδράσκειν ὀνομάζομεν.
Ὅστις δὲ ἀπίλλει τῇ θύρᾳ, ἔνδον τοῦ κλέπτου ὄντος.
Τὸ ἀπίλλειν τοῦτο ἀποκλῄειν νομίζεται, καὶ μηδὲν διὰ
τοῦτο διαφέρου.
18   Τὸ ἀργύριον στάσιμον εἶναι ἐφ᾽ ὁπόσῳ ἂν βούληται ὁ
δανείζων.
Τὸ στάσιμον τοῦτό ἐστιν, ὦ βέλτιστε, οὐ ζυγῷ ἱστάναι
ἀλλὰ τόκον πράττεσθαι ὁπόσον ἂν βούληται. Ἔτι δ᾽ ἀνάγνωθι
τουτουὶ τοῦ νόμου τὸ τελευταῖον.
19   Ὅσαι δὲ πεφασμένως πολοῦνται,
καὶ
οἰκῆος [καὶ] βλάβης τὴν διπλῆν εἶναι ὀφείλειν.
Προσέχετε τὸν νοῦν. τὸ μὲν πεφασμένως ἐστὶ φανερῶς,
20 πολεῖσθαι δὲ βαδίζειν, τὸ δὲ οἰκῆος θεράποντος. πολλὰ δὲ
τοιαῦτα καὶ ἄλλα ἐστίν, ὦ ἄνδρες δικασταί. ἀλλ᾽ εἰ μὴ σιδη-
ροῦς ἐστιν, οἴομαι αὐτὸν ἔννουν γεγονέναι ὅτι τὰ μὲν πράγματα ταῦτά ἐστι νῦν τε καὶ πάλαι, τῶν δὲ ὀνομάτων ἐνίοις οὐ
τοῖς αὐτοῖς χρώμεθα νῦν τε καὶ πρότερον. δηλώσει δέ· οἰχήσεται

---

14 καί μοι Markland: καίτοι
15 μὴ C solus
16 ποδοκάκκη O et Harpocration s.v.: ποδοκάκη CX   πέντε
   Hude coll. Dem. 24.114: δέκα   μὴ del. Auger
17 ὀμόσαντα Harpocration s.v. ἐπιορκήσαντα: ὀμόσαι
   τοῦτο Markland: τὸ
18 ἔτι δ᾽ ἀνάγνωθι P.Müller: ἐπανάγνωθι
19 πολοῦνται C: πωλοῦνται OX Thalheim   [καὶ] et διπλῆν
   Schelling: δούλην   εἶναι del. Taylor   πολεῖσθαι
   Hude: πωλεῖσθαι

150

punishment? Please read me the law.

LAW

Now I think you all know, gentlemen of the jury, that my 15
statement is correct, but this man is so slow-witted that he cannot
understand what is being said. I will therefore use other laws to
instruct him in these matters, in the hope that he can be taught even
now, while on the stand, and cause us no trouble in the future.
Please read me those ancient laws of Solon.
LAW: "He shall have his foot locked in the stocks for five days, if 16
the court shall add this to the sentence".
The "stocks" here mentioned, Theomnestus, are what we now call
"locking in the wood". So if the prisoner on release should accuse the
Eleven at their audit of having locked him not in the "stocks" but in
the "wood", would they not think him simple-minded? Read another
law.
LAW: "He is to give security vowing by Apollo. If he fears the 17
course of justice, let him flee".
Here "vow" means "swear", and for "flee" we now say "run away".
"Whoever excludes with the door, when the burglar is within.."
"Excludes" here means "shuts out"; do not argue about that.
"Money is to be set out at whatever rate the lender requires". 18
Here "setting out" does not mean "setting on the scales", my fine
fellow, but exacting such interest as one may require. Again, read
the last part of this law here.
"But such women as overtly tread abroad", and 19
"is to owe double the penalty of a serf's injury".
Pay attention: "overtly" is "openly", and "tread abroad" is "walk
about"; and "serf" is "servant". There are many other such 20
examples, gentlemen of the jury, but if he is not obdurate, I think
he has come to realise that things are the same now as they were of
old, but that in some cases we do not use the same names now as we
did formerly; and he will show his assent by leaving the stand and

21 γὰρ ἀπιὼν ἀπὸ τοῦ βήματος σιωπῇ. εἰ δὲ μή, δέομαι ὑμῶν, ὦ
    ἄνδρες δικασταί, τὰ δίκαια ψηφίσασθαι, ἐνθυμουμένους ὅτι
    πολὺ μεῖζον κακόν ἐστιν ἀκοῦσαι τὸν πατέρα ἀπεκτονέναι ἢ
    τὴν ἀσπίδα ἀποβεβληκέναι. ἐγὼ γοῦν δεξαίμην ἂν πάσας τὰς
    ἀσπίδας ἐρριφέναι ἢ τοιαύτην γνώμην ἔχειν περὶ τὸν πατέρα.
22   Οὗτος οὖν ἔνοχος μὲν ὢν τῇ αἰτίᾳ, ἐλάττονος δὲ οὔσης
    αὐτῷ τῆς συμφορᾶς, οὐ μόνον ὑφ' ὑμῶν ἠλεήθη, ἀλλὰ καὶ τὸν
    μαρτυρήσαντα ἠτίμωσεν. ἐγὼ δὲ ἑορακὼς μὲν ἐκεῖνο τοῦτον
    ποιήσαντα ὃ καὶ ὑμεῖς ἴστε, αὐτὸς δὲ σώσας τὴν ἀσπίδα,
    ἀκηκοὼς δὲ οὕτως ἀνόσιον καὶ δεινὸν πρᾶγμα, μεγίστης δὲ
    οὔσης μοι τῆς συμφορᾶς, εἰ ἀποφεύξεται, τούτῳ δ' οὐδενὸς
    ἀξίας, εἰ κακηγορίας ἁλώσεται, οὐκ ἄρα δίκην παρ' αὐτοῦ
23 λήψομαι; τίνος ὄντος ἐμοὶ πρὸς ὑμᾶς ἐγκλήματος; πότερον
    ὅτι δικαίως ἀκήκοα; ἀλλ' οὐδ' ἂν αὐτοὶ φήσαιτε. ἀλλ' ὅτι
    βελτίων καὶ ἐκ βελτιόνων ὁ φεύγων ἐμοῦ; ἀλλ' οὐδ' ἂν αὐτὸς
    ἀξιώσειεν. ἀλλ' ὅτι ἀποβεβληκὼς τὰ ὅπλα δικάζομαι κακηγο-
    ρίας τῷ σώσαντι; ἀλλ' οὐχ οὗτος ὁ λόγος ἐν τῇ πόλει κατε-
24 σκέδασται. ἀναμνήσθητε δὲ ὅτι μεγάλην καὶ καλὴν ἐκείνην
    δωρεὰν αὐτῷ δεδώκατε· ἐν ᾗ τίς οὐκ ἂν ἐλεήσειε Διονύσιον,
    τοιαύτη μὲν συμφορᾷ περιπεπτωκότα, ἄνδρα δὲ ἄριστον ἐν τοῖς
25 κινδύνοις γεγενημένον, ἀπιόντα δὲ ἀπὸ τοῦ δικαστηρίου [καὶ]
    λέγοντα ὅτι δυστυχεστάτην ἐκείνην εἶμεν στρατείαν ἐστρατευ-
    μένοι, ἐν ᾗ πολλοὶ μὲν ἡμῶν ἀπέθανον, οἱ δὲ σώσαντες τὰ
    ὅπλα ὑπὸ τῶν ἀποβαλόντων ψευδομαρτυρίων ἑαλώκασι, κρεῖττον
    δὲ ἦν αὐτῷ τότε ἀποθανεῖν ἢ οἴκαδ' ἐλθόντι τοιαύτῃ τύχῃ
26 χρῆσθαι; μὴ τοίνυν ἀκούσαντά <τε> θεόμνηστον κακῶς τὰ προσ-
    ήκοντα ἐλεεῖτε, καὶ ὑβρίζοντι καὶ λέγοντι παρὰ τοὺς νόμους
    συγγνώμην ἔχετε. τίς γὰρ ἂν ἐμοὶ μείζων ταύτης γένοιτο
    συμφορά, περὶ τοιούτου πατρὸς οὕτως αἰσχρὰν αἰτίαν ἀκηκο-
27 ότι; ὃς πολλάκις μὲν ἐστρατήγησε, πολλοὺς δὲ καὶ ἄλλους
    κινδύνους μεθ' ὑμῶν ἐκινδύνευσε· καὶ οὔτε τοῖς πολεμίοις
    τὸ ἐκείνου σῶμα ὑποχείριον ἐγένετο, οὔτε τοῖς πολίταις
    οὐδεμίαν πώποτε ὦφλεν εὐθύνην, ἔτη δὲ γεγονὼς ἑπτὰ καὶ
    ἑξήκοντα ἐν ὀλιγαρχίᾳ δι' εὔνοιαν τοῦ ὑμετέρου πλήθους
28 ἀπέθανεν. ἆρ' ἄξιον ὀργισθῆναι τῷ <τοιαῦτ'> εἰρηκότι καὶ
    βοηθῆσαι τῷ πατρί, ὡς καὶ ἐκείνου κακῶς ἀκηκοότος; τί γὰρ
    ἂν τούτου ἀνιαρότερον γένοιτο αὐτῷ, ἢ τεθνάναι μὲν ὑπὸ τῶν
    ἐχθρῶν, αἰτίαν δ' ἔχειν ὑπὸ τῶν παίδων; οὗ ἔτι καὶ νῦν, ὦ
    ἄνδρες δικασταί, τῆς ἀρετῆς τὰ μνημεῖα πρὸς τοῖς ὑμετέροις
    <ἱεροῖς> ἀνάκειται, τὰ δὲ τούτου καὶ τοῦ τούτου πατρὸς τῆς

---

21 ἀκοῦσαι Dobree: ἀκούσαντα
22 ἀνόσιον Hertlein: ἄνομον   ἀξίας, εἰ Contius: ἀξιώσει X
23 κατεσκέδασται Brulart: κατεσκεύασται
24 δωρεὰν Contius: δῶρον
25 καὶ del. Reiske   εἶμεν Hude: εὔημεν
26 τε add. Bekker   αἰσχρὰν αἰτίαν ἀκηκοότι; ὃς Reiske:
    αἰσχρᾶς αἰτίας ἀκηκοότος
28 τοιαῦτ' add. Frohberger   ἱεροῖς add. Contius coll.
    11.10

152

departing in silence. But if he does not, I beg you, gentlemen of the 21
jury, to cast your votes justly, bearing in mind that it is a far worse
insult to be accused of killing one's father than of throwing away
one's shield. For my part, I would be prepared to throw away any
number of shields rather than have any such intention towards my
father.

Now this man, who was guilty as charged, but faced less 22
damage, won not only your sympathy but even the disfranchisement
of his accuser. But I, who saw him doing what you also know he did,
and saved my own shield, have been accused of unholy and shocking
behaviour; and since the outcome for me will be utterly disastrous if
he is acquitted, whereas it will not be very serious for him if he is
condemned for slander, am I not to exact justice from him? What 23
charge against me has he brought before you? Is it that I stand
justly accused? But not even you yourselves could say that. Then is
it that the defendant and his parents are better citizens? But he
would not even claim that himself. Then is it that I have thrown away
my shield and am being prosecuted by a man who saved his? But this
is not the story that has been spread through the city. Remember 24
that you have bestowed that great and generous gift upon him, but
in that matter who could fail to find pity for Dionysius? Such a great
disaster has befallen him after he had proved his prowess in the face
of danger, and he left the courthouse saying that that had been our 25
most ill-fated campaign: for in it many of us were killed, and those
who kept their arms had been condemned through the false evidence
of those who had thrown their arms away. He added that it would
have been better for him to have died then than to have returned
home to meet such a fate. So do not pity Theomnestus when he is 26
censured as he deserves, nor forgive his arrogant behaviour and
illegal utterances. For what worse disaster could befall me after I
have listened to such shameful slander against so worthy a father as
mine? He was general many times, and shared many dangers with you 27
besides. He neither fell into enemy hands, nor was he ever fined by
his fellow-citizens as the result of an audit, but he died under the
oligarchy at the age of sixty-seven because of his devotion to your
democracy. Is it not right to feel anger against a man who has said 28
such things, and to support my father as being included in this
slander? What more painful fate could he suffer than this – to be
killed by his enemies and to be remembered with reproach for having
been killed by his sons? Even now, gentlemen of the jury, the
memorials of his valour are hung on your temple walls, while those of
this man and his father are on those of the enemy: so much is

κακίας πρὸς τοῖς τῶν πολεμίων· οὕτω σύμφυτος αὐτοῖς ἡ
29 δειλία. καὶ μὲν δή, ὦ ἄνδρες δικασταί, ὅσῳ μείζους εἰσὶ
καὶ νεανίαι τὰς ὄψεις, τοσοῦτο μᾶλλον ὀργῆς ἄξιοί εἰσι.
δῆλον γὰρ ὅτι τοῖς μὲν σώμασι δύνανται, τὰς δὲ ψυχὰς οὐκ
<εὖ> ἔχουσιν.
30   Ἀκούω δ' αὐτόν, ὦ ἄνδρες δικασταί, ἐπὶ τοῦτον τὸν
λόγον τρέψεσθαι, ὡς ὀργισθεὶς εἴρηκε ταῦτα ἐμοῦ μαρτυρή-
σαντος τὴν αὐτὴν μαρτυρίαν Διονυσίῳ. ὑμεῖς δ' ἐνθυμεῖσθε,
ὦ ἄνδρες δικασταί, ὅτι ὁ νομοθέτης οὐδεμίαν ὀργῇ συγγνώμην
δίδωσιν, ἀλλὰ ζημιοῖ τὸν λέγοντα, ἐὰν μὴ ἀποφαίνῃ ὡς ἔστιν
ἀληθῆ τὰ εἰρημένα. ἐγὼ δὲ δὶς ἤδη περὶ τούτου μεμαρτύρηκα·
οὐ γάρ πω ἤδη ὅτι ὑμεῖς τοὺς μὲν ἰδόντας τιμωρεῖσθε, τοῖς
δὲ ἀποβαλοῦσι συγγνώμην ἔχετε.
31   Περὶ μὲν οὖν τούτων οὐκ οἶδ' ὅ τι δεῖ πλείω λέγειν· ἐγὼ
δ' ὑμῶν δέομαι καταψηφίσασθαι Θεομνήστου, ἐνθυμουμένους ὅτι
οὐκ ἂν γένοιτο τούτου μείζων ἀγών μοι. νῦν γὰρ διώκω <μὲν>
κακηγορίας, τῇ δ' αὐτῇ ψήφῳ φόνου φεύγω τοῦ πατρός, ὃς
μόνος, ἐπειδὴ τάχιστα ἐδοκιμάσθην, ἐπεξῆλθον τοῖς τριάκοντα
32 ἐν Ἀρείῳ πάγῳ. ὧν μεμνημένοι καὶ ἐμοὶ καὶ τῷ πατρὶ βοηθήσατε καὶ τοῖς νόμοις τοῖς κειμένοις καὶ τοῖς ὅρκοις οἷς
ὀμωμόκατε.

---

29 εὖ add. Emperius
30 τρέψεσθαι Markland: τρέπεσθαι   οὐδεμίαν Brulart
    coll. 11.11: οὐδεμιᾶ   ἀποβαλοῦσι Cobet: ἀποβάλλουσι
31 μὲν add. Scheibe coll. 11.12

cowardice a part of their nature. And indeed, gentlemen of the jury, 29
the more impressive and dashing their appearance, the more they
deserve our resentment; for it is clear that they possess the physical
ability but their hearts are not in the right place.

I hear that he is going to resort to the argument that he made 30
these accusations in a moment of anger at my confirming Dionysius's
testimony. But you must bear in mind, gentlemen of the jury, that
the lawgiver makes no allowance for anger, but penalises the speaker
if he does not prove that his statement is true. Now I have already
borne witness concerning this man, for I did not yet realise that you
grant indulgence to those who have thrown away their weapons, while
punishing those who have seen them do so.

I do not know what more should be said on these matters. I 31
ask you to condemn Theomnestus, reflecting that no trial could be
more important to me than this one: for today I am prosecuting for
slander, but under the same verdict I am defending myself on a
charge of patricide – I who alone on being enrolled as an adult went
out to attack the Thirty on the Hill of Ares. Remember these acts, 32
and vindicate both me and my father, and the established laws which
you have sworn to obey.

ΚΑΤΑ ΕΡΑΤΟΣΘΕΝΟΥΣ

1   Οὐκ ἄρξασθαί μοι δοκεῖ ἄπορον εἶναι, ὦ ἄνδρες δικασταί,
τῆς κατηγορίας, ἀλλὰ παύσασθαι λέγοντι· τοιαῦτα αὐτοῖς τὸ
μέγεθος καὶ τοσαῦτα τὸ πλῆθος εἴργασται, ὥστε μήτ' ἂν ψευδόμενον δεινότερα τῶν ὑπαρχόντων κατηγορῆσαι, μήτε τἀληθῆ
βουλόμενον εἰπεῖν ἅπαντα δύνασθαι, ἀλλ' ἀνάγκη ἢ τὸν κατή-
2 γορον ἀπειπεῖν ἢ τὸν χρόνον ἐπιλιπεῖν. τοὐναντίον δέ μοι
δοκοῦμεν πείσεσθαι ἢ ἐν τῷ πρὸ τοῦ χρόνῳ. πρότερον μὲν γὰρ
ἔδει τὴν ἔχθραν τοὺς κατηγοροῦντας ἐπιδεῖξαι, ἥτις εἴη πρὸς
τοὺς φεύγοντας· νυνὶ δὲ παρὰ τῶν φευγόντων χρὴ πυνθάνεσθαι
ἥτις ἦν αὐτοῖς πρὸς τὴν πόλιν ἔχθρα, ἀνθ' ὅτου τοιαῦτα
ἐτόλμησαν εἰς αὐτὴν ἐξαμαρτάνειν. οὐ μέντοι ὡς οὐκ ἔχων
οἰκείας ἔχθρας καὶ συμφορὰς τοὺς λόγους ποιοῦμαι, ἀλλ' ὡς
ἅπασι πολλῆς ἀφθονίας οὔσης ὑπὲρ τῶν ἰδίων ἢ ὑπὲρ τῶν δημο-
3 σίων ὀργίζεσθαι. ἐγὼ μὲν οὖν, ὦ ἄνδρες δικασταί, οὔτ'
ἐμαυτοῦ πώποτε οὔτε ἀλλότρια πράγματα πράξας νῦν ἠνάγκασμαι
ὑπὸ τῶν γεγενημένων τούτου κατηγορεῖν, ὥστε πολλάκις εἰς
πολλὴν ἀθυμίαν κατέστην, μὴ διὰ τὴν ἀπειρίαν ἀναξίως καὶ
ἀδυνάτως ὑπὲρ τοῦ ἀδελφοῦ καὶ ἐμαυτοῦ τὴν κατηγορίαν ποιή-
σωμαι· ὅμως δὲ πειράσομαι ὑμᾶς ἐξ ἀρχῆς ὡς ἂν δύνωμαι δι'
ἐλαχίστων διδάξαι.
4   Οὑμὸς πατὴρ Κέφαλος ἐπείσθη μὲν ὑπὸ Περικλέους εἰς
ταύτην τὴν γῆν ἀφικέσθαι, ἔτη δὲ τριάκοντα ᾤκησε, καὶ οὐδενὶ πώποτε οὔτε ἡμεῖς οὔτε ἐκεῖνος δίκην οὔτε ἐδικασάμεθα
οὔτε ἐφύγομεν, ἀλλ' οὕτως ᾠκοῦμεν δημοκρατούμενοι ὥστε μήτε
εἰς τοὺς ἄλλους ἐξαμαρτάνειν μήτε ὑπὸ τῶν ἄλλων ἀδικεῖσθαι.
5 ἐπειδὴ δ' οἱ τριάκοντα πονηροὶ [μὲν] καὶ συκοφάνται ὄντες
εἰς τὴν ἀρχὴν κατέστησαν, φάσκοντες χρῆναι τῶν ἀδίκων
καθαρὰν ποιῆσαι τὴν πόλιν καὶ τοὺς λοιποὺς πολίτας ἐπ'
ἀρετὴν καὶ δικαιοσύνην τραπέσθαι, [καὶ] τοιαῦτα λέγοντες
οὐ τοιαῦτα ποιεῖν ἐτόλμων, ὡς ἐγὼ περὶ τῶν ἐμαυτοῦ πρῶτον
6 εἰπὼν καὶ περὶ τῶν ὑμετέρων ἀναμνῆσαι πειράσομαι. Θέογνις
γὰρ καὶ Πείσων ἔλεγον ἐν τοῖς τριάκοντα περὶ τῶν μετοίκων,
ὡς εἶέν τινες τῇ πολιτείᾳ ἀχθόμενοι· καλλίστην οὖν εἶναι
πρόφασιν τιμωρεῖσθαι μὲν δοκεῖν, τῷ δ' ἔργῳ χρηματίζεσθαι·
πάντως δὲ τὴν μὲν πόλιν πένεσθαι, τὴν <δ'> ἀρχὴν δεῖσθαι
7 χρημάτων. καὶ τοὺς ἀκούοντας οὐ χαλεπῶς ἔπειθον· ἀποκτιννύναι μὲν γὰρ ἀνθρώπους περὶ οὐδενὸς ἡγοῦντο, λαμβάνειν δὲ
χρήματα περὶ πολλοῦ ἐποιοῦντο. ἔδοξεν οὖν αὐτοῖς δέκα συλλαβεῖν, τούτων δὲ δύο πένητας, ἵνα αὐτοῖς ᾖ πρὸς τοὺς

---

3   ποιήσωμαι C: ποιήσομαι rell.
5   μὲν del. Reiske   καὶ del. Markland
6   πένεσθαι Markland: γενέσθαι   δ' add. Scaliger

SPEECH 12 : AGAINST ERATOSTHENES

My difficulty in this prosecution, gentlemen of the jury, is not 1
to know where to begin, but where to end. The size and number of
their crimes are so great that even if I lied I could not accuse them
of worse crimes than they have committed; nor could I describe them
all, though wishing to speak only the truth, but either the accuser
would inevitably tire, or his time run out. I think we shall have the 2
opposite experience to prosecutors of former times: for in those days
accusers were required to explain how they came to be enemies of the
defendants, but today it is necessary to enquire of defendants how
they came to be enemies of the state, whereby they dared to commit
such crimes against her. However, this statement of mine does not
arise from any lack of private grievance and damage sustained, but
from the abundance of reasons which everyone has to be angry   for
both personal reasons and those of public concern. Now I, gentlemen 3
of the jury, having never previously engaged in litigation either on
my own or another's behalf, have been forced by events to prosecute
this man. I have therefore often viewed the prospect of this with
great diffidence, fearing that I might, through inexperience, fail to
conduct the prosecution worthily and competently on my brother's and
my own behalf. Nevertheless I shall try to inform you of the facts
from the beginning as briefly as I can.
My father Cephalus was persuaded by Pericles to come to this 4
land, and lived in it for thirty years. Neither he nor we were ever
involved in litigation with anyone either as prosecutors or defendants,
but we so conducted our lives under the democracy as to avoid
offending others and suffering injustice at their hands. But when the 5
Thirty, who were men of a wicked and slanderous character, came to
power, they pretended that it was necessary to purge the city of
wrongdoers and to direct the rest towards virtue and justice. But
they had the audacity not to follow these words with the appropriate
actions, as I shall try to remind you by referring firstly to my own
and then to your experiences. Theognis and Peison spoke in a 6
meeting of the Thirty about the resident aliens, saying that some
were disaffected with their regime. This would afford an excellent
excuse to appear to be punishing them, while in reality to be making
money. At any rate, the city was impoverished, and the government
needed money. They had no difficulty in persuading their audience, 7
who thought nothing of putting men to death but a lot of acquiring
money. They therefore decided to arrest ten, but that these should
include two poor men, so that they would be able to excuse their

ἄλλους ἀπολογία, ὡς οὐ χρημάτων ἕνεκα ταῦτα πέπρακται,
ἀλλὰ συμφέροντα τῇ πολιτείᾳ γεγένηται, ὥσπερ τι τῶν ἄλλων
8 εὐλόγως πεποιηκότες. διαλαβόντες δὲ τὰς οἰκίας ἐβάδιζον·
καὶ ἐμὲ μὲν ξένους ἑστιῶντα κατέλαβον, οὓς ἐξελάσαντες
Πείσωνί με παραδιδόασιν· οἱ δὲ ἄλλοι εἰς τὸ ἐργαστήριον
ἐλθόντες τὰ ἀνδράποδα ἀπεγράφοντο. ἐγὼ δὲ Πείσωνα μὲν
9 ἠρώτων εἰ βούλοιτό με σῶσαι χρήματα λαβών· ὁ δ' ἔφασκεν,
εἰ πολλὰ εἴη. εἶπον οὖν ὅτι τάλαντον ἀργυρίου ἕτοιμος εἴην
δοῦναι· ὁ δ' ὡμολόγησε ταῦτα ποιήσειν. ἠπιστάμην μὲν οὖν
ὅτι οὔτε θεοὺς οὔτ' ἀνθρώπους νομίζει, ὅμως δ' ἐκ τῶν
παρόντων ἐδόκει μοι ἀναγκαιότατον εἶναι πίστιν παρ' αὐτοῦ
10 λαβεῖν. ἐπειδὴ δὲ ὤμοσεν, ἐξώλειαν ἑαυτῷ καὶ τοῖς παισὶν
ἐπαρώμενος, λαβὼν τὸ τάλαντόν με σώσειν, εἰσελθὼν εἰς τὸ
δωμάτιον τὴν κιβωτὸν ἀνοίγνυμι· Πείσων δ' αἰσθόμενος εἰσέρχεται, καὶ ἰδὼν τὰ ἐνόντα καλεῖ τῶν ὑπηρετῶν δύο, καὶ τὰ
11 ἐν τῇ κιβωτῷ λαβεῖν ἐκέλευσεν. ἐπεὶ δὲ οὐχ ὅσον ὡμολόγησα
εἶχεν, ὦ ἄνδρες δικασταί, ἀλλὰ τρία τάλαντα ἀργυρίου καὶ
τετρακοσίους κυζικηνοὺς καὶ ἑκατὸν δαρεικοὺς καὶ φιάλας
ἀργυρᾶς τέτταρας, ἐδεόμην αὐτοῦ ἐφόδιά μοι δοῦναι, ὁ δ'
12 ἀγαπήσειν με ἔφασκεν, εἰ τὸ σῶμα σώσω. ἐξιοῦσι δ' ἐμοὶ καὶ
Πείσωνι ἐπιτυγχάνει Μηλόβιός τε καὶ Μνησιθείδης ἐκ τοῦ
ἐργαστηρίου ἀπιόντες, καὶ καταλαμβάνουσι πρὸς αὐταῖς ταῖς
θύραις, καὶ ἐρωτῶσιν ὅποι βαδίζοιμεν· ὁ δ' ἔφασκεν εἰς τὰ
τοῦ ἀδελφοῦ τοῦ ἐμοῦ, ἵνα καὶ τὰ ἐν ἐκείνῃ τῇ οἰκίᾳ σκέψη-
ται. ἐκεῖνον μὲν οὖν ἐκέλευον βαδίζειν, ἐμὲ δὲ μεθ' αὐτῶν
13 ἀκολουθεῖν εἰς Δαμνίππου. Πείσων δὲ προσελθὼν σιγᾶν μοι
παρεκελεύετο καὶ θαρρεῖν, ὡς ἥξων ἐκεῖσε. καταλαμβάνομεν
δὲ αὐτόθι Θέογνιν ἑτέρους φυλάττοντα· ᾧ παραδόντες ἐμὲ
πάλιν ᾤχοντο. ἐν τοιούτῳ δ' ὄντι μοι κινδυνεύειν ἐδόκει,
14 ὡς τοῦ γε ἀποθανεῖν ὑπάρχοντος ἤδη. καλέσας δὲ Δάμνιππον
λέγω πρὸς αὐτὸν τάδε, 'ἐπιτήδειος μέν μοι τυγχάνεις ὤν, ἥκω
δ' εἰς τὴν σὴν οἰκίαν, ἀδικῶ δ' οὐδέν, χρημάτων δ' ἕνεκα
ἀπόλλυμαι. σὺ οὖν ταῦτα πάσχοντί μοι πρόθυμον παράσχου τὴν
σεαυτοῦ δύναμιν εἰς τὴν ἐμὴν σωτηρίαν.' ὁ δ' ὑπέσχετο ταῦτα
ποιήσειν. ἐδόκει δ' αὐτῷ βέλτιον εἶναι πρὸς Θέογνιν μνησθῆ-
ναι· ἡγεῖτο γὰρ ἅπαν ποιήσειν αὐτόν, εἴ τις ἀργύριον διδοίη.
15 ἐκείνου δὲ διαλεγομένου Θεόγνιδι (ἔμπειρος γὰρ ὢν ἐτύγχανον
τῆς οἰκίας καὶ ᾔδη ὅτι ἀμφίθυρος εἴη) ἐδόκει μοι ταύτῃ
πειρᾶσθαι σωθῆναι, ἐνθυμουμένῳ ὅτι, ἐὰν μὲν λάθω, σωθήσομαι,
ἐὰν δὲ ληφθῶ, ἡγούμην μέν, εἰ Θέογνις εἴη πεπεισμένος ὑπὸ
τοῦ Δαμνίππου χρήματα λαβεῖν, οὐδὲν ἧττον ἀφεθήσεσθαι, εἰ
16 δὲ μή, ὁμοίως ἀποθανεῖσθαι. ταῦτα διανοηθεὶς ἔφευγον, ἐκείνων ἐπὶ τῇ αὐλείῳ θύρᾳ τὴν φυλακὴν ποιουμένων· τριῶν δὲ
θυρῶν οὐσῶν, ἃς ἔδει με διελθεῖν, ἅπασαι ἀνεῳγμέναι ἔτυχον.
ἀφικόμενος δὲ εἰς Ἀρχένεω τοῦ ναυκλήρου ἐκεῖνον πέμπω εἰς
ἄστυ, πευσόμενον περὶ τοῦ ἀδελφοῦ· ἥκων δὲ ἔλεγεν ὅτι
Ἐρατοσθένης αὐτὸν ἐν τῇ ὁδῷ λαβὼν εἰς τὸ δεσμωτήριον

---

11 δαρεικοὺς Maussac: καρικοὺς
15 ᾔδη Hude: ᾔδειν

action against the others by saying that it had been carried out not for money, but to benefit the state, just as if it were like any other reasonable action. They allocated the houses among themselves and proceeded. They found me entertaining guests, and after driving them out they handed me over to Peison. The rest went to the factory and made a list of the slaves. I asked Peison whether he was prepared to accept money in return for my safety. He said he would, if it was a large sum. So I said I was prepared to give him a talent of silver, and he agreed to my proposal. Now I knew that he paid no regard to gods or men, yet considering the situation it seemed to me absolutely essential to obtain a pledge from him. When he had taken the oath to take the talent and save me, calling down destruction upon himself and his children, I entered my bedroom and opened the chest. Peison noticed it and came in, and on seeing its contents called two of his assistants and ordered them to seize what was in the chest. As he now had not the amount which I had agreed, gentlemen of the jury, but three talents of silver, four hundred cyzicenes, a hundred darics and four silver cups, I begged him to give me money for my journey. But he said I should be content if I saved my skin. As Peison and I went out we were met by Melobius and Mnesitheides, who were leaving the factory. They caught up with us at the very doors, and asked us where we were going. Peison said, to my brother's house to examine the contents of that house also. So they told him to carry on, but ordered me to follow them to the house of Damnippus. Peison came up and urged me to remain silent and be reassured, as he would come there. There we found Theognis guarding some other men. They handed me over to him and made off again. Such was my position that I decided to take a chance, as I already seemed doomed to die. I called Damnippus and said to him: "You are a friend of mine and I have come into your house. I have done no wrong but am being destroyed for my money. As I am in this plight, provide me with your active assistance to escape". He promised to do so; but he decided that it was better to mention it to Theognis, as he thought he would do anything if anyone offered him money. While he was talking with Theognis, (I happened to be familiar with the house and knew that it had doors at both front and back) I decided to make my bid for safety this way, reflecting that if I were undiscovered, I should be saved, while if I were caught I thought that if Theognis had been persuaded by Damnippus to accept money, I should be released none the less, and if not I should die just the same. With these thoughts I began to escape, while they were guarding the courtyard door. There were three doors for me to pass through, and all happened to be open. When I arrived at the house of Archeneos the ship-captain, I sent him to town to enquire about my brother. When he returned he said that Eratosthenes had arrested him in the street and taken him off to

8

9

10

11

12

13

14

15

16

17 ἀπαγάγοι. καὶ ἐγὼ τοιαῦτα πεπυσμένος τῆς ἐπιούσης νυκτὸς
διέπλευσα Μεγαράδε. Πολεμάρχῳ δὲ παρήγγειλαν οἱ τριάκοντα
τοὔπ' ἐκείνων εἰθισμένον παράγγελμα, πίνειν κώνειον, πρὶν
τὴν αἰτίαν εἰπεῖν δι' ἥντινα ἔμελλεν ἀποθανεῖσθαι· οὕτω
18 πολλοῦ ἐδέησε κριθῆναι καὶ ἀπολογήσασθαι. καὶ ἐπειδὴ ἀπε-
φέρετο ἐκ τοῦ δεσμωτηρίου τεθνεώς, τριῶν ἡμῖν οἰκιῶν οὐσῶν
οὐδ' ἐκ μιᾶς εἴασαν ἐξενεχθῆναι, ἀλλὰ κλεισίον μισθωσάμενοι
προὔθεντο αὐτόν. καὶ πολλῶν ὄντων ἱματίων αἰτοῦσιν οὐδὲν
ἔδοσαν εἰς τὴν ταφήν, ἀλλὰ τῶν φίλων ὁ μὲν ἱμάτιον, ὁ δὲ
προσκεφάλαιον, ὁ δὲ ὅ τι ἕκαστος ἔτυχεν ἔδωκεν εἰς τὴν
19 ἐκείνου ταφήν. καὶ ἔχοντες μὲν ἑπτακοσίας ἀσπίδας τῶν
ἡμετέρων, ἔχοντες δὲ ἀργύριον καὶ χρυσίον τοσοῦτον, χαλκὸν
δὲ καὶ κόσμον καὶ ἔπιπλα καὶ ἱμάτια γυναικεῖα ὅσα οὐδεπώποτε ᾤοντο κτήσεσθαι, καὶ ἀνδράποδα εἴκοσι καὶ ἑκατόν, ὧν
τὰ μὲν βέλτιστα ἔλαβον, τὰ δὲ λοιπὰ εἰς τὸ δημόσιον ἀπέδοσαν, εἰς τοσαύτην ἀπληστίαν καὶ αἰσχροκέρδειαν ἀφίκοντο
καὶ τοῦ τρόπου τοῦ αὐτῶν ἀπόδειξιν ἐποιήσαντο· τῆς γὰρ
Πολεμάρχου γυναικὸς χρυσοῦς ἑλικτῆρας, οὓς ἔχουσα ἐτύγχανεν, ὅτε τὸ πρῶτον ἦλθεν εἰς τὴν οἰκίαν, Μηλόβιος ἐκ τῶν
20 ὤτων ἐξείλετο. καὶ οὐδὲ κατὰ τὸ ἐλάχιστον μέρος τῆς οὐσίας
ἐλέου παρ' αὐτῶν ἐτυγχάνομεν. ἀλλ' οὕτως εἰς ἡμᾶς διὰ τὰ
χρήματα ἐξημάρτανον, ὥσπερ ἂν ἕτεροι μεγάλων ἀδικημάτων
ὀργὴν ἔχοντες, οὐ τούτων ἀξίους γε ὄντας τῇ πόλει, ἀλλὰ
πάσας <μὲν> τὰς χορηγίας χορηγήσαντας, πολλὰς δ' εἰσφορὰς
εἰσενεγκόντας, κοσμίους δ' ἡμᾶς αὐτοὺς παρέχοντας καὶ πᾶν
τὸ προσταττόμενον ποιοῦντας, ἐχθρὸν δ' οὐδένα κεκτημένους,
πολλοὺς δ' Ἀθηναίων ἐκ τῶν πολεμίων λυσαμένους· τοιούτων
ἠξίωσαν οὐχ ὁμοίως μετοικοῦντας ὥσπερ αὐτοὶ ἐπολιτεύοντο.
21 οὗτοι γὰρ πολλοὺς μὲν τῶν πολιτῶν εἰς τοὺς πολεμίους
ἐξήλασαν, πολλοὺς δ' ἀδίκως ἀποκτείναντες ἀτάφους ἐποίησαν,
πολλοὺς δ' ἐπιτίμους ὄντας ἀτίμους [τῆς πόλεως] κατέστησαν,
22 πολλῶν δὲ θυγατέρας μελλούσας ἐκδίδοσθαι ἐκώλυσαν. καὶ εἰς
τοσοῦτόν εἰσι τόλμης ἀφιγμένοι ὥσθ' ἥκουσιν ἀπολογησόμενοι,
καὶ λέγουσιν ὡς οὐδὲν κακὸν οὐδ' αἰσχρὸν εἰργασμένοι εἰσίν.
ἐγὼ δ' ἐβουλόμην ἂν αὐτοὺς ἀληθῆ λέγειν· μετῆν γὰρ ἂν καὶ
23 ἐμοὶ τούτου τἀγαθοῦ οὐκ ἐλάχιστον μέρος. νῦν δὲ οὔτε πρὸς
τὴν πόλιν αὐτοῖς τοιαῦτα ὑπάρχει οὔτε πρὸς ἐμέ· τὸν ἀδελφὸν
γάρ μου, ὥσπερ καὶ πρότερον εἶπον, Ἐρατοσθένης ἀπέκτεινεν,
οὔτε αὐτὸς ἰδίᾳ ἀδικούμενος οὔτε εἰς τὴν πόλιν ὁρῶν ἐξαμαρ-
τάνοντα, ἀλλὰ τῇ ἑαυτοῦ παρανομίᾳ προθύμως ἐξυπηρετῶν.

---

17 τοὔπ' Fritzsche: τὸ ὑπ': τὸ ἐπ' Aldus
18 οὐδ' ἐκ μιᾶς Weidner: οὐδεμιᾶς   κλεισίον W.Dindorf:
   κλίσιον
19 κτήσεσθαι Dobree: κτήσασθαι
20 γε ὄντας Thalheim, Hude: ἔχοντας   μὲν add. Reiske
   εἰσενεγκόντας Markland: ἐνεγκόντας
21 τῆς πόλεως del. Markland

prison. With this news of his fate I sailed the next night across to 17
Megara. The Thirty gave Polemarchus their customary command to
drink hemlock, with no prior statement as to the reason for his
execution, let alone a trial and a chance to make his defence. And as 18
he was being carried dead from the prison they did not allow a
funeral to be conducted from any one of our three houses, but they
laid him out in a small hut they had hired. We also had many cloaks,
yet they refused their request for one for his burial; but one of our
friends supplied a cloak, another a pillow, and others what they each
happened to have, for the burial. They had seven hundred shields of 19
ours, they had all that silver and gold, with bronze, jewellery,
furniture and women's clothes, all in quantities exceeding their
greatest expectations, and a hundred and twenty slaves, the best of
which they took for themselves and the rest they handed over to the
public treasury. But the action which illustrates their character and
the extremes of insatiable greed that they reached was this: on first
entering the house, Melobius tore from her ears the gold earrings
which Polemarchus's wife happened to be wearing. Thus we received 20
no pity from them regarding even the smallest part of our property.
But they wronged us for our wealth as others would act in anger for
great injuries done, though we did not deserve such treatment at the
city's hands, but had performed all our duties as theatre-producers,
paid many special taxes, and in general behaved as responsible and
obedient men, incurring no private enmities and ransoming many
Athenians from the enemy. Such was their reward to us for behaving
as resident aliens far otherwise than they did as citizens. For these 21
men drove many of their fellow-citizens into the enemy camp, killed
many unjustly and left them unburied, deprived many of the civic
rights they possessed, and prevented the daughters of many from
being married. And such is the degree of audacity they have reached 22
that they have come to make their defence and say that they have
done nothing wicked or even shameful. Personally, I would that they
were speaking the truth, for I should share the benefit of that in no
small measure. But in fact matters are not so as far as both the city 23
and myself are concerned: for my brother, as I said before, was
killed by Eratosthenes, who had no private grievance against him and
saw him committing no crime against the state, but was actively

24 ἀναβιβασάμενος δ' αὐτὸν βούλομαι ἐρέσθαι, ὦ ἄνδρες δικασταί.
τοιαύτην γὰρ γνώμην ἔχω· ἐπὶ μὲν τῇ τούτου ὠφελείᾳ καὶ πρὸς
ἕτερον περὶ τούτου διαλέγεσθαι ἀσεβὲς εἶναι νομίζω, ἐπὶ δὲ
τῇ τούτου βλάβῃ καὶ πρὸς αὐτὸν τοῦτον ὅσιον καὶ εὐσεβές.
ἀνάβηθι οὖν μοι καὶ ἀπόκριναι, ὅ τι ἄν σε ἐρωτῶ.
25 Ἀπήγαγες Πολέμαρχον ἢ οὔ; Τὰ ὑπὸ τῶν ἀρχόντων προσταχθέντα δεδιὼς ἐποίουν. Ἦσθα δ' ἐν τῷ βουλευτηρίῳ, ὅτε οἱ
λόγοι ἐγίγνοντο περὶ ἡμῶν; Ἦ. Πότερον συνηγόρευες τοῖς
κελεύουσιν ἀποκτεῖναι ἢ ἀντέλεγες; Ἀντέλεγον. Ἵνα ἀποθάνωμεν < ἢ μή >; Ἵνα μὴ ἀποθάνητε. Ἡγούμενος ἡμᾶς ἄδικα πάσχειν
ἢ δίκαια; Ἄδικα.
26 Εἶτ', ὦ σχετλιώτατε πάντων, ἀντέλεγες μὲν ἵνα σώσειας,
συνελάμβανες δὲ ἵνα ἀποκτείνῃς; καὶ ὅτε μὲν τὸ πλῆθος ἦν
ὑμῶν κύριον τῆς σωτηρίας τῆς ἡμετέρας, ἀντιλέγειν φῂς τοῖς
βουλομένοις ἡμᾶς ἀπολέσαι, ἐπειδὴ δὲ ἐπὶ σοὶ μόνῳ ἐγένετο
καὶ σῶσαι Πολέμαρχον καὶ μή, εἰς τὸ δεσμωτήριον ἀπήγαγες;
εἶθ' ὅτι μέν, ὡς φῄς, ἀντειπὼν οὐδὲν ὠφέλησας, ἀξιοῖς
χρηστὸς νομίζεσθαι, ὅτι δὲ συλλαβὼν ἀπέκτεινας, οὐκ [οἴει]
ἐμοὶ καὶ τουτοισὶ δοῦναι δίκην;
27 Καὶ μὴν οὐδὲ τοῦτο εἰκὸς αὐτῷ πιστεύειν, εἴπερ ἀληθῆ
λέγει φάσκων ἀντειπεῖν, ὡς αὐτῷ προσετάχθη. οὐ γὰρ δήπου
ἐν τοῖς μετοίκοις πίστιν παρ' αὐτοῦ ἐλάμβανον. ἔπειτα τῷ
ἧττον εἰκὸς ἦν προσταχθῆναι ἢ ὅστις ἀντειπών γε ἐτύγχανε
καὶ γνώμην ἀποδεδειγμένος; τίνα γὰρ εἰκὸς ἦν ἧττον ταῦτα
ὑπηρετῆσαι ἢ τὸν ἀντειπόντα οἷς ἐκεῖνοι ἐβούλοντο πραχθῆναι;
28 Ἔτι δὲ τοῖς μὲν ἄλλοις Ἀθηναίοις ἱκανή μοι δοκεῖ πρόφασις
εἶναι τῶν γεγενημένων εἰς τοὺς τριάκοντα ἀναφέρειν τὴν
αἰτίαν· αὐτοὺς δὲ τοὺς τριάκοντα, ἂν εἰς σφᾶς αὐτοὺς ἀνα-
29 φέρωσι, πῶς ὑμᾶς εἰκὸς ἀποδέχεσθαι; εἰ μὲν γάρ τις ἦν ἐν τῇ
πόλει ἀρχὴ ἰσχυροτέρα [αὐτῆς], ὑφ' ἧς αὐτῷ προσετάττετο
παρὰ τὸ δίκαιον ἀνθρώπους ἀπολλύναι, ἴσως ἂν εἰκότως αὐτῷ
συγγνώμην εἴχετε· νῦν δὲ παρὰ τοῦ ποτε καὶ λήψεσθε δίκην,
εἴπερ ἐξέσται τοῖς τριάκοντα λέγειν ὅτι τὰ ὑπὸ τῶν τριά-
30 κοντα προσταχθέντα ἐποίουν; Καὶ μὲν δὴ οὐκ ἐν τῇ οἰκίᾳ ἀλλ'
ἐν τῇ ὁδῷ, σῴζειν τε αὐτὸν καὶ τὰ τούτοις ἐφηφισμένα παρόν,
συλλαβὼν ἀπήγαγεν. ὑμεῖς δὲ πᾶσιν ὀργίζεσθε, ὅσοι εἰς τὰς
οἰκίας ἦλθον τὰς ὑμετέρας ζήτησιν ποιούμενοι ἢ ὑμῶν ἢ τῶν
31 ὑμετέρων τινός. καίτοι, εἰ χρὴ τοῖς διὰ τὴν ἑαυτῶν σωτηρίαν

---

24 ὅσιον Stephanus: ὅσον   ὅ τι Brunck: εἴ τι
25 ἢ μή addidi: ἢ μὴ ἀποθάνωμεν add. Reiske
26 οἴει del. Madvig
27 προσετάχθη Reiske: ἐτάχθη   ἧττον ante εἰκὸς Canter:
   πίστιν X: οὐ πιστὸν C
29 αὐτῆς del. Dobree   παρὰ τοῦ Canter: παρ' αὐτοῦ
30 σῴζειν . . . παρόν Sauppe: σῴζοντα αὐτὸν . . . ὃν X:
   σῴζων αὐτὸν . . . C: σῴζοντα αὐτὸν, κατὰ . . . Baiter
   πᾶσιν Reiske: πάντες
31 τοῖς Reiske: τούτοις

pursuing his own lawless aims. I wish to put him on the stand and question him, gentlemen of the jury. For my opinion is this: I think it impious to argue with a third party about this man for his benefit, but a holy and pious act actually to address him directly to harm him. So please mount the stand and answer what I ask you.

Did you arrest Polemarchus or not?

I was acting in fear, on the orders of the government.

Were you in the Council when discussions about us took place?

I was.

Did you support or oppose those who urged our death?

I opposed them.

Were you for our death or against it?

Against it.

Thinking we were being **unjustly or justly treated**?

Unjustly.

So, most wicked of all men, you opposed them to save us, but took part in our arrest to kill us? And when a majority of you had the power to save us, you say you opposed those who wished to destroy us, but when it was in your power alone to save Polemarchus or not, you led him off to prison? Then you expect to be thought good because, according to your account, you opposed his death to no avail, but for your action in arresting and killing him you should not pay the penalty to me and this court?

Furthermore, supposing his alleged opposition to be true, it is not even reasonable to believe his statement that he was ordered to act as he did. For presumably it was not in his treatment of resident aliens that they would seek proof of his loyalty. Then who was less likely to be given that order than a man who had been an avowed opponent of the action proposed, or who was likely to be less energetic in assisting in its execution than the man who had opposed what they wanted to do? And again, other Athenians seem to me to have sufficient cause to blame the Thirty for what happened; but if the Thirty actually assign the blame to themselves, how can you reasonably accept that? For if there had been a stronger source of authority in the city, which gave orders to him for men to be destroyed unjustly, perhaps you might reasonably accord him indulgence; but as it is, from whom are you ever going to exact justice if the Thirty are to be allowed to say that they carried out the orders of the Thirty? Now again, it was not in the house that he arrested him and took him away, but in the street, where it was possible to let him escape without disobeying their decrees. You express anger against all those who entered your houses in search of any of you or your families; and yet if there is to be pardon for

163

ἑτέρους ἀπολέσασι συγγνώμην ἔχειν, ἐκείνοις ἂν δικαιότερον
ἔχοιτε· κίνδυνος γὰρ ἦν πεμφθεῖσι μὴ ἐλθεῖν καὶ καταλαβοῦ-
σιν ἐξάρνοις γενέσθαι. τῷ δὲ Ἐρατοσθένει ἐξῆν εἰπεῖν ὅτι
οὐκ ἀπήντησεν, ἔπειτα ὅτι οὐκ εἶδεν· ταῦτα γὰρ οὔτε ἔλεγχον
οὔτε βάσανον εἶχε, ὥστε μηδ᾽ ὑπὸ τῶν ἐχθρῶν βουλομένων οἷόν
32 τε εἶναι ἐξελεγχθῆναι. χρῆν δέ σε, ὦ Ἐρατόσθενες, εἴπερ
ἦσθα χρηστός, πολὺ μᾶλλον τοῖς μέλλουσιν ἀδίκως ἀποθανεῖσθαι μηνυτὴν γενέσθαι ἢ τοὺς ἀδίκως ἀπολουμένους συλλαμβά-
νειν. νῦν δέ σου τὰ ἔργα φανερὰ γεγένηται οὐχ ὡς ἀνιωμένου
33 ἀλλ᾽ ὡς ἡδομένου τοῖς γιγνομένοις, ὥστε τούσδε ἐκ τῶν ἔργων
χρὴ μᾶλλον ἢ ἐκ τῶν λόγων τὴν ψῆφον φέρειν, ἃ ἴσασι γεγενη-
μένα τῶν τότε λεγομένων τεκμήρια λαμβάνοντας, ἐπειδὴ μάρτυρας περὶ αὐτῶν οὐχ οἷόν τε παρασχέσθαι. οὐ γὰρ μόνον ἡμῖν
παρεῖναι οὐκ ἐξῆν, ἀλλ᾽ οὐδὲ παρ᾽ αὐτοῖς εἶναι, ὥστ᾽ ἐπὶ
τούτοις ἐστὶ πάντα τὰ κακὰ εἰργασμένοις τὴν πόλιν πάντα
34 τἀγαθὰ περὶ αὐτῶν λέγειν. τοῦτο μέντοι οὐ φεύγω, ἀλλ᾽ ὁμολογῶ σοι, εἰ βούλει, ἀντειπεῖν. θαυμάζω δὲ τί ἄν ποτ᾽
ἐποίησας συνειπών, ὁπότε ἀντειπεῖν φάσκων ἀπέκτεινας Πολέμαρχον.

Φέρε δή, τί ἄν, εἰ καὶ ἀδελφοὶ ὄντες ἐτύχετε αὐτοῦ ἢ
καὶ ὑεῖς; ἀπεψηφίσασθε <ἄν>; δεῖ γάρ, ὦ ἄνδρες δικασταί,
Ἐρατοσθένη δυοῖν θάτερον ἀποδεῖξαι, ἢ ὡς οὐκ ἀπήγαγεν
αὐτόν, ἢ ὡς δικαίως τοῦτ᾽ ἔπραξεν. οὗτος δὲ ὡμολόγηκεν
ἀδίκως συλλαβεῖν, ὥστε ῥᾳδίαν ὑμῖν τὴν διαψήφισιν περὶ
35 αὐτοῦ πεποίηκε. Καὶ μὲν δὴ πολλοὶ καὶ τῶν ἀστῶν καὶ τῶν
ξένων ἥκουσιν εἰσόμενοι τίνα γνώμην περὶ τούτων ἕξετε. ὧν
οἱ μὲν ὑμέτεροι ὄντες πολῖται μαθόντες ἀπίασιν ὅτι ἢ δίκην
δώσουσιν ὧν ἂν ἐξαμάρτωσιν, ἢ πράξαντες μὲν ὧν ἐφίενται
τύραννοι τῆς πόλεως ἔσονται, δυστυχήσαντες δὲ τὸ ἴσον ὑμῖν
ἕξουσιν· ὅσοι δὲ ξένοι ἐπιδημοῦσιν, εἴσονται πότερον ἀδίκως
τοὺς τριάκοντα ἐκκηρύττουσιν ἐκ τῶν πόλεων ἢ δικαίως. εἰ
γὰρ δὴ αὐτοὶ οἱ κακῶς πεπονθότες λαβόντες ἀφήσουσιν, ἦ που
σφᾶς <γ᾽> αὐτοὺς ἡγήσονται περιέργους ὑπὲρ ὑμῶν τηρουμένους.
36 οὐκ οὖν δεινὸν εἰ τοὺς μὲν στρατηγούς, οἳ ἐνίκων ναυμαχοῦν-
τες, ὅτε διὰ χειμῶνα οὐχ οἷοί τ᾽ ἔφασαν εἶναι τοὺς ἐκ τῆς
θαλάττης ἀνελέσθαι, θανάτῳ ἐζημιώσατε, ἡγούμενοι χρῆναι τῇ
τῶν τεθνεώτων ἀρετῇ παρ᾽ ἐκείνων δίκην λαβεῖν, τούτους δέ,
οἳ ἰδιῶται μὲν ὄντες καθ᾽ ὅσον ἐδύναντο ἐποίησαν ἡττηθῆναι
ναυμαχοῦντας, ἐπειδὴ δὲ εἰς τὴν ἀρχὴν κατέστησαν, ὁμολογοῦσιν ἑκόντες πολλοὺς τῶν πολιτῶν ἀκρίτους ἀποκτιννύναι, οὐκ
ἄρα χρὴ αὐτοὺς καὶ τοὺς παῖδας ὑφ᾽ ὑμῶν ταῖς ἐσχάταις
ζημίαις κολάζεσθαι;
37 Ἐγὼ τοίνυν, ὦ ἄνδρες δικασταί, ἠξίουν ἱκανὰ εἶναι τὰ

---

34 ποτ᾽ ἐποίησας Dobree: ποτε ποιήσαις   ἄν add. Fritzsche
35 ὑμέτεροι Cs: ἡμέτεροι C¹X   γ᾽ add. Fuhr
    τηρουμένους] τιμωρουμένους Markland: τιμωροῦντας Froh-
    berger
36 ὑφ᾽ C: ἀφ᾽ X

164

those who have destroyed others to save themselves, it would be fairer to pardon these intruders, for it was dangerous for them not to go where they had been sent and to deny finding their victims at home. But Eratosthenes could have said that he did not meet him, and then that he did not see him. Such statements could not be disproved or tested, so that even if his enemies wanted to convict him they could not do so. But if you were a good man, Eratosthenes, 32 you ought to have been much readier to be an informer for those who were about to suffer unjust death than to join in arresting those about to be destroyed unjustly. But as it is, your actions have been shown to be those of a man who was not vexed but pleased by what was happening. The jury must therefore pass its verdict on your 33 deeds rather than your words. They should take what they know to have happened as evidence of what was said at the time, since it is not possible to furnish witnesses to the words. For it was not only impossible for us to be present at their meetings, but we could not even be in our own homes; so that these men can have committed every crime against the city, but can give a wholly favourable account of themselves. However, I do not try to evade this difficulty, 34 but concede, if you like, that you did oppose the murder. But I wonder what you would have done if you had supported it, seeing that when you say you opposed it you killed Polemarchus.

Come now, what would you do if you happened to be brothers or even sons of this man? Would you acquit? For Eratosthenes, gentlemen of the jury, must prove one of two things, either that he did not arrest him, or that he did so justly. But this man has admitted that he arrested him unjustly, so he has presented you with an easy verdict in his case. And furthermore, many townspeople and 35 foreigners have come here to learn what your judgment on these men is to be. Of these, your own fellow-citizens will depart with the knowledge either that they will pay the penalty for any crimes they commit, or that they will either achieve their end when they aim at tyranny over the city or, on failing to do so, will be treated equally with you. As for such foreigners as are visiting the city, they will learn whether they do wrongly to exclude the Thirty from their cities, or rightly. For clearly, if the very victims of their crimes are going to arrest them and then release them, of course they will regard their own vigilance on your behalf as wasted labour. Would it 36 not therefore be shocking, when you have punished with death those captains who won the sea-battle, thinking, in spite of their plea that they were unable to rescue the men in the sea because of a storm, that the valour of the dead should be requited by exacting satisfaction from them; to have done this, and not feel obliged to punish with extreme penalties these men and their children – men who, as private citizens did all they could to bring about our naval defeat and, on assuming government, freely admit to putting many of their fellow-citizens to death without trial?

At this point, gentlemen of the jury, I might claim that the 37

κατηγορημένα· μέχρι γὰρ τούτου νομίζω χρῆναι κατηγορεῖν, ἕως ἂν θανάτου δόξῃ τῷ φεύγοντι ἄξια εἰργάσθαι. ταύτην γὰρ ἐσχάτην δίκην δυνάμεθα παρ' αὐτῶν λαβεῖν. ὥστ' οὐκ οἶδ' ὅ τι δεῖ πολλὰ κατηγορεῖν τοιούτων ἀνδρῶν, οἳ οὐδ' ὑπὲρ ἑνὸς ἑκάστου τῶν πεπραγμένων δὶς ἀποθανόντες <ἱκανὴν> δίκην
38 δοῦναι δύναιντ' ἄν. οὐ γὰρ δὴ οὐδὲ τοῦτο αὐτῷ προσήκει ποιῆσαι, ὅπερ ἐν τῇδε τῇ πόλει εἰθισμένον ἐστί, πρὸς μὲν τὰ κατηγορημένα μηδὲν ἀπολογεῖσθαι, περὶ δὲ σφῶν αὐτῶν ἕτερα λέγοντες ἐνίοτε ἐξαπατῶσιν, ὑμῖν ἀποδεικνύντες ὡς στρατιῶται ἀγαθοί εἰσιν, ἢ ὡς πολλὰς τῶν πολεμίων ναῦς ἔλαβον τριηραρ-
39 χήσαντες, <ἢ> πόλεις πολεμίας οὔσας φίλας ἐποίησαν· ἐπεὶ κελεύετε αὐτὸν ἀποδεῖξαι ὅπου τοσούτους τῶν πολεμίων ἀπέκ-τειναν ὅσους τῶν πολιτῶν, ἢ ναῦς ὅπου τοσαύτας ἔλαβον ὅσας αὐτοὶ παρέδοσαν, ἢ πόλιν ἥντινα τοιαύτην προσεκτήσαντο οἵαν
40 τὴν ὑμετέραν κατεδουλώσαντο. ἀλλὰ γὰρ ὅπλα τῶν πολεμίων <τοσαῦτα> ἐσκύλευσαν ὅσα περ ὑμῶν ἀφείλοντο, ἀλλὰ τεύχη τοιαῦτα εἷλον οἷα τῆς ἑαυτῶν πατρίδος κατέσκαψαν; οἵτινες καὶ τὰ περὶ τὴν Ἀττικὴν φρούρια καθεῖλον, καὶ ὑμῖν ἐδήλω-σαν ὅτι οὐδὲ τὸν Πειραιᾶ Λακεδαιμονίων προσταττόντων περι-εῖλον, ἀλλ' ὅτι ἑαυτοῖς τὴν ἀρχὴν οὕτω βεβαιοτέραν ἐνόμιζον εἶναι.
41 Πολλάκις οὖν ἐθαύμασα τῆς τόλμης τῶν λεγόντων ὑπὲρ αὐτοῦ, πλὴν ὅταν ἐνθυμηθῶ ὅτι τῶν αὐτῶν ἐστιν αὐτούς τε
42 πάντα τὰ κακὰ ἐργάζεσθαι καὶ τοὺς τοιούτους ἐπαινεῖν. οὐ γὰρ νῦν πρῶτον τῷ ὑμετέρῳ πλήθει τὰ ἐναντία ἔπραξεν, ἀλλὰ καὶ ἐπὶ τῶν τετρακοσίων ἐν τῷ στρατοπέδῳ ὀλιγαρχίαν καθιστὰς ἔφευγεν ἐξ Ἑλλησπόντου τριήραρχος καταλιπὼν τὴν ναῦν, μετὰ Ἰατροκλέους καὶ ἑτέρων, ὧν τὰ ὀνόματα οὐδὲν δέομαι λέγειν. ἀφικόμενος δὲ δεῦρο τἀναντία τοῖς βουλομένοις δημο-κρατίαν εἶναι ἔπραττε. Καὶ τούτων μάρτυρας ὑμῖν παρέξομαι.

ΜΑΡΤΥΡΕΣ

43 Τὸν μὲν τοίνυν μεταξὺ βίον αὐτοῦ παρήσω· ἐπειδὴ δὲ ἡ ναυμαχία καὶ ἡ συμφορὰ τῇ πόλει ἐγένετο, δημοκρατίας ἔτι οὔσης, ὅθεν τῆς στάσεως ἦρξαν, πέντε ἄνδρες ἔφοροι κατέστη-σαν ὑπὸ τῶν καλουμένων ἑταίρων, συναγωγεῖς μὲν τῶν πολιτῶν, ἄρχοντες δὲ τῶν συνωμοτῶν, ἐναντία δὲ τῷ ὑμετέρῳ πλήθει
44 πράττοντες· ὧν Ἐρατοσθένης καὶ Κριτίας ἦσαν. οὗτοι δὲ φυλάρχους τε ἐπὶ τὰς φυλὰς κατέστησαν, καὶ ὅ τι δέοι χειρο-τονεῖσθαι καὶ οὕστινας χρείη ἄρχειν παρήγγελλον, καὶ εἴ τι

---

37 ἱκανὴν add. Cobet: ἀξίαν add. Frohberger
38 κατηγορημένα C: κατηγορουμένα X   ἢ add. Markland
39 ὑμετέραν Reiske: ἡμετέραν
40 τοσαῦτα add. Reiske   ὅτι ἑαυτοῖς Sluiter: οἷς αὐτοῖς
41 αὐτοῦ Dobree: αὐτῶν
42 ἔπραξεν C: ἔπραξαν X
43 ὑμετέρῳ C: ἡμετέρῳ X
44 φυλὰς Taylor: φυλακὰς   χρείη Bekker: χρὴ

case for the prosecution is complete; for I think it needs to be carried only as far as to establish that the defendant has committed crimes which deserve death, for this is the extreme penalty that we can exact from them. So I doubt whether further accusations need be made against such men, for they could not pay an adequate penalty even if they were to die twice for each of their crimes. Nor indeed is 38 it open to him, as has been customary in this city, to make no defence against the charges but to make unrelated statements about themselves and so, on occasion, to deceive you by representing themselves to you as good soldiers, who served as captains and captured many enemy ships, or secured the friendship of cities which were hostile. Just you tell him to show where they killed as many of 39 our enemies as of our citizens, or where they captured as many ships as they surrendered, or what city they won over to compare with your own which they enslaved. No, he cannot: but did they strip the 40 enemy of as many arms as they took from you, or capture walls as strong as those of their native land which they dismantled? They are the men who stripped Attica of her surrounding forts, and made it clear to you that, even in their demolition of the Piraeus walls, they were acting not on the orders of the Lakedaimonians but because they thought their regime would thereby be more secure.

I have often wondered at the audacity of those who speak for 41 him, except when I reflect that it is characteristic of men who commit every sort of crime to praise those like themselves. For this is not 42 the first time he has opposed your people by his actions, but under the Four Hundred also he tried to establish an oligarchy in the army and fled from the Hellespont, where he was a captain but abandoned his ship, along with Iatrocles and others whose names I need not mention. On arriving here he opposed those who wanted democracy. I will furnish you with witnesses to these facts.

WITNESSES

Now I shall pass over his life between these periods. After the 43 sea-battle and the disaster it brought upon the city, the continued existence of the democracy was the starting point of the revolution. Five men were appointed as overseers by the so-called "club-men", to be organisers of the citizens and leaders of the conspiracy against your democracy; and Eratosthenes and Critias were among them. These men appointed tribal leaders over the tribes and passed on to 44 them instructions on how to vote and who should hold office; and they had the power to dictate any policy they wished. Thus you were

ἄλλο πράττειν βούλοιντο, κύριοι ἦσαν· οὕτως οὐχ ὑπὸ τῶν
πολεμίων μόνων ἀλλὰ καὶ ὑπὸ τούτων πολιτῶν ὄντων ἐπεβουλεύ-
εσθε ὅπως μήτ' ἀγαθὸν μηδὲν ψηφιεῖσθε πολλῶν τε ἐνδεεῖς
45 ἔσεσθε. τοῦτο γὰρ καλῶς ἠπίσταντο, ὅτι ἄλλως μὲν οὐχ οἷοί
τε ἔσονται περιγενέσθαι, κακῶς δὲ πραττόντων δυνήσονται·
καὶ ὑμᾶς ἡγοῦντο τῶν παρόντων κακῶν ἐπιθυμοῦντας ἀπαλλαγῆ-
46 ναι περὶ τῶν μελλόντων οὐκ ἐνθυμήσεσθαι. ὡς τοίνυν τῶν
ἐφόρων ἐγένετο, μάρτυρας ὑμῖν παρέξομαι, οὐ τοὺς τότε συμ-
πράττοντας (οὐ γὰρ ἂν δυναίμην), ἀλλὰ τοὺς αὐτοῦ 'Ερατο-
47 σθένους ἀκούσαντας. καίτοι εἰ ἐσωφρόνουν κατεμαρτύρουν ἂν
αὐτῶν, καὶ τοὺς διδασκάλους τῶν σφετέρων ἁμαρτημάτων σφόδρ'
ἂν ἐκόλαζον, καὶ τοὺς ὅρκους, εἰ ἐσωφρόνουν, οὐκ ἂν ἐπὶ μὲν
τοῖς τῶν πολιτῶν κακοῖς πιστοὺς ἐνόμιζον, ἐπὶ δὲ τοῖς τῆς
πόλεως ἀγαθοῖς ῥᾳδίως παρέβαινον. πρὸς μὲν οὖν τούτους
τοσαῦτα λέγω, τοὺς δὲ μάρτυράς μοι κάλει. Καὶ ὑμεῖς ἀνάβητε.

ΜΑΡΤΥΡΕΣ

48   Τῶν μὲν μαρτύρων ἀκηκόατε. τὸ δὲ τελευταῖον εἰς τὴν
ἀρχὴν καταστὰς ἀγαθοῦ μὲν οὐδενὸς μετέσχεν, ἄλλων δὲ πολλῶν. καίτοι εἴπερ ἦν ἀνὴρ ἀγαθός, ἐχρῆν αὐτὸν πρῶτον μὲν μὴ
παρανόμως ἄρχειν, ἔπειτα τῇ βουλῇ μηνυτὴν γίγνεσθαι περὶ
τῶν εἰσαγγελιῶν ἁπασῶν, ὅτι ψευδεῖς εἶεν, καὶ Βάτραχος καὶ
Αἰσχυλίδης οὐ τἀληθῆ μηνύουσιν, ἀλλὰ τὰ ὑπὸ τῶν τριάκοντα
πλασθέντα εἰσαγγέλλουσι, συγκείμενα ἐπὶ τῇ τῶν πολιτῶν βλάβῃ.
49 καὶ μὲν δή, ὦ ἄνδρες δικασταί, ὅσοι κακόνοι ἦσαν τῷ ὑμετέρῳ
πλήθει, οὐδὲν ἔλαττον εἶχον σιωπῶντες· ἕτεροι γὰρ ἦσαν οἱ
λέγοντες καὶ πράττοντες ὧν οὐχ οἷόν τ' ἦν μείζω κακὰ γενέσθαι τῇ πόλει. ὁπόσοι δ' εὐνοί φασιν εἶναι, πῶς οὐκ ἐνταῦθα
ἔδειξαν, αὐτοί τε τὰ βέλτιστα λέγοντες καὶ τοὺς ἐξαμαρτάνοντας ἀποτρέποντες;
50   "Ισως δ' ἂν ἔχοι εἰπεῖν ὅτι ἐδεδοίκει, καὶ ὑμῶν τοῦτο
ἐνίοις ἱκανὸν ἔσται. ὅπως τοίνυν μὴ φανήσεται ἐν τῷ λόγῳ
τοῖς τριάκοντα ἐναντιούμενος· εἰ δὲ μή, ἐνταυθοῖ δῆλος ἔσται
ὅτι ἐκεῖνά τε αὐτῷ ἤρεσκε, καὶ τοσοῦτον ἐδύνατο ὥστε ἐναν-
τιούμενος μηδὲν κακὸν παθεῖν ὑπ' αὐτῶν. χρῆν δ' αὐτὸν ὑπὲρ
τῆς ὑμετέρας σωτηρίας ταύτην τὴν προθυμίαν ἔχειν, ἀλλὰ μὴ
51 ὑπὲρ Θηραμένους, ὃς εἰς ὑμᾶς πολλὰ ἐξήμαρτεν. ἀλλ' οὗτος
τὴν μὲν πόλιν ἐχθρὰν ἐνόμιζεν εἶναι, τοὺς δ' ὑμετέρους
ἐχθροὺς φίλους, ὡς ἀμφότερα ταῦτα ἐγὼ πολλοῖς τεκμηρίοις
παραστήσω, καὶ τὰς πρὸς ἀλλήλους διαφορὰς οὐχ ὑπὲρ ὑμῶν
ἀλλ' ὑπὲρ ἑαυτῶν γιγνομένας, ὁπότεροι ταῦτα πράξουσι καὶ
52 τῆς πόλεως ἄρξουσι. εἰ γὰρ ὑπὲρ τῶν ἀδικουμένων ἐστασίαζον,

---

44 ψηφιεῖσθε Cobet: ψηφίσεσθε C
45 καλῶς Frohberger: καὶ   ὑμᾶς Markland: ἡμᾶς
48 αὐτὸν Bekker: ἂν   ἀλλὰ τὰ C: ἀλλὰ τἀληθῆ X
50 τοσοῦτον Xs: τοσαῦτα CX¹
51 ταῦτα] πάντα Reiske: τὰ πράγματα Gebauer
52 εἰ γὰρ Schottus: καὶ γὰρ

the victims of plots not only by your enemies but also by men who were your own citizens, plots designed to prevent you from voting for any beneficial policy, and to render you short of many things. For they knew very well that they would be able to gain ascendency 45 over you only when you were faring badly, not otherwise; and they thought that you, in your desire to be released from present evils, would not give thought to future ones. Now I shall furnish you with 46 witnesses to testify that he was one of the overseers. They are not those men who acted with him at that time, for I could not do that, but those who heard it from Eratosthenes himself. And yet if they 47 were prudent, they would be bearing witness against those men, and would be severely punishing those who had taught them to do wrong; and as for their oaths, if they were prudent, they would not hold them as binding to the detriment of the citizens, while readily breaking them for the advantage of the city. That is all, then, that I have to say about these men. Please call the witnesses. And you, mount the stand.

WITNESSES

You have heard the witnesses. Finally, when he was 48 established in power, he engaged in no good work, but plenty of the other kind. Yet if he was indeed a good man, he ought in the first instance to have refused to act illegally in office, and next he ought to have exposed the falsity of all the impeachments before the Council, showing that Batrachus and Aeschylides were giving information that was not true, but fabricated by the Thirty for the injury of the citizens. And furthermore, gentlemen of the jury, men 49 who wished your people ill were no worse off in remaining silent, for there were others to say and do things that caused the maximum possible damage to the city. As for those who proclaim their good will, how did they fail to show it at the time by themselves speaking to the best effect and discouraging malefactors? Perhaps he could say 50 that he was afraid, and to some of you this excuse will be sufficient. Then let him not be seen to have opposed the Thirty in the discussion, otherwise by that opposition he will be shown to have approved of their policies in general, and moreover enjoyed such authority that by his opposition he suffered no harm at their hands. He ought to have directed his zeal towards securing your safety, not that of Theramenes, who committed many crimes against you. No, this 51 man regarded the city as an enemy and your enemies as friends, and I shall support those two statements with plenty of evidence. I shall also show that their mutual disputes were not over your interests but their own, on the question of which faction should conduct affairs and rule the city. For if their quarrel had been about those who were 52

169

ποῦ κάλλιον [ἂν] ἦν ἀνδρὶ ἄρχοντι, ἢ Θρασυβούλου Φυλὴν
κατειληφότος, τότε ἐπιδείξασθαι τὴν αὑτοῦ εὔνοιαν; ὁ δ'
ἀντὶ τοῦ ἐπαγγείλασθαί τι ἢ πρᾶξαι ἀγαθὸν πρὸς τοὺς ἐπὶ
Φυλῇ, ἐλθὼν μετὰ τῶν συναρχόντων εἰς Σαλαμῖνα καὶ 'Ελευσῖ-
νάδε τριακοσίους τῶν πολιτῶν ἀπήγαγεν εἰς τὸ δεσμωτήριον,
καὶ μιᾷ ψήφῳ αὐτῶν ἁπάντων θάνατον κατεψηφίσατο.

53   'Επειδὴ δὲ εἰς τὸν Πειραιᾶ ἤλθομεν καὶ αἱ ταραχαὶ γεγε-
νημέναι ἦσαν καὶ περὶ τῶν διαλλαγῶν οἱ λόγοι ἐγίγνοντο,
πολλὰς ἑκάτεροι ἐλπίδας εἴχομεν πρὸς ἀλλήλους ἔσεσθαι, ὡς
ἀμφότεροι ἔδειξαν. οἱ μὲν γὰρ ἐκ Πειραιῶς κρείττους ὄντες
54   εἴασαν αὐτοὺς ἀπελθεῖν· οἱ δὲ εἰς τὸ ἄστυ ἐλθόντες τοὺς μὲν
τριάκοντα ἐξέβαλον πλὴν Φείδωνος καὶ 'Ερατοσθένους, ἄρχοντας
δὲ τοὺς ἐκείνοις ἐχθίστους εἵλοντο, ἡγούμενοι δικαίως ἂν ὑπὸ
τῶν αὐτῶν τούς τε τριάκοντα μισεῖσθαι καὶ τοὺς ἐν Πειραιεῖ
55   φιλεῖσθαι. τούτων τοίνυν Φείδων [ὁ τῶν τριάκοντα] γενόμενος
καὶ 'Ιπποκλῆς καὶ 'Επιχάρης ὁ Λαμπτρεὺς καὶ ἕτεροι οἱ
δοκοῦντες εἶναι ἐναντιώτατοι Χαρικλεῖ καὶ Κριτίᾳ καὶ τῇ
ἐκείνων ἑταιρείᾳ, ἐπειδὴ αὐτοὶ εἰς τὴν ἀρχὴν κατέστησαν,
πολὺ μείζω στάσιν καὶ πόλεμον ἐπὶ τοὺς ἐν Πειραιεῖ [ἢ] τοῖς
56   ἐξ ἄστεως ἐποίησαν· ᾧ καὶ φανερῶς ἐπεδείξαντο ὅτι οὐχ ὑπὲρ
τῶν ἐν Πειραιεῖ οὐδ' ὑπὲρ τῶν ἀδίκως ἀπολλυμένων ἐστασίαζον,
οὐδ' οἱ τεθνεῶτες αὐτοὺς ἐλύπουν οὐδ' οἱ μέλλοντες ἀποθανεῖσθαι, ἀλλ' οἱ μεῖζον δυνάμενοι καὶ θᾶττον πλουτοῦντες.
57   λαβόντες γὰρ τὰς ἀρχὰς καὶ τὴν πόλιν ἀμφοτέροις ἐπολέμουν,
τοῖς τε τριάκοντα πάντα κακὰ εἰργασμένοις καὶ ὑμῖν πάντα
κακὰ πεπονθόσι. καίτοι τοῦτο πᾶσι δῆλον ἦν, ὅτι εἰ μὲν
ἐκεῖνοι δικαίως ἔφευγον, ὑμεῖς ἀδίκως, εἰ δ' ὑμεῖς δικαίως,
οἱ τριάκοντα ἀδίκως· οὐ γὰρ δὴ ἑτέρων ἔργων αἰτίαν λαβόντες
58   ἐκ τῆς πόλεως ἐξέπεσον, ἀλλὰ τούτων. ὥστε σφόδρα χρὴ ὀργίζεσθαι, ὅτι Φείδων αἱρεθεὶς ὑμᾶς διαλλάξαι καὶ καταγαγεῖν
τῶν αὐτῶν ἔργων 'Ερατοσθένει μετεῖχε καὶ τῇ αὐτῇ γνώμῃ τοὺς
μὲν κρείττους αὑτῶν δι' ὑμᾶς κακῶς ποιεῖν ἕτοιμος ἦν, ὑμῖν
δὲ ἀδίκως φεύγουσιν οὐκ ἠθέλησεν ἀποδοῦναι τὴν πόλιν, ἀλλ'
ἐλθὼν εἰς Λακεδαίμονα ἔπειθεν αὐτοὺς στρατεύσασθαι, δια-
βάλλων ὅτι Βοιωτῶν ἡ πόλις ἔσται, καὶ ἄλλα λέγων οἷς ᾤετο
59   πείσειν μάλιστα. οὐ δυνάμενος δὲ τούτων τυχεῖν, εἴτε καὶ
τῶν ἱερῶν ἐμποδὼν ὄντων εἴτε καὶ αὐτῶν οὐ βουλομένων, ἑκατὸν
τάλαντα ἐδανείσατο, ἵνα ἔχοι ἐπικούρους μισθοῦσθαι, καὶ
Λύσανδρον ἄρχοντα ᾐτήσατο, εὐνούστατον μὲν ὄντα τῇ ὀλιγαρχίᾳ, κακονούστατον δὲ τῇ πόλει, μισοῦντα δὲ μάλιστα τοὺς ἐν
60   Πειραιεῖ. μισθωσάμενοι δὲ πάντας ἀνθρώπους ἐπ' ὀλέθρῳ τῆς

52   ἂν om. C
     εὔνοιαν Markland: συνουσίαν
53   ἔδειξαν Canter: ἔδοξαν
55   ὁ τῶν τριάκοντα del. Frohberger   Λαμπτρεὺς Taylor:
     Λαμπρεὺς   αὐτοὶ Markland: αὐτοὺς CX¹: αὐτοῖς Xˢ
     ἢ del. Reiske
56   ᾧ Rauchenstein: οὗ: ᾗ Reiske
57   δικαίως, οἱ τριάκοντα ἀδίκως Reiske: ἀδίκως, οἱ τριάκοντα
     δικαίως

being wronged, what better occasion was there for a leader to have shown his patriotism than after Thrasybulus had seized Phyle? But Eratosthenes, instead of offering aid or actually bringing it to those in Phyle, went with his partners in power to Salamis and Eleusis and led off three hundred of the citizens to prison, and by a single resolution condemned all of them to death.

After our return to the Piraeus and the upheavals that 53 followed, negotiations for reconciliation took place which led both sides to be very hopeful of the outcome, as they both showed. For the Piraeus party, on winning the battle, allowed the others to 54 depart, and these in turn went into town and expelled the Thirty, except Pheidon and Eratosthenes, and chose their bitterest enemies as leaders, thinking it fair to expect the same people who hated the Thirty to feel friendly towards the party of the Piraeus. Now among 55 these were included Pheidon, Hippocles and Epichares of Lamptra, and others who were reputed to be the worst enemies of Charicles and Critias and their club. But when they had themselves acceded to the government, they caused the party of the city to intensify the faction and the war against the Piraeus party, thereby showing 56 clearly that their revolution was not on behalf of the Piraeus party or indeed on behalf of those who were being unjustly destroyed, and showing too that their sense of grievance was not for the dead or those about to die, but against those who were enjoying greater power and quicker enrichment. For having seized office and control of 57 the city, they waged war on both factions, the Thirty for committing every kind of evil, and you because you had tolerated all those evils. And yet it was clear to all men that if they deserved their exile, you did not deserve yours, and if you deserved your exile, they did not deserve theirs; for it was on this and no other charge that they were exiled from the city. Hence the strongest anger should be shown that 58 Pheidon, who was chosen to reconcile and restore you, joined in the same activities as Eratosthenes and was ready, following the same plan, to damage the more powerful of their own party through you, while not being willing to return the city to you who were in unjust exile. Instead, he went to Lakedaimon and urged them to mount an expedition, alleging that the city would fall into Boeotian hands, and saying other things that he thought most likely to persuade them. When he could not achieve this, either because the sacred signs were 59 against it or the people themselves opposed it, he borrowed a hundred talents so that he could hire auxiliaries, and asked for their leader to be Lysander because he was most favourably disposed towards the oligarchy and most hostile towards the city, and reserved a special hatred for the Piraeus party. Having hired all kinds of men 60

πόλεως, καὶ πόλεις ἐπάγοντες καὶ τελευτῶντες Λακεδαιμονίους
καὶ τῶν συμμάχων ὁπόσους ἐδύναντο πεῖσαι, οὐ διαλλάξαι ἀλλ'
ἀπολέσαι παρεσκευάζοντο τὴν πόλιν εἰ μὴ δι' ἄνδρας ἀγαθούς,
οἷς ὑμεῖς δηλώσατε παρὰ τῶν ἐχθρῶν δίκην λαβόντες, ὅτι καὶ
61 ἐκείνοις χάριν ἀποδώσετε. ταῦτα δὲ ἐπίστασθε μὲν καὶ αὐτοί,
καὶ <οὐκ> οἶδ' ὅ τι δεῖ μάρτυρας παρασχέσθαι· ὅμως δέ· ἐγώ
τε γὰρ δέομαι ἀναπαύσασθαι, ὑμῶν τ' ἐνίοις ἥδιον ὡς πλείστων
τοὺς αὐτοὺς λόγους ἀκούειν.

MΑΡΤΥΡΕΣ

62 Φέρε δὴ καὶ περὶ Θηραμένους ὡς ἂν δύνωμαι διὰ βραχυτάτων διδάξω. δέομαι δ' ὑμῶν ἀκοῦσαι ὑπέρ τ' ἐμαυτοῦ καὶ τῆς
πόλεως. καὶ μηδενὶ τοῦτο παραστῇ, ὡς Ἐρατοσθένους κινδυ-
νεύοντος <οὐ προσηκόντως> Θηραμένους κατηγορῶ· πυνθάνομαι
γὰρ ταῦτα ἀπολογήσεσθαι αὐτόν, ὅτι ἐκείνῳ φίλος ἦν καὶ τῶν
63 αὐτῶν ἔργων μετεῖχε. καίτοι σφόδρ' ἂν αὐτὸν οἶμαι μετὰ
Θεμιστοκλέους πολιτευόμενον προσποιεῖσθαι πράττειν ὅπως
οἰκοδομηθήσεται τὰ τείχη, ὁπότε καὶ μετὰ Θηραμένους ὅπως
καθαιρεθήσεται. <ἀλλ'> οὐ γάρ μοι δοκοῦσιν ἴσου ἄξιοι γεγε-
νῆσθαι· ὁ μὲν γὰρ Λακεδαιμονίων ἀκόντων ᾠκοδόμησεν αὐτά,
64 οὗτος δὲ τοὺς πολίτας ἐξαπατήσας καθεῖλε. περιέστηκεν οὖν
τῇ πόλει τοὐναντίον ἢ ὡς εἰκὸς ἦν. ἄξιον μὲν γὰρ <ἦν> καὶ
τοὺς φίλους τοὺς Θηραμένους προσαπολωλέναι, πλὴν εἴ τις
ἐτύγχανεν ἐκείνῳ τἀναντία πράττων· νῦν δὲ ὁρῶ τάς τε ἀπολογίας εἰς ἐκεῖνον ἀναφερομένας, τούς τ' ἐκείνῳ συνόντας τιμᾶσθαι πειρωμένους, ὥσπερ πολλῶν ἀγαθῶν αἰτίου ἀλλ' οὐ μεγάλων
65 κακῶν γεγενημένου. ὃς πρῶτον μὲν τῆς προτέρας ὀλιγαρχίας
αἰτιώτατος ἐγένετο, πείσας ὑμᾶς τὴν ἐπὶ τῶν τετρακοσίων
πολιτείαν ἐλέσθαι. καὶ ὁ μὲν πατὴρ αὐτοῦ τῶν προβούλων ὢν
ταῦτ' ἔπραττεν, αὐτὸς δὲ δοκῶν εὐνούστατος εἶναι τοῖς πράγ-
66 μασι στρατηγὸς ὑπ' αὐτῶν ᾑρέθη. καὶ ἕως μὲν ἐτιμᾶτο, πιστὸν
ἑαυτὸν τῇ πόλει παρεῖχεν· ἐπειδὴ δὲ Πείσανδρον μὲν καὶ Κάλ-
λαισχρον καὶ ἑτέρους ἑώρα προτέρους αὐτοῦ γιγνομένους, τὸ
δὲ ὑμέτερον πλῆθος οὐκέτι βουλόμενον τούτων ἀκροᾶσθαι, τότ'
ἤδη διά τε τὸν πρὸς ἐκείνους φθόνον καὶ τὸ παρ' ὑμῶν δέος
67 μετέσχε τῶν Ἀριστοκράτους ἔργων. βουλόμενος δὲ τῷ ὑμετέρῳ
πλήθει δοκεῖν πιστὸς εἶναι Ἀντιφῶντα καὶ Ἀρχεπτόλεμον
φιλτάτους ὄντας αὐτῷ κατηγορῶν ἀπέκτεινεν, εἰς τοσοῦτον δὲ

60 οἷς Taylor: οὓς
61 οὐκ add. Weidner   πλείστων Contius: πλεῖστον
62 οὐ προσηκόντως add. Hude   ἀπολογήσεσθαι Markland:
ἀπολογήσασθαι   ἐκείνῳ Taylor: ἐκείνοις
63 ἀλλ' add. Baiter
64 ἦν add. Reiske   τοὺς ante Θηραμένους Franz: τοῦ
αἰτίου . . . γεγενημένου Bekker: αἰτίους . . . γεγενημένους
65 ταῦτ' Classen: ταῦτ'   αὐτῶν Sauppe: αὐτοῦ
66 προτέρους Canter: πραοτέρους

with a view to the city's destruction, they brought in other cities, and finally that of the Lakedaimonians, together with as many of their allies as they could persuade. They were preparing not to reconcile but to destroy the city, had it not been for some worthy men: to these you must show clearly that you intend to show gratitude for their loyalty by exacting justice from your enemies. But you are 61 yourselves aware of these facts, and I do not think I need to provide witnesses. Nevertheless I shall: for I am in need of a rest, and some of you will prefer to hear the same evidence from as many sources as possible.

WITNESSES

Well now, I shall tell you about Theramenes in as few words as I 62 can. I ask you to listen both for my own and the city's sake. And let it not occur to anyone that it is not fitting for me to accuse Theramenes when it is Eratosthenes who is on trial, for I am informed that he is going to plead in his defence that he was that man's friend and shared in the same deeds. Yet I suppose he would have been 63 very eager to lay claim to political connections with Themistocles when he built the walls, since he claims them with Theramenes in his destruction of them. He should not, since the two do not seem to me worthy of equal acclaim: for the former built them against the wishes of the Lakedaimonians, while the latter dismantled them after deceiving the citizens. Thus the opposite has happened to the city to 64 what was reasonable to expect: for it was right that Theramenes's friends should have died after him, except for those who may have opposed him; but in fact I see them resting their defence on appeals to his name, with his associates attempting to win honours, as if he had been the author of many benefits, not many evils. Firstly, it was 65 he who was responsible chiefly for the earlier oligarchy when he persuaded you to choose the constitution of the Four Hundred. And his father was one of the commissioners and pursued the same policy, while he himself was regarded as strongly in favour of these developments and was chosen general by them. And so long as he was 66 given preferment he remained loyal to the city. But when he saw Peisander, Kallaischros and others winning precedence over him and your people no longer willing to listen to these men, at that point, because he was jealous of them and afraid of you, he joined the intrigues of Aristocrates. Wishing to appear devoted to your people's 67 cause, he accused Antiphon and Archeptolemus, who were his closest friends, and had them executed, thereby reaching such a degree of

κακίας ἦλθεν, ὥστε ἅμα μὲν διὰ τὴν πρὸς ἐκείνους πίστιν ὑμᾶς
κατεδουλώσατο, διὰ δὲ τὴν πρὸς ὑμᾶς τοὺς φίλους ἀπώλεσε.
68 τιμώμενος δὲ καὶ τῶν μεγίστων ἀξιούμενος, αὐτὸς ἐπαγγειλά-
μενος σώσειν τὴν πόλιν αὐτὸς ἀπώλεσε, φάσκων πρᾶγμα ηὑρηκέ-
ναι μέγα καὶ πολλοῦ ἄξιον (ὑπέσχετο δὲ εἰρήνην ποιήσειν μήτε
ὅμηρα δοὺς μήτε τὰ τείχη καθελὼν μήτε τὰς ναῦς παραδούς)·
τοῦτο δὲ εἰπεῖν μὲν οὐδενὶ ἠθέλησεν, ἐκέλευσε δὲ αὐτῷ πισ-
69 τεύειν. ὑμεῖς δέ, ὦ ἄνδρες Ἀθηναῖοι, πραττούσης μὲν τῆς ἐν
Ἀρείῳ πάγῳ βουλῆς σωτήρια, ἀντιλεγόντων δὲ πολλῶν Θηραμέ-
νει, εἰδότες δὲ ὅτι οἱ μὲν ἄλλοι ἄνθρωποι τῶν πολεμίων ἕνεκα
τἀπόρρητα ποιοῦνται, ἐκεῖνος δ᾽ ἐν τοῖς αὐτοῦ πολίταις οὐκ
ἠθέλησεν εἰπεῖν ταῦθ᾽ ἃ πρὸς τοὺς πολεμίους ἔμελλεν ἐρεῖν,
ὅμως ἐπετρέψατε αὐτῷ πατρίδα καὶ παῖδας καὶ γυναῖκας καὶ
70 ὑμᾶς αὐτούς. ὁ δὲ ὧν μὲν ὑπέσχετο οὐδὲν ἔπραξεν, οὕτως δὲ
ἐνετεθύμητο ὡς χρὴ μικρὰν καὶ ἀσθενῆ γενέσθαι τὴν πόλιν,
ὥστε περὶ ὧν οὐδεὶς πώποτε οὔτε τῶν πολεμίων ἐμνήσθη οὔτε
τῶν πολιτῶν ἤλπισε, ταῦθ᾽ ὑμᾶς ἔπεισε πρᾶξαι, οὐχ ὑπὸ Λακεδαιμονίων ἀναγκαζόμενος, ἀλλ᾽ αὐτὸς ἐκείνοις ἐπαγγελλόμενος,
τοῦ τε Πειραιῶς τὰ τείχη περιελεῖν καὶ τὴν ὑπάρχουσαν πολιτείαν καταλῦσαι, εὖ εἰδὼς ὅτι, εἰ μὴ πασῶν τῶν ἐλπίδων
ἀποστερηθήσεσθε, ταχεῖαν παρ᾽ αὐτοῦ τὴν τιμωρίαν κομιεῖσθε.
71 καὶ τὸ τελευταῖον, ὦ ἄνδρες δικασταί, οὐ πρότερον εἴασε τὴν
ἐκκλησίαν γενέσθαι, ἕως ὁ λεγόμενος ὑπ᾽ ἐκείνων καιρὸς ἐπι-
μελῶς ὑπ᾽ αὐτοῦ ἐτηρήθη, καὶ μετεπέμψατο μὲν τὰς μετὰ
Λυσάνδρου ναῦς ἐκ Σάμου, ἐπεδήμησε δὲ τὸ τῶν πολεμίων
72 στρατόπεδον. τότε δὲ τούτων ὑπαρχόντων, καὶ παρόντος Λυσάνδρου καὶ Φιλοχάρους καὶ Μιλτιάδου, περὶ τῆς πολιτείας
τὴν ἐκκλησίαν ἐποίουν, ἵνα μήτε ῥήτωρ αὐτοῖς μηδεὶς ἐναντι-
οῖτο μηδὲ διαπειλοῖτο ὑμεῖς τε μὴ τὰ τῇ πόλει συμφέροντα
73 ἔλοισθε, ἀλλὰ τἀκείνοις δοκοῦντα ψηφίσαισθε. ἀναστὰς δὲ
Θηραμένης ἐκέλευσεν ὑμᾶς τριάκοντα ἀνδράσιν ἐπιτρέψαι τὴν
πόλιν καὶ τῇ πολιτείᾳ χρῆσθαι ἣν Δρακοντίδης ἀπέφαινεν.
ὑμεῖς δ᾽ ὅμως καὶ οὕτω διακείμενοι ἐθορυβεῖτε ὡς οὐ ποιή-
σοντες ταῦτα· ἐγιγνώσκετε γὰρ ὅτι περὶ δουλείας καὶ ἐλευθε-
74 ρίας ἐν ἐκείνῃ τῇ ἡμέρᾳ ἠκκλησιάζετε. Θηραμένης δέ, ὦ
ἄνδρες δικασταί, (καὶ τούτων ὑμᾶς αὐτοὺς μάρτυρας παρέξομαι) εἶπεν ὅτι οὐδὲν αὐτῷ μέλοι τοῦ ὑμετέρου θορύβου, ἐπειδὴ
πολλοὺς μὲν Ἀθηναίων εἰδείη τοὺς τὰ ὅμοια πράττοντας αὐτῷ,
δοκοῦντα δὲ Λυσάνδρῳ καὶ Λακεδαιμονίοις λέγοι. μετ᾽ ἐκεῖνον
δὲ Λύσανδρος ἀναστὰς ἄλλα τε πολλὰ εἶπε καὶ ὅτι παρασπόνδους
ὑμᾶς ἔχοι, καὶ ὅτι οὐ περὶ πολιτείας ὑμῖν ἔσται ἀλλὰ περὶ

---

68 τοῦτο Hamaker: ταῦτα   αὐτῷ Sauppe: αὐτῷ
69 σωτήρια Markland: σωτηρίαν
70 αὐτὸς Canter: αὐτοῖς
71 ἐκείνων Markland: ἐκείνου
72 παρόντος Xs: παρόντων CX¹   μηδὲ Emperius: μήτε
   διαπειλοῖτο Cobet: ἀπειλοῖτο
74 μέλοι edd.: μέλλοι X: μέλλει C: μέλει Contius

wickedness that he enslaved you to impress them with his loyalty, then destroyed his friends to impress you. While enjoying popularity 68 and the highest esteem, he announced that he would save the city single-handed: single-handed he destroyed it. He alleged that he had found a great and valuable expedient, and promised to secure a peace without giving hostages or dismantling the walls or surrendering the ships. He would not divulge this plan to anyone, but told them to trust him. And you, Athenians, while the council of the Areopagus 69 was working for your survival and many opposed Theramenes, also realised that, whereas other men kept secrets to thwart their enemies, that man refused to tell his own people what he was intending to say to the enemy. Nevertheless you entrusted your country, your children, your wives and yourselves to him. For his 70 part, he fulfilled none of his promises, but so rooted in his mind was the idea that the city should be small and weak, that he persuaded you to do things which none of the enemy had ever mentioned or any of the citizens had expected. Not compelled by the Lakedaimonians, but making them voluntary proposals himself, he negotiated the demolition of the Piraeus walls and the dissolution of the existing constitution, knowing full well that if you were not totally deprived of all your hope, you would swiftly take vengeance upon him. Finally, 71 gentlemen of the jury, he did not allow the assembly to be held until he had studiously awaited the moment chosen by them. He also sent for the ships of Lysander's fleet from Samos, and the enemy garrison was present in the city. This was the situation at that time, and they 72 held the assembly to debate on the constitution in the presence of Lysander, Philochares and Miltiades, so that it should be impossible for an orator either to oppose them or influence them by threats, or for you to choose measures that were beneficial to the city; you could only vote for what they wanted. Theramenes stood up and told you to 73 entrust the city to thirty men and to accept the constitution which Dracontides propounded. But you, in spite of your situation, protested loudly that you would not do these things; for you knew that the meeting that day would decide between your freedom and enslavement. But Theramenes, gentlemen of the jury (and I shall 74 make yourselves my witnesses to these facts), said that he cared nothing about your uproar, because he knew that many Athenians were pursuing the same objectives as himself, and that his proposals had the support of Lysander and the Lakedaimonians. After him Lysander stood up and spoke at great length, but in particular said that he held you responsible for breaking the truce, and that the issue for you would be not your constitution but your survival, if

75 σωτηρίας, εἰ μὴ ποιήσεθ᾽ ἃ Θηραμένης κελεύει. τῶν δ᾽ ἐν τῇ
ἐκκλησίᾳ ὅσοι ἄνδρες ἀγαθοὶ ἦσαν, γνόντες τὴν παρασκευὴν
καὶ τὴν ἀνάγκην, οἱ μὲν αὐτοῦ μένοντες ἡσυχίαν ἦγον, οἱ δὲ
ᾤχοντο ἀπιόντες, τοῦτο γοῦν σφίσιν αὐτοῖς συνειδότες, ὅτι
οὐδὲν κακὸν τῇ πόλει ἐψηφίσαντο· ὀλίγοι δέ τινες καὶ πονηροὶ καὶ κακῶς βουλευόμενοι τὰ προσταχθέντα ἐχειροτόνησαν.
76 παρήγγελτο γὰρ αὐτοῖς δέκα μὲν οὓς Θηραμένης ὑπέδειξε χειρο-
τονῆσαι, δέκα δὲ οὓς οἱ καθεστηκότες ἔφοροι κελεύοιεν, δέκα
δ᾽ ἐκ τῶν παρόντων· οὕτω γὰρ τὴν ὑμετέραν ἀσθένειαν ἑώρων
καὶ τὴν αὑτῶν δύναμιν ἠπίσταντο, ὥστε πρότερον ᾔδεσαν τὰ
77 μέλλοντα ἐν τῇ ἐκκλησίᾳ πραχθήσεσθαι. ταῦτα δὲ οὐκ ἐμοῦ δεῖ
πιστεῦσαι, ἀλλὰ ἐκείνῳ· πάντα γὰρ τὰ ὑπ᾽ ἐμοῦ εἰρημένα ἐν
τῇ βουλῇ ἀπολογούμενος ἔλεγεν, ὀνειδίζων μὲν τοῖς φεύγουσιν,
ὅτι δι᾽ αὐτὸν κατέλθοιεν, οὐδὲν φροντιζόντων Λακεδαιμονίων,
ὀνειδίζων δὲ τοῖς τῆς πολιτείας μετέχουσιν, ὅτι πάντων τῶν
πεπραγμένων τοῖς εἰρημένοις τρόποις ὑπ᾽ ἐμοῦ αὐτὸς αἴτιος
γεγενημένος τοιούτων τυγχάνοι, πολλὰς πίστεις αὐτοῖς ἔργῳ
78 δεδωκὼς καὶ παρ᾽ ἐκείνων ὅρκους εἰληφώς. καὶ τοσούτων καὶ
ἑτέρων κακῶν καὶ αἰσχρῶν καὶ πάλαι καὶ νεωστὶ καὶ μικρῶν
καὶ μεγάλων αἰτίου γεγενημένου τολμήσουσιν αὐτοὺς φίλους
ὄντας ἀποφαίνειν, οὐχ ὑπὲρ ὑμῶν ἀποθανόντος Θηραμένους ἀλλ᾽
ὑπὲρ τῆς αὐτοῦ πονηρίας, καὶ δικαίως μὲν ἐν ὀλιγαρχίᾳ δίκην
δόντος (ἤδη γὰρ αὐτὴν κατέλυσε), δικαίως δ᾽ ἂν ἐν δημοκρα-
τίᾳ· δὶς γὰρ ὑμᾶς κατεδουλώσατο, τῶν μὲν παρόντων καταφρο-
νῶν, τῶν δὲ ἀπόντων ἐπιθυμῶν, καὶ τῷ καλλίστῳ ὀνόματι χρώμενος δεινοτάτων ἔργων διδάσκαλος καταστάς.
79 Περὶ μὲν τοίνυν Θηραμένους ἱκανά μού ἐστι τὰ κατηγορη-
μένα· ἥκει δ᾽ ὑμῖν ἐκεῖνος ὁ καιρός, ἐν ᾧ δεῖ συγγνώμην καὶ
ἔλεον μὴ εἶναι ἐν ταῖς ὑμετέραις γνώμαις, ἀλλὰ παρὰ Ἐρατοσθένους καὶ τῶν τούτου συναρχόντων δίκην λαβεῖν, μηδὲ μαχο-
μένους <μὲν> κρείττους εἶναι τῶν πολεμίων, ψηφιζομένους δὲ
80 ἥττους τῶν ἐχθρῶν. μηδ᾽ ὧν φασι μέλλειν πράξειν πλείω χάριν
αὐτοῖς ἴστε, ἢ ὧν ἐποίησαν ὀργίζεσθε· μηδ᾽ ἀποῦσι μὲν τοῖς
τριάκοντα ἐπιβουλεύετε, παρόντας δ᾽ ἀφῆτε· μηδὲ τῆς τύχης,
ἢ τούτους παρέδωκε τῇ πόλει, κάκιον ὑμῖν αὐτοῖς βοηθήσητε.
81 Κατηγόρηται δὴ Ἐρατοσθένους καὶ τῶν τούτου φίλων, οἷς
τὰς ἀπολογίας ἀνοίσει καὶ μεθ᾽ ὧν αὐτῷ ταῦτα πέπρακται. ὁ
μέντοι ἀγὼν οὐκ ἐξ ἴσου τῇ πόλει καὶ Ἐρατοσθένει· οὗτος
μὲν γὰρ κατήγορος καὶ δικαστὴς αὐτὸς ἦν τῶν κρινομένων,
82 ἡμεῖς δὲ νυνὶ εἰς κατηγορίαν καὶ ἀπολογίαν καθέσταμεν. καὶ

---

74 ποιήσεθ᾽ Cobet: ποιήσαιθ᾽
76 παρήγγελτο Cobet: παρηγγέλλετο
77 δεῖ C: δοκεῖ X   αὐτὸν Sauppe: αὐτὸν   φροντιζόντων
Dobree: φροντίζων δὲ τῶν
78 αἰτίου γεγενημένου Reiske: αἴτιοι γεγενημένοι
79 μὲν add. Contius
81 κατηγόρηται Bake: κατηγορεῖτε   δὴ Scheibe: δὲ
αὐτὸς Markland: αὐτὸς
82 καὶ Dobree: καίτοι

you did not do as Theramenes said. All the worthy men in the 75
assembly, recognising the plot designed to force their compliance,
either stayed there and remained silent, or left and went away, their
conscience relieved at least at this - that they had not voted for
anything harmful to the city. But a small number of wicked men of
evil intent voted for the measures imposed. They had been instructed 76
to elect ten men whom Theramenes had nominated, ten ordered by the
appointed overseers and ten from those present. So aware were they
of your impotence, and so sure of their own power that they knew
beforehand what would be transacted in the assembly. There is no 77
need to take my word for this, but his own: for he said all I have
said in his defence before the council, when he reproached the
exiles, saying that they owed their return to him, while the
Lakedaimonians showed no interest in them; and when he reproached
his partners in the administration with the fact that, although he was
himself responsible for all the measures effected in the way I have
described, he was treated in this way after giving them many
practical reasons for trusting him and after receiving oaths from
them. And it is for this man, responsible as he has been for these 78
many wicked and shameful acts and others besides, in the past and
recently, of both a petty and important nature, that they will dare to
proclaim their friendship, in spite of the fact that Theramenes died
not on your account but on account of his own wickedness. Deserving
the just punishment he received under the oligarchy (for he had
already caused its ruin), he would have deserved it under the
democracy: for he enslaved you twice, spurning what was present
and desiring what was absent. Calling them by the fairest name, he
set himself up as mentor of the most terrible crimes.

I have now said enough in my accusation of Theramenes. The 79
time has now come for you to allow no place for sympathy or pity in
your minds, but to exact justice from Eratosthenes and those who
ruled with him. You must not show yourselves superior to your
foreign enemies in battle, then weaker than your domestic enemies
when you cast your votes. Nor again should you show more gratitude 80
for what they say they will do than anger for what they have done;
nor plot the downfall of the Thirty when they are away, but release
them when they are present; nor come to your own aid less
effectively than fortune did in delivering these men to the city.

Thus is the prosecution of Eratosthenes and his friends 81
complete. In his defence he will refer to them as his partners in
these deeds. Yet the contest between the city and Eratosthenes is an
unequal one, for he was at once accuser and judge of the men tried,
but today we are engaged as prosecutor and defendant. And these 82

οὗτοι μὲν τοὺς οὐδὲν ἀδικοῦντας ἀκρίτους ἀπέκτειναν, ὑμεῖς
δὲ τοὺς ἀπολέσαντας τὴν πόλιν κατὰ τὸν νόμον ἀξιοῦτε κρίνειν, παρ' ὧν οὐδ' ἂν παρανόμως βουλόμενοι δίκην λαμβάνειν
ἀξίαν τῶν ἀδικημάτων ὧν τὴν πόλιν ἠδικήκασι λάβοιτε. τί γὰρ
ἂν παθόντες δίκην τὴν ἀξίαν εἴησαν τῶν ἔργων δεδωκότες;
83 πότερον εἰ αὐτοὺς ἀποκτείναιτε καὶ τοὺς παῖδας αὐτῶν,
ἱκανὴν ἂν τοῦ φόνου δίκην λάβοιμεν, ὧν οὗτοι πατέρας καὶ
υἱεῖς καὶ ἀδελφοὺς ἀκρίτους ἀπέκτειναν; ἀλλὰ γὰρ εἰ τὰ χρήματα τὰ φανερὰ δημεύσαιτε, καλῶς ἂν ἔχοι ἢ τῇ πόλει, ἧς
οὗτοι πολλὰ εἰλήφασιν, ἢ τοῖς ἰδιώταις, ὧν <τὰς> οἰκίας
84 ἐξεπόρθησαν; ἐπειδὴ τοίνυν πάντα ποιοῦντες <ἱκανὴν> δίκην
παρ' αὐτῶν οὐκ ἂν δύναισθε λαβεῖν, πῶς οὐκ αἰσχρὸν ὑμῖν καὶ
ἡντινοῦν ἀπολιπεῖν, ἥντινά τις βούλοιτο παρὰ τούτων λαμβάνειν;
      Πᾶν δ' ἄν μοι δοκεῖ τολμῆσαι, ὅστις νυνί, οὐχ ἑτέρων
ὄντων τῶν δικαστῶν ἀλλ' αὐτῶν τῶν κακῶς πεπονθότων, ἥκει
ἀπολογησόμενος πρὸς αὐτοὺς τοὺς μάρτυρας τῆς τούτου πονη-
ρίας· τοσοῦτον ἢ ὑμῶν καταπεφρόνηκεν ἢ ἑτέροις πεπίστευκεν.
85 ὧν ἀμφοτέρων ἄξιον ἐπιμεληθῆναι, ἐνθυμουμένους ὅτι οὔτ' ἂν
ἐκεῖνα ἐδύναντο ποιεῖν μὴ ἑτέρων συμπραττόντων οὔτ' ἂν νῦν
ἐπεχείρησαν ἐλθεῖν μὴ ὑπὸ τῶν αὐτῶν οἰόμενοι σωθήσεσθαι, οἳ
οὐ τούτοις ἥκουσι βοηθήσοντες, ἀλλὰ ἡγούμενοι πολλὴν ἄδειαν
σφίσιν ἔσεσθαι τῶν <τε> πεπραγμένων καὶ τοῦ λοιποῦ ποιεῖν ὅ
τι ἂν βούλωνται, εἰ τοὺς μεγίστων κακῶν αἰτίους λαβόντες
86 ἀφήσετε. ἀλλὰ καὶ τῶν συνερούντων αὐτοῖς ἄξιον θαυμάζειν,
πότερον ὡς καλοὶ κἀγαθοὶ αἰτήσονται, τὴν αὐτῶν ἀρετὴν πλεί-
ονος ἀξίαν ἀποφαίνοντες τῆς <τούτων> πονηρίας (ἐβουλόμην
μέντ' ἂν αὐτοὺς οὕτω προθύμους εἶναι σῴζειν τὴν πόλιν,
ὥσπερ οὗτοι ἀπολλύναι), ἢ ὡς δεινοὶ λέγειν ἀπολογήσονται
καὶ τὰ τούτων ἔργα πολλοῦ ἄξια ἀποφανοῦσιν. ἀλλ' οὐχ ὑπὲρ
ὑμῶν οὐδεὶς αὐτῶν οὐδὲ τὰ δίκαια πώποτε ἐπεχείρησεν εἰπεῖν.
87 Ἀλλὰ τοὺς μάρτυρας ἄξιον ἰδεῖν, οἳ τούτοις μαρτυροῦν-
τες αὐτῶν κατηγοροῦσι, σφόδρα ἐπιλήσμονας καὶ εὐήθεις νομίζοντες ὑμᾶς εἶναι, εἰ διὰ μὲν τοῦ ὑμετέρου πλήθους ἀδεῶς
ἡγοῦνται τοὺς τριάκοντα σώσειν, διὰ δὲ Ἐρατοσθένη καὶ τοὺς
συνάρχοντας αὐτοῦ δεινὸν ἦν καὶ τῶν τεθνεώτων ἐπ' ἐκφορὰν
88 ἐλθεῖν. καίτοι οὗτοι μὲν σωθέντες πάλιν ἂν δύναιντο τὴν
πόλιν ἀπολέσαι· ἐκεῖνοι δέ, οὓς οὗτοι ἀπώλεσαν, τελευτήσαν-
τες τὸν βίον πέρα ἔχουσι τῆς παρὰ τῶν ἐχθρῶν τιμωρίας. οὐκ
οὖν δεινὸν εἰ τῶν μὲν ἀδίκως τεθνεώτων οἱ φίλοι συναπώλλυν-

83 ἀποκτείναιτε Bekker: ἀποκτείνοιτε C   δημεύσαιτε Reiske:
    δημεύσετε
84 τὰς add. Scheibe   ἱκανὴν add. Hirschig   ·δύναισθε
    Bekker: δύνησθε   ἢ post τοσοῦτον Reiske: δ'
85 ἐδύναντο Markland: δύναιντο   τε add. Reiske
86 συνερούντων Reiske: ξυνεργούντων   κἀγαθοὶ Canter: ἢ
    ἀγαθοὶ X: καὶ ἀγαθοὶ C   τούτων add. Markland
    ἀπολλύναι Markland: ἀποδοῦναι   οὐδὲ Reiske: οὔτε X
88 πέρα vel πέρᾳ coniecit Hude: πέρας

men killed without trial men who were doing no wrong, but you are only exercising your right to pass judgment according to the law on men who ruined the city, from whom you could not exact a penalty worthy of their crimes against the city even if you were willing to act illegally. For what could they suffer to pay in full the penalty they deserve for their deeds? If you put them and their children to death, 83 do you think we, whose fathers, sons and brothers these men slew without trial, would thereby receive sufficient compensation for their murder? Or if you confiscated their material property, would this be adequate for the city, from which these men have taken so much, or for the private citizens, whose houses they plundered? So since all 84 possible action on our part would not enable us to exact adequate compensation from them, how would it not be shameful for you to discountenance any punishment that one might wish to exact from them?

But he seems to me capable of any sort of rashness when he comes here today, when the judges are not different men but the very ones who have been badly treated, to make his defence before the very witnesses of his wickedness. Such has been his contempt of you or his confidence in others. In both these possible cases you 85 should be on your guard, bearing in mind that they would not have been able to achieve those things without the collaboration of others, nor would they now have chanced coming to trial unless they thought they would be saved by the same people, who in turn have come not to help these men but because they think they themselves will enjoy a large measure of immunity for their past actions and licence to do whatever they like in the future if, after arresting those guilty of the greatest crimes, you let them go. But you may well be wondering 86 about those who intend to support them, whether they will present their pleas as loyal gentlemen, showing their own good character as outweighing the wickedness of these men – though I should have preferred them to be as keen on saving the city as these men were on destroying it – or whether they will use their oratorical skill in presenting a defence and portraying these men's actions as meritorious. But none of these has ever tried to advocate anything on your behalf, even what is rightly yours.

But it is worth observing the witnesses. In testifying for these 87 men they accuse themselves, but imagine you to be remarkably forgetful and naïve if they think they are going to save the Thirty through your people's court with impunity, when it was because of Eratosthenes and his partners in power that it was dangerous even to attend the funerals of the dead. Yet these men, if acquitted, could 88 once again destroy the city, whereas those they destroyed, having ended their lives, are beyond seeking requital from their enemies. Is it not therefore shocking that the friends of those unjustly killed

το, αὐτοῖς δὲ τοῖς τὴν πόλιν ἀπολέσασι δήπου ἐπ' ἐκφορὰν
89 πολλοὶ ἥξουσιν, ὁπότε βοηθεῖν τοσοῦτοι παρασκευάζονται; καὶ
μὲν δὴ πολὺ ῥᾷον ἡγοῦμαι εἶναι ὑπὲρ ὧν ὑμεῖς ἐπάσχετε ἀντειπεῖν, ἢ ὑπὲρ ὧν οὗτοι πεποιήκασιν ἀπολογήσασθαι. καίτοι
λέγουσιν ὡς Ἐρατοσθένει ἐλάχιστα τῶν τριάκοντα κακὰ εἴργασται, καὶ διὰ τοῦτο αὐτὸν ἀξιοῦσι σωθῆναι· ὅτι δὲ τῶν
ἄλλων Ἑλλήνων πλεῖστα εἰς ὑμᾶς ἐξημάρτηκεν, οὐκ οἴονται
90 χρῆναι αὐτὸν ἀπολέσθαι; ὑμεῖς δὲ δείξατε ἥντινα γνώμην
ἔχετε περὶ τῶν πραγμάτων. εἰ μὲν γὰρ τούτου καταψηφιεῖσθε,
δῆλοι ἔσεσθε ὡς ὀργιζόμενοι τοῖς πεπραγμένοις· εἰ δὲ ἀποψη-
φιεῖσθε, ὀφθήσεσθε τῶν αὐτῶν ἔργων ἐπιθυμηταὶ τούτοις ὄντες,
καὶ οὐχ ἕξετε λέγειν ὅτι τὰ ὑπὸ τῶν τριάκοντα προσταχθέντα
91 ἐποιεῖτε· νυνὶ μὲν γὰρ οὐδεὶς ὑμᾶς ἀναγκάζει παρὰ τὴν
ὑμετέραν γνώμην ψηφίζεσθαι. ὥστε συμβουλεύω μὴ τούτων ἀπο-
ψηφισαμένους ὑμῶν αὐτῶν καταψηφίσασθαι. μηδ' οἴεσθε κρύβδην
τὴν ψῆφον εἶναι· φανερὰν γὰρ τῇ πόλει τὴν ὑμετέραν γνώμην
ποιήσετε.
92   Βούλομαι δὲ ὀλίγα ἑκατέρους ἀναμνήσας καταβαίνειν, τούς
τε ἐξ ἄστεως καὶ τοὺς ἐκ Πειραιῶς, ἵνα τὰς ὑμῖν διὰ τούτων
γεγενημένας συμφορὰς παραδείγματα ἔχοντες τὴν ψῆφον φέρητε.
καὶ πρῶτον μὲν ὅσοι ἐξ ἄστεώς ἐστε, σκέψασθε ὅτι ὑπὸ τούτων
οὕτω σφόδρα ἤρχεσθε ὥστε ἀδελφοῖς καὶ ὑέσι καὶ πολίταις
ἠναγκάζεσθε πολεμεῖν τοιοῦτον πόλεμον, ἐν ᾧ ἡττηθέντες μὲν
τοῖς νικήσασι τὸ ἴσον ἔχετε, νικήσαντες δ' ἂν τούτοις ἐδου-
93 λεύετε. καὶ τοὺς ἰδίους οἴκους οὗτοι μὲν ἂν ἐκ τῶν πραγμάτων
μεγάλους ἐκτήσαντο, ὑμεῖς δὲ διὰ τὸν πρὸς ἀλλήλους πόλεμον
ἐλάττους ἔχετε· συνωφελεῖσθαι μὲν γὰρ ὑμᾶς οὐκ ἠξίουν, συν-
διαβάλλεσθαι δ' ἠνάγκαζον, εἰς τοσοῦτον ὑπεροψίας ἐλθόντες
ὥστε οὐ τῶν ἀγαθῶν κοινούμενοι πιστοὺς ὑμᾶς ἐκτῶντο, ἀλλὰ
94 τῶν ὀνειδῶν μεταδιδόντες εὔνους ᾤοντο εἶναι. ἀνθ' ὧν ὑμεῖς
νῦν ἐν τῷ θαρραλέῳ ὄντες, καθ' ὅσον δύνασθε, καὶ ὑπὲρ ὑμῶν
αὐτῶν καὶ ὑπὲρ τῶν ἐκ Πειραιῶς τιμωρήσασθε, ἐνθυμηθέντες
μὲν ὅτι ὑπὸ τούτων πονηροτάτων ὄντων ἤρχεσθε, ἐνθυμηθέντες
δὲ ὅτι μετ' ἀνδρῶν νῦν ἀρίστων πολιτεύεσθε καὶ τοῖς πολεμίοις μάχεσθε καὶ περὶ τῆς πόλεως βουλεύεσθε, ἀναμνησθέντες
δὲ τῶν ἐπικούρων, οὓς οὗτοι φύλακας τῆς σφετέρας ἀρχῆς καὶ
95 τῆς ὑμετέρας δουλείας εἰς τὴν ἀκρόπολιν κατέστησαν. καὶ
πρὸς ὑμᾶς μὲν ἔτι πολλῶν ὄντων εἰπεῖν τοσαῦτα λέγω. ὅσοι δ'
ἐκ Πειραιῶς ἐστε, πρῶτον μὲν τῶν ὅπλων ἀναμνήσθητε, ὅτι
πολλὰς μάχας ἐν τῇ ἀλλοτρίᾳ μαχεσάμενοι οὐχ ὑπὸ τῶν πολεμίων
ἀλλ' ὑπὸ τούτων εἰρήνης οὔσης ἀφῃρέθητε τὰ ὅπλα, ἔπειθ' ὅτι
ἐξεκηρύχθητε μὲν ἐκ τῆς πόλεως, ἣν ὑμῖν οἱ πατέρες παρέδο-

---

88 δήπου Sauppe: ἤπου X: om. C
89 ῥᾷον Stephanus: ῥάδιον
91 ψηφίζεσθαι Bekker: ἀποψηφίζεσθαι
94 πονηροτάτων Reiske: πονηροτέρων   σφετέρας Markland:
    ὑμετέρας

were destroyed with them, whereas there will be many to attend the funerals of the very men who destroyed the city: or so one must suppose, since so many are preparing to help them? Furthermore, I 89 think it was much easier to speak in deprecation of your sufferings at the time than to defend what they have done now. And yet they say that of the Thirty Eratosthenes has committed the least serious crimes, and for this reason they demand that he should be acquitted. But since compared with all other Greeks he has committed the most offences against you, do they not think he ought to be destroyed? It 90 is for you to show what opinion you hold on these matters: for if you cast your votes against this man, you will clearly show that you are angry at what has been done; but if you acquit him, you will be seen to be aspirants to the same deeds as they, and you will not be able to say that you acted under orders from the Thirty, since today 91 nobody is compelling you to vote contrary to your own true opinion. So I advise you not to condemn yourselves by acquitting them. Nor indeed should you suppose that your vote is secret: you will be making your opinion manifest to the city.

I wish to remind both parties, that of the Town and that of the 92 Piraeus, of a few points, and then step down. You may then cast your votes with the precedents of those disasters caused by them in your minds. Firstly, all of you from the Town party, consider that you were governed so repressively by these men that you were forced to fight a war against brothers, sons and fellow-citizens, in which defeat has brought you equal rights with the victors, but victory would have made you these men's slaves. And they would have 93 acquired enlarged estates as a result of their conduct, but what you have now is diminished because of internecine war. For they would not let you share their benefits, but compelled you to share the brickbats they received. Such was the degree of contempt they reached that they did not obtain your loyalty by sharing their benefits, but expected you to be well-disposed towards them when they tried to give you a share of the reproaches. In return for this 94 it is for you now to be confident and use your full powers to obtain revenge, on both your own behalf and that of the Piraeus party, reflecting that you were ruled by these men, who were the most villainous on earth; and reflecting too that you now share the government with the best men, that it is with them that you are fighting our enemies and making political decisions; and remembering the auxiliaries whom these men stationed on the Acropolis to support their rule and secure your slavery. There are still many things that I 95 could say to you, but I shall say no more. All of you of the Piraeus party, remember first your arms, how, after fighting many battles on foreign soil, you were deprived of your arms not by the enemy but by these men in peacetime, and then that you were banished from the

96 σαν, φεύγοντας δὲ ὑμᾶς ἐκ τῶν πόλεων ἐξητοῦντο. ἀνθ' ὧν
ὀργίσθητε μὲν ὥσπερ ὅτ' ἐφεύγετε, ἀναμνήσθητε δὲ καὶ τῶν
ἄλλων κακῶν ἃ πεπόνθατε ὑπ' αὐτῶν, οἳ τοὺς μὲν ἐκ τῆς ἀγορᾶς
τοὺς δ' ἐκ τῶν ἱερῶν συναρπάζοντες βιαίως ἀπέκτειναν, τοὺς
δὲ ἀπὸ τέκνων καὶ γονέων καὶ γυναικῶν ἀφέλκοντες φονέας
αὐτῶν ἠνάγκασαν γενέσθαι καὶ οὐδὲ ταφῆς τῆς νομιζομένης
εἴασαν τυχεῖν, ἡγούμενοι τὴν αὐτῶν ἀρχὴν βεβαιοτέραν εἶναι
97 τῆς παρὰ τῶν θεῶν τιμωρίας. ὅσοι δὲ τὸν θάνατον διέφυγον,
πολλαχοῦ κινδυνεύσαντες καὶ εἰς πολλὰς πόλεις πλανηθέντες
καὶ πανταχόθεν ἐκκηρυττόμενοι, ἐνδεεῖς ὄντες τῶν ἐπιτηδείων,
οἱ μὲν ἐν πολεμίᾳ τῇ πατρίδι τοὺς παῖδας καταλιπόντες, οἱ
δ' ἐν ξένῃ γῇ, πολλῶν ἐναντιουμένων ἤλθετε εἰς τὸν Πειραιᾶ.
πολλῶν δὲ καὶ μεγάλων κινδύνων ὑπαρξάντων ἄνδρες ἀγαθοὶ
γενόμενοι τοὺς μὲν ἠλευθερώσατε, τοὺς δ' εἰς τὴν πατρίδα
98 κατηγάγετε. εἰ δὲ ἐδυστυχήσατε καὶ τούτων ἡμάρτετε, αὐτοὶ
μὲν ἂν δείσαντες ἐφεύγετε μὴ πάθητε τοιαῦτα οἷα καὶ πρότερον, καὶ οὔτ' ἂν ἱερὰ οὔτε βωμοὶ ὑμᾶς ἀδικουμένους διὰ
τοὺς τούτων τρόπους ὠφέλησαν, ἃ καὶ τοῖς ἀδικοῦσι σωτήρια
γίγνεται· οἱ δὲ παῖδες ὑμῶν, ὅσοι μὲν ἐνθάδε ἦσαν, ὑπὸ
τούτων ἂν ὑβρίζοντο, οἱ δ' ἐπὶ ξένης μικρῶν ἂν ἕνεκα συμ-
βολαίων ἐδούλευον ἐρημίᾳ τῶν ἐπικουρησόντων.
99   Ἀλλὰ γὰρ οὐ τὰ μέλλοντα ἔσεσθαι βούλομαι λέγειν, τὰ
πραχθέντα ὑπὸ τούτων οὐ δυνάμενος εἰπεῖν· οὐδὲ γὰρ ἑνὸς
κατηγόρου οὐδὲ δυοῖν ἔργον ἐστίν, ἀλλὰ πολλῶν. ὅμως δὲ τῆς
ἐμῆς προθυμίας <οὐδὲν> ἐλλέλειπται, ὑπέρ <τε> τῶν ἱερῶν, ἃ
οὗτοι τὰ μὲν ἀπέδοντο τὰ δ' εἰσιόντες ἐμίαινον, ὑπέρ τε τῆς
πόλεως, ἣν μικρὰν ἐποίουν, ὑπέρ τε τῶν νεωρίων, ἃ καθεῖλον,
καὶ ὑπὲρ τῶν τεθνεώτων, οἷς ὑμεῖς, ἐπειδὴ ζῶσιν ἐπαμῦναι
100 οὐκ ἐδύνασθε, ἀποθανοῦσι βοηθήσατε. οἶμαι δ' αὐτοὺς ἡμῶν τε
ἀκροᾶσθαι καὶ ὑμᾶς εἴσεσθαι τὴν ψῆφον φέροντας, ἡγουμένους,
ὅσοι μὲν ἂν τούτων ἀποψηφίσησθε, αὐτῶν θάνατον κατεψηφισμένους ἔσεσθαι, ὅσοι δ' ἂν παρὰ τούτων δίκην λάβωσιν, ὑπὲρ
αὐτῶν τιμωρίας πεποιημένους.
        Παύσομαι κατηγορῶν. ἀκηκόατε, ἑοράκατε, πεπόνθατε,
ἔχετε· δικάζετε.

---

95 ἐξητοῦντο Contius: ἐζητοῦντο
96 ἀπέκτειναν Reiske: ἀπέκτενον   ἀφέλκοντες Reiske:
   ἀφελόντες
99 οὐδὲν add. Canter   τε add. Sauppe
100 ἡμῶν Auger: ὑμῶν   κατεψηφισμένους ἔσεσθαι Kayser:
   καταψηφιεῖσθαι

city which your fathers had bequeathed you, and when you were in exile they demanded your extradition from the several cities. In 96 return for this you should show the same anger as when you were in exile, and remember also the other ills which you suffered from these men, who seized upon people, some in the market-place and others in the temples, and put them to violent death; while others they dragged away from their children, parents and wives and forced them to commit suicide, and did not even allow them to receive the customary rites of burial, considering their own authority to be too securely established to be touched by divine vengeance. Those of you 97 who escaped death, after facing dangers in many lands and wandering to many cities, from all of which you were banished, suffering shortage of necessities, some leaving their children in a hostile homeland, others in foreign lands, though opposed by numerous enemies, you finally returned to the Piraeus. The dangers that faced you were many and great, but you proved yourselves brave men and liberated one party and restored the other to its fatherland. If you 98 had been unfortunate and failed to achieve these objectives, you would yourselves have become exiles, in fear of suffering as before; and because of these men's methods neither temples nor altars would have protected you against attempts to injure you, places which provide refuge even to wrongdoers. And your children who were here would be suffering wanton abuse at these men's hands, and those in foreign parts would be serving as slaves on account of small debts in the absence of anyone to come to their aid.

But I do not wish to talk about things which might have 99 happened, when I cannot give a complete account of what these men have actually done: that would be a task not for one accuser or two, but for many. Nevertheless, there has been no failure of zeal on my part in defence of the temples whose contents these men have sold or which they have defiled by entering; of the city, which they tried to make insignificant; of the dockyards., which they destroyed; and of the dead, whom you were unable to protect when they were alive, and so must vindicate now they are dead. I imagine that they are 100 listening to us and will take cognisance of the verdict you give. They will consider that those of you who vote to acquit these men will have confirmed their own condemnation to death, but that those who exact justice from them have taken vengeance on their behalf.

I shall conclude my prosecution. You have heard; you have seen; you have suffered; you hold the guilty men. Deliver your judgment.

ΥΠΕΡ ΜΑΝΤΙΘΕΟΥ

1   Εἰ μὴ συνῄδη, ὦ βουλή, τοῖς κατηγόροις βουλομένοις ἐκ
παντὸς τρόπου κακῶς ἐμὲ ποιεῖν, πολλὴν ἂν αὐτοῖς χάριν εἶχον
ταύτης τῆς κατηγορίας· ἡγοῦμαι γὰρ τοῖς ἀδίκως διαβεβλημέ-
νοις τούτους εἶναι μεγίστων ἀγαθῶν αἰτίους, οἵτινες ἂν
αὐτοὺς ἀναγκάζωσιν εἰς ἔλεγχον τῶν αὐτοῖς βεβιωμένων κατα-
2 στῆναι. ἐγὼ γὰρ οὕτω σφόδρα ἐμαυτῷ πιστεύω, ὥστ' ἐλπίζω καὶ
εἴ τις πρός με τυγχάνει ἀηδῶς [ἢ κακῶς] διακείμενος, ἐπειδὰν ἐμοῦ λέγοντος ἀκούσῃ περὶ τῶν πεπραγμένων, μεταμελήσειν
αὐτῷ καὶ πολὺ βελτίω με εἰς τὸν λοιπὸν χρόνον ἡγήσεσθαι.
3 ἀξιῶ δέ, ὦ βουλή, ἐὰν μὲν τοῦτο μόνον ὑμῖν ἐπιδείξω, ὡς
εὔνους εἰμὶ τοῖς καθεστηκόσι πράγμασι καὶ ὡς ἠνάγκασμαι τῶν
αὐτῶν κινδύνων μετέχειν ὑμῖν, μηδέν πώ μοι πλέον εἶναι· ἐὰν
δὲ φαίνωμαι <καὶ> περὶ τὰ ἄλλα μετρίως βεβιωκὼς καὶ πολὺ
παρὰ τὴν δόξαν καὶ [παρὰ] τοὺς λόγους τοὺς τῶν ἐχθρῶν,
δέομαι ὑμῶν ἐμὲ μὲν δοκιμάζειν, τούτους δὲ ἡγεῖσθαι χείρους
εἶναι. πρῶτον δὲ ἀποδείξω ὡς οὐχ ἵππευον οὐδ' ἐπεδήμουν ἐπὶ
τῶν τριάκοντα, οὐδὲ μετέσχον τῆς τότε πολιτείας.
4   Ἡμᾶς γὰρ ὁ πατὴρ πρὸ τῆς ἐν Ἑλλησπόντῳ συμφορᾶς ὡς
Σάτυρον τὸν ἐν τῷ Πόντῳ διαιτησομένους ἐξέπεμψε, καὶ οὔτε
τῶν τειχῶν καθαιρουμένων <ἐπεδημοῦμεν> οὔτε μεθισταμένης
τῆς πολιτείας, ἀλλ' ἤλθομεν πρὶν τοὺς ἀπὸ Φυλῆς εἰς τὸν
5 Πειραιᾶ κατελθεῖν πρότερον πένθ' ἡμέραις. καίτοι οὔτε ἡμᾶς
εἰκὸς ἦν εἰς τοιοῦτον καιρὸν ἀφιγμένους ἐπιθυμεῖν μετέχειν
τῶν ἀλλοτρίων κινδύνων, οὔτ' ἐκεῖνοι φαίνονται τοιαύτην
γνώμην ἔχοντες ὥστε καὶ τοῖς ἀποδημοῦσι καὶ τοῖς μηδὲν ἐξ-
αμαρτάνουσι μεταδιδόναι τῆς πολιτείας, ἀλλὰ μᾶλλον ἠτίμαζον
6 καὶ τοὺς συγκαταλύσαντας τὸν δῆμον. ἔπειτα δὲ ἐκ μὲν τοῦ
σανιδίου τοὺς ἱππεύσαντας σκοπεῖν εὐηθές ἐστιν· ἐν τούτῳ
γὰρ πολλοὶ μὲν τῶν ὁμολογούντων ἱππεύειν οὐκ ἔνεισιν, ἔνιοι
δὲ τῶν ἀποδημούντων ἐγγεγραμμένοι εἰσίν. ἐκεῖνος δ' ἐστὶν
ἔλεγχος μέγιστος· ἐπειδὴ γὰρ κατήλθετε, ἐψηφίσασθε τοὺς
φυλάρχους ἀπενεγκεῖν τοὺς ἱππεύσαντας, ἵνα τὰς καταστάσεις
7 ἀναπράξητε παρ' αὐτῶν. ἐμὲ τοίνυν οὐδεὶς ἂν ἀποδείξειεν οὔτ'
ἀπενεχθέντα ὑπὸ τῶν φυλάρχων οὔτε παραδοθέντα τοῖς συνδίκοις
οὔτε κατάστασιν καταβαλόντα. καίτοι πᾶσι ῥάδιον τοῦτο γνῶναι, ὅτι ἀναγκαῖον ἦν τοῖς φυλάρχοις, εἰ μὴ ἀποδείξειαν τοὺς

---

2 ἢ κακῶς del. Reiske
3 καὶ add. Reiske   παρὰ om. C   οὐδ' Turr.: οὔτ'
4 ἐπεδημοῦμεν add. Kayser (post πολιτείας Markland)
6 ἐγγεγραμμένοι Markland: ἐπιγεγραμμένοι   ἀναπράξητε
   Harpocration s.v. κατάστασις: ἀναπράττηται X: ἀναπράττητε
   C
7 καταβαλόντα Bake: παραλαβόντα   ὅτι Kayser: διότι

SPEECH 16 : FOR MANTITHEUS

If I were not aware of my opponents' desire, councillors, to 1
harm me by every possible means, I should be very grateful to them
for bringing this accusation. For I think that such men as these
confer the greatest benefits upon those they have unjustly slandered
whenever they compel them to submit to an examination of the lives
they have led. So great is my confidence in myself that, if anyone 2
should happen to be disagreeably disposed towards me, I hope that
when he has heard me speak about my past conduct, he will regret
his attitude and think much more highly of me in the future. What I 3
claim, councillors, is this: if I succeed in proving to you only that I
support the existing state of affairs and that I have had to share in
the same dangers as you, I ask for no further favour; but if I am
seen to have led a moderate life in all other respects, quite contrary
to both the opinion and the statements of my enemies, I ask you to
approve my audit and think the worse of these men. But first I shall
prove that I did not serve in the cavalry or even reside under the
Thirty, nor play any part in the administration at that time.

Before the disaster at the Hellespont, our father sent us abroad 4
to live at the court of Satyrus in the Pontus; and we were not
residing in the city either when the walls were being dismantled or
when the constitution was being changed, but we arrived back five
days before those at Phyle returned to the Piraeus. Yet it was surely 5
not reasonable to expect us to desire to share in other men's dangers
after arriving at such a critical time; and the tyrants were clearly
not of a mind to share the government with men who were living
abroad and were guilty of no crime. Rather, they were disfranchising
even those who had helped them destroy the democracy. Next, it is 6
naïve to consult the register for the names of those who served in
the cavalry, for it does not contain many who themselves admit to
serving in the cavalry, while some names are included of men who
were living abroad. But the strongest proof is this: when you had
returned, you voted that the tribal officers should make a list of
those who had served as cavalry, so that you could recover the
allowances from them. Now nobody could show that I was either 7
included in the tribal officers' lists or reported to the financial
officers or made to refund an allowance. And yet everybody can
easily ascertain that the tribal officers were themselves liable to be
penalised if they did not reveal the receivers of allowances. So it

ἔχοντας τὰς καταστάσεις, αὐτοῖς ζημιοῦσθαι. ὥστε πολὺ ἂν
δικαιότερον ἐκείνοις τοῖς γράμμασιν ἢ τούτοις πιστεύοιτε·
ἐκ μὲν γὰρ τούτων ῥᾴδιον ἦν ἐξαλειφθῆναι τῷ βουλομένῳ, ἐν
ἐκείνοις δὲ τοὺς ἱππεύσαντας ἀναγκαῖον ἦν ὑπὸ τῶν φυλάρχων
8 ἀπενεχθῆναι. ἔτι δέ, ὦ βουλή, εἴπερ ἵππευσα, οὐκ ἂν ἦ ἔξαρνος ὡς δεινόν τι πεποιηκώς, ἀλλ' ἠξίουν, ἀποδείξας ὡς
οὐδεὶς ὑπ' ἐμοῦ τῶν πολιτῶν κακῶς πέπονθε, δοκιμάζεσθαι.
ὁρῶ δὲ καὶ ὑμᾶς ταύτῃ τῇ γνώμῃ χρωμένους, καὶ πολλοὺς μὲν
τῶν τότε ἱππευσάντων βουλεύοντας, πολλοὺς δ' αὐτῶν στρατη-
γοὺς καὶ ἱππάρχους κεχειροτονημένους. ὥστε μηδὲν δι' ἄλλο
με ἡγεῖσθε ταύτην ποιεῖσθαι τὴν ἀπολογίαν, ἢ ὅτι περιφανῶς
ἐτόλμησάν μου καταψεύσασθαι. Ἀνάβηθι δέ μοι καὶ μαρτύρησον.

MARTYRIA

9   Περὶ μὲν τοίνυν αὐτῆς τῆς αἰτίας οὐκ οἶδ' ὅ τι δεῖ πλείω
λέγειν· δοκεῖ δέ μοι, ὦ βουλή, ἐν μὲν τοῖς ἄλλοις ἀγῶσι περὶ
αὐτῶν μόνων τῶν κατηγορημένων προσήκειν ἀπολογεῖσθαι, ἐν δὲ
ταῖς δοκιμασίαις δίκαιον εἶναι παντὸς τοῦ βίου λόγον διδόναι. δέομαι οὖν ὑμῶν μετ' εὐνοίας ἀκροάσασθαί μου. ποιήσομαι
δὲ τὴν ἀπολογίαν ὡς ἂν δύνωμαι διὰ βραχυτάτων.
10 Ἐγὼ γὰρ πρῶτον μέν, οὐσίας μοι οὐ πολλῆς καταλειφθείσης
διὰ τὰς συμφορὰς καὶ τὰς τοῦ πατρὸς καὶ τὰς τῆς πόλεως, δύο
μὲν ἀδελφὰς ἐξέδωκα ἐπιδοὺς τριάκοντα μνᾶς ἑκατέρᾳ, πρὸς τὸν
ἀδελφὸν δ' οὕτως ἐνειμάμην ὥστ' ἐκεῖνον πλέον ὁμολογεῖν
ἔχειν ἐμοῦ τῶν πατρῴων, καὶ πρὸς τοὺς ἄλλους ἅπαντας οὕτως
βεβίωκα ὥστε μηδεπώποτέ μοι μηδὲ πρὸς ἕνα μηδὲν ἔγκλημα
11 γενέσθαι. καὶ τὰ μὲν ἴδια οὕτως διῴκηκα· περὶ δὲ τῶν κοινῶν
μοι μέγιστον ἡγοῦμαι τεκμήριον εἶναι τῆς ἐμῆς ἐπιεικείας,
ὅτι τῶν νεωτέρων ὅσοι περὶ κύβους ἢ πότους ἢ [περὶ]τὰς τοι-
αύτας ἀκολασίας τυγχάνουσι τὰς διατριβὰς ποιούμενοι, πάντας
αὐτοὺς ὄψεσθέ μοι διαφόρους ὄντας, καὶ πλεῖστα τούτους περὶ
ἐμοῦ λογοποιοῦντας καὶ ψευδομένους. καίτοι δῆλον ὅτι, εἰ
τῶν αὐτῶν ἐπεθυμοῦμεν, οὐκ ἂν τοιαύτην γνώμην εἶχον περὶ
12 ἐμοῦ. ἔτι δ', ὦ βουλή, οὐδεὶς ἂν ἀποδεῖξαι περὶ ἐμοῦ δύναιτο
οὔτε δίκην αἰσχρὰν οὔτε γραφὴν οὔτε εἰσαγγελίαν γεγενημένην·
καίτοι ἑτέρους ὁρᾶτε πολλάκις εἰς τοιούτους ἀγῶνας καθεστηκότας. πρὸς τοίνυν τὰς στρατείας καὶ τοὺς κινδύνους τοὺς
πρὸς τοὺς πολεμίους σκέψασθε οἷον ἐμαυτὸν παρέχω τῇ πόλει.
13 πρῶτον μὲν γάρ, ὅτε τὴν συμμαχίαν ἐποιήσασθε πρὸς [τοὺς]
Βοιωτοὺς καὶ εἰς Ἁλίαρτον ἔδει βοηθεῖν, ὑπὸ Ὀρθοβούλου
κατειλεγμένος ἱππεύειν, ἐπειδὴ πάντας ἑώρων τοῖς μὲν ἱππεύ-
ουσιν ἀσφάλειαν εἶναι δεῖν νομίζοντας, τοῖς δ' ὁπλίταις
κίνδυνον ἡγουμένους, ἑτέρων ἀναβάντων ἐπὶ τοὺς ἵππους ἀδοκι-
μάστων παρὰ τὸν νόμον ἐγὼ προσελθὼν ἔφην τῷ Ὀρθοβούλῳ
ἐξαλεῖφαί με ἐκ τοῦ καταλόγου, ἡγούμενος αἰσχρὸν εἶναι τοῦ

---

8 ὥστε μηδὲν δι' ἄλλο με Taylor: ὥστ' εἰ μηδὲν διαβάλλομαι
9 αὐτῆς Frohberger: ταύτης
11 διῴκηκα Sauppe: διῴκησα   περὶ del. Fuhr

would be much fairer if you relied upon those lists than upon the register, for any one who wished could easily have his name erased from the latter, but there was an obligation upon the tribal officers to record in the former the names of those who served as cavalry. And besides, councillors, if I had served in the cavalry, I should not   8 deny it as if I had done something terrible, but expect to be approved on showing that no citizen has suffered harm at my hands. And I observe that you also hold this view, and that many who served in the cavalry at that time are now serving on the Council, and many of these have been elected generals and cavalry-commanders. So you are not to suppose that I am making this defence for any other reason than their audacity in exposing me blatantly to false charges. Please step up and bear witness.

TESTIMONY

Now regarding the charge itself I do not know what more needs   9 to be said. But I think, councillors, that whereas in other kinds of trial the defence should be confined only to the charges made, in cases of scrutiny it is right to give an account of the whole of one's life. Therefore I ask you to listen to me with good will. I shall make my defence in as few words as I can.

In the first place, when because of the disasters that struck   10 both my father and the city little property was left to me, I gave two sisters in marriage, providing a dowry of thirty minae for each, and I so distributed the estate between my brother and myself that he acknowledges possessing more of our patrimony than I; and towards everyone else I have so conducted my life that no charge has ever been brought against me by a single complainant before any magistrate. Such has been the conduct of my private life: as to my   11 public life I think the most convincing proof of my respectable conduct is that you will see that all the younger men who are found passing their time in dice-playing or drinking or other such excesses are hostile to me, and these people tell many false stories about me. And yet it is obvious that if we had similar pursuits they would not have such an opinion of me. Again, councillors, no one could point to   12 any shameful private or public suit or any impeachment in which I have been involved, yet you frequently see others concerned in such trials.

Now consider my record of service to the city in military campaigns and dangers in face of the enemy. The first occasion was   13 when you made your alliance with the Boeotians and we had to go to relieve Haliartus. I had been enrolled in the cavalry by Orthobulus, but when I became aware that everyone thought the cavalry were sure to be safe, but considered that the infantry would have to face danger, and other men had taken to horseback illegally and without passing the scrutiny, I approached Orthobulus and told him to strike me off the roll, believing it shameful to go on a campaign with my

πλήθους μέλλοντος κινδυνεύειν ἄδειαν ἐμαυτῷ παρασκευάσαντα
στρατεύεσθαι. Καί μοι ἀνάβηθι, 'Ορθόβουλε.

14   Συλλεγέντων τοίνυν τῶν δημοτῶν πρὸ τῆς ἐξόδου, εἰδὼς
αὐτῶν ἐνίους πολίτας μὲν χρηστοὺς ὄντας καὶ προθύμους,
ἐφοδίων δὲ ἀποροῦντας, εἶπον ὅτι χρὴ τοὺς ἔχοντας παρέχειν
τὰ ἐπιτήδεια τοῖς ἀπόρως διακειμένοις. καὶ οὐ μόνον τοῦτο
συνεβούλευον τοῖς ἄλλοις, ἀλλὰ καὶ αὐτὸς ἔδωκα δυοῖν ἀνδροῖν
τριάκοντα δραχμὰς ἑκατέρῳ, οὐχ ὡς πολλὰ κεκτημένος, ἀλλ' ἵνα
παράδειγμα τοῦτο τοῖς ἄλλοις γένηται. Καί μοι ἀνάβητε.

ΜΑΡΤΥΡΕΣ

15   Μετὰ ταῦτα τοίνυν, ὦ βουλή, εἰς Κόρινθον ἐξόδου γενομέ-
νης καὶ πάντων προειδότων ὅτι δεήσει κινδυνεύειν, ἑτέρων
ἀναδυομένων ἐγὼ διεπραξάμην ὥστε τῆς πρώτης τεταγμένος μάχεσθαι τοῖς πολεμίοις· καὶ μάλιστα τῆς ἡμετέρας φυλῆς δυσ-
τυχησάσης, καὶ πλείστων ἐναποθανόντων, ὕστερος ἀνεχώρησα
τοῦ σεμνοῦ Στειριῶς τοῦ πᾶσιν ἀνθρώποις δειλίαν ὠνειδικότος.
16 καὶ οὐ πολλαῖς ἡμέραις ὕστερον μετὰ ταῦτα ἐν Κορίνθῳ χωρίων
ἰσχυρῶν κατειλημμένων, ὥστε τοὺς πολεμίους μὴ δύνασθαι παριέναι, 'Αγησιλάου δ' εἰς τὴν Βοιωτίαν ἐμβαλόντος ψηφισαμένων
τῶν ἀρχόντων ἀποχωρίσαι τάξεις αἵτινες βοηθήσουσι, φοβουμέ-
νων ἁπάντων (εἰκότως, ὦ βουλή· δεινὸν γὰρ ἦν ἀγαπητῶς ὀλίγῳ
πρότερον σεσωσμένους ἐφ' ἕτερον κίνδυνον ἰέναι) προσελθὼν
ἐγὼ τὸν ταξίαρχον ἐκέλευον ἀκληρωτὶ τὴν ἡμετέραν τάξιν πέμ-
17 πειν. ὥστ' εἴ τινες ὑμῶν ὀργίζονται τοῖς τὰ μὲν τῆς πόλεως
ἀξιοῦσι πράττειν, ἐκ δὲ τῶν κινδύνων ἀποδιδράσκουσιν, οὐκ
ἂν δικαίως περὶ ἐμοῦ τὴν γνώμην ταύτην ἔχοιεν· οὐ γὰρ μόνον
τὰ προσταττόμενα ἐποίουν προθύμως, ἀλλὰ καὶ κινδυνεύειν
ἐτόλμων. καὶ ταῦτ' ἐποίουν οὐχ ὡς οὐ δεινὸν ἡγούμενος εἶναι
Λακεδαιμονίοις μάχεσθαι, ἀλλ' ἵνα, εἴ ποτε ἀδίκως εἰς κίνδυνον καθισταίμην, διὰ ταῦτα βελτίων ὑφ' ὑμῶν νομιζόμενος
ἁπάντων τῶν δικαίων τυγχάνοιμι. Καί μοι ἀνάβητε τούτων
μάρτυρες.

ΜΑΡΤΥΡΕΣ

18   Τῶν τοίνυν ἄλλων στρατειῶν καὶ φρουρῶν οὐδεμιᾶς ἀπελεί-
φθην πώποτε, ἀλλὰ πάντα τὸν χρόνον διατετέλεκα μετὰ τῶν
πρώτων μὲν τὰς ἐξόδους ποιούμενος, μετὰ τῶν τελευταίων δὲ
ἀναχωρῶν. καίτοι χρὴ τοὺς φιλοτίμως καὶ κοσμίως πολιτευομένους ἐκ τῶν τοιούτων σκοπεῖν, ἀλλ' οὐκ εἴ τις κομᾷ, διὰ
τοῦτο μισεῖν· τὰ μὲν γὰρ τοιαῦτα ἐπιτηδεύματα οὔτε τοὺς

---

13 παρασκευάσαντα marg. Ald.: παρασκευάσαντι
15 ἐναποθανόντων Markland: ἐνθανόντων   ὕστερος Contius:
    ὕστερον
16 παριέναι Herbst: προσιέναι
18 κομᾷ Hamaker: τολμᾷ

own safety provided for when the majority was about to face danger. Please mount the stand, Orthobulus.

TESTIMONY

Now when my fellow-demesmen had been mustered before our departure, knowing that some of them, though good and patriotic citizens, lacked subsistence-money, I said that those with means should provide supplies for those who were lacking them. And I not only recommended this course to others, but myself gave two men thirty drachmae each, not because I had plenty but so that this should be an example to the others. Please mount the stand. 14

WITNESSES

Now after this, councillors, an expedition to Corinth took place. Everybody knew beforehand that dangers would have to be met, but while others tried to shirk them, I arranged to be positioned in the front line and do battle with the enemy. And after our tribe had borne the greatest casualties and many men had died on the field, I left it after that proud man from Steiria, who has been reproaching everybody with cowardice. Not many days after this battle, some strong positions had been secured at Corinth to prevent the enemy from passing through. Agesilaus had forced his way through to Boeotia, and the commanders decided to send off some battalions to the rescue. Everyone was afraid (and reasonably so, councillors, for it was a grim prospect, after feeling the relief of getting off safe a short time before, to go out and face a new danger); but I approached my captain and told him to send our battalion without drawing lots. So if any of you resent men who expect to run the city's affairs but try to escape its dangers, they would be wrong to hold this opinion of me: for I not only obeyed orders wholeheartedly, but also had the boldness to face dangers. And I did this not because I did not find doing battle with the Lakedaimonians a daunting matter, but in order that if at some time I should be exposed to an unjust prosecution, my actions would give you a better opinion of me and I should receive all my rights. Witnesses to these facts, please mount the stand. 15 16 17

WITNESSES

Now in all other expeditions and garrisons I never once failed in my duty, but on every occasion I have followed my practice of setting out in the van of an expedition and returning with the rear guard. Now surely it is on such behaviour that the respectable aspirant to office should be judged, and you should not take a man's habit of wearing his hair long as a reason to hate him. For such habits do 18

189

ἰδιώτας οὔτε τὸ κοινὸν τῆς πόλεως βλάπτει, ἐκ δὲ τῶν κινδυνεύειν ἐθελόντων πρὸς τοὺς πολεμίους ἅπαντες ὑμεῖς ὠφε-
19 λεῖσθε. ὥστε οὐκ ἄξιον ἀπ' ὄψεως, ὦ βουλή, οὔτε φιλεῖν οὔτε
μισεῖν οὐδένα, ἀλλ' ἐκ τῶν ἔργων σκοπεῖν· πολλοὶ μὲν γὰρ
μικρὸν διαλεγόμενοι καὶ κοσμίως ἀμπεχόμενοι μεγάλων κακῶν
αἴτιοι γεγόνασιν, ἕτεροι δὲ τῶν τοιούτων ἀμελοῦντες πολλὰ
κἀγαθὰ ὑμᾶς εἰσιν εἰργασμένοι.
20   Ἤδη δέ τινων ἠσθόμην, ὦ βουλή, καὶ διὰ ταῦτα ἀχθομένων
μοι, ὅτι νεώτερος ὢν ἐπεχείρησα λέγειν ἐν τῷ δήμῳ. ἐγὼ δὲ
τὸ μὲν πρῶτον ἠναγκάσθην ὑπὲρ τῶν ἐμαυτοῦ πραγμάτων δημηγο-
ρῆσαι, ἔπειτα μέντοι καὶ ἐμαυτῷ δοκῶ φιλοτιμότερον διατεθῆ-
ναι τοῦ δέοντος, ἅμα μὲν τῶν προγόνων ἐνθυμούμενος, ὅτι
21 οὐδὲν πέπαυνται τὰ τῆς πόλεως πράττοντες, ἅμα δὲ ὑμᾶς ὁρῶν
(τὰ γὰρ ἀληθῆ χρὴ λέγειν) τοὺς τοιούτους μόνους <τινὸς>
ἀξίους νομίζοντας εἶναι, ὥστε ὁρῶν ὑμᾶς ταύτην τὴν γνώμην
ἔχοντας τίς οὐκ ἂν ἐπαρθείη πράττειν καὶ λέγειν ὑπὲρ τῆς
πόλεως; ἔτι δὲ τί ἂν τοῖς τοιούτοις ἄχθοισθε; οὐ γὰρ ἕτεροι
περὶ αὐτῶν κριταί εἰσιν, ἀλλ' ὑμεῖς.

---

19 ἀμπεχόμενοι Dobree: ἀπερχόμενοι
20 τὰ Dobree: τῶν
21 τοὺς τοιούτους Francken: τούτους   τινὸς add. Dobree

190

harm neither to individuals nor to the state at large, but you all derive benefit from those who undergo danger willingly in the face of the enemy. Thus it is not right, councillors, to let your liking or 19
hatred for anyone be decided by appearance, but by their deeds. For many men who engage little in debate and wear sober dress have been responsible for great evils, while others unconcerned over such matters have done you many worthy services.

I have noticed before, councillors, some people expressing 20
annoyance with me for trying my hand at speaking in the assembly when I was too young to do so. But in the first place I was forced to speak in public to defend my own interests, though as my second point I admit that I was inclined to be more ambitious than I ought because I was thinking of my ancestors, who have followed an unbroken career of public service, and because at the same time I 21
observe that you (for I must speak the truth) consider only men of such character as worthy of regard. So who would not be inspired to act and speak for the city when he sees you holding this view? Besides, how could you be annoyed with such people, since none other than yourselves are judges of their worth?

ΚΑΤΑ ΤΩΝ ΣΙΤΟΠΩΛΩΝ

1   Πολλοί μοι προσεληλύθασιν, ὦ ἄνδρες δικασταί, θαυμάζον-
τες ὅτι ἐγὼ τῶν σιτοπωλῶν ἐν τῇ βουλῇ κατηγόρουν, καὶ λέγοντες ὅτι ὑμεῖς, εἰ ὡς μάλιστα αὐτοὺς ἀδικεῖν ἡγεῖσθε,
οὐδὲν ἧττον καὶ τοὺς περὶ τούτων ποιουμένους <τοὺς> λόγους
συκοφαντεῖν νομίζετε. ὅθεν οὖν ἠνάγκασμαι κατηγορεῖν αὐτῶν,
περὶ τούτων πρῶτον εἰπεῖν βούλομαι.
2   Ἐπειδὴ γὰρ οἱ πρυτάνεις ἀπέδοσαν εἰς τὴν βουλὴν περὶ
αὐτῶν, οὕτως ὠργίσθησαν αὐτοῖς, ὥστε ἔλεγόν τινες τῶν ῥητό-
ρων ὡς ἀκρίτους αὐτοὺς χρὴ τοῖς ἕνδεκα παραδοῦναι θανάτῳ
ζημιῶσαι. ἡγούμενος δὲ ἐγὼ δεινὸν εἶναι τοιαῦτα ἐθίζεσθαι
ποιεῖν τὴν βουλήν, ἀναστὰς εἶπον ὅτι μοι δοκοίη κρίνειν τοὺς
σιτοπώλας κατὰ τὸν νόμον, νομίζων, εἰ μέν εἰσιν ἄξια θανάτου
εἰργασμένοι, ὑμᾶς οὐδὲν ἧττον ἡμῶν γνώσεσθαι τὰ δίκαια, εἰ
δὲ μηδὲν ἀδικοῦσιν, οὐ δεῖν αὐτοὺς ἀκρίτους ἀπολωλέναι.
3   πεισθείσης δὲ τῆς βουλῆς ταῦτα, διαβάλλειν ἐπεχείρουν με
λέγοντες ὡς ἐγὼ σωτηρίας ἕνεκα τῆς τῶν σιτοπωλῶν τοὺς λόγους
τούτους ἐποιούμην. πρὸς μὲν οὖν τὴν βουλήν, ὅτ' ἦν αὐτοῖς ἡ
κρίσις, ἔργῳ ἀπελογησάμην· τῶν γὰρ ἄλλων ἡσυχίαν ἀγόντων
ἀναστὰς αὐτῶν κατηγόρουν, καὶ πᾶσι φανερὸν ἐποίησα ὅτι οὐχ
ὑπὲρ τούτων ἔλεγον, ἀλλὰ τοῖς νόμοις τοῖς κειμένοις ἐβοή-
4   θουν. ἠρξάμην μὲν οὖν τούτων ἕνεκα, δεδιὼς τὰς αἰτίας·
αἰσχρὸν δ' ἡγοῦμαι πρότερον παύσασθαι, πρὶν ἂν ὑμεῖς περὶ
αὐτῶν ὅ τι ἂν βούλησθε ψηφίσησθε.
5   Καὶ πρῶτον μὲν ἀνάβητε. εἰπὲ σὺ ἐμοί, μέτοικος εἶ; Ναί.
Μετοικεῖς δὲ πότερον ὡς πεισόμενος τοῖς νόμοις τοῖς τῆς
πόλεως, ἢ ὡς ποιήσων ὅ τι ἂν βούλῃ; Ὡς πεισόμενος. Ἄλλο
τι οὖν ἢ ἀξιοῖς ἀποθανεῖν, εἴ τι πεποίηκας παρὰ τοὺς νόμους,
ἐφ' οἷς θάνατος ἡ ζημία; Ἔγωγε. Ἀπόκριναι δή μοι, εἰ ὁμο-
λογεῖς πλείω σῖτον συμπρίασθαι πεντήκοντα φορμῶν, ὧν ὁ
νόμος ἐξεῖναι κελεύει. Ἐγὼ τῶν ἀρχόντων κελευόντων συν-
επριάμην.
6   Ἂν μὲν τοίνυν ἀποδείξῃ, ὦ ἄνδρες δικασταί, ὡς ἔστι
νόμος ὃς κελεύει τοὺς σιτοπώλας συνωνεῖσθαι τὸν σῖτον, ἂν
οἱ ἄρχοντες κελεύωσιν, ἀποψηφίσασθε· εἰ δὲ μή, δίκαιον ὑμᾶς
καταψηφίσασθαι. ἡμεῖς γὰρ ὑμῖν παρεσχόμεθα τὸν νόμον, ὃς
ἀπαγορεύει μηδένα τῶν ἐν τῇ πόλει πλείω σῖτον πεντήκοντα
φορμῶν συνωνεῖσθαι.
7   Χρῆν μὲν τοίνυν, ὦ ἄνδρες δικασταί, ἱκανὴν εἶναι ταύτην

---

1   τοὺς add. Hirschig
4   τὰς αἰτίας· αἰσχρὸν δ' Dobree: δὲ τὰς αἰτίας αἰσχρὸν
5   ἀνάβητε Frohberger: ἀνάβηθι   ἢ ἀξιοῖς Reiske: ἀξιοῖς ἢ
7   χρῆν Reiske: χρὴ

SPEECH 22 : AGAINST THE CORN-DEALERS

Many men have approached me, gentlemen of the jury, 1
expressing surprise that I accused the corn-dealers in the Council,
and saying that, even if you think they are entirely culpable, you
nevertheless take the view that those conducting the case against
them are making false charges. I therefore wish to speak first of the
grounds on which I have been obliged to accuse them.

When the presiding committee referred their case to the Council, 2
there was so much anger against them that some speakers said that
they ought to be handed over to the Eleven without trial to suffer
the death penalty. But I, thinking it alarming that the Council should
habituate itself to such practices, stood up and said that in my
opinion the corn-dealers should be tried according to the law,
because I thought that if their actions deserved the death penalty,
you would be no less likely to pass the right judgment than we,
whereas if they are guilty of no crime they ought not to perish
without trial. This argument convinced the Council, but some tried to 3
discredit me, saying that I was putting forward these arguments in
order to save the corn-dealers. Now I defended my action before the
Council in a practical way when the case came before them: while the
rest kept silent I stood up and accused the men, and made it clear to
everyone that my arguments were made not to protect them but in
support of the established laws. So these are the reasons I began my 4
task, because I feared those accusations; and I think it would be
shameful to stop before you have passed upon them whatever verdict
you desire.

Firstly, then, mount the stand. Tell me, are you a resident 5
alien? Yes. Do you regard obedience to the laws of the city as a
condition of your residence? Or do you intend to do as you please? I
will obey them. Do you expect any other penalty than death if you
have done anything illegal that carries the death penalty? I expect
death. Now answer me, do you admit to having bought up more than
fifty baskets of corn, which the law prescribes as the limit allowable?
I bought it up on orders from the magistrates.

Well, gentlemen of the jury, if he proves that a law exists which 6
requires corn-dealers to buy up corn if the magistrates so order
them, acquit him; if not, it is right for you to condemn him. For we
have produced to you the law which forbids anyone in the city to buy
up more than fifty baskets of corn.

Now this prosecution of mine ought to have been sufficient, 7

τὴν κατηγορίαν, ἐπειδὴ οὗτος μὲν ὁμολογεῖ συμπρίασθαι, ὁ δὲ
νόμος ἀπαγορεύων φαίνεται, ὑμεῖς δὲ κατὰ τοὺς νόμους ὀμωμόκατε ψηφιεῖσθαι· ὅμως δ' ἵνα πεισθῆτε ὅτι καὶ κατὰ τῶν
ἀρχόντων ψεύδονται, ἀνάγκη καὶ μακρότερον εἰπεῖν περὶ αὐτῶν.
8 ἐπειδὴ γὰρ οὗτοι τὴν αἰτίαν εἰς ἐκείνους ἀνέφερον, παρακαλέ-
σαντες τοὺς ἄρχοντας ἠρωτῶμεν. καὶ οἱ μὲν νῦν οὐδὲν ἔφασαν
εἰδέναι τοῦ πράγματος, Ἄνυτος δ' ἔλεγεν ὡς τοῦ προτέρου
χειμῶνος, ἐπειδὴ τίμιος ἦν ὁ σῖτος, τούτων ὑπερβαλλόντων
ἀλλήλους καὶ πρὸς σφᾶς αὐτοὺς μαχομένων συμβουλεύσειεν
αὐτοῖς παύσασθαι φιλονικοῦσιν, ἡγούμενος συμφέρειν ὑμῖν
τοῖς παρὰ τούτων ὠνουμένοις ὡς ἀξιώτατον τούτους πρίασθαι·
9 δεῖν γὰρ αὐτοὺς ὀβολῷ μόνον πωλεῖν τιμιώτερον. ὡς τοίνυν οὐ
συμπριαμένους καταθέσθαι ἐκέλευεν αὐτούς, ἀλλὰ μὴ ἀλλήλοις
ἀντωνεῖσθαι συνεβούλευεν, αὐτὸν ὑμῖν Ἄνυτον μάρτυρα παρέξομαι.

MARTYPIA

Καὶ [ὡς] οὗτος μὲν ἐπὶ τῆς προτέρας βουλῆς τούτους εἶπε
τοὺς λόγους, οὗτοι δ' ἐπὶ τῆσδε συνωνούμενοι φαίνονται.
10 Ὅτι μὲν τοίνυν οὐχ ὑπὸ τῶν ἀρχόντων κελευσθέντες συν-
επρίαντο τὸν σῖτον, ἀκηκόατε· ἡγοῦμαι δ', ἐὰν ὡς μάλιστα
περὶ τούτων ἀληθῆ λέγωσιν, οὐχ ὑπὲρ αὐτῶν αὐτοὺς ἀπολογήσεσθαι, ἀλλὰ τούτων κατηγορήσειν· περὶ γὰρ ὧν εἰσι νόμοι διαρρήδην γεγραμμένοι, πῶς οὐ χρὴ διδόναι δίκην καὶ τοὺς μὴ
πειθομένους καὶ τοὺς κελεύοντας τούτοις τἀναντία πράττειν;
11 Ἀλλὰ [μὲν] γάρ, ὦ ἄνδρες δικασταί, οἴομαι αὐτοὺς ἐπὶ
μὲν τοῦτον τὸν λόγον οὐκ ἐλεύσεσθαι· ἴσως δ' ἐροῦσιν, ὥσπερ
καὶ ἐν τῇ βουλῇ, ὡς ἐπ' εὐνοίᾳ τῆς πόλεως συνεωνοῦντο τὸν
σῖτον, ἵν' ὡς ἀξιώτατον ὑμῖν πωλοῖεν. μέγιστον δ' ὑμῖν ἐρῶ
12 καὶ περιφανέστατον τεκμήριον ὅτι ψεύδονται· ἐχρῆν γὰρ αὐτούς,
εἴπερ ὑμῶν ἕνεκα ἔπραττον ταῦτα, φαίνεσθαι τῆς αὐτῆς τιμῆς
πολλὰς ἡμέρας πωλοῦντας, ἕως ὁ συνεωνημένος αὐτοὺς ἐπέλιπε·
νῦν δ' ἐνίοτε τῆς αὐτῆς ἡμέρας ἐπώλουν δραχμῇ τιμιώτερον,
ὥσπερ κατὰ μέδιμνον συνωνούμενοι. καὶ τούτων ὑμᾶς μάρτυρας
13 παρέχομαι. δεινὸν δέ μοι δοκεῖ εἶναι, εἰ ὅταν μὲν εἰσφορὰν
εἰσενεγκεῖν δέῃ, ἣν πάντες εἴσεσθαι μέλλουσιν, οὐκ ἐθέλουσιν
ἀλλὰ πενίαν προφασίζονται, ἐφ' οἷς δὲ θάνατός ἐστιν ἡ ζημία
καὶ λαθεῖν αὐτοῖς συνέφερε, ταῦτα ἐπ' εὐνοίᾳ φασὶ τῇ ὑμετέρᾳ
παρανομῆσαι. καίτοι πάντες ἐπίστασθε ὅτι τούτοις ἥκιστα
προσήκει τοιούτους ποιεῖσθαι λόγους. τἀναντία γὰρ αὐτοῖς
καὶ τοῖς ἄλλοις συμφέρει· τότε γὰρ πλεῖστα κερδαίνουσιν,
ὅταν κακοῦ τινος ἀπαγγελθέντος τῇ πόλει τίμιον τὸν σῖτον
14 πωλῶσιν. οὕτω δ' ἄσμενοι τὰς συμφορὰς τὰς ὑμετέρας ὁρῶσιν,
ὥστε τὰς μὲν πρότεροι τῶν ἄλλων πυνθάνονται, τὰς δ' αὐτοὶ

---

8 νῦν Thalheim: δύο: τέσσαρες Bergk
11 μὲν om. Aldus
    ὑμῖν C: ἡμῖν X et Suidas s.v. ἄξιον
12 νῦν Hofmeister: νυνὶ
14 αὐτοὶ Markland: οὗτοι

gentlemen of the jury, since this man admits that he bought up the corn, and the law manifestly forbids him to do so; and you have sworn to vote according to the law. Nevertheless, in order that you may be convinced that they are lying against the magistrates too, I must speak at some length also about them. When they tried to shift   8 the blame on to them, we summoned the magistrates and questioned them. Two of them denied any knowledge of the matter, but Anytus said that during the previous winter, when corn was dear, as the dealers were outbidding one another and fighting among themselves, he had advised them to stop their competition, regarding it as beneficial to you, their customers, that they should buy as cheaply as possible; for they were bound in selling it to raise the price by only one obol. Now I shall produce Anytus himself to you as witness   9 to the fact that he did not tell them to buy it up and store it, but only advised them not to bid against one another.

TESTIMONY

This man made these statements at the time of the earlier **Council**, whereas these men clearly bought up the corn during the present one. Well, you have heard that they bought up the corn   10 under no orders from the magistrates. But I consider that, however true their statements on these matters may be, they will not be establishing a defence for themselves but accusing the magistrates: for in cases for which laws are specifically written, how should penalties not be exacted both from those who disobey and from those who order them to act counter to them? However, I do not expect   11 them to resort to this argument, gentlemen of the jury; but perhaps they will say, as they did in the Council, that they bought up the corn out of patriotism, in order to sell it to you as cheaply as possible. I shall give you the strongest and clearest proof that they are lying. If they were doing this for your benefit, they ought to   12 have been seen selling at the same price for a number of days, until the stock bought up by them ran out. But in fact there were times during the same day when they were selling it at the higher profit of **a drachma, as though they were buying up by the medimnus at a time. I** make you yourselves the witnesses to these facts. It seems shocking   13 to me if, whenever a special levy has to be paid, which everyone is going to know about, they decline, pleading poverty as their excuse. But in committing offences for which the penalty is death and when it was to their advantage to employ secrecy, they say that they broke the law out of good will towards you. Yet you all know that such arguments are highly inappropriate coming from them. Their interests and those of the rest of us are opposite, for they achieve the greatest gain when some bad news has reached the city, and they can sell their corn at a high price. Such is the pleasure with which they   14 view your misfortunes that they come to hear about them before the rest of us, and they fabricate other rumours themselves, saying that

195

λογοποιοῦσιν, ἢ τὰς ναῦς διεφθάρθαι τὰς ἐν τῷ Πόντῳ, ἢ ὑπὸ
Λακεδαιμονίων ἐκπλεούσας συνειλῆφθαι, ἢ τὰ ἐμπόρια κεκλῆσ-
θαι, ἢ τὰς σπονδὰς μέλλειν ἀπορρηθήσεσθαι, καὶ εἰς τοῦτ'
15 ἔχθρας ἐληλύθασιν, ὥστ' ἐν τοῖς αὐτοῖς καιροῖς ἐπιβουλεύουσιν ὑμῖν, ἐν οἷσπερ οἱ πολέμιοι. ὅταν γὰρ μάλιστα σίτου
τυγχάνητε δεόμενοι, συναρπάζουσιν οὗτοι καὶ οὐκ ἐθέλουσι
πωλεῖν, ἵνα μὴ περὶ τῆς τιμῆς διαφερώμεθα, ἀλλ' ἀγαπῶμεν ἂν
ὁποσουτινοσοῦν πριάμενοι παρ' αὐτῶν ἀπέλθωμεν· ὥστ' ἐνίοτε
16 εἰρήνης οὔσης ὑπὸ τούτων πολιορκούμεθα. οὕτω δὲ πάλαι περὶ
τῆς τούτων πανουργίας καὶ κακονοίας ἡ πόλις ἔγνωκεν, ὥστ'
ἐπὶ μὲν τοῖς ἄλλοις ὠνίοις ἅπασι τοὺς ἀγορανόμους φύλακας
κατεστήσατε, ἐπὶ δὲ ταύτῃ μόνῃ τῇ τέχνῃ χωρὶς σιτοφύλακας
ἀποκληροῦτε· καὶ πολλάκις ἤδη παρ' ἐκείνων πολιτῶν ὄντων
δίκην τὴν μεγίστην ἐλάβετε, ὅτι οὐχ οἷοί τ' ἦσαν τῆς τούτων
πονηρίας ἐπικρατῆσαι. καίτοι τί χρὴ αὐτοὺς τοὺς ἀδικοῦντας
ὑφ' ὑμῶν πάσχειν, ὁπότε καὶ τοὺς οὐ δυναμένους φυλάττειν
ἀποκτείνετε;
17 Ἐνθυμεῖσθαι δὲ χρὴ ὅτι ἀδύνατον ὑμῖν ἐστιν ἀποψηφίσασθαι. εἰ γὰρ ἀπογνώσεσθε ὁμολογούντων αὐτῶν ἐπὶ τοὺς ἐμπόρους
συνίστασθαι, δόξεθ' ὑμεῖς ἐπιβουλεύειν τοῖς εἰσπλέουσιν. εἰ
μὲν γὰρ ἄλλην τινὰ ἀπολογίαν ἐποιοῦντο, οὐδεὶς ἂν εἶχε τοῖς
ἀποψηφισαμένοις ἐπιτιμᾶν· ἐφ' ὑμῖν γὰρ ὁποτέροις βούλεσθε
πιστεύειν· νῦν δὲ πῶς οὐ δεινὰ ἂν δόξαιτε ποιεῖν, εἰ τοὺς
18 ὁμολογοῦντας παρανομεῖν ἀζημίους ἀφήσετε; ἀναμνήσθητε δέ, ὦ
ἄνδρες δικασταί, ὅτι πολλῶν ἤδη ἐχόντων ταύτην τὴν αἰτίαν,
ἀλλ' ἀρνουμένων καὶ μάρτυρας παρεχομένων, θάνατον κατέγνωτε,
πιστοτέρους ἡγησάμενοι τοὺς τῶν κατηγόρων λόγους. καίτοι πῶς
ἂν οὐ θαυμαστὸν εἴη, εἰ περὶ τῶν αὐτῶν ἁμαρτημάτων δικάζον-
τες μᾶλλον ἐπιθυμεῖτε παρὰ τῶν ἀρνουμένων δίκην λαμβάνειν;
19 καὶ μὲν δή, ὦ ἄνδρες δικασταί, πᾶσιν ἡγοῦμαι φανερὸν εἶναι
ὅτι οἱ περὶ τῶν τοιούτων ἀγῶνες κοινότατοι τυγχάνουσιν ὄντες
τοῖς ἐν τῇ πόλει, ὥστε πεύσονται ἥντινα γνώμην περὶ αὐτῶν
ἔχετε, ἡγούμενοι, ἂν μὲν θάνατον τούτων καταγνῶτε, κοσμιω-
τέρους ἔσεσθαι τοὺς λοιπούς· ἂν δ' ἀζημίους ἀφῆτε, πολλὴν
ἄδειαν αὐτοῖς ἐφηφισμένοι ἔσεσθε ποιεῖν ὅ τι ἂν βούλωνται.
20 χρὴ δέ, ὦ ἄνδρες δικασταί, μὴ μόνον τῶν παρεληλυθότων ἕνεκα
αὐτοὺς κολάζειν, ἀλλὰ καὶ παραδείγματος ἕνεκα τῶν μελλόντων
ἔσεσθαι· οὕτω γὰρ ἔσονται μόγις ἀνεκτοί. ἐνθυμεῖσθε δὲ ὅτι
ἐκ ταύτης τῆς τέχνης πλεῖστοι περὶ τοῦ σώματός εἰσιν ἠγωνισ-
μένοι· καὶ οὕτω μεγάλα ἐξ αὐτῆς ὠφελοῦνται, ὥστε μᾶλλον
αἱροῦνται καθ' ἑκάστην ἡμέραν περὶ τῆς ψυχῆς κινδυνεύειν ἢ
21 παύεσθαι παρ' ὑμῶν ἀδίκως κερδαίνοντες. καὶ μὲν δὴ οὐδ' ἐὰν
ἀντιβολῶσιν ὑμᾶς καὶ ἱκετεύωσι, δικαίως ἂν αὐτοὺς ἐλεήσαιτε,

15 τοῖς αὐτοῖς Cobet: τούτοις τοῖς   συναρπάζουσιν Cobet:
    ἀναρπάζουσιν
18 ἀλλ' ἀρνουμένων Sauppe: λαμβάνειν
19 τούτων Kayser: αὐτῶν
20 παύεσθαι Scheibe: παύσεσθαι

the ships on the Pontus route have been wrecked or have been captured by the Lakedaimonians as they sailed out, or that the markets have been blockaded or the peace treaty was about to be broken. And to such lengths have they carried their personal war 15 against you that they use the same crises to plot against you as the enemy. For it is at times when you are shortest of corn that they snap it up and refuse to sell it, in order that we may not dispute about the price but would be glad to come away having bought it from them at any price. Thus there are times when, even when there is peace, we are besieged by these men. But the city has known 16 about their villainy and malevolence for so long that, whereas you appointed the market-officers as controllers of all other items for sale, you elect separately corn-controllers by lot to supervise this trade alone. And there have been many occasions already when you have exacted the most extreme penalties from these officers, fellow-citizens though they were, because they were unable to overcome these men's villainy. Yet what should the wrongdoers themselves suffer at your hands, when you even execute those who cannot control them?

You ought to reflect that it is impossible for you to vote an 17 acquittal. For if you reject the charge when they themselves admit to forming a combine against the merchants, you in turn will be regarded as forming designs against the importers. Now if they had made some other defence, nobody would have had grounds for criticising those who acquitted them, since it is up to you to decide which side you want to believe. But as it is, how could your action appear other than shocking, if you release unpunished men who admit they are breaking the law? And remember, gentlemen of the jury, 18 that in the past you have condemned to death many who have been accused of the same offence, though they have denied the charge and produced witnesses in their defence, because you placed more trust in the statements of their prosecutors. And yet how would it not be surprising if, in passing judgment on the same crimes, you show a greater desire to exact justice from those who deny committing them? And besides, gentlemen of the jury, I assume it to be obvious to all 19 that lawsuits on matters of this kind are of the most communal concern to everyone in the city, so that they will be wanting to know what your view on them is, since they consider that if you condemn these men to death, the others will behave in a more responsible way, whereas if you release them unpunished, you will have voted them complete licence to do whatever they like. They ought to be 20 punished, gentlemen of the jury, not only because of the past, but also to set an example for the future: by this action they will become bearable, though barely so. And remember that a very large number from this profession have faced lawsuits on capital charges: so great is the profit they make from it that they choose to risk their lives each day rather than cease making illegal gains at your expense. Furthermore, you would not do right to pity them even if they 21

ἀλλὰ πολὺ μᾶλλον τῶν τε πολιτῶν οἳ διὰ τὴν τούτων πονηρίαν
ἀπέθνησκον, καὶ τοὺς ἐμπόρους ἐφ' οὓς οὗτοι συνέστησαν· οἷς
ὑμεῖς χαριεῖσθε καὶ προθυμοτέρους ποιήσετε, δίκην παρὰ τούτων λαμβάνοντες. εἰ δὲ μή, τίν' αὐτοὺς οἴεσθε γνώμην ἕξειν,
ἐπειδὰν πύθωνται ὅτι τῶν καπήλων, οἳ τοῖς εἰσπλέουσιν ὡμο-
λόγησαν ἐπιβουλεύειν, ἀπεψηφίσασθε;

22   Οὐκ οἶδ' ὅ τι δεῖ πλείω λέγειν· περὶ μὲν γὰρ τῶν ἄλλων
τῶν ἀδικούντων, ὅτε δικάζονται, δεῖ παρὰ τῶν κατηγόρων πυ-
θέσθαι, τὴν δὲ τούτων πονηρίαν ἅπαντες ἐπίστασθε. ἂν οὖν
τούτων καταψηφίσησθε, τά τε δίκαια ποιήσετε καὶ ἀξιώτερον
τὸν σῖτον ὠνήσεσθε· εἰ δὲ μή, τιμιώτερον.

---

21 οὓς Taylor: οἷς   παρὰ τούτων Taylor: παρ' αὐτῶν
    τίν' αὐτοὺς Reiske: τίνα αὐτοὺς C: τὴν αὐτὴν X
    εἰσπλέουσιν Reiske: ἐκπλέουσιν

beseech and implore you: much more readily should you pity those of our citizens who died because of these men's villainy, and the merchants against whom they combined. But you will gratify and encourage these men by exacting justice from the accused. If you fail to do this, what do you think their opinion will be when they learn that you have acquitted the retailers who admitted conspiring against the importers?

I do not think any more needs to be said. When other wrongdoers are brought to trial, it is necessary to ask the prosecutors to explain the charges. But all of you are acqainted with the villainy of the present defendants. Therefore if you condemn them you will both be doing what is just and securing a cheaper price for the corn you buy; if you do not, it will be dearer.

22

ΠΕΡΙ ΤΟΥ ΑΔΥΝΑΤΟΥ

1   Οὐ πολλοῦ δέω χάριν ἔχειν, ὦ βουλή, τῷ κατηγόρῳ, ὅτι μοι
παρεσκεύασε τὸν ἀγῶνα τουτονί. πρότερον γὰρ οὐκ ἔχων πρόφασιν ἐφ' ἧς τοῦ βίου λόγον δοίην, νυνὶ διὰ τοῦτον εἴληφα. καὶ
πειράσομαι τῷ λόγῳ τοῦτον μὲν ἐπιδεῖξαι ψευδόμενον, ἐμαυτὸν
δὲ βεβιωκότα μέχρι τῆσδε τῆς ἡμέρας ἐπαίνου μᾶλλον ἄξιον ἢ
φθόνου· διὰ γὰρ οὐδὲν ἄλλο μοι δοκεῖ παρασκευάσαι τόνδε μοι
2   τὸν κίνδυνον οὗτος ἢ διὰ φθόνον. καίτοι ὅστις τούτοις φθονεῖ
οὓς οἱ ἄλλοι ἐλεοῦσι, τίνος ἂν ὑμῖν ὁ τοιοῦτος ἀποσχέσθαι
δοκεῖ πονηρίας; εἰ μὲν γὰρ ἕνεκα χρημάτων με συκοφαντεῖ—·
εἰ δ' ὡς ἐχθρὸν ἑαυτοῦ με τιμωρεῖται, ψεύδεται· διὰ γὰρ τὴν
πονηρίαν αὐτοῦ οὔτε φίλῳ οὔτε ἐχθρῷ πώποτε ἐχρησάμην αὐτῷ.
3   ἤδη τοίνυν, ὦ βουλή, δῆλός ἐστι φθονῶν, ὅτι τοιαύτη κεχρη-
μένος συμφορᾷ τούτου βελτίων εἰμὶ πολίτης. καὶ γὰρ οἶμαι
δεῖν, ὦ βουλή, τὰ τοῦ σώματος δυστυχήματα τοῖς τῆς ψυχῆς
ἐπιτηδεύμασιν ἰᾶσθαι [καλῶς]. εἰ γὰρ ἐξ ἴσου τῇ συμφορᾷ καὶ
τὴν διάνοιαν ἕξω καὶ τὸν ἄλλον βίον διάξω, τί τούτου διοίσω;
4   Περὶ μὲν οὖν τούτων τοσαῦτά μοι εἰρήσθω· ὑπὲρ ὧν δέ μοι
προσήκει λέγειν, ὡς ἂν οἷόν τε διὰ βραχυτάτων ἐρῶ. φησὶ γὰρ
ὁ κατήγορος οὐ δικαίως με λαμβάνειν τὸ παρὰ τῆς πόλεως ἀργύ-
ριον· καὶ γὰρ τῷ σώματι δύνασθαι καὶ οὐκ εἶναι τῶν ἀδυνάτων,
καὶ τέχνην ἐπίστασθαι τοιαύτην ὥστε καὶ ἄνευ τοῦ διδομένου
5   τούτου ζῆν. καὶ τεκμηρίοις χρῆται τῆς μὲν τοῦ σώματος ῥώμης,
ὅτι ἐπὶ τοὺς ἵππους ἀναβαίνω, τῆς δ' ἐν τῇ τέχνῃ εὐπορίας,
ὅτι δύναμαι συνεῖναι δυναμένοις ἀνθρώποις ἀναλίσκειν. τὴν
μὲν οὖν ἐκ τῆς τέχνης εὐπορίαν καὶ τὸν ἄλλον τὸν ἐμὸν βίον,
οἷος τυγχάνει, πάντας ὑμᾶς οἴομαι γιγνώσκειν· ὅμως δὲ κἀγὼ
6   διὰ βραχέων ἐρῶ. ἐμοὶ γὰρ ὁ μὲν πατὴρ κατέλιπεν οὐδέν, τὴν
δὲ μητέρα τελευτήσασαν πέπαυμαι τρέφων τρίτον ἔτος τουτί,
παῖδες δέ μοι οὔπω εἰσὶν οἵ με θεραπεύσουσι. τέχνην δὲ
κέκτημαι βραχέα δυναμένην ὠφελεῖν, ἣν αὐτὸς μὲν ἤδη χαλεπῶς
ἐργάζομαι, τὸν διαδεξόμενον δ' αὐτὴν οὔπω δύναμαι κτήσασθαι.
πρόσοδος δέ μοι οὐκ ἔστιν ἄλλη πλὴν ταύτης, ἣν ἂν ἀφέλησθέ
με, κινδυνεύσαιμ' ἂν ὑπὸ τῇ δυσχερεστάτῃ γενέσθαι τύχῃ.
7   μὴ τοίνυν, ἐπειδή γε ἔστιν, ὦ βουλή, σῶσαί με δικαίως, ἀπο-
λέσητε ἀδίκως· μηδὲ ἃ νεωτέρῳ καὶ μᾶλλον ἐρρωμένῳ ὄντι
ἔδοτε, πρεσβύτερον καὶ ἀσθενέστερον γιγνόμενον ἀφέλησθε·
μηδὲ πρότερον καὶ περὶ τοὺς οὐδὲν ἔχοντας κακὸν ἐλεημονέστα-
τοι δοκοῦντες εἶναι νυνὶ διὰ τοῦτον τοὺς καὶ τοῖς ἐχθροῖς

---

1   οὐ πολλοῦ C: πολλοῦ X
3   καλῶς del. Cobet: καλοῖς Markland: εἰκότως P. Müller
6   ἣν ante ἂν Contius: ἧς
7   τοὺς καὶ Reiske: καὶ τοὺς

SPEECH 24 : FOR THE INVALID

I am almost grateful to my accuser, councillors, for devising this 1
case against me. For before this I had no excuse for giving an
account of my life, but now because of him I have obtained one. I
shall try in my speech to prove this man to be lying, and that to this
day I have lived a life worthy of praise rather than envy: for it
seems to me that it is for no reason other than envy that he has
devised this plot to endanger me. Now tell me, what villainy do you 2
think a man would shrink from, who envies those whom others pity?
If it is for my money that he is slandering me...! While if he is
representing me as a personal enemy against whom he is seeking
revenge, he is lying, because I have never had anything to do with
him as a friend or an enemy because of his wicked character. So it is 3
now clear, councillors, that he is envious because, in spite of my
great misfortune, I am a better citizen than he is. For it is my belief,
councillors, that one should remedy the afflictions of the body by
exercising the powers of the spirit, since if I am to maintain my
mental attitude and my life in general at the same level as my
misfortune, in what way shall I differ from this man?

Let those, then, be my only words on these matters: as to the 4
facts relevant to my case, I shall speak in as few words as possible.
The prosecutor says that I am receiving the state pension illegally
because I am able-bodied and not to be classed as an invalid, and
that I am skilled in a trade which enables me to live without this
pension. As proof of my physical fitness he adduces my riding on 5
horseback, and of the prosperity I derive from my trade, the fact
that I am able to associate with men who have money to spend. Now I
think you all know how much prosperity my trade brings me and how
I conduct my life in general, but even so I shall give you my own
brief account. My father left me nothing, and it is only two years 6
since I ceased supporting my mother on her death, and I do not yet
have any children to look after me. The trade I possess can provide
only limited assistance; I now have difficulty in practising it myself,
and am as yet unable to procure someone to take it over. I have no
other income than this pension, and if you deprive me of it, I could
risk being subjected to the most intolerable misfortune. Do not 7
therefore, councillors, destroy me unjustly when you can save me
justly, nor deprive me as I grow older and weaker of what you
granted me when I was younger and stronger; and again, do not
undo your earlier reputation for the greatest compassion, even in
cases where there was no hardship, by now heeding my opponent and

ἐλεινοὺς ὄντας ἀγρίως ἀποδέξησθε· μηδ᾽ ἐμὲ τολμήσαντες
ἀδικῆσαι καὶ τοὺς ἄλλους τοὺς ὁμοίως ἐμοὶ διακειμένους
8 ἀθυμῆσαι ποιήσητε. καὶ γὰρ ἂν ἄτοπον εἴη, ὦ βουλή, εἰ ὅτε
μὲν ἁπλῆ μοι ἦν ἡ συμφορά, τότε μὲν φαινοίμην λαμβάνων τὸ
ἀργύριον τοῦτο, νῦν δ᾽ ἐπειδὴ καὶ γῆρας καὶ νόσοι καὶ τὰ
τούτοις ἑπόμενα κακὰ προσγίγνεταί μοι, τότε ἀφαιρεθείην.
9 δοκεῖ δέ μοι τῆς πενίας τῆς ἐμῆς τὸ μέγεθος ὁ κατήγορος ἂν
ἐπιδεῖξαι σαφέστατα μόνος ἀνθρώπων. εἰ γὰρ ἐγὼ κατασταθεὶς
χορηγὸς τραγῳδοῖς προκαλεσαίμην αὐτὸν εἰς ἀντίδοσιν, δεκάκις
ἂν ἕλοιτο χορηγῆσαι μᾶλλον ἢ ἀντιδοῦναι ἅπαξ. καὶ πῶς οὐ
δεινόν ἐστι νῦν μὲν κατηγορεῖν ὡς διὰ πολλὴν εὐπορίαν ἐξ
ἴσου δύναμαι συνεῖναι τοῖς πλουσιωτάτοις, εἰ δὲ ὧν ἐγὼ λέγω
τύχοι τι γενόμενον, τοιοῦτόν μ᾽ εἰδέναι καὶ ἔτι πονηρότερον;
10 Περὶ δὲ τῆς ἐμῆς ἱππικῆς, ἧς οὗτος ἐτόλμησε μνησθῆναι
πρὸς ὑμᾶς, οὔτε τὴν τύχην δείσας οὔτε ὑμᾶς αἰσχυνθείς, οὐ
πολὺς ὁ λόγος. ἐγὼ γάρ, ὦ βουλή, πάντας οἶμαι τοὺς ἔχοντάς
τι δυστύχημα τοῦτο ζητεῖν καὶ τοῦτο φιλοσοφεῖν, ὅπως ὡς
ἀλυπότατα μεταχειριοῦνται τὸ συμβεβηκὸς πάθος. ὧν εἷς ἐγώ,
καὶ περιπεπτωκὼς τοιαύτῃ συμφορᾷ ταύτην ἐμαυτῷ ῥᾳστώνην
11 ἐξηῦρον εἰς τὰς ὁδοὺς τὰς μακροτέρας τῶν ἀναγκαίων. ὃ δὲ
μέγιστον, ὦ βουλή, τεκμήριον ὅτι διὰ τὴν συμφορὰν ἀλλ᾽ οὐ
διὰ τὴν ὕβριν, ὡς οὗτός φησιν, ἐπὶ τοὺς ἵππους ἀναβαίνω
[ῥᾴδιόν ἐστι μαθεῖν]· εἰ γὰρ ἐκεκτήμην οὐσίαν, ἐπ᾽ ἀστράβης
ἂν ὠχούμην, ἀλλ᾽ οὐκ ἐπὶ τοὺς ἀλλοτρίους ἵππους ἀνέβαινον·
νυνὶ δ᾽ ἐπειδὴ τοιοῦτον οὐ δύναμαι κτήσασθαι, τοῖς ἀλλοτρί-
12 οις ἵπποις ἀναγκάζομαι χρῆσθαι πολλάκις. καίτοι πῶς οὐκ
ἄτοπόν ἐστιν, ὦ βουλή, τοῦτον ἄν, εἰ μὲν ἐπ᾽ ἀστράβης ὀχού-
μενον ἑώρα με, σιωπᾶν (τί γὰρ ἂν καὶ ἔλεγεν;), ὅτι δὲ ἐπὶ
τοὺς ᾐτημένους ἵππους ἀναβαίνω, πειρᾶσθαι πείθειν ὑμᾶς ὡς
δυνατός εἰμι; καὶ ὅτι μὲν δυοῖν βακτηρίαιν χρῶμαι, τῶν ἄλλων
μιᾷ χρωμένων, μὴ κατηγορεῖν ὡς καὶ τοῦτο τῶν δυναμένων ἐστίν,
ὅτι δ᾽ ἐπὶ τοὺς ἵππους ἀναβαίνω, τεκμηρίῳ χρῆσθαι πρὸς ὑμᾶς
ὡς εἰμὶ τῶν δυναμένων; οἷς ἐγὼ διὰ τὴν αὐτὴν αἰτίαν ἀμφοτέροις χρῶμαι.
13 Τοσοῦτον δὲ διενήνοχεν ἀναισχυντίᾳ τῶν ἁπάντων ἀνθρώπων,
ὥστε ὑμᾶς πειρᾶται πείθειν, τοσούτους ὄντας εἷς ὤν, ὡς οὐκ
εἰμὶ τῶν ἀδυνάτων ἐγώ. καίτοι εἰ τοῦτο πείσει τινὰς ὑμῶν, ὦ
βουλή, τί με κωλύει κληροῦσθαι τῶν ἐννέα ἀρχόντων, καὶ ὑμᾶς

8   ἑπόμενα Reiske: ἐχόμενα
9   προκαλεσαίμην Reiske: προσκαλεσαίμην   τι Emperius:
τις   τοιοῦτόν μ᾽ εἰδέναι coniecit Erbse: εἶναι:
ὁμολογεῖν ἄν με ante τοιοῦτον Thalheim: ἂν ἐμὲ κρῖναι
post τοιοῦτον Heldmann: εἶναι; καὶ τί πονηρότερον;
Halm: καὶ ἔστι τι πονηρότερον; Scheibe: ἀπορώτερον
Kayser
10   τοῦτο ante ζητεῖν Stephanus: τοιοῦτο X
11   ῥᾴδιόν ἐστι μαθεῖν del. Scheibe
12   ἄν post τοῦτον Weidner: αὐτὸν   εἰμὶ post
δυνατός Kayser: εἴην

treating savagely those who are pitied even by their enemies. And do
not cause despondency in those similarly placed to myself by rashly
doing me wrong. For it would be absurd, councillors, if I were to be   8
seen receiving this money when I had a single disability, but now, as
age, illness and their consequences are added to my problems, I
should be deprived of it. I think my accuser would be in a better   9
position than anybody else on earth to show the extent of my
poverty: for if I were to be appointed producer of the tragic dramas
and challenged him to an exchange, he would choose to be a producer
ten times rather than make a single change of property. And how is
it not shocking for him to accuse me now of being able to associate on
equal terms with the richest men because of my great wealth, whereas
in the event of one of the possibilities I describe, he would recognise
my condition to be such, or even worse?

As to my riding horses, which he has been rash enough to bring   10
to your attention, showing no fear of fortune or shame before you,
there is not much to say. For I assume, councillors, that all those
who have some affliction make it their aim and object of study to
manage the misfortune that has befallen them as painlessly as
possible. I am one of these; and when I found myself caught up in
such a disaster, I contrived for myself this easy way of travelling on
the longer journeys I had to make. But the strongest proof,   11
councillors, that I ride horses because of my misfortune, not from
arrogance as this man alleges, is this: if I possessed wealth, I should
travel on a saddled mule, and not ride on other men's horses; but as
it is, since I am unable to afford such a mount, I am frequently
obliged to use other men's horses. Yet how is it not absurd,   12
gentlemen, that this man would say nothing if he saw me riding a
saddled mule (for what could he say?) but because I ride hired
horses, he tries to persuade you that I am able-bodied? And from the
fact that I use two sticks, whereas others use one, he does not argue
that this also is what able-bodied men do, but he uses the fact that I
ride horses as proof to you that I am to be classed as able-bodied? I
use both aids for the same reason.

He has so surpassed the whole human race in shamelessness as   13
to try to persuade you, on his own in face of so many, that I am not
one of the disabled class. Yet if he should persuade some of you of
this, councillors, what is there to prevent me from drawing lots for
one of the nine archonships, and you from depriving me of the obol

ἐμοῦ μὲν ἀφελέσθαι τὸν ὀβολὸν ὡς ὑγιαίνοντος, τούτῳ δὲ ψηφίσασθαι ἐλεήσαντας ὡς ἀναπήρῳ; οὐ γὰρ δήπου τὸν αὐτὸν ὑμεῖς
μὲν ὡς δυνάμενον ἀφαιρήσεσθε τὸ διδόμενον, οἱ δὲ <θεσμοθέ-
14 ται> ὡς ἀδύνατον ὄντα κληροῦσθαι κωλύσουσιν. ἀλλὰ γὰρ οὔτε
ὑμεῖς τούτῳ τὴν αὐτὴν ἔχετε γνώμην, οὔθ᾽ οὗτος εὖ φρονῶν. ὁ
μὲν γὰρ ὥσπερ ἐπικλήρου τῆς συμφορᾶς οὔσης ἀμφισβητήσων ἥκει
καὶ πειρᾶται πείθειν ὑμᾶς ὡς οὐκ εἰμὶ τοιοῦτος οἷον ὑμεῖς
ὁρᾶτε πάντες· ὑμεῖς δέ (ὃ τῶν εὖ φρονούντων ἔργον ἐστί)
μᾶλλον πιστεύετε τοῖς ὑμετέροις αὐτῶν ὀφθαλμοῖς ἢ τοῖς τούτου λόγοις.
15   Λέγει δ᾽ ὡς ὑβριστής εἰμι καὶ βίαιος καὶ λίαν ἀσελγῶς
διακείμενος, ὥσπερ, εἰ φοβερῶς ὀνομάσειε, μέλλων ἀληθῆ
λέγειν, ἀλλ᾽ οὐκ, ἂν πάνυ πραόνως μηδὲ ψεύδηται, ταῦτα ποιήσων. ἐγὼ δ᾽ ὑμᾶς, ὦ βουλή, σαφῶς οἶμαι δεῖν διαγιγνώσκειν
οἷς τ᾽ ἐγχωρεῖ τῶν ἀνθρώπων ὑβρισταῖς εἶναι καὶ οἷς οὐ
16 προσήκει. οὐ γὰρ <τοὺς> πενομένους καὶ λίαν ἀπόρως διακειμένους ὑβρίζειν εἰκός, ἀλλὰ τοὺς πολλῷ πλείω τῶν ἀναγκαίων
κεκτημένους· οὐδὲ τοὺς ἀδυνάτους τοῖς σώμασιν ὄντας, ἀλλὰ
τοὺς μάλιστα πιστεύοντας ταῖς αὐτῶν ῥώμαις· οὐδὲ τοὺς ἤδη
προβεβηκότας τῇ ἡλικίᾳ, ἀλλὰ τοὺς ἔτι νέους καὶ νέαις ταῖς
17 διανοίαις χρωμένους. οἱ μὲν γὰρ πλούσιοι τοῖς χρήμασιν
ἐξωνοῦνται τοὺς κινδύνους, οἱ δὲ πένητες ὑπὸ τῆς παρούσης
ἀπορίας σωφρονεῖν ἀναγκάζονται· καὶ οἱ μὲν νέοι συγγνώμης
ἀξιοῦνται τυγχάνειν παρὰ τῶν πρεσβυτέρων, τοῖς δὲ πρεσβυτέ-
18 ροις ἐξαμαρτάνουσιν ὁμοίως ἐπιτιμῶσιν ἀμφότεροι· καὶ τοῖς
μὲν ἰσχυροῖς ἐγχωρεῖ μηδὲν αὐτοῖς πάσχουσιν, οὓς ἂν βουληθῶσιν, ὑβρίζειν, τοῖς δὲ ἀσθενέσιν οὐκ ἔστιν οὔτε ὑβριζομέ-
νοις ἀμύνεσθαι τοὺς ὑπάρξαντας οὔτε ὑβρίζειν βουλομένοις
περιγίγνεσθαι τῶν ἀδικουμένων. ὥστε μοι δοκεῖ ὁ κατήγορος
εἰπεῖν περὶ τῆς ἐμῆς ὕβρεως οὐ σπουδάζων ἀλλὰ παίζων, οὐδ᾽
ὑμᾶς πεῖσαι βουλόμενος ὡς εἰμὶ τοιοῦτος, ἀλλ᾽ ἐμὲ κωμῳδεῖν
βουλόμενος, ὥσπερ τι καλὸν ποιῶν.
19   Ἔτι δὲ καὶ συλλέγεσθαί φησιν ἀνθρώπους ὡς ἐμὲ πονηροὺς
καὶ πολλούς, οἳ τὰ μὲν ἑαυτῶν ἀνηλώκασι, τοῖς δὲ τὰ σφέτερα
σῴζειν βουλομένοις ἐπιβουλεύουσιν. ὑμεῖς δὲ ἐνθυμήθητε πάντες ὅτι ταῦτα λέγων οὐδὲν ἐμοῦ κατηγορεῖ μᾶλλον ἢ τῶν ἄλλων
ὅσοι τέχνας ἔχουσιν, οὐδὲ τῶν ὡς ἐμὲ εἰσιόντων μᾶλλον ἢ τῶν
20 ὡς τοὺς ἄλλους δημιουργούς. ἕκαστος γὰρ ὑμῶν εἴθισται προσφοιτᾶν ὁ μὲν πρὸς μυροπώλιον, ὁ δὲ πρὸς κουρεῖον, ὁ δὲ πρὸς
σκυτοτομεῖον, ὁ δ᾽ ὅποι ἂν τύχῃ, καὶ πλεῖστοι μὲν ὡς τοὺς
ἐγγυτάτω τῆς ἀγορᾶς κατεσκευασμένους, ἐλάχιστοι δὲ ὡς τοὺς
πλεῖστον ἀπέχοντας αὐτῆς· ὥστ᾽ εἴ τις ὑμῶν πονηρίαν κατα-
γνώσεται τῶν ὡς ἐμὲ εἰσιόντων, δῆλον ὅτι καὶ τῶν παρὰ τοῖς

·13 ἐλεήσαντας Frohberger: ἐάσαντας Suidas s.v. ἀνάπηρος:
πάντας   θεσμοθέται add. Frohberger
14 φρονῶν Markland: φρονεῖ Hude: εὔνοιαν Erbse: ποιῶν
15 πραόνως Turr.: πρᾶον ὡς
16 τοὺς add. Reiske
17 πρεσβυτέροις Frohberger: ἑτέροις

204

because I am of sound health, but voting it to this man from pity at his being a cripple? For surely you cannot be intending to deprive a man of his pension on the ground that he is able-bodied, and then the law-officers will prevent that same man from drawing lots for election on the ground that he is disabled? No: neither do you hold 14 the same view as this man, nor does he believe it when he is in his right mind. For he has come to argue about my misfortune as if over an heiress, and he is trying to persuade you that I am not such as you all see me to be. But you – and this is what all men in their right minds should do – prefer to trust your own eyes than this man's words.

He says that I am overbearing, violent and of an utterly 15 unrestrained character, as if he could tell the truth only by using these frightening words, and that he could not do so by using wholly inoffensive terms and avoiding falsehood. But I think, councillors, that you ought clearly to distinguish between those men who are free to behave insolently and those who are not allowed. Now it is not the 16 poor and those with very limited means who are likely to behave insolently, but those whose possessions greatly exceed the bare necessities; again, not those who are physically disabled, but those with complete confidence in their bodily strength; nor indeed those of advanced age, but those still young and of a youthful mentality. For 17 the wealthy buy off with their money the consequences of their dangerous actions, but the poor are compelled by their lack of means to behave with restraint. And young men expect to meet with indulgence from their elders, but when older men misbehave both ages alike reproach them. The strong are free to act violently 18 towards anyone they wish with impunity, but the weak, when insulted, can neither fend off the aggressors nor, when they wish to retaliate, can they get the better of their victims. So I think that the prosecutor's words about my overbearing behaviour are spoken not seriously but in jest: indeed, it is not his desire to persuade you that I am of that nature, but to make me into a comic character, as a kind of artistic touch.

He says further that wicked men meet at my shop, and many 19 who have wasted their own resources and plot against those who wish to preserve theirs. But you should all reflect that in saying this he is not accusing me any more than the other shopkeepers, or my customers any more than those of any others who have trades. For 20 each of you habitually visits the perfumer's, the barber's, the shoe-maker's, or wherever he may happen to go. Most of you visit those who have their businesses nearest the market-place, with only a small minority going to those farthest away from it. Therefore if any of you is going to find my customers guilty of villainy, the same judgment clearly applies to those who pass their time in other men's

ἄλλοις διατριβόντων· εἰ δὲ κἀκείνων, ἁπάντων Ἀθηναίων·
ἅπαντες γὰρ εἴθισθε προσφοιτᾶν καὶ διατρίβειν ἀμοῦ γέ που.
21   Ἀλλὰ γὰρ οὐκ οἶδ' ὅ τι δεῖ λίαν με ἀκριβῶς ἀπολογούμε-
νον πρὸς ἓν ἕκαστον ὑμῖν τῶν εἰρημένων ἐνοχλεῖν πλείω χρόνον. εἰ γὰρ ὑπὲρ τῶν μεγίστων εἴρηκα, τί δεῖ περὶ τῶν φαύλων
ὁμοίως τούτῳ σπουδάζειν; ἐγὼ δ' ὑμῶν, ὦ βουλή, δέομαι πάντων
τὴν αὐτὴν ἔχειν περὶ ἐμοῦ διάνοιαν, ἥνπερ καὶ πρότερον.
22   μηδ' οὗ μόνου μεταλαβεῖν ἔδωκεν ἡ τύχη μοι τῶν ἐν τῇ πατρίδι,
τούτου διὰ τουτονὶ ἀποστερήσητέ με· μηδ' ἃ πάλαι κοινῇ πάντες
ἔδοτέ μοι, νῦν οὗτος εἷς ὢν πείσῃ πάλιν ὑμᾶς ἀφελέσθαι.
ἐπειδὴ γάρ, ὦ βουλή, τῶν μεγίστων [ἀρχῶν] ὁ δαίμων ἀπεστέρησεν ἡμᾶς, ἡ πόλις ἡμῖν ἐψηφίσατο τοῦτο τὸ ἀργύριον, ἡγουμένη
κοινὰς εἶναι τὰς τύχας τοῖς ἅπασι καὶ τῶν κακῶν καὶ τῶν
23   ἀγαθῶν. πῶς οὖν οὐκ ἂν δειλαιότατος εἴην, εἰ τῶν μὲν καλ-
λίστων καὶ μεγίστων διὰ τὴν συμφορὰν ἀπεστερημένος εἴην, ἃ
δ' ἡ πόλις ἔδωκε προνοηθεῖσα τῶν οὕτως διακειμένων, διὰ τὸν
κατήγορον ἀφαιρεθείην; μηδαμῶς, ὦ βουλή, ταύτῃ θῆσθε τὴν
24   ψῆφον. διὰ τί γὰρ ἂν καὶ τύχοιμι τοιούτων ὑμῶν; πότερον ὅτι
δι' ἐμέ τις εἰς ἀγῶνα πώποτε καταστὰς ἀπώλεσε τὴν οὐσίαν;
ἀλλ' οὐδ' ἂν εἷς ἀποδείξειεν. ἀλλ' ὅτι πολυπράγμων εἰμὶ καὶ
θρασὺς καὶ φιλαπεχθήμων; ἀλλ' οὐ τοιαύταις ἀφορμαῖς τοῦ βίου
25   πρὸς τὰ τοιαῦτα τυγχάνω χρώμενος. ἀλλ' ὅτι λίαν ὑβριστὴς καὶ
βίαιος; ἀλλ' οὐδ' ἂν αὐτὸς φήσειεν, εἰ μὴ βούλοιτο καὶ τοῦτο
ψεύδεσθαι τοῖς ἄλλοις ὁμοίως. ἀλλ' ὅτι ἐπὶ τῶν τριάκοντα
γενόμενος ἐν δυνάμει κακῶς ἐποίησα πολλοὺς τῶν πολιτῶν; ἀλλὰ
μετὰ τοῦ ὑμετέρου πλήθους ἔφυγον εἰς Χαλκίδα [τὴν ἐπ' Εὐρί-
πῳ], καὶ ἐξόν μοι μετ' ἐκείνων ἀδεῶς πολιτεύεσθαι, μεθ' ὑμῶν
26   εἱλόμην κινδυνεύειν ἁπάντων. μὴ τοίνυν, ὦ βουλή, μηδὲν ἡμαρ-
τηκὼς ὁμοίως ὑμῶν τύχοιμι τοῖς πολλὰ ἠδικηκόσιν, ἀλλὰ τὴν
αὐτὴν ψῆφον θέσθε περὶ ἐμοῦ ταῖς ἄλλαις βουλαῖς, ἀναμνησθέντες ὅτι οὔτε χρήματα διαχειρίσας τῆς πόλεως δίδωμι λόγον
αὐτῶν, οὔτε ἀρχὴν ἄρξας οὐδεμίαν εὐθύνας ὑπέχω νῦν αὐτῆς,
27   ἀλλὰ περὶ ὀβολοῦ μόνον ποιοῦμαι τοὺς λόγους. καὶ οὕτως ὑμεῖς
μὲν τὰ δίκαια γνώσεσθε πάντες, ἐγὼ δὲ τούτων ὑμῖν τυχὼν ἕξω
τὴν χάριν, οὗτος δὲ τοῦ λοιποῦ μαθήσεται μὴ τοῖς ἀσθενεσ-
τέροις ἐπιβουλεύειν ἀλλὰ τῶν ὁμοίων αὐτῷ περιγίγνεσθαι.

---

20 ἀμοῦ Bekker: ἄλλου
21 φαύλων ὁμοίως τούτῳ Dobree: ὁμοίως τούτῳ φαύλων
22 μόνου Markland: μόνον   ἀρχῶν del. Frohberger
23 δειλαιότατος Markland: δικαιότατος   θῆσθε Bekker:
    θέσθε   τὴν ψῆφον Contius: τῇ ψήφῳ
25 τὴν ἐπ' Εὐρίπῳ del. Frohberger   ἁπάντων] ἀπαντῶν
    Westermann: ἀπελθών Baeker

shops; and if these men are condemned, all Athenians are condemned with them, for all of you are in the habit of frequenting and spending your time in some shop or other.

But I really see no need to weary you any longer with an 21 excessively detailed defence against each individual charge. For if I have spoken about the most important points, why should I treat trifling matters with the same seriousness as my accuser? I beg all of you, councillors, to view my situation in the same way as before. Do 22 not deprive me because of this man of the only state benefit of which fortune granted me a share; nor let him single-handed persuade you today to take back what all of you gave me long ago by common agreement. It was because heaven had deprived me of her greatest bounties, councillors, that the city voted this money to me, deeming the chances of good or evil to be the common lot of all. Therefore 23 how would I not be most pitiable if I were to be deprived of the fairest and greatest things because of my misfortune, and also see taken away from me because of my accuser that which the city, in her provident concern for men in my condition, granted me? Do not be induced to cast your vote in this way, councillors. For why should I find you so disposed? Is it because anyone has ever been brought 24 to court through me and lost his property? But not a single man could prove that. Or is it because I am meddlesome, aggressive and quarrelsome? But I do not happen to use my means of livelihood, such as they are, for that purpose. Or is it because I am grossly 25 overbearing and violent? But even my opponent would not allege this unless he wished to lie about this as he did about other matters. Or is it because under the Thirty I held a position of power and harmed many of the citizens? But I went into exile to Chalcis along with your people, and when I could have lived securely as a citizen with those men I chose to face danger with all of you. Therefore, councillors, as 26 I have committed no offence, let me not receive the same treatment from you as those who have done many wrongs, but pass the same verdict as did the other **Councils in my case**, remembering that I am not giving an account of public money that I have handled, nor have I held any state office for which I am now submitting an audit: my speech is about a mere obol. With this in mind you will all arrive at a 27 just decision, and I shall receive it with gratitude; while for the future this man will learn not to plot against those weaker than himself but only to try to overreach his equals.

ΔΗΜΟΥ ΚΑΤΑΛΥΣΕΩΣ ΑΠΟΛΟΓΙΑ

1   'Υμῖν μὲν πολλὴν συγγνώμην ἔχω, ὦ ἄνδρες δικασταί, ἀκούουσι τοιούτων λόγων καὶ ἀναμιμνησκομένοις τῶν γεγενημένων,
ὁμοίως ἅπασιν ὀργίζεσθαι τοῖς ἐν ἄστει μείνασι· τῶν δὲ κατηγόρων θαυμάζω, οἳ ἀμελοῦντες τῶν οἰκείων τῶν ἀλλοτρίων ἐπι-
μελοῦνται, εἰ σαφῶς εἰδότες τοὺς μηδὲν ἀδικοῦντας καὶ τοὺς
πολλὰ ἐξημαρτηκότας ζητοῦσι [κερδαίνειν ἤ] ὑμᾶς πείθειν περὶ
2   ἁπάντων ἡμῶν τὴν γνώμην ταύτην ἔχειν. εἰ μὲν οὖν οἴονται,
ὅσα ὑπὸ τῶν τριάκοντα γεγένηται τῇ πόλει, ἐμοῦ κατηγορηκέναι,
ἀδυνάτους αὐτοὺς ἡγοῦμαι λέγειν· οὐδὲ γὰρ πολλοστὸν μέρος
τῶν ἐκείνοις πεπραγμένων εἰρήκασιν· εἰ δὲ ὡς ἐμοῦ τι προσῆκον περὶ αὐτῶν ποιοῦνται τοὺς λόγους, ἀποδείξω τούτους μὲν
ἅπαντα ψευδομένους, ἐμαυτὸν δὲ τοιοῦτον ὄντα οἷόσπερ ἂν τῶν
3   ἐκ Πειραιῶς <ὁ> βέλτιστος ἐν ἄστει μείνας ἐγένετο. δέομαι δ'
ὑμῶν, ὦ ἄνδρες δικασταί, μὴ τὴν αὐτὴν γνώμην ἔχειν τοῖς
συκοφάνταις. τούτων μὲν γὰρ ἔργον ἐστὶ καὶ τοὺς μηδὲν ἡμαρτηκότας εἰς αἰτίαν καθιστάναι (ἐκ τούτων γὰρ ἂν μάλιστα
χρηματίζοιντο), ὑμέτερον δὲ τοῖς μηδὲν ἀδικοῦσιν ἐξ ἴσου
τῆς πολιτείας μεταδιδόναι· οὕτω γὰρ ἂν τοῖς καθεστηκόσι
4   πράγμασι πλείστους συμμάχους ἔχοιτε. ἀξιῶ δέ, ὦ ἄνδρες δικασταί, ἐάνπερ φανῶ συμφορᾶς μὲν μηδεμιᾶς αἴτιος γεγενημένος,
πολλὰ δὲ κἀγαθὰ εἰργασμένος τὴν πόλιν καὶ τῷ σώματι καὶ τοῖς
χρήμασι, ταῦτα γοῦν μοι παρ' ὑμῶν ὑπάρχειν, ὧν οὐ μόνον τοὺς
εὖ πεποιηκότας ἀλλὰ καὶ τοὺς μηδὲν ἀδικοῦντας τυγχάνειν
5   δίκαιόν ἐστι. μέγα μὲν οὖν ἡγοῦμαι τεκμήριον εἶναι, ὅτι,
εἴπερ ἐδύναντο οἱ κατήγοροι ἰδίᾳ με ἀδικοῦντα ἐξελέγξαι, οὐκ
ἂν τὰ τῶν τριάκοντα ἁμαρτήματα ἐμοῦ κατηγόρουν, οὐδ' ἂν ᾤοντο
χρῆναι ὑπὲρ τῶν ἐκείνοις πεπραγμένων ἑτέρους διαβάλλειν,
ἀλλ' αὐτοὺς τοὺς ἀδικοῦντας τιμωρεῖσθαι· νῦν δὲ νομίζουσι
τὴν πρὸς ἐκείνους ὀργὴν ἱκανὴν εἶναι καὶ τοὺς μηδὲν κακὸν
6   εἰργασμένους ἀπολέσαι. ἐγὼ δὲ οὐχ ἡγοῦμαι δίκαιον εἶναι οὔτε
εἴ τινες τῇ πόλει πολλῶν ἀγαθῶν αἴτιοι γεγένηνται, ἄλλους
τινὰς ὑπὲρ τούτων τιμὴν ἢ χάριν κομίσασθαι παρ' ὑμῶν, οὔτ'
εἴ τινες πολλὰ κακὰ εἰργασμένοι εἰσίν, εἰκότως ἂν δι' ἐκείνους τοὺς μηδὲν ἀδικοῦντας ὀνείδους καὶ διαβολῆς τυγχάνειν·
ἱκανοὶ γὰρ οἱ ὑπάρχοντες ἐχθροὶ τῇ πόλει καὶ μέγα κέρδος

---

1   εἰ Reiske: οἳ   μηδὲν Reiske: μὲν X: om. C
    κερδαίνειν ἤ del. Dobree
2   ὅσα Herwerden: ἃ   γεγένηται Jacobs: γεγένηνται
    ἅπαντα Stephanus: ἅπαντας
3   καθιστάναι Coraes: καθιστάνειν   χρηματίζοιντο Coraes:
    χρηματίζειν τὸ
4   ἐάνπερ φανῶ Dobree: ἐὰν ἀποφανῶ

208

SPEECH 25 : DEFENCE AGAINST A CHARGE
OF SUBVERTING THE DEMOCRACY

I feel much sympathy for you, gentlemen of the jury, if, on   1
hearing such statements and recalling the events, you should
feel equal anger against all who remained in the city. But I am
amazed at my accusers, that through their habit of minding other
people's business at the expense of their own they know clearly who
are the innocent men and who are the habitual wrongdoers, yet seek to peruade you to take the same view of all of us.
Now if they think they have accused me of all that happened   2
to the city under the Thirty, I consider them ineffective speakers, as
they have not mentioned the smallest fraction of what they
did. But if their statement about them implies that I had some
part in the regime, I shall prove that all their words are false, and
that I behaved as the best man in the Piraeus party would have done
if he had remained in the city. I beg of you, gentlemen of the jury,   3
not to share the opinion of the slander-mongers: for it is their
function to incriminate the innocent, as they are the most likely
source of money; but it is yours to afford the innocent equal
enjoyment of their rights as citizens, for by so doing you may secure
the greatest support for the established order of things. And I claim,   4
gentlemen of the jury, that if I am shown to be responsible for none
of the disasters but to have brought many benefits to the city both
physically and fiscally, I should receive from you at least that
treatment to which not only the city's benefactors but also those
merely innocent of any crime have a right. I think it a strong proof   5
of my good record that if my accusers could prove me guilty with
private charges, they would not be laying the Thirty's crimes at my
door; nor would they think it necessary to accuse others falsely of
their deeds, but would seek requital from the wrongdoers themselves.
But in fact they believe your anger against them to be sufficient also
to destroy those who have committed no crime. But I do not think it   6
just either that, if some men have been responsible for many benefits
to the city, others should receive from you the honour or gratitude
for them, or that if some men have committed many crimes, those
innocent of wrongdoing would deserve to receive abuse and false
accusation through them. The city has enough enemies as it is, men

νομίζοντες εἶναι τοὺς ἀδίκως ἐν ταῖς διαβολαῖς καθεστηκότας.
7   Πειράσομαι δ᾽ ὑμᾶς διδάξαι, οὓς ἡγοῦμαι τῶν πολιτῶν
προσήκειν ὀλιγαρχίας ἐπιθυμεῖν καὶ <οὓς> δημοκρατίας. ἐκ
τούτου γὰρ καὶ ὑμεῖς γνώσεσθε, κἀγὼ περὶ ἐμαυτοῦ τὴν ἀπολογίαν ποιήσομαι, ἀποφαίνων ὡς οὔτε ἐξ ὧν ἐν δημοκρατίᾳ οὔτε
ἐξ ὧν ἐν ὀλιγαρχίᾳ πεποίηκα, οὐδέν μοι προσῆκον κακόνουν
8   εἶναι τῷ πλήθει τῷ ὑμετέρῳ. πρῶτον μὲν οὖν ἐνθυμηθῆναι χρὴ
ὅτι οὐδείς ἐστιν ἀνθρώπων φύσει οὔτε ὀλιγαρχικὸς οὔτε δημο-
κρατικός, ἀλλ᾽ ἥτις ἂν ἑκάστῳ πολιτεία συμφέρῃ, ταύτην προ-
θυμεῖται καθεστάναι· ὥστε οὐκ ἐλάχιστον ἐν ὑμῖν ἐστι μέρος
ὡς πλείστους ἐπιθυμεῖν τῶν παρόντων νυνὶ πραγμάτων. καὶ
ταῦτα ὅτι οὕτως ἔχει, οὐ χαλεπῶς ἐκ τῶν πρότερον γεγενημένων
9   μαθήσεσθε. σκέψασθε γάρ, ὦ ἄνδρες δικασταί, τοὺς προστάντας
ἀμφοτέρων <τῶν> πολιτειῶν, ὁσάκις δὴ μετεβάλοντο. οὐ Φρύνι-
χος μὲν καὶ Πείσανδρος καὶ οἱ μετ᾽ ἐκείνων δημαγωγοί, ἐπειδὴ
πολλὰ εἰς ὑμᾶς ἐξήμαρτον, τὰς περὶ τούτων δείσαντες τιμωρίας
τὴν προτέραν ὀλιγαρχίαν κατέστησαν, πολλοὶ δὲ τῶν τετρακοσίων
μετὰ τῶν ἐκ Πειραιῶς συγκατῆλθον, ἔνιοι δὲ τῶν ἐκείνους ἐκ-
βαλόντων αὐτοὶ αὖθις τῶν τριάκοντα ἐγένοντο; εἰσὶ δὲ οὕτινες
τῶν Ἐλευσῖνάδε ἀπογραψαμένων, ἐξελθόντες μεθ᾽ ὑμῶν, ἐπολι-
10 όρκουν τοὺς μεθ᾽ αὑτῶν. οὔκουν χαλεπὸν γνῶναι, ὦ ἄνδρες
δικασταί, ὅτι οὐ περὶ πολιτείας εἰσὶν αἱ πρὸς ἀλλήλους
διαφοραί, ἀλλὰ περὶ τῶν ἰδίᾳ συμφερόντων ἑκάστῳ. ὑμᾶς οὖν
χρὴ ἐκ τούτων δοκιμάζειν τοὺς πολίτας, σκοποῦντας μὲν ὅπως
ἦσαν ἐν τῇ δημοκρατίᾳ πεπολιτευμένοι, ζητοῦντας δὲ εἴ τις
αὐτοῖς ἐγίγνετο ὠφέλεια τῶν πραγμάτων μεταπεσόντων· οὕτως
11 γὰρ ἂν δικαιοτάτην <τὴν> κρίσιν περὶ αὐτῶν ποιοῖσθε. ἐγὼ
τοίνυν ἡγοῦμαι, ὅσοι μὲν ἐν τῇ δημοκρατίᾳ ἄτιμοι ἦσαν εὐθύνας δεδωκότες ἢ τῶν ὄντων ἀπεστερημένοι ἢ ἄλλῃ τινὶ συμφορᾷ
τοιαύτῃ κεχρημένοι, προσήκειν αὐτοῖς ἑτέρας ἐπιθυμεῖν πολιτείας, ἐλπίζοντας τὴν μεταβολὴν ὠφέλειάν τινα αὐτοῖς ἔσεσθαι·
ὅσοι δὲ τὸν δῆμον πολλὰ κἀγαθὰ εἰργασμένοι εἰσί, κακὸν δὲ
μηδὲν πώποτε, ὀφείλεται δὲ αὐτοῖς χάριν κομίσασθαι παρ᾽ ὑμῶν
μᾶλλον ἢ δοῦναι δίκην τῶν πεπραγμένων, οὐκ ἄξιον κατὰ τούτων
ἀποδέχεσθαι διαβολάς, οὐδ᾽ ἐὰν πάντες οἱ τὰ τῆς πόλεως πράττοντες ὀλιγαρχικοὺς αὐτοὺς φάσκωσιν εἶναι.
12   Ἐμοὶ τοίνυν, ὦ ἄνδρες δικασταί, οὔτ᾽ ἰδίᾳ οὔτε δημοσίᾳ
συμφορὰ ἐν ἐκείνῳ τῷ χρόνῳ οὐδεμία πώποτε ἐγένετο, ἀνθ᾽ ἧσ-
τινος ἂν προθυμούμενος τῶν παρόντων κακῶν ἀπαλλαγῆναι ἑτέρων
ἐπεθύμουν πραγμάτων. τετριηράρχηκά τε γὰρ πεντάκις, καὶ τετ-

---

7   οὓς add. Contius
8   καθεστάναι Fuhr: καθιστάναι
9   τῶν add. Reiske   αὖθις Brulart: αὐτοῖς X: αὐτῶν C
    ἐπολιόρκουν τοὺς Scheibe: ἐπολιορκοῦντο
10 τὴν add. Rauchenstein
11 κατὰ Madvig: τὰς X: τὰς κατὰ C   ἀποδέχεσθαι Taylor:
    ὑποδέχεσθαι
12 τετριηράρχηκα Scheibe: ἐτριηράρχησα   τε Gebauer: μὲν

who think it a great gain to have persons arraigned on false charges.

I shall try to describe to you which of your citizens may in my 7 view be expected to desire democracy, and which oligarchy, for it is from this that you, for your part, will reach your decision, while I shall make my own defence by showing that neither under democracy nor oligarchy have my actions indicated any personal interest in being disloyal to your people. Now firstly it must be borne in mind that no 8 human being is naturally either an oligarch or a democrat: each man strives to establish whichever constitution works to his advantage, so that it is largely up to you to see that as many men as possible desire the present constitution. You will have no difficulty in discovering that this is so from past events. For consider, gentlemen 9 of the jury, how many times the leaders of both parties changed sides. Did not Phrynichus and Peisander and the demagogues in their party, when they had offended against you many times, establish the first oligarchy in fear of punishment for their misdeeds? And did not many of the Four Hundred return from exile along with the Piraeus party, and some of those who had expelled them come themselves to be numbered among the Thirty? And some of those enlisted for Eleusis marched out with you and besieged their own side. So it is 10 not difficult to realise, gentlemen of the jury, that disagreements between men are not about constitutions but about their own individual interests. It is therefore from these criteria that you should examine citizens, noting their political behaviour under democracy and trying to discover what advantage they gained by a revolution. By this process you may reach the fairest judgment concerning them. Now I think all of those who were disfranchised 11 under the democracy after submitting to audit, or had their property confiscated or suffered any other such kind of misfortune should be expected to desire a different constitution, in the hope that the change would be in some way advantageous to them. But those who have done the people much good and never any harm, and deserve to receive thanks from you rather than punishment for their actions, should not be the victims of slanderous charges, not even if all the politicians should allege that they favour oligarchy.

Now as for myself, gentlemen of the jury, during that time I 12 never suffered any disaster, either private or public, that might cause me, through a desire to be relieved of present ills, to long for a different state of affairs. For I equipped a trireme five times,

211

ράκις νεναυμάχηκα, καὶ εἰσφορὰς ἐν τῷ πολέμῳ πολλὰς εἰσενή-
νοχα, καὶ τἆλλα λελητούργηκα οὐδενὸς χεῖρον τῶν πολιτῶν.
13 καίτοι διὰ τοῦτο πλείω τῶν ὑπὸ τῆς πόλεως προσταττομένων
ἐδαπανώμην, ἵνα καὶ βελτίων ὑφ' ὑμῶν νομιζοίμην, καὶ εἴ πού
μοί τις συμφορὰ γένοιτο, ἄμεινον ἀγωνιζοίμην. ὧν ἐν τῇ ὀλιγαρχίᾳ ἁπάντων ἀπεστερούμην· οὐ γὰρ τοὺς τῷ πλήθει ἀγαθοῦ
τινος αἰτίους γεγενημένους χάριτος παρ' αὐτῶν ἠξίουν τυγχάνειν, ἀλλὰ τοὺς πλεῖστα κακὰ ὑμᾶς εἰργασμένους εἰς τὰς τιμὰς
καθίστασαν, ὡς ταύτην παρ' ἡμῶν πίστιν εἰληφότες. ἃ χρὴ
πάντας ἐνθυμουμένους μὴ τοῖς τούτων λόγοις πιστεύειν, ἀλλὰ
14 [καὶ]ἐκ τῶν ἔργων σκοπεῖν ἃ ἑκάστῳ τυγχάνει πεπραγμένα. ἐγὼ
γάρ, ὦ ἄνδρες δικασταί, οὔτε [ἐπὶ]τῶν τετρακοσίων ἐγενόμην·
ἢ τῶν κατηγόρων ὁ βουλόμενος παρελθὼν ἐλεγξάτω· οὐ τοίνυν
οὐδ' ἐπειδὴ οἱ τριάκοντα κατέστησαν, οὐδείς με ἀποδείξει
οὔτε βουλεύσαντα οὔτε ἀρχὴν οὐδεμίαν ἄρξαντα. καίτοι εἰ μὲν
ἐξόν μοι ἄρχειν μὴ ἐβουλόμην, ὑφ' ὑμῶν νυνὶ τιμᾶσθαι δίκαιός
εἰμι· εἰ δὲ οἱ τότε δυνάμενοι μὴ ἠξίουν μοι μεταδιδόναι τῶν
πραγμάτων, πῶς ἂν φανερώτερον ἢ οὕτως ψευδομένους ἀποδείξαιμι
τοὺς κατηγόρους;
15   Ἔτι τοίνυν, ὦ ἄνδρες δικασταί, καὶ ἐκ τῶν ἄλλων τῶν
ἐμοὶ πεπραγμένων ἄξιον σκέψασθαι. ἐγὼ γὰρ τοιοῦτον ἐμαυτὸν
ἐν ταῖς τῆς πόλεως συμφοραῖς παρέσχον ὥστε, εἰ πάντες τὴν
αὐτὴν γνώμην εἶχον ἐμοί, μηδένα ἂν ὑμῶν μηδεμιᾷ χρῆσθαι συμφορᾷ. ὑπ' ἐμοῦ γὰρ ἐν τῇ ὀλιγαρχίᾳ οὔτε ἀπαχθεὶς οὐδεὶς
φανήσεται, οὔτε τῶν ἐχθρῶν οὐδεὶς τετιμωρημένος, οὔτε τῶν
16 φίλων εὖ πεπονθώς (καὶ τοῦτο μὲν οὐκ ἄξιον θαυμάζειν· εὖ
μὲν γὰρ ποιεῖν ἐν ἐκείνῳ τῷ χρόνῳ χαλεπὸν ἦν, ἐξαμαρτάνειν
δὲ τῷ βουλομένῳ ῥᾴδιον). οὐ τοίνυν οὐδ' εἰς τὸν κατάλογον
Ἀθηναίων καταλέξας οὐδένα φανήσομαι, οὐδὲ δίαιταν κατα-
διαιτησάμενος οὐδενός, οὐδὲ πλουσιώτερος ἐκ τῶν ὑμετέρων
γεγονὼς συμφορῶν. καίτοι εἰ τοῖς τῶν γεγενημένων κακῶν
αἰτίοις ὀργίζεσθε, εἰκὸς καὶ τοὺς μηδὲν ἡμαρτηκότας βελτί-
17 ους ὑφ' ὑμῶν νομίζεσθαι. καὶ μὲν δή, ὦ ἄνδρες δικασταί,
μεγίστην ἡγοῦμαι περὶ ἐμαυτοῦ τῇ δημοκρατίᾳ πίστιν δεδωκέναι.
ὅστις γὰρ τότε οὐδὲν ἐξήμαρτον οὕτω πολλῆς δεδομένης ἐξου-
σίας, ἦ που νῦν σφόδρα προθυμηθήσομαι χρηστὸς εἶναι, εὖ
εἰδὼς ὅτι, ἐὰν ἀδικῶ, παραχρῆμα δώσω δίκην. ἀλλὰ γὰρ τοιαύτην
διὰ τέλους γνώμην ἔχω, ὥστε ἐν ὀλιγαρχίᾳ μὲν μὴ ἐπιθυμεῖν
τῶν ἀλλοτρίων, ἐν δημοκρατίᾳ δὲ τὰ ὄντα προθύμως εἰς ὑμᾶς
ἀναλίσκειν.
18   Ἡγοῦμαι δέ, ὦ ἄνδρες δικασταί, οὐκ ἂν δικαίως ὑμᾶς
μισεῖν τοὺς ἐν τῇ ὀλιγαρχίᾳ μηδὲν πεπονθότας κακόν, ἐξὸν
ὀργίζεσθαι τοῖς εἰς τὸ πλῆθος ἐξημαρτηκόσιν, οὐδὲ τοὺς μὴ
φυγόντας ἐχθροὺς νομίζειν, ἀλλὰ τοὺς ὑμᾶς ἐκβαλόντας, οὐδὲ

13 ἐδαπανώμην Stephanus: ἐδαπανώμεν X   καὶ del. Emperius
14 ἐπὶ del. Markland   οἱ τριάκοντα Markland: οὔδε
15 εἶχον Hude: ἔσχον
16 ὀργίζεσθε Aldus: ὀργίζοισθε

fought in four sea-battles, paid many war-taxes and performed my other public services no less adequately than my fellow-citizens. Yet 13 the reason why I spent more than what was demanded by the city was in order that I should have a better reputation with you, and that if I should suffer a misfortune at any time I should be able to defend myself better. But I was stripped of all this under the oligarchy, for they determined not to grant favours to those responsible for some benefit to the people, but to set in high office those who had caused you the most harm, as if this was the proof of loyalty that they had exacted from us. You should all ponder these facts and not trust the words of these men but examine the record of each from his deeds. For 14 my part, gentlemen of the jury, I was not one of the Four Hundred: let any one of my accusers who wishes come forward and convict me. Nor again will anyone be able to prove that when the Thirty were established I served either on the Council or in the offices of government. And yet if I had the chance of office and refused it, do I not now deserve to be honoured by you? And if those in power then thought me unworthy to participate in public life, what clearer way could I have than this of showing my accusers to be lying?

And furthermore, gentlemen of the jury, conclusions should be 15 drawn from my other actions. During the city's disasters, my behaviour was such that if everyone had taken the same attitude as I did none of you would have suffered any misfortune. For it will be clear that under the oligarchy nobody was arrested by me, nor was any of my enemies visited with my vengeance, nor did any of my friends receive any favours (and this should not be surprising, for 16 at that time it was difficult to bestow favours, but easy for anyone so inclined to do mischief). Nor indeed will you find that I added anyone's name to the list of Athenian citizens or have anyone condemned by an arbitrator, or become richer as a result of your misfortunes. Yet if you show anger against those responsible for the evils that occurred, it is also reasonable for you to have a better opinion of those who did no wrong. And furthermore, gentlemen of 17 the jury, I think I have given the democracy the greatest proof of my own loyalty: for since I committed no crime then, when ample means were provided, surely now I shall be very keen to be a good citizen when I know well that, if I do wrong, I shall immediately pay the penalty. But in fact that has been my constant resolve – under oligarchy not to covet others' possessions and under democracy eagerly to spend my own resources upon you.

I consider, gentlemen of the jury, that you would not be 18 justified in hating those who suffered no evil under the oligarchy, when you have the means of expressing anger towards those who offended against the people. And you should regard as enemies not those who did not go into exile, but those who exiled you; not those

τοὺς προθυμουμένους τὰ ἑαυτῶν σῶσαι, ἀλλὰ τοὺς τὰ τῶν ἄλλων
ὑφῃρημένους, οὐδὲ οἳ τῆς σφετέρας αὐτῶν σωτηρίας ἕνεκα ἔμει-
ναν ἐν τῷ ἄστει, ἀλλ' οἵτινες ἑτέρους ἀπολέσαι βουλόμενοι
μετέσχον τῶν πραγμάτων. εἰ δὲ οἴεσθε χρῆναι, οὓς ἐκεῖνοι
παρέλιπον ἀδικοῦντες, ὑμεῖς ἀπολέσαι, οὐδεὶς τῶν πολιτῶν
ὑπολειφθήσεται.
19   Σκοπεῖν δὲ χρὴ καὶ ἐκ τῶνδε, ὦ ἄνδρες δικασταί. πάντες
γὰρ ἐπίστασθε ὅτι ἐν τῇ προτέρᾳ δημοκρατίᾳ τῶν τὰ τῆς πόλεως
πραττόντων πολλοὶ μὲν τὰ δημόσια ἔκλεπτον, ἔνιοι δ' ἐπὶ τοῖς
ὑμετέροις ἐδωροδόκουν, οἱ δὲ συκοφαντοῦντες τοὺς συμμάχους
ἀφίστασαν. καὶ εἰ μὲν οἱ τριάκοντα τούτους μόνους ἐτιμω-
ροῦντο, ἄνδρας ἀγαθοὺς καὶ ὑμεῖς ἂν αὐτοὺς ἡγεῖσθε· νῦν δέ,
ὅτι ὑπὲρ τῶν ἐκείνοις ἡμαρτημένων τὸ πλῆθος κακῶς ποιεῖν
ἠξίουν, ἠγανακτεῖτε, ἡγούμενοι δεινὸν εἶναι τὰ [τῶν] ὀλίγων
20   ἀδικήματα πάσῃ τῇ πόλει κοινὰ γίγνεσθαι. οὐ τοίνυν ἄξιον
χρῆσθαι τούτοις, οἷς ἐκείνους ἑωρᾶτε ἐξαμαρτάνοντας, οὐδὲ ἃ
πάσχοντες ἄδικα ἐνομίζετε πάσχειν, ὅταν ἑτέρους ποιῆτε,
δίκαια ἡγεῖσθαι, ἀλλὰ τὴν αὐτὴν κατελθόντες περὶ αὐτῶν γνώμην ἔχετε, ἥνπερ φεύγοντες περὶ ὑμῶν αὐτῶν εἴχετε· ἐκ τούτων
γὰρ καὶ ὁμόνοιαν πλείστην ποιήσετε, καὶ ἡ πόλις ἔσται μεγίστη, καὶ τοῖς ἐχθροῖς ἀνιαρότατα ψηφιεῖσθε.
21   Ἐνθυμηθῆναι δὲ χρή, ὦ ἄνδρες δικασταί, καὶ τῶν ἐπὶ τῶν
τριάκοντα γεγενημένων, ἵνα τὰ τῶν ἐχθρῶν ἁμαρτήματα ἄμεινον
ὑμᾶς ποιήσῃ περὶ τῶν ὑμετέρων αὐτῶν βουλεύσασθαι. ὅτε μὲν
γὰρ ἀκούοιτε τοὺς ἐν ἄστει τὴν αὐτὴν γνώμην ἔχειν, μικρὰς
ἐλπίδας εἴχετε τῆς καθόδου, ἡγούμενοι τὴν ἡμετέραν ὁμόνοιαν
22   μέγιστον κακὸν εἶναι τῇ ὑμετέρᾳ φυγῇ· ἐπειδὴ δὲ ἐπυνθάνεσθε
τοὺς μὲν τρισχιλίους στασιάζοντας, τοὺς δὲ ἄλλους πολίτας
ἐκ τοῦ ἄστεως ἐκκεκηρυγμένους, τοὺς δὲ τριάκοντα μὴ τὴν
αὐτὴν γνώμην ἔχοντας, πλείους δ' ὄντας τοὺς ὑπὲρ ὑμῶν δεδιό-
τας ἢ τοὺς ὑμῖν πολεμοῦντας, τότ' ἤδη καὶ κατιέναι προσεδο-
κᾶτε καὶ παρὰ τῶν ἐχθρῶν λήψεσθαι δίκην. ταῦτα γὰρ τοῖς
θεοῖς ηὔχεσθε, ἅπερ ἐκείνους ἑωρᾶτε ποιοῦντας, ἡγούμενοι διὰ
τὴν τῶν τριάκοντα πονηρίαν πολὺ μᾶλλον σωθήσεσθαι ἢ διὰ τὴν
23   τῶν φευγόντων δύναμιν κατιέναι. χρὴ τοίνυν, ὦ ἄνδρες δικασταί, τοῖς πρότερον γεγενημένοις παραδείγμασι χρωμένους
βουλεύεσθαι περὶ τῶν μελλόντων ἔσεσθαι, καὶ τούτους ἡγεῖσθαι
δημοτικωτάτους, οἵτινες ὁμονοεῖν ὑμᾶς βουλόμενοι τοῖς ὅρκοις
καὶ ταῖς συνθήκαις ἐμμένουσι, νομίζοντες καὶ τῆς πόλεως
ταύτην ἱκανωτάτην εἶναι σωτηρίαν καὶ τῶν ἐχθρῶν μεγίστην
τιμωρίαν· οὐδὲν γὰρ ἂν εἴη αὐτοῖς χαλεπώτερον τούτων, ἢ πυνθάνεσθαι μὲν ἡμᾶς μετέχοντας τῶν πραγμάτων, αἰσθάνεσθαι δὲ
οὕτως διακειμένους τοὺς πολίτας ὥσπερ μηδενὸς ἐγκλήματος
24   πρὸς ἀλλήλους γεγενημένου. χρὴ δὲ εἰδέναι, ὦ ἄνδρες δικασταί,

18 ὑφῃρημένους **Sauppe**: ἀφῃρημένους   ὑπολειφθήσεται **Dob-**
    ree: ἀπολειφθήσεται
19 τῶν del. **Vischer**   ὀλίγων X¹: λόγων
22 ἐπυνθάνεσθε **Markland**: πυνθάνοισθε   ἄστεως **edd.**: ἄστεος

who were energetic in preserving their own possessions, but those who filched other men's; not those who remained in the city for their own safety, but those who shared in the administration from a desire to destroy others. If you think you should yourselves destroy those passed over by these men in the course of their misdeeds, none of the citizens will be left.

You ought to draw conclusions from these further points, 19 gentlemen of the jury. You all know that in the previous democracy many of those who administered the city's affairs stole public money, some accepted bribes at your expense, and others by slanderous accusations alienated your allies. Now if the Thirty had punished these alone, even you would have considered them worthy men. But in fact, because they saw fit to injure the people for these men's misdeeds, you resented it, considering it shocking that the crimes of the few should be imputed to the whole city. Therefore it is not right 20 to resort to those crimes which you saw them committing, nor to think it just to inflict on others sufferings which you yourselves thought unjust when you were experiencing them. No: you should hold the same opinion of them on your return as you did of yourselves when you were in exile. For by this attitude you will create the greatest concord; the city will be supreme, and your vote will cause your enemies the greatest pain.

And you should reflect, gentlemen of the jury, on what 21 happened under the Thirty, so that the crimes of your enemies should make you plan your own affairs better. For whenever you heard that those in the Town shared the same views, you had but slight hopes of return, judging that our unanimity was the greatest of your misfortunes in exile. But when you heard that the Three 22 Thousand were feuding, that the rest of the citizens had been banished from the city, and that the Thirty were not of one mind, and that more men were fearing on your behalf than making war on you, then straightway you began to look forward both to your return and the exaction of justice from your enemies. This was your prayer to the gods, that these men should continue what you saw them doing, because you thought you were much more likely to be saved by the wickedness of the Thirty than return through the power of the exiles. Well, gentlemen of the jury, you should base your 23 deliberations on the future upon examples from the past, and regard as the most devoted to democracy those who, from a desire for your concord, adhere to their oaths and agreements, considering this to be the surest salvation of the city and the most effective means of punishing her enemies. For there could be nothing more bitter for them than to learn that we are participating in the government, and to see that the citizens are behaving as though they had never made any charges against one another. And you should realise, gentlemen 24

ὅτι οἱ φεύγοντες τῶν ἄλλων πολιτῶν ὡς πλείστους καὶ διαβε-
βλῆσθαι καὶ ἠτιμῶσθαι βούλονται, ἐλπίζοντες τοὺς ὑφ' ὑμῶν
ἀδικουμένους ἑαυτοῖς ἔσεσθαι συμμάχους, τοὺς δὲ συκοφάντας
εὐδοκιμεῖν δέξαιντ' ἂν παρ' ὑμῖν καὶ μέγα δύνασθαι ἐν τῇ
πόλει· τὴν γὰρ τούτων πονηρίαν ἑαυτῶν ἡγοῦνται σωτηρίαν.
25 "Αξιον δὲ μνησθῆναι <καὶ> τῶν μετὰ τοὺς τετρακοσίους
πραγμάτων· εὖ γὰρ εἴσεσθε ὅτι, ἃ μὲν οὗτοι συμβουλεύουσιν,
οὐδεπώποτε ὑμῖν ἐλυσιτέλησεν, ἃ δ' ἐγὼ παραινῶ, ἀμφοτέραις
ἀεὶ ταῖς πολιτείαις συμφέρει. ὥστε γὰρ Ἐπιγένη καὶ Δημόφαντον καὶ Κλειγένη ἰδίᾳ μὲν καρπωσαμένους τὰς τῆς πόλεως συμ-
26 φοράς, δημοσίᾳ δὲ ὄντας μεγίστων κακῶν αἰτίους. ἐνίων μὲν
γὰρ ἔπεισαν ὑμᾶς ἀκρίτων θάνατον καταψηφίσασθαι, πολλῶν δὲ
ἀδίκως δημεῦσαι τὰς οὐσίας, τοὺς δ' ἐξελάσαι καὶ ἀτιμῶσαι
τῶν πολιτῶν· τοιοῦτοι γὰρ ἦσαν ὥστε τοὺς μὲν ἡμαρτηκότας
ἀργύριον λαμβάνοντες ἀφιέναι, τοὺς δὲ μηδὲν ἠδικηκότας εἰς
ὑμᾶς εἰσιόντες ἀπολλύναι. καὶ οὐ πρότερον ἐπαύσαντο, ἕως τὴν
μὲν πόλιν εἰς στάσεις καὶ τὰς μεγίστας συμφορὰς κατέστησαν,
27 αὐτοὶ δ' ἐκ πενήτων πλούσιοι ἐγένοντο. ὑμεῖς δὲ οὕτως διετέ-
θητε ὥστε τοὺς μὲν φεύγοντας κατεδέξασθε, τοὺς δ' ἀτίμους
ἐπιτίμους ἐποιήσατε, τοῖς δ' ἄλλοις περὶ ὁμονοίας ὅρκους
ὤμνυτε· τελευτῶντες ἥδιον ἂν τοὺς ἐν τῇ δημοκρατίᾳ συκοφαντοῦντας ἐτιμωρήσασθε ἢ τοὺς ἄρξαντας ἐν τῇ ὀλιγαρχίᾳ. καὶ
εἰκότως, ὦ ἄνδρες δικασταί· πᾶσι γὰρ ἤδη φανερόν ἐστιν ὅτι
διὰ τοὺς μὲν ἀδίκως πολιτευομένους ἐν τῇ ὀλιγαρχίᾳ δημο-
κρατία γίγνεται, διὰ δὲ τοὺς ἐν τῇ δημοκρατίᾳ συκοφαντοῦντας
ὀλιγαρχία δὶς κατέστη. ὥστε οὐκ ἄξιον τούτοις πολλάκις χρῆσ-
28 θαι συμβούλοις, οἷς οὐδὲ ἅπαξ ἐλυσιτέλησε πιθομένοις. σκέψασθαι δὲ χρὴ ὅτι καὶ τῶν ἐκ Πειραιῶς οἱ μεγίστην δόξαν ἔχοντες
καὶ μάλιστα κεκινδυνευκότες καὶ πλεῖστα ὑμᾶς ἀγαθὰ εἰργασμένοι πολλάκις ἤδη τῷ ὑμετέρῳ πλήθει διεκελεύσαντο τοῖς ὅρκοις
καὶ ταῖς συνθήκαις ἐμμένειν, ἡγούμενοι ταύτην δημοκρατίας
εἶναι φυλακήν· τοῖς μὲν γὰρ ἐξ ἄστεως ὑπὲρ τῶν παρεληλυθότων
ἄδειαν ποιήσειν, τοῖς δ' ἐκ Πειραιῶς οὕτως πλεῖστον χρόνον
29 τὴν πολιτείαν <ἂν> παραμεῖναι. οἷς ὑμεῖς πολὺ ἂν δικαιότερον
πιστεύοιτε ἢ τούτοις, οἳ φεύγοντες μὲν δι' ἑτέρους ἐσώθησαν,
κατελθόντες δὲ συκοφαντεῖν ἐπιχειροῦσιν. ἡγοῦμαι δέ, ὦ
ἄνδρες δικασταί, τοὺς μὲν τὴν αὐτὴν γνώμην ἔχοντας ἐμοὶ τῶν
ἐν ἄστει μεινάντων φανεροὺς γεγενῆσθαι καὶ ἐν ὀλιγαρχίᾳ καὶ
30 ἐν δημοκρατίᾳ, ὁποῖοί τινές εἰσι πολῖται· τούτων δ' ἄξιον
θαυμάζειν, ὅ τι ἂν ἐποίησαν, εἴ τις αὐτοὺς εἴασε τῶν τριάκοντα γενέσθαι, οἳ νῦν δημοκρατίας οὔσης ταὐτὰ ἐκείνοις
πράττουσι, καὶ ταχέως μὲν ἐκ πενήτων πλούσιοι γεγένηνται,
πολλὰς δὲ ἀρχὰς ἄρχοντες οὐδεμιᾶς εὐθύνην διδόασιν, ἀλλ'
ἀντὶ μὲν ὁμονοίας ὑποψίαν πρὸς ἀλλήλους πεποιήκασιν, ἀντὶ δὲ

25 καὶ add. Baiter   Ἐπιγένη Hude: Ἐπιγένην
   Δημόφαντον καὶ Κλειγένη Schwartz: Δημοφάνην καὶ Κλεισθένην
27 πιθομένοις Cobet: πειθομένοις
28 διεκελεύσαντο Taylor: διελύσαντο   ἂν add. Taylor

of the jury, that the exiles want as many other citizens as possible to be slandered and disfranchised also, in the hope that those wronged by you will become their allies, and they would welcome the success of slanderers among you. and their influence in the city, for they regard their wickedness as their own salvation.

It is also worth recalling the events following the rule of the 25 Four Hunded, for you will be well aware that the measures these men recommended have never brought you any advantage, whereas those which I propose have always benefited both parties. For you know that Epigenes, Demophantus and Cleigenes reaped private gain from the city's misfortunes, while by their public actions they were responsible for the greatest of evils. They persuaded you to condemn 26 some men to death without trial, to confiscate the property of many others unjustly, and to exile and disfranchise other citizens. For their character was such that they would accept bribes for the release of wrongdoers, and, coming before you, destroy the innocent. And they did not stop until they had subjected the city to seditions and the greatest disasters, and converted themselves from rags to riches. But you were disposed to take the exiles back and reinstate 27 the disfranchised, and you swore oaths proclaiming concord with the rest. In the end you would have been happier to punish those who had laid false charges under the democracy than those who held office under the oligarchy. And reasonably so, gentlemen of the jury; for it is by now clear to everyone that democracy arises because of unjust administrators in the oligarchy, and that oligarchy has been established twice through the activities of slanderous accusers in the democracy. So it is not right to employ these men as your regular advisers, when it has never even once benefited you to obey them. You should observe that those of the highest reputation in the 28 Piraeus party, men who have run the greatest risks and conferred on you the greatest benefits, have frequently before urged your assembly to abide by their oaths and agreements, regarding this as a safeguard of democracy. They saw this as the means of securing for the Town party immunity for past deeds, and for the Piraeus party the longest life for their government. You would be far more justified 29 in trusting these men than those who were restored from exile through others, but on returning take up slander-mongering as their profession. But I consider, gentlemen of the jury, that the men sharing my views who remained in the city have made manifest, under both oligarchy and democracy, what kind of citizens they are. But 30 the men who should make us wonder what they would have done if they had been allowed to join the Thirty are those who, even now under democracy, do the same as they did: swiftly rising from rags to riches, holding many offices but submitting to audit for none, they have created mutual suspicion instead of concord, and declared war

εἰρήνης πόλεμον κατηγγέλκασι, διὰ τούτους δὲ ἄπιστοι τοῖς
31 Ἕλλησι γεγενήμεθα. καὶ τοσούτων κακῶν καὶ ἑτέρων πολλῶν
ὄντες αἴτιοι, καὶ οὐδὲν διαφέροντες τῶν τριάκοντα πλὴν ὅτι
ἐκεῖνοι μὲν ὀλιγαρχίας οὔσης ἐπεθύμουν ὧνπερ οὗτοι, οὗτοι δὲ
καὶ δημοκρατίας τῶν αὐτῶν ὧνπερ ἐκεῖνοι, ὅμως οἴονται χρῆναι
οὕτως ῥᾳδίως ὃν ἂν βούλωνται κακῶς ποιεῖν, ὥσπερ τῶν μὲν
32 ἄλλων ἀδικούντων, ἄριστοι δὲ ἄνδρες αὐτοὶ γεγενημένοι (καὶ
τούτων μὲν οὐκ ἄξιον θαυμάζειν, ὑμῶν δέ, ὅτι οἴεσθε μὲν
δημοκρατίαν εἶναι, γίγνεται δὲ ὅ τι ἂν οὗτοι βούλωνται, καὶ
δίκην διδόασιν οὐχ οἱ τὸ ὑμέτερον πλῆθος ἀδικοῦντες, ἀλλ' οἱ
τὰ σφέτερα αὐτῶν μὴ διδόντες). καὶ δέξαιντ' ἂν μικρὰν εἶναι
33 τὴν πόλιν μᾶλλον ἢ δι' ἄλλους μεγάλην καὶ ἐλευθέραν, ἡγούμενοι νῦν μὲν διὰ τοὺς ἐκ Πειραιῶς κινδύνους αὐτοῖς ἐξεῖναι
ποιεῖν ὅ τι ἂν βούλωνται, ἐὰν δ' ὕστερον ὑμῖν δι' ἑτέρων
σωτήρια γένηται, αὐτοὶ μὲν καταλύσεσθαι, ἐκείνους δὲ μεῖζον
δυνήσεσθαι· ὥστε τὸ αὐτὸ πάντες ἐμποδών εἰσιν, ἐάν τι δι'
34 ἄλλων ἀγαθὸν ὑμῖν φαίνηται. τοῦτο μὲν οὖν οὐ χαλεπὸν τῷ
βουλομένῳ κατανοῆσαι· αὐτοί τε γὰρ οὐκ ἐπιθυμοῦσι λανθάνειν,
ἀλλ' αἰσχύνονται μὴ δοκοῦντες εἶναι πονηροί, ὑμεῖς τε τὰ μὲν
αὐτοὶ ὁρᾶτε τὰ δ' ἑτέρων πολλῶν ἀκούετε. ἡμεῖς δέ, ὦ ἄνδρες
δικασταί, δίκαιον μὲν ἡγούμεθ' εἶναι πρὸς πάντας ὑμᾶς τοὺς
35 πολίτας ταῖς συνθήκαις καὶ τοῖς ὅρκοις ἐμμένειν, ὅμως δέ,
ὅταν μὲν ἴδωμεν τοὺς τῶν κακῶν αἰτίους δίκην διδόντας, τῶν
τότε περὶ ὑμᾶς γεγενημένων μεμνημένοι συγγνώμην ἔχομεν, ὅταν
δὲ φανεροὶ γένησθε τοὺς μηδὲν αἰτίους ἐξ ἴσου τοῖς ἀδικοῦσι
τιμωρούμενοι, τῇ αὐτῇ ψήφῳ πάντας ἡμᾶς εἰς ὑπο<ψίαν καταστή-
σετε>. . .

31 ὅμως Reiske: ὁμοίως
33 σωτήρια Frohberger: σωτηρία   αὐτοὶ μὲν καταλύσεσθαι
    Herwerden: αὐτοὺς μὲν ἐπιλύσεσθαι C: τούτους μὲν ἐπι-
    λύσασθαι X
34 τε post ὑμεῖς Reiske: δὲ
    ὑπο<ψίαν καταστήσετε> coniecit Francken

instead of peace. It is these men who have caused us to be
mistrusted among the Greeks. The cause of all those evils and many   31
others, and no different from the Thirty except that the latter
pursued the same aims under oligarchy as they, while these men even
under democracy have the same objectives as the tyrants, they
nevertheless think they should be free to harm anyone they wish as
readily as if all others were the wrongdoers and they themselves had
been excellent men. (And it is not they who should cause wonder,   32
but you, because you think there is democracy, whereas in fact what
they want is being done, and it is not those who are injuring your
people that are paying the penalty, but those who will not give up
their own possessions.) And they would prefer to have the city
insignificant rather than great and free through the efforts of others.
They think that under present conditions, because of the dangers   33
they faced in advancing from the Piraeus, they can do as they like;
but that later, if you obtain deliverance through others, they
themselves will be deposed and the others will be more powerful. So
they make common cause to obstruct any benefit you seem likely to
receive through the efforts of others. Now this plan of theirs is easy   34
for any willing person to perceive, for they are not themselves
desirous of concealing it, but actually feel ashamed if they are not
thought to be villainous; while you see some of their actions
yourselves and hear of some from many other sources. But we,
gentlemen of the jury, think it right that you should abide by your
agreements and oaths in your dealings with all citizens. Nevertheless,   35
whenever we see those responsible for your troubles paying the
penalty, we remember your experiences at that time and sympathise
with you. But whenever you openly punish the innocent and the
guilty even-handedly, by the same vote you will be exposing us all to
suspicion....

SPEECH 1 : THE KILLING OF ERATOSTHENES

Euphiletus, a farm labourer in whose defence Lysias wrote this clever and lively speech, was the victim of a conflict between ancient law and contemporary custom. He had caught his wife's adulterer in the act and killed him before witnesses in her bedroom, confident that the law supported his action. The relatives of the dead man tried to prove that Euphiletus had prepared a trap for Eratosthenes by enticing or even forcing him into the house, both of which actions would have been illegal. But in his refutation of these allegations Euphiletus enjoys the great advantage over his prosecutors that the most telling evidence arises from his own actions, which he is in a much better position than they to describe convincingly. He is able to show clearly at each stage of the narrative, and to reaffirm in the proof, that a minimum of planning preceded the killing. Much more serious and intractable a problem for him is the fact that cuckolded husbands customarily accepted monetary compensation from adulterers instead of exacting the extreme penalty allowed by the law. Although self-help remained a practical resort for victims of crime, the growth of prejudice against summary justice, especially when it involved the taking of life, seems to have outpaced changes in the law; and it was with this prejudice that Euphiletus had to contend.

Lysias' solution to this problem is the construction of a narrative which not only supplies the facts essential for the refutation of the charge of premeditated entrapment, but also the portrayal, limned in subtly cumulative detail, of the defendant's character. This narrative begins with a simple account of the early years of Euphiletus' marriage and his stable, harmonious relationship with his wife, whose qualities he praises. But her corruption by Eratosthenes is mentioned immediately afterwards (8), and thereafter the tone of the narrative changes, being shot through with bitter asides while he describes, in an apparently natural succession of domestic scenes, how his wife deceived him: how she took advantage of his allowing her to sleep downstairs for convenience in nursing their baby; how she locked him in the bedroom, feigning play; how the doors creaked at night and he noticed her wearing cosmetics even though her brother had died recently. All this contributes little to the purely technical requirements of his defence, but the jury is gradually forming an impression of the defendant's character: he is a simple man, the easy victim of deceit rather than a cunning deviser of it. His bitter observations also mark him as a man capable of anger. These feelings assume particular prominence as he describes his discovery of his wife's liaison, and how the tell-tale signs flashed through his mind and their significance became clear (17). This seems to be the point at which Lysias intends that the jury should feel the strongest sympathy for Euphiletus, since in what follows it is impossible for him to conceal some potentially damaging evidence. Euphiletus confronts his wife's maidservant with his knowledge, and forces her to aid him in his pursuit of revenge. At this point the jury might be prompted to ask why he did not also confront his wife, as a simple man might be expected to do. Lysias has already supplied the answer with the second side of his characterisation: confrontation with his wife would have put an end to the affair, but it would not have assuaged the anger that was as much a part of his client's character as his simplicity. Only revenge could do that. But Lysias is careful to describe how Euphiletus' arrangement with the maidservant was no more than that she should inform him when Eratosthenes had entered the house (not, as the prosecution had alleged, that she should seek him out and bring him there). The narrative draws attention to the lack of preparation prior to Eratosthenes' entry and discovery. The bedroom scene serves to enlarge upon the motive of revenge, which is, however, made to appear civic and judicial quite as much as personal. Euphiletus is made to say: "It is not I who am going to kill you, but the city's law". He sounds and behaves like an officer of the law punishing a malefactor, and the narrative concludes on the same theme as the prooemion, which stresses the universal detestation of adulterers. There could be no more effective way to combat the jury's prejudice against a man who has acted contrary to custom and allowed an affair to continue so that he could catch the adulterer *in flagrante delicto*.

After this masterly narrative, original in its attention to characterisation and vivid and fresh in its descriptive detail, all that is necessary in the proof is to draw inferences, making them seem as inescapable as possible. Also, the theme of the introduction is explored further: adultery is more serious than rape because it involves the corruption of the mind as well as the body; and it endangers family life by creating doubts as to paternity (32-33). The need to punish adulterers with the maximum severity is also the main theme of the short epilogue, in which the defendant solemnly reminds the jury that the law upholds his action. The noun *timōria* and the verb *timōreisthai* occur seven times outside the narrative. It is a key concept, ranging in meaning between 'punishment', 'revenge' and 'requital'. In the speech there is an interesting ambivalence between Euphiletus' simple character, which prompted him to take revenge as the opportunity arose, and his posture as an agent of state justice, which led him to rely on the law rather than follow custom.

1-5   PROOEMIUM: The conventional elements are the universalising theme and the summary of charges and counter-charges. Absent is any attempt to flatter the jury: rather the tone is uncompromising, even demanding.

1   I should much appreciate it: this and the tentative tone imparted by the conditional and potential forms of the verbs immediately following are the only traces of conventional deference. Characterisation has already begun.

if you had faced a similar experience: Euphiletus sets out to identify the jury with his cause. For this *locus indignationis ab auditoribus* see Cic.*Inv*.1.54.105.

engage in such practices: censoriously describing the habitual criminal who is a continual menace to ordered society. Cf. 16 *tekhnēn*, and 29.

2 the whole of Greece: the attitude of other Greek states at this time is not known, but there is no reason to suppose that the Athenian law on adultery was exceptionally severe. For the punishment of adulterers in earlier Greece, see Bonner & Smith, *AJHA* 1, 12-13, 52. The introduction of an authority (*locus ab auctoritate*, (*Ad.Herenn*.2.30.48)) which is universal serves to reinforce the hyperbole of the previous sentence, in which it is suggested that death is too lenient a punishment for adulterers.

humblest.....most eminent: both individually and in their mutual dealings. In practice, however, the establishment of the custom of compensatory payment to the cuckolded husband afforded the wealthy philanderer the greater scope. (For the advantages enjoyed by the wealthy, see Lys.24 *Inv*. 16).

4 I consider that my task is to show: the summary of the issues of the case (*katastasis*), regularly given towards the end of the prooemium in Lysias and later orators, but not in Antiphon. Since the killing is not denied, the case was probably tried in the Delphinium, the court of justified homicide. The listing of the side-effects of Eratosthenes' act is rhetorically effective.

insulted me: the use of the word *hubrisen* is semi-technical, since *hubris* was an offence actionable at law (see MacDowell,*LCA*, 129 and n.280).

no enmity...not...for money: two charges regularly brought by prosecutors and listed for dismissal by defendants (see e.g. Ant. 5 *Her*.57-8). Only the first could possibly apply to Euphiletus, since he had shown his indifference to money by refusing compensation (25,29).

5 all my actions.....complete account of the events: not 'as briefly as possible' or one of the other normal transitional formulae with which narratives are introduced (e.g. Lys.12 *Erat*.62; 24 *Inv*.4), for the following narrative is one of Lysias' longest and most detailed, affording scope for characterisation. Also the intimate description of familiar domestic scenes serves well the defendant's purpose of carrying his audience along with him.

6-26 NARRATIVE: Before describing the events surrounding the case, Lysias gives a preliminary narrative (*prodiēgēsis*) designed to portray a harmonious marriage (6-7), to anticipate its destruction (8) and to explain the domestic arrangements which facilitated the adultery (9).

6 Now: narratives in Attic Oratory after Antiphon commonly begin with *gar*.

harass....watched....paid attention: the Athenian husband exercised legal control (*kurieia*) over his wife. The male jury, with its prejudices against female frailties (see Dover,*GPM*, 100ff.) would have found Euphiletus' attitude reasonable. For popular opinions see further Ar. *Thesm*. 225,390-432; Plato Comicus frg.2.2. 648(Meineke). It is significant that the wife is not blamed at any stage, and Euphiletus finds it necessary to explain the relaxation of his supervision by the arrival of the child.

when a child was born to me: the fulfilment of the purpose of marriage, according to the conventional view (Lacey,*FCG*, 110). The wife presented the child to the husband, who acknowledged it as his and registered it with his phratry. Note the historic present *gignetai*, marking an event of special significance.

6-7 all my affairs....best wife in the world: the hyperbole and the superlative serve to crown this short description of an ideal marriage and to confer maximum effect on what follows. It also emphasises and rationalises Euphiletus' trust. On women in charge of domestic matters, see Xen.*Oec*.3.8; Plato *Meno* 71e; [Dem.] 59 *Neair*.122.

8 funeral: one of the rare occasions when Athenian women were seen in public.

corrupted by him: morally as well as physically, the former being the more serious in the husband's view. Hence the idea that seduction was a more serious crime than rape (MacDowell,*LCA*,124-5; Dover,*GPM*, 147). See 32-3 and commentary.

9 equal in area: i.e. the house contained other rooms on the ground floor, but the men's and women's quarters were equal in area. In two-storied houses the women's quarters were usually upstairs (Homer *Il*.2.514; 16.184; Eur.*Phoen*.89; Ar.*Eccl*.693,961). In Lys. 3 *Sim*. 7 an intruder (the defendant Simon) forces his way into the women's quarters at night, which suggests that they may have been on the ground floor; in Xen.*Oec*. 9.4 men's and women's quarters seem to have been on the same floor and separated by a heavily barred door, but these appear to be servants' quarters. Women certainly spent some time in ground-floor rooms performing various household duties, and not all houses were on two levels. Hence perhaps Euphiletus' use of the diminutive *oikidion* to minimise the impression of size. On ancient Greek houses, see esp. B.C. Rider, *Ancient Greek Houses* (repr.Chicago, 1954); and on this house, G. Morgan, 'Euphiletus' House: Lysias 1', *TAPA* 112 (1982) 115-123.

10 naïve: the self-characterisation required for the chosen line of defence; and the first of several bitter asides which punctuate this simple narrative, in which Euphiletus is portrayed as an easy victim of deceit who has nevertheless behaved reasonably. See 13: I thought nothing of this...; 14: I made no comment and supposed her story to be true...I said nothing about the matter; 15: remained quite unaware of the wrongs being done to me.

11   estate: perhaps the safest translation of *agros* ("land", "country" as opposed to "town" (sing.), "fields" (plur.)). It is not known whether Euphiletus owned land or worked as a labourer for someone else.

12   as if: *hōs an* implies pretence. The wife carries her deceit to an extreme by acting out the part of the affectionate but suspicious wife. The high irony of the scene is enhanced by the easy and cordial tone of a conversation held while the seducer was actually in the house.

13   turned the key: Euphiletus was occupying the women's quarters, which were secured from the outside.

14   powdered: or perhaps 'painted', with white lead (cf. female figures on pottery). See Ar.*Eccl.*878,929,1072; *Plutus*,1064; Xen.*Oec.*10.12; Pliny *Nat.Hist.*34.54.
     thirty days: the usual period of mourning the death of a relative, concluded by a ceremony. (Harpocration and Suidas s.v. *triakas*; Pollux 1.66; D.C. Kurtz and J.Boardman, *Greek Burial Customs* (London,1971) 147.)

15   came up: historic or graphic present (see 6 note). Most of the action has been described in the imperfect, the tense of animated narrative (see 17 below), in which emotions accompany actions (*eboa ...eduskolainen...ekeleuon...ouk ēthelen.....ōrgizomēn...egelōn... ephaske...esiōpōn...hēgoumēn*).

16   meddlesome motive: the first of three passages written in a very artificial style, the others being 18 (on which see note) and 26. The phrase *mēdemiai polupragmosunēi* is reminiscent of a litigant's commonplace claim that he is not litigious (e.g.Lys.24 *Inv*.24; Dem.39 *Boiot.On*.1) and the politician's claim that he is not ambitious (e.g. Ar.*Thesm*.383-4).
     practises....profession: cf. 1,29,47.
     Eratosthenes of Oe: identified by Kirschner (*PA* and *RE*) with the tyrant prosecuted by Lysias in Speech 12. But absence of all reference to his political activities renders this identification improbable, even though the two men may have belonged to the same tribe Oineis. See Davies,*APF*, 184-5.

17   I was at once thrown into confusion: in this passage Euphiletus' astonishment is mirrored in the style, with tense variation (*apēllagē...etarattomēn...eiseiei*), repeated *kai...kai* and the repetition of a whole clause (*panta.....hupopsias*). It is as if Euphiletus' character suddenly reveals its other side: naïve trust gives way to anger and a righteous desire for revenge. A convincing portrayal of this change is essential in order to prepare the jury for the most difficult and potentially damaging part of his story.

18   to the market.....to a friend's house: i.e. to a private place away from his home. Euphiletus had decided quickly to conceal his knowledge from his wife, thereby exposing his motives to suspicion. (See Dihle 53).

choice from two alternatives: in his emotional state of mind, what did Euphiletus actually say? Why does Lysias make him speak with such studied formality? The published speech was to be read as literature, and this imposed limits upon realism. Also, in the actual trial, the speaker is trying to impress the jury rather than present an account that is accurate in every detail. For other examples of formalised live speech in Lysias and discussion, see Usher (1965) 104-5 and (1976) 39-40.

Do not lie at all: for the future (*pseusēi*) as an imperative, see *GMT* 69-70; and with negative *mē* rather than *ou*, showing its modal force, Lys.29 *Philoc*.13.

19   suffer no harm: perhaps this included sparing her from torture, thereby preventing her from giving evidence. Once again the question of premeditation may be raised. Had Euphiletus already decided what he was going to do and how much concealment would be necessary? Dover rightly points out that the slave-girl's evidence could have decided the issue of this trial either way (*LCL*,188). On other motives, see MacDowell, *AHL*, 106.

20   Thesmophoria: a women's festival held in the autumn. The association of the two women in religious ceremonies suggests that the liaison was, or was becoming, close and stable.

21   see to it that: the Greek construction is elliptical, the fear or warning not being expressed. It is used especially as a colloquial form of command by a person addressing someone familiar. Cf.Lys.12 *Erat*.50. See *GMT* 271-9.

22   will be valid: another somewhat stiff locution in live speech. Cf. 18 note.

I...want a clear exposure: the only explanation that Euphiletus gives for his course of action. Erbse (1958) 57 accepts it because eyewitnesses were necessary to establish the crime; but Euphiletus' subsequent action suggests that he had no intention of bringing Eratosthenes to court.

23   entered: historic present marking the first action leading to the *dénouement* (cf. 15 *proserkhetai*). Note subsequent tense variation between present and aorist, with one imperfect (*ebadizon*). Most of the action was not continuous because it was abortive: the chief point being made in this part of the narrative is that Euphiletus had made no preparations to apprehend Eratosthenes, and he later argues this point in the proof (40-42).

24   still lying: note the hyperbaton *eti*.....*katakeimenon*, emphasising the fulfilment of the requirement of the law (30) that the adulterer must be caught in the act. The rest of the description is designed to rebut the charge that Eratosthenes had been dragged from the hearth, where he had sought refuge (27).

25   struck...knocked...asked: a physical display of anger and an irrational question: a vitally important piece of characterisation. Euphiletus, the guileless man, is also a man of quick temper (see 12) and tumultuous emotion (17 note). Lysias' idea of including venial flaws in his client's character never found its way into the

mainstream of rhetorical *ēthos*-theory in spite of its sound rational basis. A man cannot help his own nature.

25 **monetary settlement**: probably the commonest outcome of a discovered adultery (e.g. [Dem.] 59 *Neair*.65. For a mythological precedent, see Homer *Od*. 8.332. Here, however, recourse to the extreme penalty against Ares was not open to his fellow-immortal Hephaestus.) Blass (*AB* 1,572) believes that the slaying of an adulterer in historical times was the exception, not the rule, though a lost speech of Lysias, the *pros Philōna* (frg.14), may have concerned such a case. See also Harrison, *LA* 1,33; MacDowell,*LCA*, 124-5.

26 **It is not I...**: Euphiletus' words are formal and dignified, even hieratic or judicial, like a judge pronouncing sentence. They articulate his self-appointed role of guardian of the city's laws against habitual transgressors (cf.4,29,47).

27 **enjoin**: other sources are less positive. In Dem.23 *Aristoc*.53, the law simply exempts the adulterer's killer from prosecution. In Plut.*Sol*. 23.1 it 'grants' (*dedōken*) him the right to kill. See note on 30 below.

seized from the street: hence not caught in the act, but forcibly detained, exposing Euphiletus to a charge of wrongful imprisonment (*dikē heirgmou*: see Harrison,*LA* 2,241).

at the hearth: from which, as the centre of domestic religious observance, he could not be dragged without incurring divine wrath. The other details serve to prove that the killing took place in violation of no laws, human or divine. The narrative ends argumentatively by subjecting, in a rhetorical question, the most telling facts to the test of probability, and rebutting the weakest of the prosecution's charges.

the city's law: for the effectiveness of this argument see Bateman (1962) 171-2.

your prescribed it: the law (see 30n) was at least 190 years old. For the device of representing present jurors as sponsors of past legislation, cf. Ant.5 *Her*.90.

28-40 **PROOF**: The relevant laws are stated to show that Eratosthenes has infringed them. Lysias then turns to the significant events of the narrative and interprets them.

30 **stated categorically.......should not be convicted of murder**: i.e. the law specifies an exemption from punishment, not a penalty to be exacted for adultery or an obligation upon anyone to impose it. So Dem.23 *Aristoc*.53, who adds that it was a law of Draco.

31 **mistresses**: the full text of the law states "...taken with a view to fathering free children" (Dem.23 *Aristoc*.53). Inclusion of this would have weakened Lysias' comparative argument.

And yet.....being unable to discover a more severe one: this sentiment may be traceable to the original lawgiver's reasoning, if he was Draco and his proverbial severity is historical (Plut. *Sol*. 17.2). The homicide laws were the only laws of Draco that were said to have been left unaltered by Solon. See Ant.5 *Her*. 14n.

32 double the damages: the comparison is between slaves and free citizens. So Glotz 393; Harrison, *LA* 1,34-5. The alternative interpretation, "double the value of the injury sustained" (Lipsius, *AR*, 639; P. Vianello, *Lisias: Sobre el Asesinato de Eratóstenes Defensa* (Mexico,1980)lxxv) is unsatisfactory because it discounts the reference to the *free* adult, the purpose of which is apparently to imply that violation of slaves carried lesser penalties, as might be expected. See 10.19n for further evidence; and the law on *hubris* quoted by Demosthenes (21.*Meid*.47), in which distinction is made between free victims of *hubris* and slave victims: only in the case of free victims could the offender be imprisoned until he paid the fine. (Aeschines in 1 *Tim*. 16-17 makes no such distinction, but it would weaken his argument to have done so.)

for whose seduction: *eph' hais* picks up *epi tais gametais* and *epi tais pallakais*, in which the choice of preposition might have been influenced by the text of the law, ...*epi damarti*. Lysias refers back to the extreme penalty for seduction in order to emphasise the lesser severity of the law on rape, but he does not complete the argument by mentioning the penalty for the seduction of slaves. Regarding rape, Bateman (1958) 277-8 says that a rapist could be punished by death, but no extant Athenian law states this. Nevertheless a husband discovering another man with his wife might not wait to establish the distinction, and an Athenian jury would have been unlikely to punish him. Cf. the argument in 36, and see Harrison,*LA* 1, 34-5. Of course, Lysias's reason for discussing these laws is to make the jury forget that adulterers were not normally killed.

33 the whole family comes under their control: in the next generation, on the succession of sons fathered by the adulterer, not the husband. The integrity of the family and estate depended on the wife's, not the husband's marital fidelity, and the law protected this by requiring him to divorce her if she was unfaithful ([Dem.] 59 *Neair*. 87). Note also Lysias' insistence on the psychological injury inflicted by the adulterer.

34 acquit....command: periphrastic perfect indicative forms, used to emphasise the completeness of the action, and hence the rightness of the speaker's position. Cf.45 *heorakōs ē, ē...ēdikēmenos* (pluperfect). See 27n and 30n.

35 all cities make their laws for this reason: a subtle attempt to get the best of both worlds by arguing that he has obeyed the letter of the law but also acted according to nature. Bateman suggests that the argument reflects the contemporary debate about the proper status of law in society. Another point of reference is the origin of the law on adultery in the primitive idea of self-help: before laws could be enforced, individuals were accorded the right to defend their own property. In spite of his reliance here on the law (which does not in fact unequivocally uphold his action (see 27n and 30n)), Euphiletus later shows a more ambivalent attitude to it (38n).

227

36 burglars: the closest parallel is to be here understood, i.e. between adulterers and burglars both caught in the act (*ep' autophōrōi*). The latter could be punished with summary execution either by the victim (Plato *Laws* 874b-c) or by the Eleven as criminals (*kakourgoi*) (Dem.24 *Tim*.113; [Arist.] *Ath.Pol*.52.1). A lesser punishment imposed for burglary, the return of the property stolen and a five-day period in the stocks at the discretion of the jury (Lys.10 *Theomn.* 10; Dem.24 *Tim*.105, 114) was probably applied in less serious cases, or cases brought after a lapse of time (*dikai klopēs*).
nobody will touch them: the same practical improbabilities apply as to rape and seduction (see 32n *sub fin.*). Lysias does well to sandwich this flawed argument between stronger ones. Perhaps the intention is comic (Blass, *AB* 1,575); if so, it is a bold stroke. See Cic. *Inv.* 1.53.101.

37 servant-girl: she would have been a key witness, but see 19n.

38 catch him by any means available: the jury would readily concede this much, because the laws governing the arrest of wrongdoers allowed considerable latitude (see MacDowell, *LCA*, 148). But Euphiletus is on trial for murder, not wrongful arrest.

40 advantage: one of the tests applied to actions in probability argument, to which Lysias now subjects all the events of the fateful night (40-42). He shows that Euphiletus neither encouraged nor expected Eratosthenes to enter his home.
so that....punish: for past tenses of the indicative with *hina* in purpose clauses dependent on unreal conditions, see *GMT* 333. So also *hin'*...*eiseia* in 42.

43 enmity...44:...false charges....private suits.....money: the usual summary dismissal of the standard motives of enmity (*ekhthra*), fear (*deos*) and hope of gain (*kerdos*) (cf.Ant.5 *Her*.57-8n; *Ad Herenn*.2.2.3). False political charges were the speciality of *sukophantai*, professional blackmailers who traded on their victims' reluctance to go to court.

46 impious act: referring to the accusation that he had dragged Eratosthenes from the hearth (27).
calling witnesses: for this commonplace, cf.Ant.5 *Her*. 43n.
unjustly: by means involving stealth, since he has said (42) that it was unsafe for him to confront Eratosthenes alone and openly.

7-50 EPILOGUE: This contains only one of the three topics listed by the handbooks, Amplification (*deinōsis*). Lysias concentrates the jury's attention upon Euphiletus' reliance on the law and the effect which his conviction would have upon society. Of the other two topics, Summary (*anakephalaiōsis*) is superfluous because the main evidence has been covered twice (22-26,39-42); and Appeal for Pity (*eleos*) would be totally out of character, just as *captatio benevolentiae* would have been in the Prooemium.

47 the whole city: the universalising topic again (cf.1-2). For its use in the epilogue, cf.Lys.12 *Erat*.35n; 22 *Corn*. 19.

prizes: a strikingly ironic metaphor (cf. Lys.31 *Phil*.32 for the same metaphor used without irony). See also entrapped ('caught by ambush') in 49.

49 however he wishes: an adulterer could be subjected to various painful indignities, such as having a radish thrust up his anus and his pubic hairs removed with hot ashes (Ar.*Clouds* 1083 and Dover *ad.loc*.). But the law provided for the extreme penalty also.

SPEECH 10 : AGAINST THEOMNESTUS

The unnamed prosecutor in this case of slander (*kakēgoria*) had been accused by Theomnestus of patricide. In order to qualify as an offence, a slander had to be public (Plut.*Sol.* 21.2). In this case Theomnestus uttered it at his own trial on a charge of speaking in the assembly when he was disqualified from doing so, because he had shown cowardice in battle by throwing his shield away to facilitate his flight from the field. The present speaker was a witness at this trial, at which Theomnestus was acquitted (22), presumably because the ground for his disqualification was successfully disputed. Evidence found in the speech and elsewhere (Davies,*APF*,355,610) suggests that political rivalry may lie behind the case. It was brought after Theomnestus had followed up his success in his own trial by prosecuting two of his accusers (12,24-5) for slander, perhaps using these trials as opportunities to promote his own political career by parading his virtues before the juries. There may also be an element of class rivalry in the conflict between Theomnestus, on the one hand, and Lysitheus, Dionysius and the present prosecutor on the other. These men were members of the wealthier class (27) (Davies.*loc.cit.*), whereas the name of Theomnestus appears on no magistrate lists of the period. He may therefore have been a "new man" trying to make his way in politics, and Lysias is aiding one of his wealthier opponents by taking advantage of Theomnestus' impetuosity in making a rash public accusation against one of his political opponents.

Theomnestus' defence appears to be weak. He has not denied accusing the prosecutor of murdering his father, but has taken forlorn refuge in the form of words in which he uttered the accusation. He has appealed to the original text of the ancient law and has argued that a charge of slander could be sustained only if the accused had used the 'forbidden words' contained in it. Since many of these words were obsolete or archaic, the prosecutor can easily reduce Theomnestus' argument to absurdity by showing that slanderers who use words which are in current use stand to escape prosecution, though their guilt is patent. Nevertheless, the case may have afforded a test of the application of the law of slander at the time. It is likely that prosecution for slander was not common, being considered excessively litigious (2) in a society in which vilification was both everyday currency and prominent in literature, especially comedy. Perhaps the concept of 'forbidden words' originated in a practical need to restrict the number of slander charges that could be brought, and the present speaker has to show that his case is exceptionally serious.

After a short prooemium (1-3) and an even shorter narrative in which the charge of patricide against him is summarily refuted (4-5), the prosecutor's main argument (6-21) shows how the normal legal processes could not operate if the language used in bringing charges were restricted to the actual wording of the laws. Much of the discussion concerns the use of current vocabulary, a subject which is said to have interested Lysias in its own right and was reflected in his language and style (D.H. *Lys.*3). Another issue raised is that of the relation between the spirit and the letter of the law (see 7n). These matters could be dealt with coolly and clinically, even at times scornfully (e.g. 9,11,15,19,20). But occasion had to be found to magnify Theomnestus' crime and emphasise the danger it posed for the speaker. Lysias provides this in 22-9, one of his most powerful passages of emotional appeal (*deinōsis*) which also serves to minimise the effect of Theomnestus' secondary plea, that he uttered the slander in anger, which is made to follow (30). In the short epilogue, he reaffirms his own danger and calls for vindication of both himself and his father. One of Lysias' mature speeches (384/3 B.C., see 4n.), *Against Theomnestus* combines thoroughness of argument with powerful pleading to produce a well-balanced speech.

1-3 PROOEMIUM: In a few sentences Lysias aims to establish maximum rapport with the jury and their hostility towards his client's opponent by focusing on the seriousness of the charge of patricide. This is necessary because Theomnestus admits the charge but pleads that he uttered the slander in anger (30). It also serves to rebut a possible charge of malicious prosecution (*sukophantia*). Revenge (3), by contrast, was an acceptable as well as a powerful motive for litigation. (See Sp.1 Introd. *sub.fin.*)

1   any shortage of witnesses: cf. ...*ouk aporon* at the beginning of Speech 12. Both are variant formulae of the *prooimion ek periousias*, setting a confident tone at the start.

many of you: some of these 'witnesses' would also remember that Theomnestus was acquitted at that trial (22).

prosecuted Theomnestus.....disqualified: his acquittal must mean that the original charge of fleeing from the battlefield was rejected, though there had been no previous trial on that issue alone. This suggests that summary judgment was regularly passed, on the evidence of a number of a man's battle-comrades, and that it was up to him to challenge it by defying one or more of the restrictions placed upon him as an *atimos* ('disfranchised man', on which see MacDowell (1962) 110-112). Lysitheus'

230

prosecution was thus the first occasion on which a jury examined the evidence, and *eisangelia* would seem the appropriate procedure in such a situation. But the passage presents difficulties in relation to the subject of impeachment. On these see P.J.Rhodes, 'Eisangelia in Athens', *JHS* 99(1979)103-114, whose view that the procedure might have had wider application than that allowed it by Hansen (1975) and *JHS* 100 (1980) 89-95 seems well-founded.

2   Now if.....excusable....But in the present case: a standard antithetical formula. For close parallels see Lys.12 *Erat*.29, 18 *Nik*.20. Hermogenes, *On Invention*,4.2 notes its suitability for prooemia and quotes Dem.4 *Phil*.1.1. In Lysias see also 3 *Sim*.31; 4 *Traum*.3; 5 *Kall*.1; 7 *Sac.01*.1,12; 8 *Kak*.9; 13 *Agor*.36; 31 *Phil*.1. In Antiphon, 5 *Her*. 1n.

3   shameful.....father: after conventionally expressing his reluctance to litigate, the speaker uses his father's good reputation to magnify and discredit Theomnestus' charge of patricide. Though illogical and apt to rebound on him, this line of attack should have provided useful short-term ammunition. Cf.Ant.5 *Her*.74n.

4-5   NARRATIVE: The charge of patricide is dismissed in four sentences in which chronological facts are stated and probabilities are swiftly drawn.

4   I am thirty-two years old.....nineteen years....you returned: 'you' are the democratic party, which restored itself to power in 403 B.C. Thus the speaker was born in 416/5 and delivered this speech in 384/3 B.C.

5   took over everything: i.e. assumed executive powers over the estate. All legitimate sons shared equally (Is. 6 *Philoc*.25) on coming of age (17 or 18). So Pantaleon, the second of many unscrupulous guardians (*epitropoi*) in the Attic Orators, had about five years in which to plot his younger brother's disinheritance. The prosecution of Diogeiton (Lysias 32) is to be dated 401 or 400 B.C., and there are some undatable fragments of Lysianic inheritance speeches.

6-21   REFUTATION: The prosecutor seeks to establish that a charge of slander does not depend on the offender's use of the actual words forbidden in the law, many of which are obsolete. Other laws containing archaic words are quoted to illustrate the absurdity of Theomnestus' argument. Its weakness suggests that he may not have made it his main plea.

6   he will not attempt a defence......arbitrator: anticipation (*prokatalepsis, occupatio*) of the defendant's argument was regularly introduced by 'perhaps' (*isos*) (cf.12 *Erat*.50; 13 *Agor*.52,55; 22 *Corn*.11.) This was misleading, however, since the prosecutor knew that the defendant would use the main arguments which he had put before the arbitrator at the prior hearing. On arbitration see Harrison,*LA* 2,64-6; MacDowell, *LCA*,201-211.

7   meaning: i.e. the intention of the legislator. The relation of the letter of the law to its spirit was of perennial interest to lawyers and rhetoricians (Quint.7.6; *Ad Herenn*.2.9.13; Cic.*Inv*. 2.42.121 - 48.143). See S.F. Bonner, *Education in Ancient Rome* (London,1977) 300-1. An early view was that doubts as to the intention of a law should be resolved by applying principles of equity (*to epieikes*) (Arist. *Rhet*. 1.13.13-17).
    all those who have killed people....have also killed people: this change of subject and predicate (*antimetabolē*, cf.Ant.5 *Her*. 14n) produces a fallacious legal argument, which ignores the distinction between intentional and unintentional homicide. But because of the serious view taken of all forms of homicide, the jury might have accepted this argument. Moreover, the exact sense of *androphonos* in the law is uncertain, since it originally referred to killing in battle.

8   *ou gar dēpou* negates the whole sentence:'...it cannot be the case that....whereas...'.
    father-beater...mother-beater: forbidden words, like 'murderer' above.

9   I should like...: continuing the *apostrophē* (direct address to a second person) with a touch of sarcasm. The formula is common in Isocrates (e.g. 6 *Arch*.88,8 *On the Peace* 37), but it is used only here in Lysias.
    flung....thrown: a clever analogy, since the old law uses the weaker verb: *apoballein* could mean merely 'to lose' by this time. The question of whether a man had shown unpardonable cowardice, or incompetence, or merely discretion in the face of the enemy must have made these cases difficult to decide. Plato *Laws* 944b proposes to distinguish between a 'loser' (*apoboleus*) and a 'thrower-away' of arms (*rhipsaspis*). The latter was evidently the popular word, applied occasionally in official contexts, in the time of Lysias and Aristophanes (see *Clouds* 353,*Peace* 1186), but the old law was still quoted later (Isoc.8 *On the Peace* 143 (355 B.C.); Aesch.1 *Tim*.29 (345 B.C.)).

10 Eleven: one official appointed from each of the ten tribes, plus a secretary, to supervise the administration of justice, law and order, including the custody of malefactors. See Harrison, *LA* 2, 17-18,222-32; and Ant.5 *Her*.17n.
    arrest by a citizen: on *apagōgē*, or summary 'citizen's arrest' for offences involving theft and violence, see [Arist.]*Ath.Pol*. 52.1, who lists thieves, slavedealers or kidnappers (see below) and clothes-stealers (or highwaymen) as the commonest types of criminal subject to *apagōgē*. See Hansen, *AEE*.
    child....slave-dealer: most slaves were, or were descended from, children sold or abducted, or war-captives. Hence the usual purpose of child abduction and of kidnapping in general was the procurement of slaves, and it was one of the slave-dealer's activities.

12 Lysitheus: Frohberger's emendation seems preferable to the

232

introduction of a second accuser of Theomnestus on the same charge.

13   **is it not shocking..?**: for this formula introducing a type of *reductio ad absurdum*, cf. 12 *Erat.*87; 24 *Inv.* 8,12; 30 *Nicomach.*32; Bateman (1962) 161-2.

  so influential: in view of his successful prosecution of Dionysius, perhaps he was.

16   **stocks**: an additional punishment optionally imposed on the initiative of the prosecutor. See note on 1 *Caed.Erat.*36 and Harrison, *LA* 2,166-7.

  Eleven: see 10n above. Like all other officials, the Eleven underwent an audit (*euthuna*) before the Heliaea on concluding their term of office. See [Arist.]*Ath.Pol.*48.3-5 and Rhodes *ad.loc.*; Harrison, *LA* 2,208-11.

17   **vowing**: in this example a key word, *epiorkein*, means 'to swear falsely' in Lysias' time, so that literal invocation of the law would lead to absurdity. The law in this case appears to concern the regularisation of contracts sworn under oath. A section of the text is then omitted. When it resumes with the clause containing the archaic word *draskazein*, it deals with the provision, available even for the most serious crimes (see Ant.5 *Her.*13), that an offender be allowed to go into exile.

  excludes: 'forces back', 'bars the way'. The root verb *eilō*, *illō* or *eillō* means 'to coop up'; so that although the unnamed object of *apillei* is probably 'a rescuer', it retains this original sense by referring also to the trapped burglar. The law gave the citizen the right to detain and even kill a burglar caught in the act. The concluding clause of this law may therefore have been'...is not to be punished' (*azēmios estō*). Shuckburgh (226) takes the opposite view, viz. that the door is barred to protect the thief from within, a less probable interpretation involving a third party in an action which must have ended in failure.

18   **set out**: i.e. made available for borrowing. The act of setting the money on the scales was a necessary part of the transaction in early times before the weight and fineness of coinage was regularised. But the contemporary meaning of *stasimon* was 'fixed', 'stable', whereas Solon's law clearly envisaged the operation of market forces, with the rate varying according to the lender's judgment of what he could obtain.

19   **But.....tread abroad**: to ply the oldest profession. Being mostly owned by brothel-keepers, prostitutes (*hetairai*) were similar in status to slaves. Hence the juxtaposition of the two laws. The *de* ('but') may correspond with a *men* in a preceding clause describing the penalties for assault on free women in their homes. *pephasmenōs* and *polountai* are poetical words in Lysias' time.

  serf: the text is uncertain, but with minimum emendation it can be seen to relate to the law cited in 1 *Caed.Erat.*32. Understand *zēmian* ('penalty') with *diplēn*, which can take the genitive to mean 'double the amount..'(cf.Plato,*Tim.*35b). Redress for injury to slaves was pursued by their masters, since they could not normally litigate on their own behalf (Plato, *Gorg*.483b). On their legal status, see Harrison, *LA* 1,163-80.

22   **won**: Theomnestus' success in two previous lawsuits, one as defendant, the other as prosecutor, is Lysias' chief problem. He therefore uses his grandest style to complete the case against him in 22-29.

    utterly disastrous.....not very serious: antithetical (cf.this man...But I above) commonplace to elicit sympathy by saying that the defendant has more to lose than the prosecutor (cf. 7 *Sac. Ol.* 37).

23   **What charge..?...Is it that...?....But...**: *hypophora* (*subiectio*), a figure in which the speaker poses and answers his own questions (*Ad Herenn*. 4.33-4). Here it provides an effective contrast with the periodic sentences in 22 and 24-5. Its use as a device of emotional appeal between proof and epilogue is paralleled in 24 *Inv*.24-5, 2 *Epitaph*.74; *Ant*.5 *Her*.58 (**see** n); *And*.1 *Myst*.148, suggesting a common origin in the handbooks.

24   **that great and generous gift**: the condemnation and disfranchisement of Dionysius.

    pity for Dionysius: invoked in Lysias' grandest style, with its periodic and interrogative structure and description of Dionysius' bitter feelings as he left the courthouse.

27   **general many times**: Attic litigants recited not only their own services (*leitourgiai*) but those of their parents. Similarly they were required to clear their parent's name if any suspicion surrounded it (see *Ant*.5 *Her*. 74-80 and notes). The prominence given to the present speaker's father is especially appropriate, not least because, at thirty-two years of age, he may have few of his own services to recall. Note the assonance *pollakis...pollous* and the hyperbaton *oudemian....euthunēn* and *etē...hepta*.

28   **memorials....on your temple walls**: Lysias uses *pros* rather than *en*, implying placement near the temples or on their outside walls (cf.Thuc.3.57.1). In Thuc.3.114 war-spoils are 'in the Attic temples', but this may be abnormal, because they were placed there as dedicatory offerings by the general Demosthenes, who had received them as a personal share of the spoils. On the dedication of booty at temples, see W.K. Pritchett, *The Greek State at War 1* (Los Angeles,1971) 93-100.

29   **impressive.....appearance**: further evidence that Theomnestus was a formidable and influential adversary.

30   **I hear..**: *prokatalēpsis* (see n. on 6).

    in a moment of anger: the aorist *orgistheis* denotes a sudden action of brief duration.

    the lawgiver makes no allowance for anger: nor did the handbooks regard it as an excuse, since anger was thought to show a defect of character (*Ad Herenn*.2.16.24). *Rhet.ad Alex*. 1429a says that anger should be pleaded only as a last resort. See also Dover, *GPM*,147.

for I did not yet realise: an astounding piece of sarcasm at this, the most sensitive stage of the speech.

31   patricide: acquittal of Theomnestus would uphold the charge he had made.

alone on being enrolled as an adult...: soon after his eighteenth birthday ([Arist.]*Ath.Pol.*42.1 and Rhodes *ad loc.*). As he was thirteen years old in 404-3 (4) the 'attack' on the Thirty here described took place in 399/8 B.C., and was forensic, not military, the Hill of Ares being the seat of the Areopagus homicide court. His reference to 'the Thirty' probably includes their adherents, since only Eratosthenes (see Lysias 12) and possibly Pheidon were alive in Athens by that time (Cloché, *RDA*, 325-30).

SPEECH 12 : AGAINST ERATOSTHENES

The only speech in the corpus certainly spoken by Lysias himself, *Against Eratosthenes* has two distinct parts. The case against the defendant is complete by ch.40, for the sketch of Eratosthenes' earlier career (41-61) adds little of substance other than a description of his character. Thereafter the main victim of Lysias' pen is Theramenes. Thus over half of the speech concerns the politics of the Thirty. But the orator faces a major problem: his attack is of necessity levelled against men who were generally admitted to have been among the more moderate of the Thirty, Theramenes and his adherent Eratosthenes. Furthermore, as Lysias' own narrative shows, Eratosthenes was not directly responsible for the murder of his brother Polemarchus, but only for his arrest.

Further estimation of the difficulty facing Lysias depends on establishing the date of the speech. Since metics were not allowed to appear in their own lawsuits (Harrison, *LA* 2, 193-9), the best conclusion seems to be that Lysias made the speech in 403 B.C., during the brief period when he was a citizen, i.e. after the decree of Thrasybulus granting citizenship to all who returned with the democrats ([Arist.]*Ath.Pol.*40.2; Aesch.3 *Ctes.*195), and before it was revoked on the initiative of Archinus. The broad front on which Lysias conducted his attack is best explained by the assumption that Eratosthenes, in an attempt to clear himself of association with the excesses of the Thirty, had submitted to an audit in compliance with the conditions of the amnesty (And.1 *Myst.*90; [Arist.]*Ath.Pol.*39.6). He would have had good reason for promptness in his attempt to restore his status as a citizen with full franchise, while the spirit of reconciliation and the authority of its sponsor Thrasybulus were still at their height. Acceptance of the following sequence of events: the amnesty (Sept.403)(Plut.*Glor.Ath.*7); Lysias' temporary citizenship granted under a decree of Thrasybulus ([Arist.]*Ath.Pol.*40.2;

[Plut.]*Vit.X.Or.*835f); Eratosthenes' submission of his audit (around the same time or a little earlier); Lysias' speech *Against Eratosthenes*; Archinus' revocation of Thrasybulus' citizenship decree;- would do no violence to the known facts and place the speech in the final weeks of 403 B.C.

Lysias' handling of the case was influenced by the later career of Theramenes and his popularity at the time of the speech. The manner of his death had made a deep impression on the popular mind (as it did upon Xenophon (*Hell.*2.3.56), who was otherwise not sympathetic towards him), and many had recent memories of his resistance to the excesses of the Thirty under Critias and the other extremists. Lysias himself remarks in his speech that men who had supported him were hoping for political advancement on the strength of that support (64); and a pro-Theramenean literary tradition arose in opposition to Lysias, which was preserved in Diodorus and Aristotle and a document called the 'Theramenes Papyrus' (P.Mich.5982). Lysias' only hope of success in his prosecution of Theramenes' adherent Eratosthenes was a frontal attack on Theramenes' career. But he had to be selective in his choice of episodes. After giving a very short and sketchy account of his career between 411 and 404 B.C. (66-7) (the period during which he gradually formed for himself a reputation for moderation), Lysias concentrates mainly upon his peace negotiations with Lysander and the Spartans. This is, of course, because their outcome was the Athenian surrender, and it was possible for a skilful rhetorician to make this simple fact obscure the diplomatic finesse which enabled Theramenes to achieve the best settlement possible in the circumstances (see n. on ch.70). In dealing with the Thirty in general, Lysias aims at maximum effect by emphasising that they were motivated by pure material greed rather than by ideology. He saw this as the best way of finding common ground with members of the jury who may not, at every stage of their reign, have been hostile to the aims of the Thirty. (Sources are agreed that the Thirty were deemed by many to have started well by ridding the city of some of the most detestable features of democracy ([Arist.] *Ath.Pol.*35.2; Diod.14.4.2; Xen.*Hell.*2.3.12)). In order to establish this motive, Lysias found it necessary to suppress reference to the Spartan garrison on the Acropolis and the need for money to maintain it. He represents the Thirty as purely self-seeking, and enemies of their own people; but a more profound analysis of their political aims is not to be expected from him, either in order to meet the rhetorical requirements of his case or as a manifestation of his own understanding of the objective distinctions between democracy, oligarchy and tyranny. His main aims in this speech are simple: to secure the posthumous condemnation of the Thirty by successfully prosecuting one of their survivors, while doing minimum damage to the spirit of concord that was to nurture the renascent democracy. It was a difficult and delicate task. By attempting it Lysias may have harmed his own chances of becoming a full Athenian citizen, and, if the majority of commentators since

Rauchenstein are to be followed, lost the case as well. The speech must nevertheless have impressed its audience and its readers sufficiently to launch him upon his career as a speechwriter.

1-3 PROOEMIUM: Though full of conventional topics, these opening chapters point firmly towards the general political attack into which the speech is to evolve. There is no summary of the specific charges against the defendant.

1 difficulty.....size and number: a subtle blend and adaptation of two topics assigned to prooemia by the handbooks. For the latter, see 10.1n.: there witnesses are said to be numerous, here crimes (see their crimes (below)). *Difficulty* is more commonly represented as due to the problems inherent in the case or created by an opponent's behaviour (as in Lys.7 *Sac. Ol.*2 and Lys.19 *Arist.*). See also Cic.*Pro Lege Manilia*,3.
their crimes: Eratosthenes is being tried for only one crime, and is the sole defendant. Neither he nor his crime is mentioned in the prooemium (contrast 1.4). But reference to a plurality of crimes and wrongdoers at this early stage establishes the broad front on which the attack is to be conducted.
time run out: this was measured by the water-clock (*klepsudra*) ([Arist.] *Ath.Pol.*67.2 and Rhodes *ad.loc.* (719-721)).

2 opposite...former times...enemies: enmity was one of the motives considered in private cases (Ant.5 *Her.*57-8; Lys.1 *Caed.Erat.*4,43; Lys.31 *Phil.*2). Lysias thus establishes the picture of the state's enemies in the dock.
today...enemies of the state: an artificial inversion, since defendants would be concerned primarily with proving their innocence; but historically interesting because it underlines the political character of trials following the removal of the Thirty.
private grievance: Lysias makes this minimum concession to the practical need of specifying the subject of the trial.

3 inexperience: as both speechwriter and speaker, Lysias invests this commonplace (cf.Ant.5 *Her.*1 (and n.);Lys.19 *Arist.*2; And.1 *Myst.*1; Isoc.15 *Ant.*26; Is.10 *Arist.*1; [Dem.] 58 *Theok.*3) with double significance: for clients, the anxiety they expressed concerned only their ability to *present* the speech effectively. If this was Lysias' first speech, then Speech 20 in the corpus, *Against Polystratus*, must be spurious.

4-20 NARRATIVE: A model of clear simplicity, but containing many personal reflections (e.g. in 7,26,31) designed to arouse sympathy and indignation, the narrative has two main objectives: the specific and practical one of establishing Eratosthenes' personal responsibility for the death of his brother Polemarchus; and the general one of representing the Thirty as motivated purely by greed. It begins with a preliminary narrative (*prodiēgēsis*(Arist.*Rhet.*3.13.5)) describing his family's status in Athens prior to the events that led to Polemarchus' murder (4-5) (cf. 1 *Caed Erat.*6).

237

Cephalus: The opening scene of Plato's *Republic* is set in his house in the Piraeus. Though a metic of Syracusan birth, he was a friend of the great at Athens, including Pericles, with whom he had ties of friendship and hospitality ([Plut.] *Vit.X.Or.* 835c). See Dover, *LCL*, 29-30; Davies, *APF*, 587-8.

under the democracy: i.e. politically, as grammatically, passive. They professed *apragmosunē* (non-participation in public affairs), a convenient virtue for men of property who, at least publicly, claimed to admire self-restraint, respectability and the maintenance of the *status quo*.

5   my.....your experiences: a clear reference to the bipartite division of the speech.

virtue and justice: the Thirty may have made positive attempts at moral reform by means of some sort of propaganda. See L. Gianfrancesco, 'Aspetti propagandistici della politica dei Trenti Tiranni', *Contributi dell' Istituto di storia antico* 2 (1974) 20-35.

6   Note *gar* beginning the main narrative (cf. Lys.24 *Inv.*6).

resident aliens: Xenophon notes (*Hell.*2.3.40-1) that Theramenes opposed this attack on the metics, saying that it would create disaffection. But the wealth of some of them gave rise to jealousy, making them vulnerable to extremists. On their status, see M. Clerc, *Les Metèques athéniens* (Paris, 1893); Harrison, *LA* 2, 187-199.

making money: Lysias implies that this was solely for personal aggrandizement, but this is only partly true. The rule of the Thirty was maintained through the presence of a Spartan garrison under Kallibius stationed on the Acropolis (Xen.*Hell.*2.3.13-14,21; Diod.14.4.4; [Arist.]*Ath.Pol.*37.2,who misplaces the time of its installation (see Rhodes *ad.loc.*)).

7   thought nothing....but a lot: note synonyms *hēgounto..epoiounto* used to create balanced clauses with assonance; so too *pepraktai....gegenētai*. Note also *hina....ēi*, subjunctive rather than optative in historic sequence after aorist *edoxen*, used to reflect the force with which the justification was presented.

8   made a list of the slaves: with a view to assessing their value when sold. There were 120 (19).

large sum: Lysias was described as 'the richest of the metics' at this time (P.Oxy.1606 lines 153-5), and the value of the family's property, the main asset of which was a shield-factory, was 70 talents when sold by the Thirty (*id*.lines 29-30).

10   calling down destruction....children: 'the greatest and most binding oath known' (Ant.5 *Her*.11). For the religious implications of oaths, see Dover, *GPM*, 248.

11   cyzicenes: *staters* struck at the Hellespontine market-port of Cyzicus. They were coins of electrum (gold and silver alloy) worth about 28 Attic drachmae.

darics: Persian gold coins named after Darius I, in wide circulation throughout the Eastern Mediterranean and Aegean, and worth about 20 Attic drachmae.

money for my journey: *ephodion* (Lat.*viaticum*) originally meant rations for a soldier on the march.

saved my skin: note the *parēchēsis* (*sōma sōsō*) rendered by alliteration in the translation: lit. "saved my body".

12 met....caught up: historic present. Note the tense variation in the whole of this dramatic part of the narrative, starting with *paradidoasi* in 8 and continuing with *anoignumi* ...*eiserkhetai*...*kalei* interlaced with past tenses (10). Even more striking is the sequence *erōtōsin*....*badizoimen* and *ephasken*.....*skepsētai*, the first following the normal practice of regarding the historic present as a secondary tense (*GMT* 21,33), the second either using the vivid subjunctive after an historic main verb or understanding *ephasken hoti badizei*.

Melobius and Mnesitheides: like Peison and Theognis, members of the Thirty (Xen.*Hell*.2.3.2). Damnippus, though apparently trusted by them, was not of their number.

14 into your home: thereby becoming a guest and imposing the obligation of protection upon his host. Lysias' action was also a form of supplication (*hiketeia*), but J.P.Gould ('Hiketeia', *JHS* (93) 1973 101) writes: "By the end of the fifth century, supplication.....was becoming increasingly a ritual whose binding force was weakening in the face of the counterstrain of political realities". Lysias' plight and his remedy for it support Gould's view.

15 reflecting....I thought: *anacolouthon* with imperfect indicative *hēgoumēn* following dative participle *enthumoumenōi*, interrupting the second of two conditional sentences dependent on it, and governing future infinitives instead of future indicative. For Lysias' occasional lapses into loose construction, see Blass,*AB* 1, 419-421. Here the purpose may be to portray the swift passage of thoughts through Lysias' mind during the actions described.

16 three doors: that of the room in which he was being detained, and two leading out of the back of the house, corresponding with the two (*auleios* and *metaulos*) in the front (see 1.17).

17 Eratosthenes.....in the street: the defendant is mentioned for the first time, together with the most damning piece of evidence against him. See Lys.26 *Euand*.30.

hemlock: perhaps introduced for executions by the Thirty (Bonner and Smith, *AJHA* 2, 284-5). For its effects prior to death, see C. Gill, 'The Death of Socrates',*CQ* 23(1973) 25-6.

18 funeral: the Thirty's desire to avoid a public spectacle of grief is understandable, because it would attract sympathetic crowds and perhaps lead to serious disorder. But Lysias makes the most of the pathos and outrage implicit in the scene. Refusal of burial rites amounted to sacrilege.

19 they had...., they had....: *anaphora*, highlighting the *leitmotif* of the whole narrative - the pure material greed, devoid of ideology, of the Thirty. It leads to a single instance which shows their greed in its extreme form in an act of gross *hubris*, at

239

which the narrative proper ends on a highpoint of indignation.
handed over....treasury: for sale or service as public slaves
(*dēmosioi*).

20   **duties**: reference to these was made by defendants rather than
prosecutors, usually towards the end of the proof (e.g. Ant.5
Her.77n; Lys.7 *Sac.Ol*.31; 19 *Arist*.57. In showing the full range
of his family's *leitourgiai* Lysias incidentally reveals its wealth.
But here, sandwiched between the climax of the narrative and an
amplification (*deinōsis*) of the Thirty's crimes (21-2) the recital
points a most effective contrast.

21   **many...many...many**: the *anaphora* adds cumulative weight to the
Thirty's misdeeds. This is necessary to counteract the envy
which Lysias' wealth (20) may have aroused in some of the jury.
enemy camp: so Xen.*Hell*. 2.3.42-3, in Theramenes' speech
against Critias. Thebes sheltered the exiled democrats.
deprived....civic rights: by disfranchisement and/or exile.

22   **I would that...But as it is**: a form of antithesis favoured by
rhetoricians, especially for use in prooemia (cf.Lys.4 *Traum*.3; 31
Phil.1; 32 *Diog*.1; Hermogenes, *On Invention*, 4 (Sp.2.237).

23   **his own lawless aims**: the language is still strong as Eratosthenes
is linked with the rest of the Thirty in a final statement of
charge and motive. *exupēretōn* is a very rare intensive.

24   **third party....for his benefit**: a false witness who might have
been bribed to exonerate Eratosthenes who, according to Lysias,
was alone when he arrested Polemarchus (26,30-31).
impious: because the case was one of murder; and a suspected
murderer was defiled (*miaros*) and accursed (*enagēs*) until his
innocence was proved. (See Is.9.*Ast*.20).
benefit...to harm him: the antithesis seems somewhat strained,
but Lysias means that Eratosthenes' personal responsibility for
the murder of Polemarchus will be established most fairly by
confronting him with a few simple questions rather than by
allowing other witnesses' testimony to obscure the issue. In fact
no witnesses to the arrest and execution are introduced. On the
conventional morality of doing good to one's friends and harm to
one's enemies, see Lys.9 *Sold*.20; Eur. *Ion* 1045-7; Xen.
Mem.2.6.35, *Anab*.1.3.6, *Cyr*.1.4.25; Ar. *Birds* 420ff; Soph.
Ant.643ff.
answer what I ask you: on this type of evidence, see Harrison,
LA 2,138. Questioning (*erōtēsis*) aimed to lead the defendant
from his own statements (as here) or from agreed premises, into
an absurdity (*atopon*). See Arist.*Rhet*.3.18.1, with Cope's
Introduction (Cambridge,1867)362-3; and E.M.Carawan, '*Erōtēsis*:
Interrogation in the Courts', *GRBS* 24 (1983) 214; (on 22.5,
218-9).

25   **in fear**: Eratosthenes' main defence is based on this plea, so it
seems unlikely that his reply would have been as short as Lysias
makes it here. Eratosthenes surely made much more of his
subordinate role and the pressure to which he was subjected by

the extremist leadership under Critias. For an admission that the
Thirty compelled many to act evilly, see Isoc.18 *Kall.* 17.

26   **so**: *eita* gives a tone of indignation.
<u>in your power alone</u>: elsewhere (16,30) Lysias says that
Eratosthenes met Polemarchus *in the street*, and claims that this
enabled him to let him go free. But the important question was
whether Eratosthenes was unaccompanied, and Lysias' phrase
(above) only implies that he was in a position of authority. In
practice, he could not have hoped to effect an arrest without
assistance; and even if the Thirty had ordered only a
house-search, his companions would be witnesses to an escape,
wherever it took place.

27   <u>proof of his loyalty</u>: evidence that Eratosthenes had argued that
he had acted from fear because he was suspected (rightly) of not
favouring extremism. The other point is that greater loyalty to
the Thirty would have been required to induce a man to kill
Athenian citizens than to kill metics. The passage is a good
example of *eikos* (probability)-argument.

28   <u>the Thirty</u>: for the flaws in this argument see Bateman (1962)
168, who points out that the Thirty are here represented as a
concerted body, when one of Eratosthenes' main contentions is
that, though nominally one of them, he disagreed with their
leaders but was powerless to oppose them.

29   <u>For if.....but as it is</u>: a variant of the form of antithesis in 22,
q.v.

30   <u>in the street</u>:   see 26.

31   <u>could not be disproved</u>: this would be true only if Eratosthenes
was unaccompanied: see 26n.

32   <u>suffer unjust death....be destroyed unjustly</u>:   superfluous
variation. For other examples see 7n. Here used to reinforce an
apostrophē (direct address of adversary).

33   <u>deeds....words</u>: on this antithesis, see Ant.5 *Her.*3n.
<u>meetings</u>: of the Thirty, like that described in 6. Though initially
appointed as legislators, they exercised power through a council
which they had themselves appointed (Xen.*Hell*.2.3;
[Arist.]*Ath.Pol*.35.1; Diod.14.4.1-2).
<u>not even...own homes</u>: because the actions of the Thirty had
driven them into exile. After the death of Theramenes the Thirty
excluded from Athens all whose names did not appear on the list
of 'those who were to participate in the government, three
thousand in number' (Xen.*Hell*.2.3.18,4.1).

34   <u>concede</u>: the figure of thought whereby an opponent's argument
is allowed (*consensio*: see Quint.9.2.51, quoting Cic.*Pro
Cluent*.63). Cf. **Ant.5** *Her*.27,62.
<u>supported it.....opposed it</u>: a form of argument by comparison,
here of opposites, but possible also with the greater and the
lesser (*a fortiori*), the part and the whole. See
Arist.*Rhet*.2.19.1-15; Quint.5.10.87-91. The argument in 1.31
belongs to this category. Cf. **Ant.5** *Her*.43n.

what would you do...?: compare this appeal to the jury with Euphiletus' opening plea (1.1).

one of two things: the question of fact (*status conjecturalis*) and the question of justification (*status juridicialis*). This is the earliest extant reference to the standpoints (*staseis, status, quaestiones*) of cases as defined by later rhetoricians. It strongly indicates that the *stasis*- theory attributed to Hermagoras of Temnos (2nd century B.C.) had its roots in the practice, and perhaps also the theory of the 5th century. This has been largely discounted by modern commentators, in spite of Quintilian's statement that the Greeks did not regard Hermagoras as the inventor of *stasis*-theory (3.6.3). For a similar division of the case, see Lys.29 *Philoc*.5.

35   foreigners: especially, since these would measure the prospects of safe residence by the treatment accorded a distinguished family of resident aliens by an Athenian court.

what your judgment...is to be: for the same formula see 26 *Euand*.14;27 *Epicr*.7. For the importance of a verdict as a guide for future behaviour, see 1 *Caed.Erat*.36;14 *Alc*.A 12;28 *Erg*.10; and as a precedent for future legal usage, 1.*Caed.Erat*.48; 12 *Erat*.85;14 *Alc. A* 4 (esp.). Other passages: 22 *Corn*. 19; 30 *Nicom*. 23.

36   Would it not therefore be shocking..?: the commonest Lysianic formula used to introduce argument by comparison (see n on 34,88). For other examples, see 4 *Traum*.13;7 *Sac.Ol*.29,35; 14 *Alc.A* 17,31; 18 *Nic*.12; 22 *Corn*.13; 24 *Inv*. 9; 28 *Erg*.3;29 *Philoc*.4,9,11; 30 *Nicom*.8,16,32; 31 *Phil*.24. The sequel to the Battle of Arginusae (406 B.C.) is particularly well-chosen: in spite of heavy seas caused by a violent storm, ten of the victorious captains were condemned to death, and six executed, for failing to rescue survivors and salvage bodies from foundering ships.

private citizens.....defeat: this refers to the alleged activities of an oligarchic fifth-column. But the antithesis 'private.......government' strains the historical probabilities: as private citizens, the oligarchs could not have done much to affect the outcome of the Battle of Aegospotami, which ended the war. But the presence there of some of them as captains could have been a factor. See Xen.*Hell*.2.1.32 and Underhill *ad.loc*. (44); Isoc.*Phil*.62.

37   the case....is complete: a standard formula to mark the end of the proof (cf. Lys. 30 *Nicom*.31; 31 *Phil*.34). The next chapters (37-40), charged with emotion, serve as an epilogue to the main speech in the case. *Against Eratosthenes* thus comprises two distinct orations, not one. See 41 below and Introd.

extreme penalty: cf. Lys. 1 *Caed.Erat*.31.

die twice: cf. Lys.13 *Agor*.91, 28 *Erg*.1. For a discussion of the order of words in this sentence, particularly the unusual position of *an*, see S. Fogelmark, 'Lysias 12.37: an unexplained case of κακοφωνία ', _Hermes_ 116 (1981) 294-300.

38 has been customary: the periphrastic form _eithismenon esti_ instead of _eithistai_ emphasises the idea of state. Note the anacolouthon in the change from infinitive _apologeisthai_ (after _prosēkei_) to indicative _exapatōsin_. See Blass, _AB_ 1, 420-1 and Introd.

they are good soldiers...: the topics of the conventional _pistis ek biou_ are listed. Lysias repudiates their use, as here, in 14 _Alc.A_ 24 and 30 _Nicom_.1 (both prosecution speeches); but uses them to defend his clients in 21 _Brib.Def_.2-10,19 _Arist_.57,62; and to defend his own family's record in this speech (20).

39 Just..: _epei_ is here used to explain the whole of the previous sentence. Its use with the imperative is colloquial. **Cf. Plato,** _Gorg_.473e5; Soph._Elect_.352; Ar._Wasps_ 73.

40 not on the orders of the Lakedaimonians: as it stands, this is contradicted by Xen. _Hell_.2.2.20, in whose account the dismantling of the Piraeus fortifications and the Long Walls is one of the peace terms exacted by the Spartans before the Thirty came into power. Lysias himself gives a similar account to this in 13 _Agor_., where he describes two sets of peace terms, an earlier set (8) in which the Long Walls were to be demolished over a distance of ten stades, and the ultimatum (14) whereby the fortifications were to be demolished in their entirety. See also 68n. But here Lysias may merely be making a rhetorical (_ouk...alla_) antithesis, i.e. 'not because the L. ordered it (though they did), but...'. Again he may be trying to introduce a more striking (false) example beside the genuine instance of the Thirty's policy of disarming the Attic forts.

41 I have often wondered...: so Isocrates begins his _Panegyricus_ and Xenophon his _Memorabilia of Socrates_. Very similar formulae are used by Isocrates to begin other epideictic discourses (_Philippus, Archidamus, Areopagiticus_). The impression that a fresh start is being made in a more expansive, epideictic style is enhanced by a change to more periodic, antithetically balanced sentences.

42 Four Hundred: the earlier oligarchy of 412-1 B.C. It was initiated in the Athenian camp at Samos, where 'certain men entered into negotiation with Alcibiades' (Thuc.8.48.1), to explore his plan for securing Persian aid in return for establishing oligarchy at Athens. Eratosthenes may have been one of these men, or an adherent, and his desertion is explained by the fact that the army rejected oligarchy (Thuc.8.75-6). He naturally wanted to be in Athens to enjoy the oligarchic regime which he had helped to introduce. But see next note.

from the Hellespont: specifically Sestos, where a garrison had been recently installed (Thuc.8.62) to defend the whole of the Hellespont. This garrison was probably not established until late spring, 411. (For the chronology, see Gomme, _HCT_ 5, 185ff). The meetings at Athens at which democracy was replaced by oligarchy probably took place about June 411 (*op.cit.* 187), so Eratosthenes could have been present, but a later arrival seems more likely, especially in view of the following statement: opposed those who wanted democracy: suggesting that the counter-revolution was already under way on his arrival. Lysias also ignores the compromise-constitution of the Five Thousand proposed by Eratosthenes' friend Theramenes, which replaced the Four Hundred in September 411 (see A. Andrewes, 'The Generals in the Hellespont,410-407 B.C.', *JHS* 73(1953) 2). Full democracy was restored in June 410.

43 the sea battle and the disaster: the Battle of Aegospotami (405) and the subsequent blockade and surrender of Athens which ended the Peloponnesian War (404).
overseers: Lysias is our only source for this temporary appointment of a committee named deferentially after the five *ephors* at Sparta. Although Lysias makes a rhetorical point of saying that the democracy was still in being, its fate was by now sealed, since peace must have been signed and exiles recalled, the latter including Critias, the leading radical oligarch.
"club-men": oligarchs, whose secret societies were bound together by oath.

44 tribal leaders: by nominating these from among their own supporters the oligarchs dictated the measures to be ratified by the Council of Five Hundred, which consisted of fifty members from each of the ten tribes. The Council was being prepared, in effect, to vote itself out of power. Lysias' 13th Speech is against an agent of the oligarchs, Agoratus, who disclosed a plot by the democrats to prevent this transference of power. See also 16 *Mant*.6-7.

46 for I could not do that: of the four other overseers, Critias was dead. Those of the other three who were still alive may have cleared themselves by submitting to a scrutiny, whereupon, like other citizens, they were bound by the amnesty oath. See next note.

47 oaths: the amnesty oath, sworn by all citizens, included only those of the Thirty who submitted themselves to scrutiny and were cleared (And.1 *Myst*.90;[Arist.]*Ath.Pol*. 39.6).
they would not hold them as binding....while...: *ouk an* negatives the whole proposition, which consists of two antithetical clauses, and makes it unreal. Lysias is arguing that the oaths should not inhibit men from bringing private suits for offences committed during the tyranny, since they considered the public interest when they discriminated against men of known oligarchic sympathies in making appointments to state offices. On court cases brought in defiance of the amnesty, see Rhodes,*CAAP*, 471-2.
refused to act illegally in office: rather than 'decline unconstitutional powers' (Lamb), which would require an ingressive aorist infinitive. Moreover, this part of the argument begins at a

point where Eratosthenes has already entered office as one of the Thirty.

impeachments: the word *eisangelia* described a formal procedure for making a variety of charges of a specific nature before the Council and/or the Assembly (see Lys. 13 *Agor*. 9-22); but it could be used to describe more general verbal denunciation, as in Lys.10 *Theomn*.1n. The case here referred to appears to be in an intermediate category: the charges against Lysias and many others were notably unspecific (see 6), yet they led to conviction by the Council acting under the direction of the Thirty. But in these cases the accused did not stand trial, the normal legal procedure following impeachment.

Batrachus: also denounced as an informer in [Lys.]6 Andoc.45.

Aeschylides: otherwise unknown.

49 those who proclaim their goodwill...show it at the time: Lysias must have known that such action was dangerous; and the jury would surely recall the fate of Theramenes (see 50n).

50 let him not be seen...: colloquial use of *hopōs mē* in an independent clause, analogous to *mē* in prohibitions, but introducing a note of caution (i.e. not 'do not' but 'see to it that you do not'; hence following the construction used with verbs denoting precaution, like *epimeloumai, skopeō* (*GMT* 278,339).Cf. Lys.1 *Caed.Erat*.21.

policies in general: *ekeina*. Lysias is trying to represent Eratosthenes as a member of the Thirty who was respected by the extremist leadership sufficiently to obtain a hearing in the debate. But Eratosthenes has only argued that he survived because he withdrew his opposition in fear.

Theramenes: when Eratosthenes interceded on his behalf is not known, if indeed he was able to. Xenophon's narrative of Theramenes' trial and death leaves little opportunity for intercession (*Hell*.2.3.24-56).

51 which faction: the extremists under Critias or the moderates under Theramenes. This struggle was very short-lived, and ended with Theramenes' death.

52 Thrasybulus....Phyle: in September 404 B.C. It was the first move towards the restoration of democracy. Lysias' suggestion is, of course, preposterous, since at this stage Thrasybulus had only 700 men, whereas the Thirty held most of Attica and enjoyed Spartan support.

went....to Salamis and Eleusis: to secure them as places of refuge. As such they must be purged of possible enemies (Xen.*Hell*.2.4.8-10).

three hundred: all the citizens, according to Xenophon, who may have been an eyewitness at Eleusis; so too Diodorus (14.32.4). If this was true, it is surprising that Lysias does not say so.

single resolution: the same procedure as that by which the Ten Generals had been condemned (Xen.*Hell*.1.7.21-37; *Mem*.1.1.18). Block trial certainly violated the individual's constitutional rights, but since it was proposed and debated at the above trial, it may not have been technically illegal. It does not appear that the Decree of Kannonus, which was invoked by Euryptolemus (*Hell*.1.7.20), and which ordained that a man accused of wronging the Athenian people should make his defence before them in chains, itself contained a reference to separate trial. (See Underhill 332). There is also uncertainty about the question of a block *verdict* as an issue distinct from the conduct of the trial itself. There can, however, be little doubt that Lysias' jury would have found the Thirty's action repugnant. Once again Xenophon adds a detail surprisingly omitted by Lysias: that the votes were, on Critias' orders, cast in open view.

53   our return: Lysias identifies himself with the democrats, and in fact gave material aid to their cause ([Plut.]*Vit.X.Or.* 835f; Justin 5.9.9; Orosius 2.17.9), supplying arms and hiring mercenaries.

54   expelled the Thirty: i.e. those who had survived the Battle of Mounichia, in which the extremists Critias, Hippomachus and Charmides were killed.
    leaders: the Ten (Xen.*Hell*.2.4.23-4), one from each tribe. They were expected to initiate peace moves (Diod.14.33.5; [Arist.]*Ath.Pol.* 38.1); but see 55-61. The continued presence of Eratosthenes in Athens proves once again that he was not regarded as an extremist.

55   Pheidon, Hippocles and Epichares of Lamptra: Pheidon was one of the Thirty; the other two are unknown, the latter being distinguished by his deme because of possible confusion with another Epichares.

58   reconcile and restore you: see previous note, and Cloché, *RDA*,61-136. For a summary of opposing views, see Rhodes,*CAAP*, 456. The sources agree that the Ten made no moves towards reconciliation, and the expectation that they would may have been mere wishful thinking on the part of the democrats. Lysias' argument in 57 is rhetorically neat in its antithesis of the two parties, but politically simplistic.
    joined.....Eratosthenes: he was now acting in a private capacity, as he was not one of the Ten (*pace* Underhill 71), or he would have been named in 53.
    Boeotian hands: a rational fear, since the Athenian democrats had been given refuge by the Thebans, and Thebes had been Thrasybulus' base for the seizure of Phyle (Diod.14.32.1). The Thebans were anxious that Attica should not fall under direct Spartan rule (Xen.*Hell*.2.4.30).
    went to Lakedaimon: as also did the Thirty from Eleusis (Xen.*Hell*.2.4.28), which suggests that Lysias may be correct in implicating Eratosthenes in Pheidon's action on behalf of the Ten.

59   sacred signs: invoked by the Spartans before they set out on campaigns (Xen.*Lac.Pol.*13.2-5). See Hdt.6.106 for a famous example of unfavourable signs delaying a Spartan expedition.

60 **worthy men**: unspecified democrats. But the city was saved from a Spartan reoccupation and reimposition of oligarchy by rivalry between Lysander and the Spartan king Pausanias, the latter favouring the democrats (Xen.*Hell*.2.4.29; Diod.14.33.6). On divided Spartan policies and clashes of personality at this time, see C.Hamilton, *Sparta's Bitter Victories. Politics and Diplomacy in the Corinthian War* (Ithaca & London,1979) 82–98; W.E. Thompson, 'Observations on Spartan Politics', *Riv.Stor.Ant.* 3(1973) 47–58; P. Krentz, *The Thirty Tyrants at Athens in 404–3 B.C.* (Princeton,1982) 95–6.

61 **Nevertheless I shall**: ellipsis of "provide witnesses".

62 **in as few words as I can**: a transitional formula marking the beginning of a new narrative (cf. 16 *Mant*.9; 24 *Inv*.4). The change of subject is foreshadowed in 61, where there is evidently an intermission as a number of witnesses are introduced. The new subject is the career of Theramenes (62–78). It is traced chronologically but selectively (see Introd.), with a much more liberal interlarding of political and moral comment than that to be found in the earlier narrative.

63 **Themistocles**: using delaying tactics in negotiating with the Spartans after the Persian War, Themistocles built fortifications around the Acropolis to secure Athens from invasion (Thuc.1.90–92). Unfavourable comparison of Theramenes with Themistocles in the matter of the fortifications was actually made by the orator Cleomenes in the debate on the terms Theramenes had secured from the Spartans (Plut.*Lys*.14). Theramenes replied that both the earlier building and the present demolition were carried out to secure the city's survival. Lysias reproduces only Cleomenes' argument, in the form of a sarcastic *a fortiori* comparison.

64 **defence....appeals to his name**: see Introd.

65 **responsible chiefly**: because he ensured a smooth transition through his persuasive powers, not because he was the prime mover of the oligarchic revolution of 411 B.C. Lysias is thus not in conflict with Thucydides (8.68), who names Theramenes fourth of the leaders after Antiphon, Peisander and Phrynichus and describes him as 'a man not wanting in ability at speaking and deliberation'. As its most skilful popular advocate, Theramenes was 'prominent' (*prōtos* (Thuc.8.68.4: see Gomme, *HCT*5,178)) in promoting the revolution. Similarly in Lysias his responsibility, though described in the superlative (*aitiōtatos*), is not sole (i.e. he is not *ho aitiōtatos*) or entire, but is limited to his part in effecting the change itself.

 father.....commissioners: Hagnon was a close associate of Pericles. On his career, see Davies, *APF*,227–8; Gomme, *HCT*5,177–8. His appointment as one of the ten *sungrapheis autokratores* (legislators with plenary powers)(Thuc.8.67.1) was designed to give an appearance of balanced respectability to the board as a whole. The poet Sophocles was one of his colleagues.

Neither was likely to prove an enthusiastic oligarch (*op.cit.*165).
Peisander, **Kallaischros** on Peisander, see 25 *Def.Sub.Dem.*9n.
Kallaischros was one of the Four Hundred and possibly the father
of Critias. For full discussion of other possible identifications,
with references, see Davies,*APF*, 327.

66   Aristocrates: originally a leading proponent of the revolution who,
when he saw that the extremists were aiming to make peace with
Sparta, began intriguing for their downfall (Thuc.8.89.2-3). Fear
of the army at Samos and of Alcibiades were other factors, but
personal rivalry is mentioned by Thucydides without reference to
individuals. For a balanced discussion of the problem, see
Gomme, *HCT*5, 298, concluding that Thucydides had probably
not formed a firm opinion of Theramenes. See also
[Arist.]*Ath.Pol.* 33.2 and Rhodes *ad.loc.*, 413.

67   Antiphon: See Introd. It is highly suspicious that this alleged act
of treachery is not mentioned in Critias' speech against
Theramenes in Xen.*Hell.*2.3.24-34, or in the biographical
tradition. See B. Perrin, 'The Rehabilitation of Theramenes',
Amer.Hist.Rev. 9 (1904) 655, who refuses to accept Lysias'
isolated testimony.
Archeptolemos: unknown independently of this association. See
also [Plut.]*Vit.X.Or.* 833f-834b.

68   While enjoying popularity...: some five to six years have been
passed over, including the Trial of the Ten Generals after the
Battle of Arginusae, in which Theramenes played an important
and mainly discreditable part, but not one which made him appear
an enemy of democracy.
secure a peace: with Sparta after the final defeat at Aegospotami
(405 B.C.). Lysias' short account (68-70) fails to reveal that
Theramenes made two missions to Sparta, and stayed with
Lysander only on the first mission, for three months. On the
second, decisive mission he shared authority with nine others
(Xen.*Hell.*2.2.16-17).
without.....ships: Xenophon, who is generally unsympathetic
towards Theramenes, has him making no such undertaking, but
merely offering to go to Sparta in order to ascertain the scope
for negotiations (*Hell.*2.2.16).

69   Areopagus: acting not as a body but as individuals. Some of the
aristocrats who were its members had long-standing personal
connections with leading Spartans, and may have conducted
private soundings and negotiations. No other source mentions any
constitutional part played by the Areopagus prior to the
reaffirmation of its function of 'guardian of the laws' under the
Decree of Teisamenos in 403 B.C., on which see And.1 *Myst.*84
and MacDowell *ad.loc.*(124).
refused to tell: secrecy was necessary because the people,
misguided by the demagogue Cleophon, had passed a decree
forbidding the discussion of any proposal to demolish the walls
(Lys 13 *Agor.*8; Xen.*Hell.*2.2.15; Aesch.2 *Fals.Leg.* 76).

Not compelled by the Lakedaimonians: see 40n. Here, however, there is no ambiguity. The antithesis ('..making them voluntary proposals himself') explains the vaguer paradox that precedes it, and stands at the centre of a period containing falsehood ('fulfilled none of his promises') and unsubstantiated allegation ('..small and weak'). Some members of Lysias' audience might recall that Theramenes accepted Spartan terms after hearing Theban and Corinthian demands for the total destruction of Athens (Xen. *Hell*.2.2.19); but both the original and the final pressure came from Sparta, who was leader of the anti-Athenian alliance.

were not totally deprived..: note the vivid future indicative *aposterēsesthe* and *komieisthe*.

71   by them: i.e. the Spartans. This refers not to the assembly held immediately after Theramenes' return from Sparta, which agreed to accept their terms (Xen.*Hell*.2.2.21-22), but to the assembly held after some time during which some democrats tried to preserve the existing constitution (Lys.13.*Agor*.15-43; [Arist.]*Ath.Pol.* 34.3), and the oligarchs countered their efforts by sending for Lysander; who, if these accounts are to be reconciled with that of Xenophon, visited Athens twice in these months, the first time to preside over the demolition of the walls, the second to intimidate the Athenians into accepting the other terms. Although this version of events is contradicted by Plut.*Lys*.15, it is the most satisfactory. For discussions of the problems, see Hignett,*HAC*,378-383,esp.381; Rhodes,*CAAP*,433-4.

72   Philochares and Miltiades: Spartan admirals.

73   Drakontides: one of the Thirty (Xen.*Hell*.2.3.2; [Arist].*Ath.Pol*.34.3). His decree gave the Thirty a definite and specific task, to draft a code of laws (Xen.*Hell*.2.3.11; Diod.14.4.1), which they never carried out.

74   responsible for breaking the truce: Lysias' account is closely followed by Plutarch (*Lys*.15). Diodorus' pro-Theramenean source has Theramenes implausibly opposing Lysander.

75   plot....force: lit. 'the preparation and the need (to comply with it)'. A kind of *hendiadys*, in which two ideas are given equal status, though the second is dependent upon the first.

small number: nevertheless, a majority of those present.

76   ten: chosen probably by tribes. Lysias is our only source for this information. For the full list, see Xen.*Hell*.2.3.2-3, and D. Whitehead, 'The Tribes of the Thirty Tyrants', *JHS* 100(1980)208-212.

77   his defence: Xenophon's version of Theramenes' speech contains none of these topics. But his purpose is to represent Theramenes as a champion of moderation; that of Lysias is to emphasise his loyalty to the oligarchs. Again, in Xenophon, Theramenes is answering charges laid against him by Critias. On the two speeches, see S. Usher, 'Xenophon, Critias and Theramenes', *JHS* 88(1968) 128-135.

249

78   past...recently...petty...important: Lysias uses amplification by
means of opposites, antithesis and anaphora
(deserving...deserved) to bring his invective (*psogos*) against
Theramenes to a resounding conclusion. Note also the cumulative
effect (*synathroismos*) of repeated *kai*.
fairest name: perhaps an allusion to the idea that the 'best'
should rule under an ancestral constitution
(Xen.*Hell.*2.3.19).Cf.94.
mentor: cf. 47 and Lys.14 *Alc.*A 30 ('...of the city's evils',
describing Alcibiades).

79   accusation against Theramenes: rather a *damnatio memoriae*.
Lysias provides the most influential hostile tradition. Xenophon is
mainly neutral or slightly antipathetic until the end, when he
praises his courage in face of death (*Hell.*2.3.56). Diodorus'
source is favourable. Aristotle tries to reconcile the extremes.
See M.C.R. Giammarco, 'Teramene di Stiria', *Parola del Pasato*
28(1973) 419-425.

80   Thirty....away: most of the Thirty retired initially to Eleusis.
Eratosthenes and Pheidon stayed in Athens.

81   prosecution....complete: the fiction of a plurality of defendants is
maintained. 81-91 contains no new evidence, but is designed to
re-focus attention on the accused, and by means of *deinōsis* to
counter arguments that Eratosthenes was not one of the
extremists.
unequal...: an inversion of the *paraskeuē-topos* employed by
defendants (e.g. in Lys.7 *Sac.Ol.*36; 19 *Arist.*2; And.1 *Myst.*1,6;
Ar.*Frogs* 867). In this case the prosecutor, claiming to have
right on his side as he exposes the defendant's crimes, has
prepared his case thoroughly. See also Ant.5 *Her.*19n.

82   penalty....illegally: for this type of hyperbole, cf. 1n and Lys.1
*Caed.Erat.*38.
could...in full: translating the potential force given by *an* to the
periphrastic perfect optative, which indicates an ideal future
state. The following sequence of rhetorical questions maintains the
hyperbole (83-4).

84   capable: *an* makes the infinitive *tolmēsai* potential.

85   immunity: cf. Lys.1 *Caed.Erat.*48; 30 *Nicom.*23.
funerals of the dead: see 18n. For impiety as a *topos* in Lysias
see Voegelin 153-167, esp.160.

88   beyond seeking requital from their enemies: accepting Hude's
emendation *pera* for *peras* ('end', 'limit'). This emendation and
interpretation are challenged at great length by S. Fogelmark, 'A
Troublesome Antithesis: Lysias 12.88', *HSCP* 83 (1979) 109-141.
He translates: '(those they destroyed)... can no longer be
reached by the vengeance of the Thirty', the true antithesis
being between the murdered and the surviving citizens, who
could yet be the Thirty's victims if the defendant(s) are
pardoned. But this interpretation depends upon the assumption
that Lysias is writing elliptically. The antithesis is very strong in

the form suggested here, reading *pera*: 'The Thirty and their adherents could damage the city again if acquitted; their victims cannot even obtain vengeance for existing wrongs'. The use of the preposition *para* in the sense of 'from the hands of' with *timōria* ('vengeance') is required to validate this interpretation. Fogelmark finds this a major objection to its acceptance. Yet it is so used in 70. For the idea of the dead obtaining posthumous vengeance through their relations see Ant.5 Her. 95n.

Is it not therefore shocking...: see 36n. The prospect is represented as real by the future indicative *hēxousin*, but in order to achieve vividness rather than to suggest that the Thirty were popular.

89   in deprecation...: as Eratosthenes had claimed to have done (25-6).

90   under orders...:   see 25, 29.

92   EPILOGUE: This lacks the conventional summary (*anakephalaiōsis*) of charges made against the defendant. Its preoccupation with the aftermath of the civil war and party differences maintains the political character of the speech, as does the plurality of accusers and defendants, to the end.

the Town....the Piraeus: Lysias refers to the oligarchic remnants and the democrats (respectively) as if they were not yet reconciled, perhaps an indication that the speech was made very shortly after the restoration of the democracy in July 403 B.C. See Loening 284-7.

defeat...victory: antithesis used to produce *para prosdokian*.

94   reflecting....reflecting..: anaphora, a figure used sparingly by Lysias, e.g. (in another peroration) 3 *Sim*.46.

the auxiliaries: the garrison of 700 Spartans under Kallibius. See 6n.

95   demanded your extradition: see Diod.14.6.1; Plut.*Lys*.27; Justin 5.9.4; Orosius 2.17.8.

96   suicide: by drinking hemlock. See 17n.

customary rites of burial: See 18. In writing this appeal to the jury's emotions, Lysias reminds them of the highpoints of his own narrative.

97   Those of you...: this section is a short encomium in the second person plural, epideictic in character, with a high concentration of rhetorical figures, including *pi* alliteration and oxymoron (*polemiai tēi patridi*). It is the only *captatio benevolentiae* in the speech, a topic conventionally assigned to the prooemium. But Lysias returns grimly to the evil consequences of the Thirty's rule in the next section.

opposed....enemies: or neuter: 'despite many adversities' (Lamb).

98   would.....have become exiles: ('...and still be in that state'), the imperfect indicative with *an* denoting an unreal condition in present time; so too with 'would be suffering...' and 'would be serving...' below.

serving as slaves: this might happen to expatriate Athenians who

251

fell into debt in places where no Athenian consular presence (*proxenia*) existed to help them.

99 whose contents....sold: *hiera* could mean 'temples' or 'sacred objects'. The verb 'sold' applies to it in its latter, the verb 'defiled' to it in its former sense. There were precedents for the sale of sacred objects like temple treasures to raise money in times of extreme national emergency, the most recent being before the Battle of Arginusae (406 B.C.), when gold and silver coins were struck from the metal of the Statue of Victory and other temple treasures (schol.Ar.*Frogs* 720; [Xen.]*Rev*.4.19).

dockyards: after the fleet, all but twelve ships, had been disbanded in accordance with Lysander's terms for peace (Xen.*Hell*.2.2.20; Plut.*Lys*.15; Diod.13.107.4 (ten ships retained); Lyc.*Leocr*.17,150; Dinarch. 3 *Philoc*.13.

must vindicate: *boēthēsate*: a striking change to imperative (cf. *keleuete* 39n). The aorist tense reinforces its peremptory character, sharpening the effect of the final clause, which is longer than its predecessors, and climactic because it refers to people instead of material objects.

100 I imagine...: *personarum ficta inductio* (Cic.*de.Or*.2.53.205); *conformatio* (*Ad. Herenn*. 4.53.66). The term *prosōpopoeia*, used in English criticism to describe words and sentiments ascribed to absent, dead or imaginary characters had a wider application in ancient criticism (Quint.1.8.3; 3.8.49,52; 6.1.25; 9.2.27,29; 11.1.41). The later Attic orator Lycurgus, perhaps imitating Lysias, uses this figure at the same point in his speech *Against Leocrates* (150).

You have heard....: This laconically abrupt, elliptical ending, with its *asyndeton* (absence of connectives), *homoeoteleuton* (similar endings), and sudden change from verbs expressing state (the perfect tenses *akēkoate, heorakate, peponthate* and the present *echete*) to a final imperative (cf. *boēthēsate* above (99)), was so admired by Aristotle that he ended his *Rhetoric* with a similar sequence: *eirēka, akekoate, echete, krinate*. A vaguer meaning of *echete* ('the case is in your hands') is perhaps closer to Aristotle's adaptation, and may be preferable to the translation given. The order of the actions is also climactic.

SPEECH 16 : FOR MANTITHEUS

Mantitheus was elected to the Council but his election was challenged at his subsequent scrutiny (*dokimasia*), on the ground that his name appeared in the list (*sanidion*) of those who had served in the cavalry under the Thirty. Such service would automatically disqualify him (Lys.26 *Euand*.10). He is able to rebut this charge by showing that he was abroad during the regime of the Thirty, but this alone does not restore his position. In spite of the fact that he has actually been elected, the *dokimasia* effectively opposed him anew to other candidates for his office. His task now becomes one of emphasising those of his characteristics which might give him popular support and minimising those which his opponents might use to discredit him. His comparative youth (20) affords him some scope for exaggeration of his virtues without giving offence (see 1n), since a certain degree of boastfulness is allowed to young men. But he has also been in the habit of dressing in a manner which suggests either self-centred affectation or more sinister political affiliations (18n). He counters these imputations in advance by describing his service in the army, laying great emphasis on his willingness to face the greatest dangers as an infantryman on the battlefield; and by giving details of his generous disposition of the modest family estate.

These topics dictate the division and arrangement of this short speech. There are thus no extended narratives or proofs, only short statements of fact followed by argument intended to lead to favourable conclusions as to the speaker's character and motives. Stylistically the speech is remarkable for its polished smoothness, containing as it does very few instances of hiatus (the clashing of terminal and initial vowels). This suits the character of the speaker, who also has brief opportunities to display skill in dramatic narrative (e.g. 15-17), for which Lysias chooses a periodic style rather than the simple style favoured in Speeches 1 and 12.

1-3   PROOEMIUM: Remarkable mainly for setting a confident tone and establishing the character which the speaker is to assume, the short prooemium is otherwise conventional.

1   aware....opponents: cf. Lys.3 *Sim.*1 for the same verb *suneidōs* applied to the speaker's opponent.
very grateful.....So great is my confidence: Mantitheus' self-assurance is of a different character from that of the Pensioner in Speech 24. It is greater and more pervasive because he is a younger man. (On the impulsiveness, ambition and optimism of youth, see Arist.*Rhet.*2.12.3-11). But he is also more earnest and deferential. Cf. Isoc.15 *Ant.*7; 19 *Aeg.*2; Dem.18 *Cor.*265.

3   only....the existing state of affairs: i.e. the restored democracy. This modest aim accords with the conventional mood of this prooemium; but Mantitheus knows that he must make a positive impression, since other candidates were ready to take his place if he was rejected.
I shall prove: the summary of charges to be answered concludes the prooemium. Cf. 1.4.

4   disaster at the Hellespont: the capture of the Athenian fleet at Aegospotami in July 405 B.C., which effectively ended the Peloponnesian War.
Satyrus: king of the Cimmerian Bosporus (mod.Crimea) c.407-393 B.C. (Diod.14.93.1). Isocrates *Trapezeticus*, written for one of his subjects resident in Athens, illustrates the close relation

between Athens and his kingdom, arising from mutual trade interests and maintained by the reciprocal conferment of benefits on visiting nationals, including residence with equal rights at law and tax concessions. Dem.20 *Lept*.29ff describes the importance of the kingdom as Athens' main source of grain. On Satyrus, see Clinton, *Fasti Hellenici* 2,339-344.

walls....dismantled: described by Xenophon in *Hell*.2.2.23.

constitution...changed: by the Decree of Drakontides. See Lys. 12 *Erat*.73n; 30 *Nicom*.14.

those at Phyle: the exiled democrats under Thrasybulus.

5 reasonable....: the 'narrative' in 4 has been the baldest possible statement of Mantitheus' movements prior to the return of the democrats: appropriately so, since he wishes to establish his absence from Athens. He now interprets his actions through *eikos*-argument, linking it with two comparative arguments, one concerning behaviour to be expected of those who had gone abroad, the other concerning behaviour to be expected of the tyrants.

6 it is naïve to consult the register: the second *eikos*-argument, this time on a practical matter. The *sanidion* was a wooden board coated with gypsum and used for public notices, mainly those of a temporary character (unlike inscriptions in stone), and including names of public offenders. See Lys.9 *Sold*.6; 26 *Euand*.10; [Arist.]*Ath.Pol*.47.2,4; Isoc.15 *Ant*.237. Such notices could easily be tampered with (Cloché,*RDA*, 396).

served in the cavalry: under the Thirty, hence as opponents of the returning democrats. See 7 below.

7 tribal officers....list: rightly invoked by Mantitheus as more reliable evidence than the *sanidion*, since these officers were financially accountable for its accuracy.

financial officers: originally legal assistants, or advocates appointed to supervise the recovery or exaction of a variety of moneys on the state's behalf, including estates, as in Lys. 17, 18, 19, forfeited by condemned citizens. After the fall of the Thirty the name *sundikoi* was given to men appointed to decide, in disputed cases, what property had been confiscated by them. See Harrison,*LA* 2, 34-5.

allowance: a single payment made on enrolment to a cavalryman (knight) by the state to cover the expense of equipment and fodder. The restored democrats voted to reclaim the allowances paid to those who served as knights under the Thirty, arguing that they had not thereby served the state and should therefore not receive state payment. On the Athenian cavalry and state payment, see Xen.*Hipparch*.1.19; [Arist.]*Ath.Pol*.49.1-2 and Rhodes *ad.loc*. 564-6, and 303-4; also Rhodes, *AB*, 174-5.

8 if I had served in the cavalry: a hypothetical *consensio* (see 12 *Erat*.34n), here running a bold and seemingly unnecessary risk. The knights had fought loyally and well for the Thirty (Xen.*Hell*. 2.4.2,4,8,10,24,26-7,31-2), and they were suspected of oligarchic

sympathies as late as 400 B.C. (Xen.*Hell*.3.1.4).[Arist.]*Ath.Pol.* 38.2 describes 'some' and 'certain of' the knights as supporters of the Ten in their last stand and as 'being the most desirous of the citizens that the men from Phyle should not return'. Mantitheus' difficulty was that popular prejudice found it easier to deal in whole classes rather than examine individual cases. But it is characteristic of him, at least in Lysias' portrayal, to meet dangers head-on.

serving on the Council: as Mantitheus is applying to do. He is tacitly reminding his audience of the spirit of the amnesty which every citizen was supposed to have sworn (Xen.*Hell*.2.4.43). For a similar argument, see Lys.18 *Nic.* 17.

9   I think...in other kinds of trial the defence should be confined only to the charges made: Arist.*Rhet*.1.1.5 refers to this as a rule imposed by the Court of the Areopagus, the guardian of the law. In [Arist.]*Ath.Pol.*67.1 the obligation to speak solely to the point at issue (*eis auto to pragma*) is said to apply specifically only to private lawsuits. The present passage is interesting in that it expresses *an opinion* which distinguishes between *dokimasiai* and other kinds of lawsuit, thereby suggesting that the distinction was not embodied in a law, or at least that if it was the law was not observed in practice. Time was of course limited by the water-clock, but this did not of itself prevent litigants from introducing irrelevancies into their speeches.

in cases of scrutiny....whole of one's life: expected of both the candidate and of those who opposed his election (cf.Lys.26 *Euand.* and 31 *Phil.*). Of this passage Harrison (*LA* 2, 201n) says: "the statement.....should not be taken too literally, but shows how pleaders might be expected to argue". The implied distinction between what information candidates were expected to supply and what they were expected to use in argument seems a fine one. In practice the Council would have welcomed any evidence that enabled them to adjudicate between rival candidates. Hence the importance of the *pistis ek biou* and its wide range of subject-matter. On the questions asked in a *dokimasia*, see [Arist.]*Ath.Pol.*53.3.

with good will....as few words as I can: for a similar appeal before a narrative, see Lys.19 *Arist.*11; and for the same transitional formula, see Lys.12 *Erat.*62.

10   Note the *gar* beginning another short narrative (cf.4).

I gave....a dowry: as his sisters' *kurios* (guardian) after their father's death. There was probably no legal obligation to provide a dowry (see Harrison,*LA* 2,48,132), and the sum of 30 minae ($\frac{1}{2}$ talent) for each sister seems generous. But it is curious that Mantitheus does not say that his father died intestate.

distributed....brother: brothers inherited equally (Is.6 *Phil.*25). *eneimamēn* (middle voice) seems to imply that Mantitheus had executive powers, which makes his generosity seem even greater, at first sight. But these powers might also explain his provision of his sisters' dowries, surely from the whole estate and not from his own portion.

11 proof: on *tekmērion* see Lys.25 *Def.Sub.Dem.*5n.
dice-playing: mostly in gambling-houses (*skirapheia*), where young men wasted their time and their patrimony (Isoc.7 *Areop.*48, 15 *Ant.*286-7; Aesch.1 *Tim.*95).
false stories: cf. Lys.22 *Corn.*14; Isoc.5 *Phil.*75. For a description of the 'gossip' as a character-type, see Theophrastus, *Characters* 8 (*logopoios*). Mantitheus must, however, beware of assisting them by appearing too priggish. Young men were expected to behave with some degree of irresponsibility (see Dover,*GPM*,103): profligacy was one aspect of this, as was its good counterpart, generosity (Dem.53 *Nicostr.*12).

12 no one....suit: the commonplace of the unlitigious, quiet citizen (*apragmōn*) (cf.Lys.7 *Sac.Ol.*1, 10 *Theomn.*2; Dem.41 *Spoud.*1, 54 *Con.*24, 56 *Dionysod.*14). On the distinction between *graphē* and *dikē*, see MacDowell,*LCA*,57-61.
impeachment: see Lys.10 *Theomn.*1n.

13 Boeotians....Haliartus: the Athenians fought with the Boeotian League led by Thebes against the Spartans in this campaign (395 B.C.) in which Lysander was killed (Xen.*Hell.*3.5.16ff). Diodorus calls it the Boeotian War (14.81.1-3). Plutarch, or his source, blames Lysander for beginning it (*Lys.*27-8). Warfare was safer for cavalry against the Spartans at this time because their main strength lay in their infantry.
Orthobulus: probably a tribal officer (*phylarch*) (see 7n) but possibly a cavalry-commander (*hipparch*). See Davies, *APF*, 9667, P. 364-5. It is natural to think of a hipparch as a field commander rather than an administrator.

14 subsistence-money: on campaigns the individual had to provide his own food, usually enough to last for three days, after which armies either returned home or lived off the land (Thuc.1.48.1; Ar.*Ach.*197, *Knights* 1077, *Peace* 312).

15 to Corinth: in the Corinthian War (394 B.C.). Athens supplied about 6000 hoplites to an army of some 24000 Argives, Corinthians, Boeotians and Euboeans. Six of the ten Athenian tribes suffered heavy casualties at the hands of the Spartans (Xen.*Hell.* 4.2.17,21) in the opening battle, which took place in the valley of the stream of Nemea, east of Phlius. Mantitheus must have been in one of these tribes.
proud man from Steiria: Thrasybulus; also criticised in Lys.28 *Erg.*4ff. He had favoured the alliance with the Boeotians, and defeat in this battle and at Coronea temporarily eclipsed his political fortunes. This passage is an important source of evidence for the low state of Athenian military morale at this time. See R. Seager, 'Thrasybulus, Conon and Athenian Imperialism, 396-386 B.C.', *JHS* 87(1967) 98-99. For *semnos* used sarcastically, see Eur.*Hipp.*94.
Agesilaus: the Spartan king who had been campaigning

successfully against the Persians. He commanded the Peloponnesian forces at Coronea (394 B.C.) and shaped some of the most important events in Greece for almost a generation. See Xenophon, *Agesilaus*.

17 **And I did this....rights:** for parallels see [Lys.]20 *Polystr*.31, 25 *Def.Sub.Dem*.13. It is a logical extension of the *pistis ek biou*: in a state where the people were sovereign, and their judgment was esteemed as highly as the written law (see Lys.1 *Caed.Erat*.35n) his past services might count in a defendant's favour even if he had technically transgressed the law, and secure for him a favourable verdict. See Dover,*GPM*, 292-3; Davies, *APF*,xvii-xviii. This concept of a broader justice based on the popular will accounts for the many pleas for pity found in Attic Oratory. Its efficacy was also an insurance against miscarriages of justice arising from false testimony and legal technicalities.

18 **wearing his hair long:** *komāi* (Hamaker), supported by '...appearance'(19), is a very probable restoration of the original reading, altered on general but mistaken grounds by the scribe to *tolmāi*, because long hair was the mark of a knight, and Mantitheus has been at pains to describe how he chose to serve in the infantry in the most dangerous battles. But he does not state that he performed all his military duties in the infantry: indeed, reference to 'the van' and 'the rearguard' in 18 perhaps suggests cavalry rather than infantry. Again, Mantitheus' habit of wearing his hair long was not necessarily connected with his military service and is not discussed in that context. The unpopularity of long-haired knights (Ar.*Knights* 580) was due not only to their wealth, but also to the fact that long hair was a Spartan custom (Ar.*Birds* 1281-2), the adoption of which suggested political affinities and oligarchic tendencies.

19 **engage little in debate....:** the course of recent Athenian history had been changed more than once by men consulting and plotting in secret. One of the most influential of these was Antiphon, of whom Thucydides wrote (8.68.1): "He did not appear before the people or willingly engage in any lawsuit".

20 **Too young:** according to convention rather than law. All citizens over 20 could speak in the assembly, but young men were expected to defer to their elders and to regular speakers (*rhētores*). Even Demosthenes at the age of 33 apologised for not waiting for most of the latter to express their opinions (4 *First Philippic* 1). See also *Rhet.ad Alex*.29; Xen.*Mem*.3.6.1.
I was forced: the aorist suggests another occasion than the present *dokimasia*, as does the phrase **to defend my own interests**.
more ambitious: Mantitheus feels relatively safe in admitting to *philotimia*, a quality closely associated in the Athenian mind with patriotism. See Dover, *GPM*, 230-233.

21 **none other than yourselves:** skilfully ending by reaffirming the sovereign power of the democracy and the defendant's confidence

in a fair verdict, in a speech in which suspicion of oligarchic sympathies has been the defendant's main problem. The high tone is maintained to the end, with two rhetorical questions.

SPEECH 22 : AGAINST THE CORN-DEALERS

The Athenians relied on foreign sources for at least a third of their corn, so that trade in grain was always a sensitive political issue. It was conducted by private individuals, like all other forms of trade in Greece, but the peculiar importance of corn led to the appointment of ten state officials, called *sitophulakes*, to supervise their activities. Laws were also made to prevent the raising of corn prices purely as the result of trading operations. But these laws were difficult to enforce in the face of the widely fluctuating conditions of foreign markets, the uncertainties of navigation and political instability at home and abroad. Consequently the dealers, both retail (*sitopōloi*) and wholesale (*emporoi*) often became the objects of abuse and litigation when corn became scarce and prices rose steeply.

In the present lawsuit, the defendant has been accused of purchasing more than the legal amount of corn in order to sell it at a higher price later. It is a charge commonly brought against *sitopōloi* who, because they were unpopular and also tended to be aliens, were ideal victims for vexatious litigants. The speaker is at pains to show that he is not one of these. He succeeds in this by skilfully arguing that by insisting that the corn-dealers should face trial in the popular court instead of suffering summary condemnation at the hands of the Council, he was acting in support of the established legal procedure (3), not in consideration of personal gain.

The speech lacks a true prooemium because the speaker has already presented the essentials of his case to the Council, so that none of the usual preliminary topics is necessary. Again, there is no need to establish the guilt of the defendants, since this is admitted. The prosecutor needs only to refute their allegation that they had acted on the suggestion of the *sitophulakes*, and that their action was in the public interest. The first of these allegations the prosecutor refutes by direct testimony (7-9); the second, which was more subjective and contentious, he deals with by rhetorical means (11-16), playing on the alien status of the corn-dealers and representing them as hostile to the vital interests of the Athenian people, thriving on their misfortunes and besieging them (*poliorkoumetha* (16)) like an enemy even in peace time. This not only serves as an effective mode of attack, but also aims to distract the jury from the speaker's possible motives, which might have included collusion with the *emporoi*.

The speech is a model of clear and economic structure and

forceful argument, into which Lysias manages to inject the right amount of emotional appeal to do justice to the importance of the subject to his audience, without over-exploitation but with his usual classical restraint and sense of balance.

1-4   PROOEMIUM-NARRATIVE: The speaker needs to establish his own _bona fides_ rather than adumbrate the guilt of the accused, which is admitted. A short narrative (2-4) serves this purpose.

1   accused the corn-dealers in the Council: himself a councillor, the speaker describes the second, not the first action in the legal process (see 2), launching his speech _in medias res_ to avoid repetition when he comes to explain his actions in 2-4.

false charges: as resident aliens (_metics_) who were both wealthy and unpopular (see 14-15, and R. Seager, 'Lysias and the Corndealers', _Historia_ 15(1966) 180), the corn-dealers were potentially easy prey to professional false accusers (_sukophantai_). But the present statement suggests that _sukophantai_ were even more unpopular than corn-dealers. On this see Ant.5 _Her._ 59n; Isoc.15 _Ant._314-5; on _sukophantai_ in general see MacDowell,_LCA_, 62-66; Bonner & Smith,_AJHA_ 2, 39-74; Lofberg (1917).

I have been obliged to accuse them: i.e. he was speaking out of a sense of public duty rather than for the gain sought by a _sukophantēs_.

2   presiding committee: the Council (_Boulē_) consisted of fifty representatives elected by each of the ten Attic tribes. Each of these tribal groupings acted as an administrative standing committee for a tenth of the year, fixing the agenda for the Council's meetings, organising them and those of the Assembly (_Ekklēsia_), and receiving foreign envoys. Each day a member of this presiding committee was chosen by lot to be president (_epistatēs_), and he thereby became the supreme administrative officer of the state for one day of his life.

Eleven: see Lys.10 _Theomn._10n.

But I....according to the law: further useful self-characterisation. The Council had no legal authority to decide or inflict a penalty (Meiggs & Lewis, _A Selection of Greek Historical Inscriptions_ (Oxford, 1969) 118,1.135-9, 120). On the limits of the Council's punitive powers, see Rhodes, _AB_, 179-207.

you: the sovereign popular court. The contrast is sharpened by the two references to summary execution _without trial_, the procedure proposed for the Council, which would remind many of the manner in which it was used by the Thirty, and reflected the anxiety felt over the corn supply at the time.

3   save the corn-dealers: he thereby cleverly shows his actions as capable of appearing to have two opposite motives, rendering both questionable, and making room for a third, his concern for justice.

5   Tell me...?: this technique of questioning the defendant directly is designed to lay responsibility on him when he has claimed to have acted under constraint. So in Lys.12 _Erat._25, on which see n.

bought up: to accumulate stock for later sale; to 'stock-pile'. The limit of fifty baskets was imposed to prevent the corn-dealers from creating artificial scarcity by hoarding. The amount refers to stock held at any given time, not to quantities purchased for sale in each transaction or sold within a certain period. By interpreting this law as 'a limit on sales in any one day' Harrison (*LA* 2,26) seems to discount the fact that, except in times of real scarcity, as quick a turnover of sales between merchant (wholesaler), corn-dealer and consumer as possible was in the latter's best interests. If observed, the limit was effective because the corn-dealer could not frequently 'top-up' his stocks, especially when shipment was erratic (see 8).

on orders: the seriousness of the offence gave this plea, and others like it (e.g. in Lys.12 *Erat*.29,31; 13 *Agor*.52) little chance of a sympathetic hearing. See Dover,*GPM*, 147-8.

7 magistrates: the corn-controllers (*sitophulakes*), of whom earlier there were five in the City and five in the Piraeus, and later twenty in the City and fifteen in the Piraeus ([Arist.]*Ath.Pol*.51.3. See Rhodes *ad loc*. 577-8).

8 tried to shift: note imperfect *anepheron* denoting attempted action (conative), here unsuccessful.

Anytus: probably not the wealthy moderate politician who was an associate of Theramenes and prosecuted Socrates. (See Davies, *APF*,40-1; Rhodes,*CAAP*, 431-2).

during the previous winter: perhaps 388/7 or 387/6 B.C., when the Spartan fleet under Antalcidas was active in disrupting the Athenian corn supply. See 14.

outbidding one another: the suppliers being the merchants (*emporoi*), who purchased the corn wholesale from growers in Scythia (mod. Ukraine), Cimmeria (mod. Crimea) and elsewhere on the Pontic seaboard.

9 he did not tell them.....one another: Anytus' advice was thus to form a 'price ring', whereby every corn-dealer bought and sold at the same agreed price, refusing all higher demands by the merchants. The corn-dealers' allegation regarding the advice given by Anytus is perhaps to be explained by its practical implementation: the successful operation of a stable price-ring depended on clearing the market as each shipment arrived, because any corn that remained unsold by the wholesalers might tempt some dealers to break their agreement and pay the wholesalers higher prices for that corn in a later time of scarcity. Hence the only way to ensure a stable price was for the authorities to connive at the purchase, in times of plenty, of amounts exceeding the legal limit. 'Buying up' (*sumpriasthai*) and forming a price-ring were thus complementary activities, necessarily so because of human greed. In these circumstances the corn-dealers found it more difficult to comply with the requirement of the law when trade was erratic and there were wide fluctuations in the price of corn, because excess stocks were

difficult to sell when there was a sharp rise. For a less cynical view of the whole operation, see Seager, *art.cit.* (1n) 174-5.

10   however true..: *consensio* (cf. Lys.12 *Erat.*34, where the question, as here, is one of sole responsibility).

11   I do not expect them to resort to this argument: its use by the single corn-dealer questioned in 5 is unrelated to the defendants' speech, which will seek the jury's sympathy on broader patriotic lines, using the speechwriter's rhetorical skills.

11   as cheaply as possible: giving precedence to utility over strict legality. Lysias readily resorts to this type of argument himself when it suits his client's case, e.g. in 19 *Arist.*38. See Lavency,*ALJA*,179.

12   drachma....medimnus: i.e. at six times the legal limit of one obol profit per basket (see 8). Seager rightly deduces that the basket (*phormus*) was larger than the medimnus (*art.cit.*(1n) n.27). Corn would be bought and sold by the medimnus in times of scarcity, and at such times the corn-dealers were allowed to take a higher proportional profit in order to remain in business. It is this dispensation, which may again have been unofficial, that they are here accused of abusing.

13   It seems shocking to me if...: for this effective kind of comparative argument, see Lys.12 *Erat.*34,36,89 and notes. Here the comparison is of opposites, closely condensed in the style of the speech as a whole. They are: special levy – open - legal – declined: stock-piling – secret - illegal – admitted. Also contrasted are the genuine patriotism of accepting a special levy (*eisphora*), by which wealthier citizens paid for triremes and dramatic productions, and the falsely claimed patriotism of the corn-dealers.
      opposite....: the contrast is sustained and underlined in the strongest language and the most emotional rhetoric in the speech (plot against you like the enemy...snap it up....we are besieged by these men). The alienation of the corn-dealers from the main body of citizens is characterised by their pleasure in bad news, their fomentation of rumour and their rapacity. The striking metaphor 'besieged' reinforced the idea that the corn-dealers are like outsiders and enemies of the state. For an interesting comparison, see Demosthenes' famous characterisation of Aeschines' political behaviour in 18 *Cor.*263,307-9.

14   fabricate other rumours: on *logopoiein* see Lys. 16 *Mant.*11n.
      peace treaty: perhaps, since *spondai*, not *eirēnē* is the word used, this was a temporary cease-fire while ambassadors were gathering to consider the terms of the King's Peace. At that time the Athenian corn-supply was cut off as Antalcidas invested the Piraeus (Xen.*Hell.*5.1.28-9). Prior to this time of extremity, the Athenians had rejected Spartan peace offers in 392/1 B.C. If this distinction between *spondai* and *eirēnē* is correct, 387 B.C. is not only the earliest possible date for this speech, but also the most likely date.

16   market-officers: these officials maintained order in the market-place. Their duties included the collection of market taxes. See [Arist.]*Ath.Pol.*51.1.
by lot: because it was a dangerous office to hold, as is seen from the *a fortiori* (comparative) argument in the next sentence. On *sitophulakes* see 7n; Harrison, *LA* 2, 26; Rhodes, *CAAP*, 577–8.

17   merchants.....importers: the latter include those who manned, and in some cases owned, the ships in which the merchants transported their cargoes. Only the merchants dealt directly with the corn-dealers, but the livelihood of both would be adversely affected by any deterioration in the terms of trade. The prospect of a resultant breakdown of the corn-supply is the most powerful utility-argument that the prosecutor could have added to that of justice. On the nature of finance in Greek trade, see H. Michell, *The Economics of Ancient Greece* (Cambridge, 1957) 227–30; R. J. Hopper, *Trade and Industry in Classical Greece* (London, 1979) 58–9.
Now if.....But as it is: for this type of antithesis, contrasting an unreal condition with the real situation, see Lys.1 *Caed.Erat.*31; 3 *Sim.*2–3,31; 4 *Traum.*3; 5 *Kall.*1; 7 *Sac.Ol.*15; 12 *Erat.*22n.

18   how would it not be surprising if...: a variant of the formula introducing a comparative argument (see Lys.12 *Erat.*34,36 notes).

19   communal concern: for this rhetorical *topos* see Lys.1 *Caed.Erat.*47, where it is also near the end of the speech; and Lys.12 *Erat.*35n.

20   example for the future: both contemporary and past parallels were used as precedents to support legal arguments. See Lys.25 *Def.Sub.Dem.* 23n.

21   pity them....gratify and encourage these men: the guilt of the corn-dealers having been established beyond all doubt, the prosecutor must still guard against their acquittal on sentimental grounds, especially that of fellow-feeling (*sungnōmē*). Dover *GPM*,292 writes: 'Since the Athenian people was the source of the law, the people, as sovereign, could forgive its breach'. The occurrence 38 times of the word *sungnōmē* in the Corpus Lysiacum shows that it was a factor which defendants might exploit and prosecutors must take into account. See also Lys.16 *Mant.*17 and 25 *Def.Sub.Dem.*13, where defendants express the hope that their services to the state will protect them. Another factor was acknowledgment of human frailty, as invoked by Andocides, 1 *Myst.*57, on which see MacDowell's *Commentary* 100 and Dover, *GPM*, 272. Gratification and encouragement of the merchants and importers is sought for reasons not of justice but of expediency – to secure a steady supply of cheap corn. For a similar argument, see Lys.19 *Arist.*61.
citizens who died: of hunger. See Xen.*Hell.*5.1.29; (though the

connection between the two passages depends upon the dating of the speech soon after 387 B.C. (see 14n)).

22 just.....cheaper price: neatly combining the themes of justice and expediency. The epilogue is not merely short but elliptical: *puthesthai* needs a predicate to complete the required sense, and *ōnēsesthe* is not repeated, leaving the final clause without a verb.

SPEECH 24 : FOR THE INVALID

Athenian citizens with physical disabilities which prevented them from earning their living were paid a state pension of one obol a day at the time of this speech. This pension was reviewed annually in order to ensure that the qualifications for it still applied. The two main qualifications were continued disability and the possession of property worth less than three minae. In the present case, continued payment of the pension to the speaker had been opposed on both grounds, and there is good reason for believing that this opposition was justified. In the first place, he nowhere categorically denies that his property is worth three minae or more, and makes no attempt to give a catalogue of his possessions and a valuation. Indeed, the lack of firm evidence of any kind in this speech has baffled some commentators and exasperated others, and has led yet more to suppose that it was never delivered in an actual trial. (For a summary of criticisms, see M.D. Reeve's review of L. Roussel, *Lysias, L'Invalide* (Paris, 1966) in *CR* N.S.18(1968) 235-6). It is worth recalling, however, that Lysias' published speeches necessarily included, for the notice of potential clients, some which illustrated his technique in difficult cases (D.H. *Lys.*16). The present case appears impossible to win by any form of orthodox handling. Lysias therefore resorts to an extraordinary mixture of humour and pathos. This line of approach must have been chosen because it suited the character of his client, who seems to have been a well-known and popular figure in the busiest part of the city (5,19).

Little logical order can be discerned, though the speech has a clearly-defined prooemium in which the main ingredients of the speech are already present. There is no proper narrative, because the speaker has no relevant facts on which to base positive argument. He has no sooner given a sketchy account of his material state (4-6) than he breaks into an emotional appeal (7) followed by a bout of sarcastic humour (8-9). Humour and an assumed dignity tinge the following argument about his disability in relation to the forms of transport which he uses (10-12). This is followed by a wholly irrelevant elaboration (13-14) and refutation of two of the minor charges made against him, that he was ill-behaved (15-18) and that he kept bad company (19-20). The speech concludes with one of the most sustained emotional pleas in the whole corpus (21-27).

The style is remarkable in several respects. It contains five times as many instances of *hyperbaton* (the separation of grammatically associated words, a figure of forceful diction) as the average for the corpus, and twice as many rhetorical questions. The vocabulary includes a high proportion of nouns and verbs that have a poetic, philosophical or dignified tone. Qualities associated with the Grand Style are recalled in passages like 16-18 and 22-24, though hiatus is rare. It is certainly an enigmatic speech, but it deserves inclusion in a selection because it shows Lysias' versatility by displaying qualities not normally ascribed to him.

1-3   PROOEMIUM: Self-assertiveness, dignity and humour are already present; but so is vagueness and circumlocution regarding the charge.

1   I am almost grateful: the same statement characterising a confident defendant as that made by Mantitheus (Lys.16.1). But here the attack is carried directly to the opponent, who is accused of trumping up the charge (*pareskeuase*) through envy (*phthonou*) and wickedness (*ponērias*), being a false accuser (*sukophantei*).

2   whom others pity: this is to be the dominant theme of the speech, cunningly given prominence at the expense of relevant facts. Note the highly artificial word-order of the rhetorical question, with hyperbaton (*tinos....ponērias*).
   If....slandering me...: *aposiōpēsis* (*praecisio* in *Ad Herenn*.4.30; Quint.9.2.54), a figure more commonly associated with the omission of words of ill omen (as Dem.18 *Cor*.5) or words likely to give offence; here, unusually, with sarcastic and humorous effect: "If he is hoping to enrich himself (as a *sukophantēs*, either by being bought off or from the proceeds of a successful prosecution), he must be mad".
   personal enemy...revenge: recognised motives for attacking someone in the courts (Ant.5 *Her*.57; Lys.1 *Caed.Erat*.43).

3   For it is my belief....: the philosophical tone and Grand Style of this sentence, with one of Lysias' rare metaphors (*iasthai*, here very apt), seems designed to represent the pensioner sympathetically as stoical and high-minded, but also not unduly materialistic – a useful combination for his particular defence.
   at the same level as my misfortune: cf. Ant.5 *Her*.1.

4   in as few words as possible: here the usual transitional formula (cf. Lys.12 *Erat*.62) reflects the speaker's intention particularly well. In a case where the defendant was confident of rebutting the charges, the prosecutor's arguments could be stated at greater length. Here they are given baldly and contradicted inconclusively in a short narrative (6, beginning conventionally with *gar*), which is followed immediately by a plea for pity, a topic usually reserved for a later point in the speech.

5   Now I think you all know: an unusual statement by a defendant,

as most litigants thought it safer to pretend that they preferred to keep their affairs to themselves. The invalid is clearly a well-known figure, and since this fact could not be concealed Lysias decided to exploit it by representing him as having nothing to hide. See 19.

6 The trade I possess......I have no other income than this pension: the rhetorical exaggeration produces a contradiction. He means that the 'limited assistance' provided by his trade is insufficient, and he needs the pension to give him a reasonable livelihood. For *techne* in the sense of 'trade' see Lys. frg 1.2. Here would have been the defendant's opportunity to deny outright that his business had a capital value of three minae or above, at which level it would have disqualified him from receiving a state pension ([Arist.]*Ath.Pol.*49.4 and Rhodes *ad.loc.* 570; Aesch.1 *Tim.*103-4). Like the invalid, Aristotle refers to 'possession', which must mean capital, not income. Lysias tries to distract the jury from the value of his client's property, which he calls his 'trade', and concentrates upon his income, which would in any case be difficult to audit.
procure: the purchase of a slave to run the business is here meant. This would keep the business in the family in the absence of children. (Cf. Pasion in Isoc.*Trapeziticus*, who was given his freedom for his services, and in turn emancipated his slave Phormio to succeed him.)

7 unjustly....justly....older,weaker.....younger...stronger: the use of antithesis to reinforce an emotional argument like this one may have been pioneered by Thrasymachus. See Plato, *Phaedr.* 267c. A passage of Thrasymachus preserved by Dionysius (*Lys.*6) illustrates his use of antithesis, and Dionysius indicates possible links between the styles of Lysias and Thrasymachus in the same passage. See also Radermacher, *AS*, B IX 7, and H. Gotoff, *'Thrasymachus of Calchedon and Ciceronian Style' CP* 75(1980) 297-311,esp.299.
those similarly placed: the universalising theme, cf. Lys.1 *Caed.Erat.* 2,36.

8 For it would be absurd....: a comparative *a fortiori* argument similar to those introduced by *deinon* (see Lys.12 *Erat.*36n). *atopon* is used only once elsewhere by Lysias with comparative argument (26 *Euand.*10); though it can connote offensiveness (e.g. in Thuc. 2.49.2, where it is used to describe the breath of plague victims), it is not usually as strong as *deinon*. The argument is, of course, wholly irrelevant to the main charge, but Lysias cleverly balances failing health and growing incapacity against the charge that the defendant has become wealthier since the pension was originally granted. On the argument see Schön 99-101.

9 I think my accuser.....: with the delayed subject *katēgoros* and *monos* predicatively separated from it, and the striking contrast

265

of long and short syllables at the end (*săphestătă mŏnŏs anthrōpōn*), this sentence is as forceful and emphatic as the next is dignified and sonorous.

If I were to be appointed producer: pure hypothesis. Exchange (*antidosis*) was a legally sanctioned process by which rich men tried to avoid performing public duties (*leitourgiai*). It involved a challenge to another either to exchange property or to perform the duty. (See [Dem.]42 *Phain.passim*; Lys.4 *Traum*.1; MacDowell, *LCA*, 162–164; Harrison, *LA* 2,236–238.) As earlier, sarcastic humour is Lysias' weapon as he emphasises his client's poverty by imagining him momentarily in the category of the very wealthy. In fact the prosecutor has alleged that the invalid has associated with such men (5,9), so this is a bold stroke. Unfortunately the precise meaning of the end of his argument is uncertain. The problems of the text are discussed by Erbse (1958) 65. The reading he proposes, *toiouton m' eidenai*, makes *ponēroteron* difficult because it must refer to the defendant, not the prosecutor, and have the sense of "in a worse condition" rather than "worse" in the moral sense. Alteration to *penesteron* would meet this difficulty but parallels to the required sense of *ponēroteron* are found. The apodosis of the remote hypothetical condition *ei..tuchoi* would need *an* in a regular construction, though cases of its omission have been noted (see Erbse,*loc.cit.*).

10 showing no fear of fortune: i.e. no awareness that fortune is capricious, so that he could find himself in the defendant's predicament at any time. See Isoc.1 *Dem*.29; Dover,*GPM*,269–270.

aim and object of study: the philosophical tone and elevated style is resumed. Note especially the long words in this and the next sentence, which also contains the hyperbaton *tautēn.... rhaistōnēn*.

misfortune: i.e. being both lame and unable to afford to own a horse or a mule (see below).

11 arrogance....wealth: for *hubris* as the cardinal vice of the rich, see Dem.21 *Meid*.98,102,205; for other passages, see Dover,*GPM*, 110–111.

saddled mule......other men's horses: i.e. he would own an *astrabē*. Three categories of wealth are envisaged, in descending order: ownership of a horse; ownership of a saddled mule; hiring a horse. The invalid claims to be in the third, poorest category, although in fact an *astrabē* was a more comfortable form of transport for him, perhaps because it enabled him to ride side-saddle in the manner commonly seen in rural Greece today. Its use by women (Athenaeus, *Deipn*.528b) and in association with effeminate trappings by Demosthenes' enemy Meidias (21 *Meid*.133), also suggests this possibility. See schol. ad Dem.*ad loc*. Hesychius, s.v. describes the *astrabē* (a word of perhaps Phoenician origin) as 'the wooden trapping placed upon a horse, which those sitting on it hold on to', suggesting a pommel. It must be assumed that *astrabai* were not available for hire, to provide the invalid with the cheapest possible form of transport.

12 I use two sticks: a parallel instance of his abnormal behaviour, for which there is an equally rational explanation which both rebuts charges of *hubris* and shows the extent of his infirmity. As an amusing modern comment on the average person's dislike of physical handicap in others, on which the prosecutor has obviously played in his speech, Dickens' description of Squeers in *Nicholas Nickleby* may be quoted: "He had but one eye, and popular prejudice runs in favour of two".

he does not argue...: the argument is a little tortuous. Dealing again in parallels, he is saying that the prosecutor, having drawn the wrong conclusion about his physical state from one piece of evidence (his horse-riding), should logically have drawn the same wrong conclusion from another piece of evidence (his use of two sticks). Cf.8n.

13 drawing lots for one of the nine archonships: the method of appointment after the reforms of 487/6 B.C. (See [Arist.]*Ath.Pol.* 22.5 and Rhodes *ad loc.*) This passage is our only evidence for the ineligibility of invalids for state office. Rhodes, *AB*,2 n1 suggests that it may have applied to membership of the Council also. By using sarcasm in conjuring up absurd hypotheses involving archonships and heiresses (below), Lysias was probably relying heavily for success upon his client's appearance and performance in court.

obol: the pension was later two obols per day ([Arist.]*Ath.Pol.*49.4).

14 when he is in his right mind: reading *eu phronōn* for MSS. *eu poiōn*. The suggestion that the prosecutor is misguidedly bringing the charge in a frivolous spirit rather than a sensible one is made in 18.Cf. also *eu phronountōn* in the next sentence.

heiress: women who survived their husbands or otherwise inherited an estate were married to their nearest male relative in order to keep the estate in the family. Rich estates would attract rival claimants for the heiress's hand, and their claims were decided by a jury-court under the archon. For further details, see Harrison,*LA* 1, 9-12,132-138.

see me to be: the defendant no doubt made gestures and movements at this point in order to exaggerate his disability, heightening the quasi-comic effect of likening himself to an archon and an heiress.

15 overbearing, violent...: presented by the defendant in these general terms, the charges had probably been substantiated with examples by the prosecutor.

those men....not allowed: this passage (15-17) has the tone and appearance of a set of general arguments such as a rhetorician, perhaps Lysias himself, might have included in a collection of preparatory exercises (*paraskeuai*) describing the generally recognised characteristics of various classes of people. That a handbook containing exercises on these topics attributed to Lysias existed in the fourth century A.D. is attested by Marcellinus (*ad Hermog*.4,P.352 Walz). Blass notes the present passage as the only surviving trace of Lysias' practical use of this material (*AB* 1,381-382). The subject is discussed by Aristotle in *Rhet*.2.12-17. For other refs. see Radermacher,*AS*, C44,218-219, adding Ar.*Wealth* 564. (The *Characters* of Theophrastus were probably written for students of poetry, especially comedy, rather than for those of rhetoric.)

17 young men.....: like Mantitheus, whose reference to his youth (20) presupposes the jury's indulgence.
older men: like the rather timorous defendant in Lys.3 *Sim*., who admits that his infatuation for the Plataean boy Theodotus was 'rather foolish for one of his age' (4).

18 not seriously but in jest: the last and most overt attempt to ridicule the whole trial.
comic character...artistic touch: perhaps an attempt to excuse the line (*color*) adopted in the defence: a masterly and impudent turning of the tables on the prosecutor.

19 wicked men meet at my shop: undoubtedly one of the lesser charges. Indeed, 'keeping a disorderly house' was not an indictable offence. It is notable that Lysias divests this charge of its substance by generalising it; but in doing so he invites speculation about the main charge – that the defendant has a good income – by tacitly admitting that his shop is a popular meeting-place. For shops as meeting-places, see Ar.*Eccl*.420; Xen.*Mem*.4.2.1; Plato,*Euthyd*.300b; Athenaeus,*Deipn*.581d.

20 the barber's: as a meeting-place for the exchange of gossip: see Ar.*Wealth* 338, *Birds* 1441; Dem.25 *Aristog.A*,52.

21 the most important points: as this is followed by an appeal for pity and a brief reference to the main points made earlier in the speech, it is to be assumed that the Epilogue begins here. But it is disproportionately long compared with the speech's total length, and of course 'the most important point' for the defence, a denial, with evidence, that the defendant owns property worth three minae or more, is even now not made.

22-25 An ancient critic would have had no hesitation in proclaiming that this impassioned plea is written in the Grand Style, with its lofty references to the deity, fortune and the city, its antithesis (single-handed...all of you), its succession of rhetorical questions, including hypophora (24-25, on which see Lys.10 *Theomn*.23n), and long words but simple sentence-structure. (See Longinus *Subl*.9,18; D.H.*Comp.Verb*.22, *Dem*.38). The subject-matter is, however, repetitious (24 = 15).

25 to Chalcis: in 404 B.C., when the Thirty overthrew the democracy. The usual disclaimer of oligarchic sympathies. Cf. Lys. 16 *Mant*. 5-6; 12 *Erat*.17; 31 *Phil*.9,17 for other refugees and destinations. Adams (238) sees an element of parody in this appeal.

26   the other councils: previous annual meetings at which his
continued receipt of the pension had been ratified.
public money....handled: strictly speaking he had 'handled'
public money; but he is comparing his daily obol with the major
transactions conducted by the state treasurers, for which they
were subject to audit (*euthuna*). Thus the speech concludes with
a belittling of the charge (*meiōsis*) rather than a refutation of it.

27   those weaker than himself: on the equalising impartiality of the
law, see Lys.1 *Caed.Erat.*2. Discussion of this subject in fifth-
and fourth-century Athens usually had political undertones, the
law also being seen as the champion of democracy; whereas
extreme oligarchs like Critias objected to its power to undermine
the natural superiority of the strong. See Plato,
*Gorg.*482c-492c,ed.Dodds (Oxford,1959) 263-296; *Rep.*1 338c-end;
Critias frg. 25 Diels. The final plea is thus for sympathy. On the
effectiveness of this, see Lys.22 *Corn.*21. But the ending is
calm, typically of most Attic Oratory (so Jebb,*AO*, ciii).

SPEECH 25 : DEFENCE AGAINST A CHARGE OF
SUBVERTING THE DEMOCRACY

The circumstances surrounding this speech are not clear. In
spite of the title that appears in the manuscripts, it is not a defence
against a charge of treason, but a speech made at a *dokimasia*, like
that of Mantitheus. But whereas in that speech the defendant deals
mainly with the practicalities affecting his election, the present
speaker chooses to dilate at some length on political morality. Why?
The answer may lie in the fact that, although unknown to us, he was
a person of some political standing who was seeking to resume a
career in public life which had been interrupted by the regime of the
Thirty. In 14 he says that he chose not to hold office during the
tyranny, and although his statements in this passage contain an
element of ambiguity they imply that he was a person who could have
been considered for high office at any time. When he came to take up
the threads of his career after the restoration of the democracy he
found himself facing powerful political rivals, some of whom, unlike
himself, had played an active part in defeating the oligarchs. His
reaction to this challenge is to cast these men in the role of accusers,
and to give a detailed account of his credentials and his political
philosophy.

The only charge against him is that he remained in the city
under the Thirty. Done by an ordinary citizen, who in any case may
not have been able to leave, this action could not be interpreted in
any sinister political way. But a politician remaining to live under the
tyranny seemed to offer his opponents an inviting opportunity to

discredit him. His immediate task is to show that he held no office under the Thirty, and that he was therefore in no position to injure any of his fellow-citizens. But the passage in which he dismisses the charge of holding office under the Thirty (14-16) comes in the middle of a broadly-based discussion of political morality, the main themes of which are pragmatism and self-interest. He uses his own example to illustrate the proposition that it is natural for politicians to be time-servers, because each man will choose the form of government which will bring him the greatest benefits (8). Other themes characterise the speaker as a politician and a man of substance. He vehemently attacks his opponents and false accusers; but he also introduces deliberative themes in a statesmanlike manner, counselling his audience to foster concord (*homonoia*) by observing the oaths of amnesty (23).

      The speech has no clear division in the manner of a forensic speech. The formality of the tone, and the absence of any of the usual Lysianic lapses into looser structure, suggest that it may have been composed as a political pamphlet and published separately from the speech that was actually made at the *dokimasia*. Stylistically it is one of the most periodic speeches in the corpus and contains *parison* (balanced clauses of equal length) to the same degree as 12 *Erat*., which is considerably higher than the Lysianic average. The date of the speech has been a matter of much controversy. No internal evidence permits a safe conclusion. Its arguments suit the situation that obtained at any time between 403 and 399 B.C., but the lack of idealism that characterises the speaker's thought suggests that the early enthusiasm immediately following the restoration of democracy had given way to a more sober assessment of the problems of reconciliation, and also to a more cynical view of politics in general. This cynicism is indeed characteristic of the politics of later generations at Athens. It is therefore probably safer to follow the view of most scholars, who favour a date between 401 and 399 B.C. (For arguments in favour of 403, see Lateiner 77-79.)

1-6   PROOEMIUM: The only clearly-marked division of the speech. In it the speaker conventionally states that he is going to prove his innocence; but he also makes an unusually vehement attack on his accusers. This prooemium lacks the concision and economy of Lysianic forensic prooemia.

1   I feel much sympathy for you: conventionally trying to elicit the jury's good will (*captatio benevolentiae*), but also distancing them from his opponents.

    minding other people's business: especially by engaging full-time in litigation against them: a description of the professional informer. See Xen.*Mem*.3.7.9; Dem.9 *Third Philippic* 73; and 3 below.

    all of us: i.e. all who remained in Athens under the Thirty.

2   accused me of all that happened: the speaker cleverly takes the initiative from his opponents by saying that their description of

the horrors of the Thirty's reign is inadequate: he knows, because he was there. By this device he also affirms his own condemnation of their actions.

Piraeus party: the democrats after their return under Thrasybulus (Xen.Hell.2.4.19,23,24,26 etc.) but before the restoration of the democracy.

3 the most likely source of money: either because they buy off the sukophantēs or because he receives a portion of their forfeited property on their conviction (see Lys.1 Caed.Erat.44n; 24 Inv.2n; Isoc.18 Kall.18; Xen.Mem.2.9.1). Lateiner, 178 characterises the speaker as 'obsessed with "sycophants", his word for democratic politicians'.

5 strong proof: more strictly, a tekmērion was a premise which, when cast in an eikos-argument, produced a necessary conclusion. In rhetorical theory it was contrasted with a sēmeion which, when so cast, produced only a probable conclusion. It is not surprising that Lysias' clients almost invariably claim to have tekmēria (e.g. in 16 Mant.11); but the two are neatly contrasted in 4 Traum.12, where the sēmeion is an unfulfilled condition, but the tekmērion is a fact. See Arist.Rhet.1.2.16-18, 2.24.5; and Cope's Introduction to Aristotle's Rhetoric (London, 1867) 160-168.

private charges....the Thirty's crimes: but general political charges are all that his opponents need for their purpose of preventing his election to office. Dover is right, however, to find the amount of generalisation in this speech suspicious (LCL,188).

destroy: hyperbole, since the speaker faced, at worst, only rejection for office. Cf.18,25. See Cloché,RDA,392.

enough enemies: if 399 B.C. is the date of the speech, the allusion may be to enemies both within and without. For at this time Athens was at war with Sparta (Diod.14.39), while in the city fear and suspicion of new oligarchic and other revolutionary movements led to a number of political trials, including that of Socrates.

7 I shall try...: the prothesis, or explanatory introduction, usually to a narrative, but here to an epicheireme, or elaborated rhetorical argument, the counterpart of the syllogism in logic. See D.H. Isaeus 16 (note in Loeb ed.1974, 212-3). Simplified, the argument is: 'People decide their political affiliation according to their own personal advantage: mine lies in democracy rather than oligarchy; therefore I am a democrat'.

8 no human being is naturally either a democrat or an oligarch: cf.Isoc.8 On the Peace,133, who is more specific: 'All men desire, in each case, to establish the form of government in which they are held in honour'; and Dover reasonably suggests that the defendant in this speech means much the same (LCL,49), since his state services (12) should already have brought him some prestige. As a metic who could not aspire to the honours attendant upon state office, Lysias may have held a view

271

corresponding more closely with that stated in this speech than with the Isocratean variant of it.

9 Phrynichus: probably in his early sixties with a long public career behind him in 411 B.C., the year of the first oligarchic revolution. As recently as 412 B.C. he had opposed the recall of Alcibiades, which would have entailed the dissolution of the democracy (Thuc.8.48.4-7).

Peisander: a prominent and influential politician who had supported traditional democratic policies until the disastrous conclusion of the Sicilian Expedition. His subsequent advocacy of a change to oligarchy was not ideological but practical: it was the only form of government that would attract Persian aid (Thuc.8.53.1). For a balanced assessment of Peisander, see G. Woodhead, 'Peisander', *AJP* 75 (1954) 131-146.

offended against you.....misdeeds: the vocabulary reflects the idea that politicians were personally answerable for the outcome of their policies, and were deemed to have 'deceived the people' if they failed. For the most eloquent arguments for and against this idea, see respectively Aesch.3 *Ctes*.49ff and Dem.18 *Cor*.270ff. On the mistrust felt for politicians, see Dover,*GPM*,25-28.

Four Hundred....Piraeus party.....those who had expelled them...Thirty: i.e. oligarchs joined the democrats who returned to overthrow the Thirty, while shortly before this men who had overthrown the Four Hundred in the name of democracy had become members of the Thirty. The most famous of these latter was Theramenes.

those enlisted for Eleusis: members of the Thirty and their supporters who retired there after defeat by the democrats (Xen.*Hell*.2.4.24,38-43; Diod.14.33.6; [Arist.]*Ath.Pol*.39 (Rhodes 464-467); Cloché, *RDA*,389).

10 not difficult to realise: for this formula, cf. Lys.14 *Alc*.A 37; 23 *Pankl*.12; and the much commoner *rhaidion gnōnai* ('easy to realise') 3 *Sim*.28,35; 16 *Mant*.7; 17 *Eraton* 7; 19 *Arist*.13,18,24,27,53; 31.*Phil*.20; 35 *Erot*.231c (the latter suggesting that Plato regarded it as a Lysianic mannerism).

individual interests: hence the most durable and influential associations arose from personal rather than ideological affinities. So Dover,*LCL*,49-50.

11 submitting to audit: after tenure of an annual state office.
in the hope...: for this sentiment, see Isoc.6*Arch*.50; Ant.2 *First Tetralogy* d9.

12 Now as for myself: the speaker now applies the principles of self-interest and personal advantage to his own career in order to show that the democracy has always served his political aspirations, and he has served it in return. The Greek word-order is emphatic, with hyperbaton (*sumphora....oudemia, heterōn...pragmatōn, eisphoras....pollas, tous.....aitious*) and chiasmus (*tetriērarchēka...pentakis,kai tetrakis nenaumachēka*); and a cumulative effect is generated through repeated *kai*

(*synathroismos*).

during that time: between 410 and 404 B.C. Sea-battles fought during that period included those at Cyzicus (410 B.C.), Notium and Mytilene (407), Arginusae (406) and finally Aegospotami (405).

13   **a better reputation with you**: on this sentiment, see 16 *Mant*.17n.

was stripped: note imperfect tense *apesteroumēn* describing a continuous state of deprivation for the duration of the Thirty's regime.

grant favours: the word *charis* denoted both the favour conferred by the citizens in choosing officials, and their expression of gratitude to them on their completion of a term of office, which could take the form of rejection of charges made against them at audit. In [Lys.] 20 *Polystr*.31 the speaker refers to *charis* on which he hopes to draw in the event of a *kindunos*, by which he meant a vexatious lawsuit brought by a *sukophantēs*.

14   **will anyone be able to prove**: in Lys.16, Mantitheus reminds the jury that the corruption to which publicly posted lists of people had been subjected since the restoration of the democracy rendered them valueless as evidence (6-7). This leaves his own behaviour as the most reliable evidence. So with the present defendant.

yet if....and if: *dilēmmaton*, or 'double-trap' argument (Arist. *Rhet*.2.23.15; *Ad Herenn*.2.24.38; Cic. *Inv*.1.29.45; Hermog. *On Invention* (Spengel 2,250,Rabe 192-4).

16   **list of Athenian citizens**: two closely contemporary speeches (Isoc.18 *Kall*.16 and 21 *Euth*.2) refer to a list kept by Lysander of Athenians thought to oppose the regime of the Thirty, and it is assumed by most commentators, starting with Sauppe (*Philol*..15 (1860) 338), that this is the *katalogos* to which the speaker is referring. But the only *katalogos* described by Xenophon (*Hell*.2.3.18,51-52; 2.4.1) and [Aristotle] (*Ath.Pol*.36.2) is that of the Three Thousand enfranchised by the Thirty. It is therefore surprising that the speaker is not more precise in stating to which *katalogos* he is referring, especially as he has created ambiguity by referring to both favours and injuries. Because of this uncertainty, I have refrained from following Lamb (Loeb) in translating *katalogos* as 'blacklist'.

condemned by an arbitrator: arbitration (*diaita*) was the normal way of settling disputes, which were brought before a full jury-court only after appeal against an arbitrator's judgment. See Bonner & Smith,*AJHA* 1,282-288,346-354; Harrison, *LA* 2,64-68; MacDowell,*LCA*, 207-211; Rhodes,*CAAP*,591-595.

17   **since I committed no crime then....surely now**: *a fortiori* argument. See Lys.12 *Erat*.34n.

18   **not....but**: clusters of this highly contrived type of antithesis are very characteristic of Middle-Style Isocratean prose, but are much less common in Lysias.

those passed over: i.e. those who survived the Thirty's reign of terror in Athens. But the distinction between the active supporters of the Thirty and those who lived passively under their regime is deliberately blurred in order to sustain the hyperbole 'none of the citizens would be left'.

stole public money.....bribes: cf. Lys.21 *Brib*.13; 27 *Epicr*.6,9,11; 28 *Erg*.1; 29 *Philocr*.11; 30 *Nicom*.26; Ar.*Knights* 1127; Xen.*Anab*.4.6.16.

19   alienated your allies: for a similar complaint, see Isoc.15 *Ant*.318; 12 *Panath*.13,142. *Sukophantai* could exploit popular suspicion of disloyalty after the revolts of Mytilene (428-7 B.C.) and Scione (423-1 B.C.) and the trials at Athens before Athenian juries made litigation hazardous for individuals, like Antiphon's client Euxitheus, and for whole states when matters like the assessment of their tribute were brought before the Athenian assembly.

Now if......but in fact: for this type of antithesis, see Lys. 12 *Erat*.22n.

20   unjust when you were experiencing them: lit. 'unjust to suffer' (*adika paschein*: prolate or epexegetic infinitive after a word requiring a verbal idea to complete its sense, like Eng. 'hard to bear', 'easy to believe').

concord: *homonoia* was still a political catch-word at this time, occurring for the first time in Thuc.8.93.3. Its antonym was *stasis*. See Lateiner 157. Later it acquired an inter-state and, under Alexander the Great, an international connotation.

greatest pain: *aniarotata* is a very strong, mainly poetical word, not found in Antiphon, Andocides, Isocrates or Isaeus.

22   Three Thousand: see 16n, and Xen.*Hell*.2.4.23.

banished from the city: immediately after the death of Theramenes (Xen.*Hell*.2.4.1). They had been disarmed soon after the list of Three Thousand enfranchised citizens had been drawn up (*id*.2.3.20).

the Thirty were not of one mind: the main disagreement was between Critias and Theramenes, over the extent of the franchise and the degree of repressiveness with which their power was to be exercised. See Xen.*Hell*.2.3.15-49.

saved....return: the parallel seems forced, but the prospect of return must have appeared remote at the beginning of the Thirty's reign of terror, when it was strongly backed by the presence of a Spartan garrison.

23   examples from the past: potent weapons in the armoury of the political orator. Cf. Ant.5 *Her*.67-71 notes. For other refs. to ancient criticism see esp. Caplan's note on *Ad.Herenn*.4.49.62 (Loeb ed.1954,382-3). On their use, see J. Perlman, 'The Historical Example, its Use and Importance as Political Propaganda in the Attic Orators', *Scripta Hierosolymitana* 7 (1961) 150-166.

we: i.e. citizens like himself, who remained in Athens under the Thirty. This sentence concludes the parallel antithetical argument: 'just as the first signs of discord among the tyrants and their supporters gave hope to the exiled democrats, so will the hopes of the city's enemies be dashed when they perceive the degree of concord in the restored democracy'.

24 the exiles: surviving members of the Thirty, the Ten who temporarily succeeded them, their agents and supporters. The exiled oligarchs remained a threat, real or imagined, to the restored democracy at least until 399 B.C.

25 Epigenes, Demophantus and Cleigenes: the emendations of Schwartz (Rhein.Mus.44 (1889) 121) seem necessary, as the last two of these names appear together in And.1 Myst.96, where Demophantus is one of the drafters of a new set of laws restoring the democracy in 410 B.C., and Cleigenes is secretary of the Assembly and Council who, if he was the 'little bathman' of Ar.Frogs 709, was a supporter of the extremist demagogue Cleophon. None of the entries under Epigenes in Davies, APF fits this one. Lysias makes one of his clients remark (30 Nicom.7) that membership of the Four Hundred was a common accusation used by slanderers.

26 accept bribes for the release of wrongdoers: characterising the sukophantēs, who is motivated by purely venal considerations. Hence their preference for wealthy victims. See Lys.24 Inv.2n.
rags to riches: cf. Lys.1 Caed.Erat.4; 27 Epicr.9; 28 Erg.1. Further on the activities of sukophantai, and the encouragement they received from the authorities when the treasury was depleted, see Lys.27 Epicr.1; 29 Philocr.11; 30 Nicom.22; and A.H.M. Jones, Athenian Democracy (Oxford, 1957) 58-60.

27 oaths: including the 'amnesty' (mē mnēskakēsein, Xen.Hell.2.4.43) of 403 B.C. And.1 Myst.90 indicates by prefixing 'and' that the amnesty oath was preceded by others. The oath was also taken in different places, including the Assembly and the Council, to secure its general observance.
democracy arises.....democracy: a facile antithesis, only the first part of which even approximates to the truth. Sukophantai operated actively under both systems, and oligarchy arose mainly through the activities of secret clubs (hetaireiai) in 411 B.C. and the demands of the Spartan victors in 404 B.C. But political theorists, no less than prejudiced litigants, were prone to generalise, e.g. Arist.Polit. 5.5.1, who says that revolution in a democracy mostly (malista) occurs as a reaction against the outrageous behaviour of popular leaders.

28 Town party.....Piraeus party.....government: as these parties existed only temporarily, this passage supports a date near 403 B.C. for the speech. As victors, the Piraeus men had the most power to make the amnesty effective.

29 those who were restored from exile through others: the speaker appears to recognise three classes of democrats: (1) those, like himself, who remained in the city under the Thirty; (2) those who joined Thrasybulus and restored the democracy with armed

force; (3) those here described, who fled from the tyranny, stayed in exile until the fighting was over, and then returned. Here he is trying to distract attention from the first (his) group by calling attention to the discreditable behaviour of the third; but slander-mongering was an activity not peculiar to any one group. For a similar digression (*parekbasis*) against *sukophantai*, see Lys.21 *Brib*.20, closely preceding the epilogue, as here.

30 submitting to audit for none: only magistrates who had not handled public money could escape scrutiny by the public accountants (*logistai*). The second part of the audit involved facing charges of maladministration while in office. It was possible to avoid incurring charges either by conducting a blameless administration or by buying off potential complainants.
war instead of peace: terms usually applied to external conflict. Reference in the next sentence to 'the Greeks' confirms this sense in the present passage. Events which increased Athenian unpopularity after the Peloponnesian War are difficult to find before 399 B.C., when an Athenian contingent joined Sparta's invasion of Elis, while the Boeotians and Corinthians remained aloof (Xen.*Hell*.3.2.25). Thus the reference adds to the problem of dating the speech.

31 same aims: self-enrichment (see Lys.12 *Erat*.6).
it is not they....but you: the speaker's aggressiveness reaches a high point. On this as a feature of the speech, see Introd. For the idea here expressed that the victim of injustice is partly responsible because of inaction or naïvety, see Thuc.4.61.5.

33 in advancing from the Piraeus: the speaker now shifts his attack to the second group of democrats ((2) in 29 (above)).

34 feel ashamed: the constructions with *aischunesthai* are (1) with the infinitive, meaning 'to be ashamed to do, and therefore *not* do'; (2) with the participle, as here (agreeing with the subject), meaning 'to feel shame as one does something'. The negative *mē* rather than *ou* with *dokountes* introduces a condition ('if') or a contingency. The overtness of the activities of *sukophantai* is an ¬spect of their *hubris*, and it contributes to the fear they seek to inspire in their victims.
agreements and oaths: see 27n. For the thought, cf. Isoc.18 *Kall*. 42ff.

35 those responsible: the oath excluded the Thirty, the Ten who temporarily succeeded them, the Eleven and the Ten Magistrates in the Piraeus (And.1 *Myst*.90 and MacDowell *ad.loc.*(130-131); [Arist.]*Ath.Pol*.39.6 and Rhodes *ad.loc.* (469-470); Hignett,*HAC*,294). Aristotle adds that these men might seek to clear themselves by submitting to audit; but this procedure would have exposed them to determined attacks both by genuine victims of the regime and by *sukophantai*. The vehemence and thoroughness with which this speaker and others in *dokimasiai* deny even the remotest connection with oligarchs reminds us of the competition which they faced.

The speech breaks off on a scolding note. Comparison with a similar tone in Lys.10 *Theomn*.30 suggests that a few sentences more might bring the speech to a conclusion on a more conciliatory note.

INDEX

(Technical terms in italics)

279

homoeoteleuton, 68, 79, 98, 112, 252.
hybris, 222, 227, 239, 266, 267, 276.
hyperbaton, 82, 87, 108, 129, 225, 234, 264, 266, 272.
hypophora, 105, 108, 234, 268.
hypostasis, 129.
hysteron-proteron, 102.

in flagrante delicto (*ep'autophōrōi*) 101, 221, 228.
Isocrates, 8, 10, 12(n.19,23), 13(n.48), 129, 243, 253, 265.

kakourgia, 24ff., 73, 228.
Kallaischros, 248.
Kallibius, 238, 251.
Kannonus, Decree of, 246.
katastasis, 222.
Khalkis, 268.
Knights, Athenian, 254, 255, 257.

Lesbos, 23, 80, 81, 91, 95, 99, 101.
liturgies (*leitourgiai*), 114, 234, 240, 266.
Locrians, 77.
Long Walls, 243.
Lycinus, 23, 103ff.
Lycurgus, 123, 252.
Lysander, 236, 247, 248, 249, 252, 256.
Lysias, 9, 125–130, 132ff., 235, 236, 244, 246, 250.
Lysitheus, 229.

Mantitheus, 130, 252ff., 264, 268, 269, 273.
Megara, 126.
meiōsis, 269.
Melobius, 239.
mēnutēs, 93, 94.
merchants (*emporoi*), 258, 260, 262.
metabolē, 70, 72, 78, 112.
metaphor, 95, 97, 229, 264.

Methymna, 23, 81, 89, 115.
Miltiades (Spartan admiral), 249.
Mnesiphilus, 6.
Mnesitheides, 239.
Mytilene, 23ff., 80, 81, 89, 99, 100, 103, 110ff., 122, 274; Battle of, 273.

narrative (*diēgēsis*), 130, 237.
Nemea, 256.
Nestor, 5.
Notium, Battle of, 273.

Odysseus, 5.
Orthobulus, 256.
oxymoron, 251.

Palladium, 28(n.6), 74, 99, 121.
Pantaleon, 231.
paragraphē, 72.
para prosdokian, 251.
parēchēsis, 239.
parison, 68, 270.
paronomasia, 121.
Pasion, 265.
Pausanias, 247.
Peisander, 247, 248, 272.
Peison, 239.
Peloponnesian War, 126, 244, 276.
Pericles, 9, 77, 125, 127, 238, 247.
periphrasis, 77, 93.
Persians, 243, 257; Persian Wars, 6, 247.
Pheidon, 235, 246.
Philochares, 249.
Philoneus, 99.
Philostratus, 21.
Phlius, 256.
Phormion, 265.
Phreatto, 74.
Phrynichus, 247, 272.
Phyle, 245, 246, 254.
Piraeus, 9, 238, 243, 251, 260, 261, 276; Piraeus Party, 271, 272, 275.